Christi

with Anna Lowy
Beatriz Martín García

ENGLISH FILE

Beginner Teacher's Book

Paul Seligson and Clive Oxenden are the original co-authors of
English File 1 and *English File 2*

OXFORD
UNIVERSITY PRESS

Great Clarendon Street, Oxford, ox2 6DP, United Kingdom

Oxford University Press is a department of the University of Oxford.
It furthers the University's objective of excellence in research, scholarship,
and education by publishing worldwide. Oxford is a registered trade
mark of Oxford University Press in the UK and in certain other countries

ACKNOWLEDGEMENTS

*The publisher would like to thank the following for their permission to reproduce
photographs:* Alamy pp.142 (women, boy at desk/Wonderlandstock), 147 (3, 9,
11, 12), 151 (women at restaurant desk), 154 (4/Alexander Caminada, 5/Glow
Wellness, 11/Network Photographers, 12), 189 (guitarist/Photo Yoko Aziz 2),
202 (camping/Eric Nathan), 220 (3, 4/Jack Sullivan, 5/Alistair Heap, 7/Matthew
Chattle); Corbis pp.151 (couple talking on bus), 154 (10/Ed Bock), 174 (Dariusz
Michalczewski/Jens Wolf), 181 (Monica's sister/Jutta Klee, Amy's daughter/
Yousuke Tanaka, Amy's son/peace!), 220 (2), 230 (couple/Patrik Giardino);
Getty pp.154 (8/Jupiterimages), 174 (Paolo Coelho/Venturelli), 181 (Mario's
brother/Mel Yates), 190 (Stephanie Meyer/Andrew H. Walker); Oxford
University Press pp.142 (call centre), 143 (keys, photo, frame, umbrella,
pens, paper, dictionaries, camera), 147 (1, 5, 6), 151 (teens walking), 154 (1),
156, 162 (talking in office), 181 (Mario, Mario's sister, Mario's father, Mario's
mother, Monica, Monica's brother, Monica's daughter, Monica's husband,
Ray, Ray's wife, Ray's brother, Ray's sister, Ray's son, Charlie, Charlie's wife,
Charlie's son, Amy, Amy's mother, Amy's husband), 183 (1–4, 11), 189 (remote
control), 202 (Nick), 213 (sushi, Swiss army knife, Turkish flag, chopsticks,
Polish flag, sombrero), 217 (strawberries, tree trunk, elephant, sun, blue
sky), 218 (1–3, 5, 6, 8, 10, 12, 13, 17, 18), 228 (1–5, 7, skipping girl), 229 (girl),
230 (1–3); Rex Features pp.174 (Mesut Ozil/Action Press, Orhan Pamuk/IBO/
SIPA), 190 (Jackie Chan/Imaginechina, Kate Middleton/Tim Rooke, Kanye
West/Billy Farrell Agency), 232 (Kris Kristofferson/David Dagley); Shutterstock
pp.140 (all), 142 (senior woman on phone), 143 (coat, chairs, windows,
watches, credit card, smartphones, wallet), 147 (2, 4, 7, 8, 10), 154 (2, 3, 6, 7,
9), 162 (women talking), 174 (Salma Hayek, Ken Watanabe, Roger Federer,
Vanessa Paradis, Fernando Alonso, Anna Netrebko, Donatella Versace, Kate
Winslet), 180 (all), 181 (Charlie's father, Charlie's mother), 183 (5–10, 12), 185,
189 (woman with strawberries), 190 (Will Smith, Keira Knightley, Rihanna,,
Katy Perry, Adele, Leonardo di Caprio, Benedict Cumberbatch, Usain Bolt),
202 (Eiffel Tower, Diana, Urquart Castle, Paula and Jake), 211, 213 (castanets,
baguette, Mercedes badge), 214 (both), 217 (crow, carrots, flamingo, trees,
snowman), 218 (4, 7, 9, 11, 14, 15, 16, 19, 20), 220 (1, 6, 8, 9, 10), 228 (6, sailor,
man chopping), 229 (man), 231.

Illustrations by: Paul Boston/Meiklejohn pp.148, 221, 222, 224; Mark Duffin
pp.157 (ex b), 178, 200, 215; Anna Hymas/New Divison pp.141, 149; Sophie
Joyce pp.194, 201; Adam Larkum/Illustration Ltd pp.144, 155, 158, 219, 233;
Jérôme Mireault/Colagene pp.139, 157 (ex a), 159, 216; Roger Penwill pp.145,
150, 153, 160, 182, 186, 212; Gavin Reece pp.161, 179; Colin Shelbourne
pp.146, 192.

*The authors and publisher are grateful to those who have given permission to reproduce
the following extracts and adaptations of copyright material*: p.228 "All Together
Now" Words and Music by John Lennon and Paul McCartney © 1968,
Reproduced by permission of Sony/ATV Tunes LLC, London W1F 9LD. p.229
"That's How Much" Words and Music by Artie Kaplan, Brooks Arthur and Jack
Keller © 1960, Reproduced by permission of Colgems-EMI Music Inc, London
W1F 9LD. p.231 "Calendar Girl" Words and Music by Howard Greenfield and
Neil Sedaka © 1961, Reproduced by permission of Screen Gems-EMI Music
Inc, London W1F 9LD. p.232 "Song I'd Like to Sing" Words and Music by Kris
Kristofferson © 1973, Reproduced by permission of Combine Music Corp/
EMI Music Publishing Ltd, London W1F 9LD. p.230 "Stop the Clock" Words
and Music by Antoine Domino, Kenny James and Pee Wee Maddux © 1962,
Reproduced by permission of EMI Unart Catalog Inc, London W1F 9LD. p.233
"Somewhere Over the Rainbow" Words and Music by E Harburg and Harold
Arlen © 1938, Reproduced by permission of EMI Fiest Catalog Inc, London
W1F 9LD.

Contents

Syllabus checklist

			Grammar	Vocabulary

Pronunciation	Speaking	Listening	Reading
/h/, /aɪ/, and /iː/	Introducing yourself; Meeting people	People introducing themselves	
/ɪ/, /əʊ/, /s/, and /ʃ/	Talking about where people and things are from	Can you hear the difference?	
/dʒ/, /tʃ/, and /ʃ/	*Is dim sum Japanese?* Talking about nationalities	Understanding short conversations	People meeting for the first time
sentence rhythm	*Personal information*	Numbers; Can you hear the difference?	Online conversations
/z/ and /s/; plural endings	Things in your bag; *Memory game*	Understanding short conversations	
/ð/ and /ə/	*How much are these watches?*	At a souvenir stand	
/ʌ/, /æ/, and the /ə/ sound	Talking about your family and friends	Understanding a dialogue	
/uː/, /ɑː/, and /ɔː/; linking	Talking about preferences	Understanding a dialogue	
word stress; /tʃ/, /dʒ/, and /g/	Talking about your meals	People talking about their favourite meal of the day	Breakfast around the world
/w/, /v/, and /ɒ/; sentence rhythm and linking	Talking about your habits	Understanding a longer dialogue	On the plane
third person -s; /ɜː/; sentence rhythm	Talking about people who work	Understanding longer a dialogue	English at work?
/j/; sentence rhythm	Questionnaire: *Are you a morning person?*	An interview	A life in the day of Ivan Vasiliev

		Grammar	Vocabulary

Pronunciation	Speaking	Listening	Reading
/w/, /h/, /eə/, and /aʊ/; sentence rhythm	Talking about free time activities *Weekdays and weekends*	An interview	Football isn't the only sport
sentence rhythm and intonation	Talking about films	Understanding a dialogue	
/æ/, /ɑː/, and /ə/; sentence rhythm	Talking about what you can and can't do in a town	Taking a driving test	
/ʊ/, /uː/, and /ŋ/; sentence rhythm	What do you like doing?		What do you like doing if you have two free hours?
sentence rhythm	Talking about what people are doing *The same or different?*	Understanding short conversations	Messages
/ɜː/, /iː/, /e/, and /eə/	Talking about clothes	An interview	Undercover boss
/eə/ and /ɪə/	*Is there a TV? Where is it?*	Hotel facilities	The Craigdarroch Inn
was and *were*; sentence rhythm	Where were you yesterday?		'For me it was a game'
regular past simple endings	Talking about past activities and events		It changed my life...
sentence rhythm	Interview a partner about their 'life in a day'	Understanding a conversation	Life in a day
irregular verbs	Asking and answering questions about the past	Strangers on a train	Strangers on a train
the letters *ea*	talking about your dream city break	Three people talking about their holiday plans	

Introduction

English File third edition Beginner is for real beginners, or for false beginners who need a slower, more supportive approach. It gives you and your students the complete *English File third edition* package, with all the in-class and out-of-class components your students need to learn successfully, and with all the teacher support that accompanies other levels of the series.

As well as the main A and B lessons, the Grammar, Vocabulary, and Sound Banks, and the Communication and Writing sections in the Student's Book, there is a range of material which can be used according to your students' needs and the time available. Don't forget:

- new Practical English video and exercises (available on the Class audio CD, Class DVD, and the iTutor for home-study)
- the Revise & Check pages, with video (also available on the Class audio CD, Class DVD, and the iTutor for home-study)
- photocopiable Grammar, Vocabulary, Communicative, and Song activities.

STUDY LINK iTutor with iChecker, Workbook, Online Skills Program, Pronunciation app, and the Student's website provide multimedia review, support, and practice for students outside the classroom.

The Teacher's Book also suggests different ways of exploiting many of the Student's Book activities depending on the level of your class. We very much hope you enjoy using *English File third edition Beginner*.

What do Beginner students need?

The aim of every level *of English File third edition* is to get students talking and Beginner is no exception. To achieve this, beginners need two things above all else: motivation and support.

Beginners' language level is low, but they need interesting topics and texts just as much as Intermediate or Advanced students.

Grammar, Vocabulary, and Pronunciation

At any level, the basic tools students need to speak English with confidence are Grammar, Vocabulary, and Pronunciation (G, V, P). In *English File third edition Beginner* all three elements are given equal importance. Each lesson has clearly stated grammar, vocabulary, and pronunciation aims. This keeps lessons focused, and gives students concrete learning objectives and a sense of progress.

Grammar

Beginner students need

- clear and memorable presentations of basic structures.
- plenty of regular and varied practice in useful and natural contexts.
- student-friendly reference material.

English File third edition Beginner provides memorable contexts for new language that will engage students, using real-life stories and situations, humour, and suspense. The **Grammar Bank** gives students a single, easy-to-access grammar reference section, with clear rules, example sentences with audio, and common errors. There are then two practice exercises for each grammar point.

When explaining grammar rules to students, and sometimes when setting up complicated activities, teachers who know their students' mother tongue may wish to use it. Although you should try to keep it to a minimum, we believe that a very judicious use of students' L1 can save time and help build good teacher–class rapport. Contrasting how English grammar works with the rules in students' L1 can also help students to assimilate the rules more easily.

Vocabulary

Beginner students need

- to expand their knowledge of high-frequency words and phrases rapidly.
- to use new vocabulary in personalized contexts.
- accessible reference material to help them review and consolidate their vocabulary

Every lesson in *English File third edition Beginner* focuses on high-frequency vocabulary and common lexical areas, but keeps the language load realistic. Many lessons are linked to the **Vocabulary Banks** which help present and practise high-frequency and topic based vocabulary in class, give audio for each word to help with pronunciation, and provide a clear reference to the main unit so students can revise and test themselves in their own time.

Pronunciation

Beginner students need

- to learn the English vowel and consonant sounds and practise them intensively.
- to see where there are rules and patterns in sound–spelling relationships.
- systematic practice of other aspects of pronunciation, e.g., stress and sentence rhythm.

English File has its own unique system of teaching the sounds of English, through sound pictures, which give clear example words to help identify and produce sounds. Students visualize and remember the words and sounds together, and the word is then used as a reference point when learning the pronunciation of other words with the same sound.

Beginner learners want to speak clearly but are often frustrated by English pronunciation, particularly the sound–spelling relationships, silent letters, and weak forms.

The **Sound Bank** on pages 133–135 helps students to see the many clear sound–spelling patterns that do exist in English and gives common examples of them. The **Sound Bank** can be referred to in class – it is on the Class audio CD (tracks 4.64–4.67) and also on iTutor for home study.

Throughout *English File Beginner* we emphasize improving pronunciation by focusing on important sounds, on word stress, and on sentence rhythm. Every lesson in *English File Beginner* has an integrated pronunciation focus that focuses on one of the above aspects.

Speaking

Beginner students need

- regular opportunities to use new language orally.
- topics that will arouse their interest and prompt them to describe their experiences and express their ideas.
- realistic and achievable tasks.

English File third edition motivates students to speak by providing them with varied and motivating tasks, and the language (grammar, vocabulary, and pronunciation) that they need in order to communicate with confidence. In addition to the Speaking sections of the main units and the **Communication** activities at the back of the book, students are encouraged to speak throughout the lesson, responding to reading texts and listening activities, and practicing grammar and vocabulary orally.

Listening

Beginner students need

- to be exposed to as much aural English as possible.
- a reason to listen.
- to build their confidence by listening to short accessible texts and conversations with achievable tasks
- to learn to get the gist of what is being said by focusing on the key words in an utterance.

The listenings in *English File Beginner* are based on a variety of entertaining and realistic situations. There is a wide range of voices and accents from the UK and the rest of the English-speaking world, but all the speakers are clear and comprehensible to students at this level. The sound effects bring the listenings alive, and make the recordings easier for students to follow and more fun to listen to. The tasks focus on helping students to get the gist the first time and then be able to understand more the second time. English File Beginner also provides some exposure to authentic, unscripted English in the listening activities of the Revise and Check sections which have short street interviews with people in the UK and USA.

The majority of the audio material is available for students on iTutor, where they can listen to this in their own time, without pressure. Students can also listen while reading the script, to help them build confidence. There is also a listening activity to accompany each Workbook lesson for further practice.

Reading

Beginner students need

- engaging topics and stimulating texts.
- manageable tasks that help them to read.
- to learn how to deal with unknown words in a text.

Many students need to read in English for their work or studies, and reading is also important in helping students to build vocabulary and to consolidate grammar. The key to encouraging students to read is to give them motivating but accessible material and manageable tasks. *English File*

Beginner reading texts are staged so that they progress from one-line sentences to short articles adapted from a variety of real sources (the British press, magazines, and news websites). These articles have been chosen for their intrinsic interest. All reading texts here are available with audio, which helps build reading fluency and confidence.

Writing

Beginner students need

- clear models.
- the 'nuts and bolts' of writing on a word and sentence level.

Thanks to the internet and social media people worldwide are writing in English more than ever before, both for business and personal communication. English File Beginner provides guided writing tasks with a range of writing types from formal email to social networking posts.

Practical English

Beginner students need

- to know what to say in common situations, e.g. buying a coffee.
- to practise using functional phrases in simple roleplays.

The six *Practical English* lessons introduce and practise the key language for situations like booking a table, checking into a hotel, ordering food and drink, telling the time, talking on the phone, inviting and offering, asking and giving directions. The story line introduces the main characters of the *English File third edition* Practical English lessons, Jenny Zielinski (from New York) and Rob Walker (from London), and gives an introduction to their lives through everyday situations, which students will be familiar with. The lessons also highlight useful everyday phrases such as *Can I help you? How much is it? Don't worry. See you there.* The Practical English lessons are on the English File Beginner DVD, iTutor, and iTools. Teachers can also use the Practical English Student's Book exercises with the Class audio CD. Using the video will provide a change of focus and give the lessons a clear visual context.

Revision

Beginner students need

- regular recycling of grammar, vocabulary, and pronunciation.
- motivating reference and practice material.
- a sense of progress.

However clearly structures or vocabulary are presented, students will usually only assimilate and *remember* new language if they have the chance to see it and use it several times. Grammar, Vocabulary, and Pronunciation are recycled throughout the book. After every two Files, there is a two-page Revise and Check section. The left-hand page reviews the grammar, vocabulary, and pronunciation of each File. The right-hand page provides a series of skill-based challenges, including reading texts and listening activities to help students to measure their progress in terms of competence. These pages are designed to be used flexibly according to the needs of your students. There is also a **short film** available on the Class DVD and the iTutor for students to watch and enjoy.

Student's Book Files 1–12

The Student's Book has twelve Files. Each File is organized like this:

A and B lessons

Each File contains two two-page lessons which present and practise **Grammar**, **Vocabulary**, and **Pronunciation** with a balance of reading and listening activities, and lots of opportunities for speaking. These lessons have clear references to the Grammar Bank, Vocabulary Bank, and Sound Bank at the back of the book.

Practical English

Every two Files (starting from File 1) there is a two-page lesson which teaches high-frequency, everyday English (e.g. language for spelling your name, booking a table or telling the time) and social English (useful phrases like *That's right* and *I'm really sorry*). Integrated into every Practical English lesson is a motivating drama which can be found on the *English File Beginner* Class DVD, on iTools and on the iTutor.

Revise & Check

Every two Files (starting from File 2) there is a two-page section revising **Grammar**, **Vocabulary**, and **Pronunciation** of each File and providing **Reading**, **Listening**, and **Speaking** *Can you…?* challenges to show students what they can achieve. There are also two videos in Revise & Check: (1) *In the street* interviews which give students the opportunity to listen to and understand authentic, spontaneous language which is suitable for this level; and (2) short films that extend the Student's Book topics and which are filmed specially for *English File*. These are also available as audio files on the Class audio CD.

The back of the Student's Book

The lessons contain references to these sections: Communication, Writing, Listening, Grammar Bank, Vocabulary Bank, and Sound Bank.

For students

iTutor with iChecker

For students to review after class or catch up on a class they have missed, or to check their progress on iChecker.

iTutor – a digital companion to the Student's Book

- The audio from the main Student's Book lessons, including recordings of the reading texts.
- All the audio for the Vocabulary Banks and the Grammar Bank examples.
- All the video for Practical English and Revise & Check.
- Links to the Student's Site for more practice.
- Printable wordlists.
- Interactive Sounds Chart.
- All video and audio can be transferred to mobile devices.
- iTutor does not contain a few short listening scripts which provide a surprise ending to some listening activities. This is so that students who listen ahead cannot spoil the activity by giving away the ending.
- For copyright reasons the songs which are in the Student's Book are not on iTutor.

iChecker – a digital companion to the Workbook

- For self-testing new grammar, vocabulary, and Practical English.
- All audio from the Workbook lessons.
- A dictation exercise for every File.
- A Progress Check test for every File.

Workbook

For practice after class

- All the Grammar, Vocabulary, Pronunciation, and Practical English.
- A listening exercise for every lesson.
- Pronunciation exercises with audio.
- Useful Words and Phrases.
- Audio for Pronunciation and Listening exercises (on iChecker).
- Available with or without key.

Oxford Online Skills Program

For students to develop and practise their skills

- Reading and Listening with exercises for every File.
- Writing and Speaking models and tasks for every File.

Pronunciation app

For students to learn and practise the sounds of English.

- Individual sounds.
- Sounds in useful phrases.
- Speak and record.

Student's Site

www.oup.com/elt/englishfile

- Extra practice of Grammar, Vocabulary, Pronunciation, and Practical English.
- Learning resources.
- Games and puzzles.

For teachers

Teacher's Book

Detailed lesson plans for all the lessons, including:

- an optional 'books closed' lead-in for every lesson
- **Extra idea** suggestions for optional extra activities
- **Extra challenge** suggestions for ways of exploiting the Student's Book material in a more challenging way if you have a stronger class
- **Extra support** suggestions for ways of adapting activities or exercises to make them work with weaker students.

Extra activities are **colour-coded** so you can see at a glance what is core material and what is extra when you are planning and teaching your classes.

All lesson plans include keys and complete audio scripts.

Over seventy pages of photocopiable activities in the Teacher's Book.

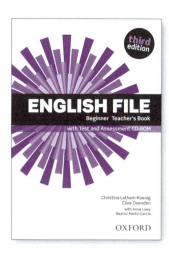

Grammar

see pp. 136–162

- An activity for every Grammar Bank, which can be used in class or for self-study extra practice.
- An Activation section to encourage students to use the new language in class.

Communicative

see pp. 163–203

- Extra speaking practice for every A and B, and Practical English lesson
- 'No cut' alternatives to reduce preparation time.

Vocabulary

see pp. 204–225

- Extra practice of new vocabulary, for every Vocabulary Bank.

Songs

see pp. 226–233

- A song for every two Files
- Provides the lyrics of the recorded song with task to do before, during, or after listening.

iTools – bring your classroom to life

- The complete Student's Book, Workbook, and Teacher's Book (photocopiables) onscreen
- Interactive activities for all Grammar and Vocabulary Banks
- All class audio (including songs) and video, with interactive scripts
- 'Click and reveal' answer keys for Student's Book, Workbook, and Teacher's Book photocopiables
- Resources including Grammar Bank PowerPoints, and Vocabulary flashcards.

Test and Assessment CD-ROM

- A Quick Test for every File
- A File test for every File covering G, V, P, Reading and Listening
- Two Progress Tests, and an End-of-course Test
- A and B versions of all the main tests
- Audio for all the Listening tests.

Class audio CDs

- All the listening materials for the Student's Book.

DVD

Practical English

- A unique teaching video that goes with the Practical English lessons in the Student's Book

In the street

- Short interviews filmed in London, New York, and Oxford to accompany the Revise & Check section

Short film

- Short documentary film for students to watch for pleasure after the Revise & Check section.

Teacher's Site

www.elt.oup.com/ teachers/englishfile

- Extra digital ideas, teaching resources, and support.

G verb *be* (singular): *I* and *you*
V numbers 0–10; days of the week
P /h/, /aɪ/, and /iː/

1A Hello!

Lesson plan

The first lesson introduces Sts to basic greetings, and the *I* and *you* forms of the verb *be* in positive and negative sentences, questions, and short answers. The context is two people meeting for the first time at a fancy dress party. The activities here also help your Sts to get to know each other's names. In Vocabulary, Sts learn numbers zero to ten. In Pronunciation, they are introduced to the *English File* system of teaching the sounds of English with three sounds, /h/, /aɪ/, and /iː/. The lesson finishes with a focus on the days of the week and ways of saying goodbye.

STUDY LINK
- Workbook 1A
- iTutor
- www.oup.com/elt/englishfile

Extra photocopiable activities
- **Grammar** verb *be* (singular): *I* and *you* p.139
- **Communicative** *Are you...?* p.173 (instructions p.163)
- **Vocabulary** Numbers and days p.210 (instructions p.204)
- www.oup.com/elt/teacher/englishfile

Optional lead-in (books closed)
- Introduce yourself to the class. Say *Hello. I'm* (…) twice. Repeat your name and write it on the board.
- Then look at one student and say *Hello. I'm* (…). Encourage him / her to respond *Hello. I'm* (…). At this stage do not correct anything they say. If the student fails to respond, move on to another student until you get the right response. Praise Sts when they respond. Say *Good* or *Very good* as often as is necessary.
- Repeat this process with other Sts round the class. With a good class you may also want to teach the phrase *Nice to meet you* at this point.
- This activity will break the ice with your class on the first day.

1 LISTENING & SPEAKING

a **1 2))** Books open. Demonstrate this by opening your own book and saying *Open your books.* Say the page number and write it on the board. Focus on the two small photos and the speech bubbles by pointing at your book and saying *Look at the photos.* Then tell Sts to listen. Demonstrate this by putting your hand to your ear, pointing to the audio player, and saying *Listen.*

Play the audio once the whole way through for Sts just to listen.

> **1 2))**
> See the script in the Student's Book on *p.4*

Now tell Sts to listen and repeat. Demonstrate with the first item. Play the audio again for Sts to repeat in chorus, allowing time for them to repeat.

! If you find the repeat pauses aren't long enough, pause the audio yourself. Encourage Sts to try to copy the rhythm. Getting the rhythm right is one of the most important aspects of good pronunciation.

Depending on the size of your class, get all or some Sts to repeat individually.

If you know your Sts' language, you may want to point out that *hi* and *hello* mean the same, although *hi* is more informal.

b Put Sts in pairs, **A** and **B**. Demonstrate the activity with a strong pair.

Now get Sts to practise the greeting in pairs.

When they have finished, tell them to swap roles. Monitor and help.

c **1 3))** Focus on the first photo and say *It's a party.* Ask Sts if they know the names of the actors in the photo.

Now focus on all three photos and the three conversations.

Play the audio once the whole way through for Sts to listen and read at the same time.

> **1 3))**
> See the conversations in the Student's Book on *p.4*

Go through the conversations, making sure the meaning is clear to Sts. Some teachers may want to do this in L1. (See **Introduction** on *p.8* for comments on use of mother tongue.) Point out that the response to *Nice to meet you* is *Nice to meet you.*

d **(1 4)))** Play conversation 1 on the audio and get Sts to repeat each phrase in chorus. Encourage Sts to copy the rhythm. Model the phrase yourself if Sts are not copying the rhythm correctly. Get individual Sts to say the sentences after you.

> **(1 4)))**
> See the conversations in the Student's Book on *p.4*

Repeat with the other two conversations.

e Put Sts in pairs, **A** and **B**. Demonstrate the activity with a good pair.

Now ask Sts to practise the conversations. When they have finished, tell them to swap roles. Listen out for general pronunciation mistakes and write them on the board, then model and drill them with choral and individual repetition.

Extra support
- With a weaker class you could work on each conversation one by one, modelling and drilling the pronunciation and then practising in pairs, before moving onto the next conversation.

Extra challenge
- Ask one student in each pair to close their book and respond to their partner from memory. **A** reads his / her lines and **B** responds from memory. Then Sts swap roles.

Focus on the **Instructions** box and go through it with the class. Model and drill the pronunciation of the five words.

2 GRAMMAR verb *be* (singular): *I* and *you*

a Focus on the instructions and get Sts to complete the two sentences.

Check answers.

> 1 I   2 You

b **(1 5)))** **(1 6)))** Before Sts go to the **Grammar Bank** you could teach them the words *positive*, *negative*, and *question*. This can be done in English by writing symbols on the board:

> ⊞ = positive   ⊟ = negative   ? = question

You could explain this in L1 if you prefer.

Tell Sts to go to **Grammar Bank 1A** on *p.92*. You could write the page number on the board to help Sts. Show Sts that all the grammar rules and exercises are in this section of the book.

Sts will have the chance to repeat all the sentences which are highlighted in the charts on *p.92*. Play the audio and ask Sts to listen and repeat the example sentences. Pause the audio as necessary.

Go through the rules with the class using the expanded information in the **Additional grammar notes** to help you. You may want to use L1 here.

Extra support
- If you have a monolingual class, don't be afraid of using your Sts' L1 to talk about the grammar rules. At this level it is unrealistic to expect Sts to fully understand grammar rules in English.

Additional grammar notes
- The **Additional grammar notes** in this Teacher's Book aim to add more or expanded information to the notes and rules on the **Grammar Bank** pages in the Student's Book. If there is no extra information in the Teacher's Book, this is because all the information needed is on the Student's Book page.

Additional grammar notes
verb *be* (singular): *I* and *you*

- In English we always use a name or pronoun with the verb.

- *I* is always written with a capital letter.

- There is only **one** form of *you* – i.e. there is no formal and informal form, unlike in many other languages.

- Native and fluent speakers of English nearly always use contractions in conversation.

- The subject usually changes position in questions in English.

- You can answer a question with a short answer in English instead of answering just *yes* or *no*. Emphasize that *you are* in the positive short answer is not contracted.

- The *you* form of the verb *be* has two possible negations: *you aren't* and *you're not*. Both forms are common, but we recommend you teach only *you aren't* so as not to confuse Sts.

Focus on the exercises for **1A** on *p.93* and get Sts to do them individually or in pairs. If they do them individually, get them to compare answers with a partner.

Check answers, getting Sts to read the full sentences.

> a
> 1 I'm   3 I'm
> 2 I'm, You're   4 You're
> b
> 1 You aren't
> 2 You aren't
> 3 I'm not
> c
> 1 Am I in room 4?
> 2 Are you Silvia?
> 3 Am I in class 3?
> d
> 1 Am, aren't   3 Are, am
> 2 Are, 'm not   4 Am, are, 'm

Tell Sts to go back to the main lesson **1A**.

Extra support
- If you think Sts need more practice, you may want to give them the Grammar photocopiable activity at this point or leave it for later as consolidation or revision.

c (1 7))) Tell Sts that they are going to practise saying contractions. Focus on the example. Remind Sts that *I'm* is the contraction of two words. Establish a gesture to remind Sts to contract verb forms, e.g. a scissor or concertina gesture. Highlight and drill the pronunciation of *I'm* /aɪm/.

Play the audio and get Sts to listen and say the contractions.

> (1 7)))
> 1 I am (*pause*) I'm
> 2 You are (*pause*) You're
> 3 I am not (*pause*) I'm not
> 4 You are not (*pause*) You aren't

Then repeat the activity, getting individual Sts to repeat the contractions.

3 VOCABULARY numbers 0–10

a (1 8))) Some Sts may already know some numbers in English, but real beginners probably won't know the correct pronunciation or spelling of all the numbers 0–10.

Focus on the two groups of numbers, A and B, and then say *Listen, is it A or B?* Play the audio once and check the answer.

> B

> (1 8)))
> **Band leader**   One, two, three, four.

Ask *What are the numbers?* Write the numbers 1, 2, 3, 4 on the board as Sts say them.

Try to elicit the numbers five to ten and zero onto the board. For 0 teach *zero* /'zɪərəʊ/. If Sts don't know <u>any</u> numbers, don't worry as they will be looking at numbers in the next exercise in the **Vocabulary Bank**.

b Tell Sts to go to **Vocabulary Bank** *Numbers and days* on *p.116*. Write the page number on the board. Highlight that these pages (**Vocabulary Banks**) are the vocabulary section, where Sts will first do all the exercises as required by the Student's Book, and will then have the pages for reference to help them remember the words.

(1 9))) Look at **1, 0–10** and focus on **a**. Play the audio for Sts to listen and repeat the numbers in chorus. Pause the audio as necessary. Give special attention to words which Sts find difficult. Give further practice as necessary, modelling and drilling the pronunciation yourself, or using the audio, and getting choral and individual responses.

> (1 9)))
> See numbers 0–10 in the Student's Book on *p.116*

In the **Vocabulary Bank** the phonetic transcription is given for all new words. Explain this to Sts and tell them that they will be learning the phonetic symbols gradually throughout the course, but not to worry about them for the time being.

Focus on the **Word stress** box and go through it with the class, demonstrating (or explaining in L1) that in English one syllable is always pronounced more strongly than the other(s) in multi-syllable words. Throughout *English File* word stress is marked by underlining the stressed syllable.

Focus on **b**. Get Sts to cover the words and say the numbers. Sts can do this individually or with a partner. Monitor and help. Make a note of any pronunciation problems they are having. Point to the numbers you wrote on the board earlier and model and drill the ones that Sts find difficult.

Tell Sts to go back to the main lesson **1A**.

Extra idea

- Count round the class from zero to ten. Point to Sts at random and encourage them to count a little bit faster each time you start from zero. Then count backwards from ten to zero.

Extra challenge

- Get Sts to count up and down in twos, i.e. *two, four, six*, etc.

c (1 10))) Focus on the instructions and example. Play the audio for Sts to hear the numbers. Now demonstrate by saying two numbers yourself and eliciting the next one from the class.

Play the audio and pause after the next pair of numbers. Ask Sts what the next number is (*nine*). Make sure Sts are clear what they have to do before continuing.

Play the rest of the audio and give Sts time to say the next number. Get a whole class response.

> (1 10)))
> one, two (*pause*) three
> seven, eight (*pause*) nine
> three, four (*pause*) five
> eight, nine (*pause*) ten
> five, six (*pause*) seven
> four, five (*pause*) six
> two, three (*pause*) four
> six, seven (*pause*) eight
> zero, one (*pause*) two

Then repeat the activity, eliciting responses from individual Sts.

Extra idea

- Give Sts more practice by doing simple sums with them on the board, e.g. *What's four and two?*

d (1 11))) Focus on the instructions and demonstrate or explain the activity.

Play the audio and get Sts to write down the numbers in digits. Pause the audio if Sts need more time to write.

Check answers by writing the numbers on the board as digits and in words.

See script 1.11

<table>
<tr><td colspan="6">(1 11)))</td></tr>
<tr><td>1</td><td>seven</td><td>5</td><td>nine</td><td>9</td><td>six</td></tr>
<tr><td>2</td><td>three</td><td>6</td><td>one</td><td>10</td><td>two</td></tr>
<tr><td>3</td><td>zero</td><td>7</td><td>four</td><td>11</td><td>ten</td></tr>
<tr><td>4</td><td>eight</td><td>8</td><td>five</td><td></td><td></td></tr>
</table>

Extra challenge

• Before writing the numbers in words on the board, get Sts to do it.

4 PRONUNCIATION /h/, /aɪ/, and /iː/

Pronunciation notes

• You may want to highlight to Sts the following sound–spelling patterns. Use Sts' L1 to do this if you know it:

– /h/ *h* at the beginning of a word is pronounced /h/, e.g. *hello*. (There are a few exceptions, but apart from *hour*, the others are not relevant for Sts at this level.)

– /aɪ/ This is actually a diphthong (literally 'two sounds'). It is usually spelled *i* before a single consonant followed by silent *e*, as in the example word *bike*.

– /iː/ Two of the most common spellings of this sound are double *e* as in *meet* and *ea* as in *repeat*.

• See also **Pronunciation** in the **Introduction**, *p.8*.

a (1 12))) Focus on the three sound pictures *house*, *bike*, and *tree*. Tell Sts that they are example words to help them to remember English sounds.

Explain that the phonetic symbol in the picture represents the sound. Phonetic symbols are used in dictionaries to help learners pronounce words correctly.

Read the **Pronunciation notes** and decide how much of the information you want to give your Sts.

Focus on the exercise and play the audio once the whole way through for Sts just to listen.

> (1 12)))
> See the words and sounds in the Student's Book on *p.5*

Focus on the sound picture *house*. Play the audio to model and drill the word and the sound (pause after the sound).

Now focus on the words after *house*. Explain that the pink letters are the /h/ sound. Play the audio, pausing after each word for Sts to listen and repeat.

Now repeat the same process for *bike* /aɪ/ and *tree* /iː/. Try to exaggerate the /iː/ so that Sts realize that it is a long sound.

If these sounds are difficult for your Sts, model them yourself so that Sts can see your mouth position, and get Sts to repeat them a few more times.

Play the audio again from the beginning, pausing after each group of words for Sts to repeat.

Give further practice as necessary.

Finally, get Sts, in pairs, to practise saying the words.

Extra support

• If you are using an interactive whiteboard, you can focus on each sound individually before moving on to the next one.

b (1 13))) Focus on the sentences and play the audio once the whole way through for Sts just to listen.

> (1 13)))
> See the sentences in the Student's Book on *p.5*

Then play the audio for Sts to listen and repeat.

Get Sts to practise saying the sentences in pairs. Monitor and help with any pronunciation problems.

5 SPEAKING

Focus on the flow chart. Demonstrate the conversation on the left side with a student whose name you remember. Do the same with two other Sts.

Demonstrate the right side of the conversation with a student whose name you pretend to have forgotten. Do the same with two other Sts.

Model and drill both conversations getting Sts to repeat them after you. Then see if Sts can remember the conversations without looking at their books.

Tell Sts to move around the class and practise the conversations from memory with other Sts.

This activity, as well as consolidating the new language, will help Sts remember each other's names.

Monitor and help, dealing with any general pronunciation problems at the end.

Extra support

• Tell Sts to close their books. Elicit the two conversations onto the board. They can refer to this during the activity if they can't remember the phrases.

Extra idea

• Before Sts start you could put music on. Tell Sts to move around the room. When the music stops, Sts should do their role-play with the person nearest them.

6 VOCABULARY days of the week

a Tell Sts to go to **Vocabulary Bank** *Numbers and days* on *p.116*.

(1 14))) Look at **2 Days of the week** and focus on **a**. Play the audio for Sts to listen and repeat the days in chorus. Pause the audio as necessary.

> (1 14)))
> See the days of the week in the Student's Book on *p.116*

Then repeat the activity, getting individual Sts to repeat the words. Make sure Sts know what the words are in their L1. Give extra practice of the words which are causing them the most problems. Highlight the silent *d* in *Wednesday* /'wenzdeɪ/, and the pronunciation of *Tuesday* /'tjuːzdeɪ/ and *Thursday* /'θɜːzdeɪ/, which Sts usually find tricky.

Focus on the **Capital letters** box and go through it with the class, explaining that in English, unlike some other languages, days of the week begin with capital letters.

Focus on **b**. Explain the words *today* and *tomorrow* by writing the actual date (not the day of the week) on the board. Point to it and say *today*. Then write the next day's date and say *tomorrow*. Ask Sts *What day is today?* Elicit the day of the week. Then ask *What day is tomorrow?* and elicit the response. See if any Sts know what *the weekend* is and elicit the days.

Drill the pronunciation of *today*, *tomorrow*, and *the weekend*. Make sure Sts don't pronounce the double **r** in *tomorrow* too strongly.

Get Sts to complete the exercise with the correct days. Make sure they start with a capital letter.

Tell Sts to go back to the main lesson **1A**.

Extra support

• If you think Sts need more practice, you may want to give them the Vocabulary photocopiable activity at this point or leave it for later as consolidation or revision.

b ①15)) Focus on the instructions and demonstrate by saying the days *Thursday* and *Friday* yourself. Gesture to indicate that the class should respond with the next day (*Saturday*).

Now play the audio and pause after the next two days. Ask Sts what the next day is (*Wednesday*). Make sure Sts are clear about what they have to do before continuing.

Play the rest of the audio and give Sts time to say the next day. Get a whole class response.

---

①15))

Thursday, Friday (*pause*) Saturday
Monday, Tuesday (*pause*) Wednesday
Saturday, Sunday (*pause*) Monday
Friday, Saturday (*pause*) Sunday
Tuesday, Wednesday (*pause*) Thursday
Sunday, Monday (*pause*) Tuesday
Wednesday, Thursday (*pause*) Friday

Then repeat the activity, getting individual Sts to say the day.

c Focus on the phrases for saying goodbye. Demonstrate by pretending that you are leaving for the day. Walk towards the door and say, for example, *Goodbye! See you tomorrow | on Wednesday*, etc.

Model and drill the pronunciation of the words and phrases and get Sts to repeat them after you. Highlight that *goodbye* has the stress on the second syllable. Show / explain that *Bye* is a shorter form of *Goodbye* and it is more informal.

Get Sts to practise by saying *Goodbye* to the person next to them. Demonstrate / explain that we often combine *bye* or *Goodbye* with another phrase such as *See you* + day.

WORDS AND PHRASES TO LEARN

④61)) Tell Sts to go to *p.130* and focus on the **Words and phrases to learn** for **1A**. Make sure Sts understand the meaning of each phrase. If necessary, remind them of the context in which the words and phrases came up in the lesson. If you speak your Sts' L1, you might like to elicit a translation for the words | phrases for the Sts to write next to them. Play the audio, pausing after each phrase for Sts to repeat. You may also like to ask Sts to test each other on the phrases.

G verb *be* (singular): *he, she, it*
V countries
P /ɪ/, /əʊ/, /s/, and /ʃ/

1B Where are you from?

Lesson plan

In this lesson Sts continue with the verb *be* and here they learn the *he, she*, and *it* form.

In the first part of the lesson Sts learn 15 country words and then they practise asking where people are from and where places are. *He is, She is*, and *It is* are presented in Grammar through a conversation about where a film director and an actress are from. Pronunciation introduces Sts to four new sounds – /ɪ/, /əʊ/, /s/, and /ʃ/. Finally, in the last activity Sts first practise distinguishing between the pronunciation of *he* and *she*, and then they identify the nationality of different people and things.

Note that because Sts are beginners we have restricted the number of countries taught in the **Vocabulary Bank** to 15 and these same countries are then recycled and revised in subsequent lessons. Teachers will probably also want to teach Sts their own and neighbouring countries if these do not appear in the **Vocabulary Bank**.

STUDY LINK
- Workbook 1B
- iTutor
- iChecker on iTutor
- www.oup.com/elt/englishfile

Extra photocopiable activities
- **Grammar** verb *be* (singular): *he, she, it p.140*
- **Communicative** Where are they from? *p.174* (instructions *p.163*)
- **Vocabulary** Countries *p.211* (instructions *p.204*)
- www.oup.com/elt/teacher/englishfile

Optional lead-in (books closed)
- Pin a world map to the wall or project one onto the board. Point to Sts' country / countries and elicit the name(s). Write it / them on the board. Model and drill the pronunciation.
- Point to England and elicit the name. Write it on the board. Model and drill the pronunciation.
- Finally, if you are from a different country, point to it on the map and elicit the name. Write it on the board. Model and drill the pronunciation.

1 VOCABULARY countries

a (1 16)) Books open. Focus on the six countries and use a map or Sts' L1 to elicit what the countries are. Tell Sts that they are going to hear a short piece of music from each of the countries on the list. They have to guess where each one is from. Tell them to write the number of their guess in the box.

Play the first piece of music on the audio and pause.

When you are sure that Sts understand the task, play the rest of the audio. Pause as needed for Sts to write their answers.

> **(1 16))**
> *Extracts of:*
> 1 *Spanish flamenco music*
> 2 *US country music*
> 3 *Chinese music*
> 4 *Brazilian samba*
> 5 *Turkish music*
> 6 *Russian Cossack-type music*

b (1 17)) Play the audio for Sts to listen and check their guesses.

Check answers. Ask how many Sts were able to guess all of the countries.

> 2 the United States   4 Brazil   6 Russia
> 3 China   5 Turkey

> **(1 17))**
> 1 *Spanish flamenco music*, Spain
> 2 *US country music*, the United States
> 3 *Chinese music*, China
> 4 *Brazilian samba*, Brazil
> 5 *Turkish music*, Turkey
> 6 *Russian Cossack-type music*, Russia

c Tell Sts to go to **Vocabulary Bank** *Countries and nationalities* on *p.117*. Write the page number on the board.

(1 18)) Look at **1 Countries** and focus on **a**. Play the audio for Sts to listen and repeat the countries in chorus. Pause the audio as necessary. Highlight the word stress and the pronunciation of the more difficult words. Give further practice as necessary, modelling and drilling the pronunciation yourself, or using the audio.

> **(1 18))**
> See the list of countries in the Student's Book on *p.117*

Explain that *the United States* is the shortened form of the *United States of America*. You could also point out that Americans usually say *the US*, but both are possible.

Then play the audio again, getting individual Sts to repeat the countries.

Focus on the **Capital letters** box and go through it with the class, explaining that in English countries always begin with capital letters.

Now do **b**. Get Sts to cover the words in **a**, look at the photos, and say the countries. Sts can do this individually or with a partner. Monitor and help. Listen for any general pronunciation mistakes. Write the words on the board, and model and drill them with choral and individual repetition.

Focus on **c**. Teach Sts the name of their country if it is not in the list and you didn't do the Optional lead-in. Write it on the board and model and drill the word. Tell Sts to write it in the gap.

Tell Sts to go back to the main lesson **1B**.

Extra support

• If you think Sts need more practice, you may want to give them the Vocabulary photocopiable activity at this point or leave it for later as consolidation or revision.

d (**1**`19`)) Sts have already seen that one syllable in a multi-syllabic word is pronounced more strongly than others (= word stress). Here they see that certain words (the ones which carry the important information in a sentence) are pronounced more strongly than others (= sentence rhythm), e.g. in *Where are you from?* **where** and **from** are pronounced more strongly than *are* and *you*. *Where* and *from* are important to understand the question. In the answer *I'm from Toledo*, **Toledo** is stressed as it is important to understand the answer.

Focus on the instructions and the conversation. Demonstrate / explain to Sts in their L1 if you know it that the bigger bold words in the conversation are stressed more strongly than the others.

Then play the audio once the whole way through for Sts just to listen.

> (**1**`19`))
> See the conversation in the Student's Book on *p.6*

Elicit / explain / demonstrate the meaning of each phrase. Make sure Sts know that Toledo is a city.

Now play the audio again, pausing after each line for Sts to listen and repeat. Encourage them to get the rhythm right.

Extra support

• Get Sts on one side of the classroom to repeat the questions in chorus. Then have Sts on the other side repeat the answers. Finally, repeat, swapping roles.

e Put Sts in pairs, **A** and **B**. Focus on the instructions and demonstrate that they are going to practise the conversation using their own countries and cities. Get a good pair to demonstrate the activity.

Get Sts to practise with their partner, inserting their own town / city and country.

Now ask Sts to get up and practise the conversation with other Sts.

Extra idea

• If your Sts all come from the same place, you could ask them to choose a different country and city.

f Tell Sts that they are going to ask each other where certain places are. Focus on the question in the speech bubble and the three possible answers. Model and drill the pronunciation.

Now put Sts in pairs, **A** and **B**, and tell them to go to **Communication *Where is it?*, A** on *p.76* and **B** on *p.80*.

Go over the instructions and make sure Sts understand what they have to do. Stress that they must answer each question using one of the three options in the speech bubbles depending on whether they know the answer. Demonstrate by asking *Where's Manchester?* (*It's in England*).

When they have finished find out who got most of the answers right.

Extra support

• If Sts are having trouble understanding the name of the places their partner is saying, tell them to write the name on a piece of paper.

Tell Sts to go back to the main lesson **1B**.

2 GRAMMAR verb *be* (singular): *he, she, it*

a (**1**`20`)) Focus on the photo and the conversation. You could ask Sts if they know any of the people. Alfonso Cuarón is a Mexican film director, screenwriter, and producer best known for his films *Y Tu Mamá También* (2001), *Harry Potter and the Prisoner of Azkaban* (2004), *Children of Men* (2006), and *Gravity* (2013). Sandra Bullock is an American actress; she won many awards for her role in *The Blind Side* (2009) and *Gravity* (2013). Elicit the meaning of *fantastic*. Then tell Sts to read and listen to the conversation and complete each gap with a country.

Play the audio once for Sts to complete the conversation.

Play the audio again, as necessary.

Check answers.

1 Mexico	2 England	3 the USA

> (**1**`20`))
> A Where's he from?
> B He's from Mexico.
> A Is she from England?
> B No, she isn't. She's from the USA.
> A Is she good?
> B Yes, she is. She's fantastic.

b (**1**`21`)) Play the audio again, pausing for Sts to listen and repeat. Try to get Sts to pronounce the *s* in *Where's* and *He's* as /z/ and the letters *sh* in *She* as /ʃ/.

> (**1**`21`))
> See script 1.20

c Put Sts in pairs, **A** and **B**. Focus on the instructions and get a good pair to demonstrate the activity.

Now ask Sts to practise the conversation.

Make sure they swap roles. Monitor and help.

Write any pronunciation mistakes on the board and correct them afterwards.

d Focus on the photos. Ask *he, she, or it?* for each photo. Tell Sts to match each word with a photo.

Check answers. Make sure Sts understand that *he* is used for a male, *she* for a female and *it* for places, things, etc.

1 he	2 she	3 it

e Here Sts see where the new forms of the verb *be*, which they have just learnt, fit into the chart along with the forms they already know (*I* and *you*). Focus on the chart and make sure Sts understand *singular*. Point out the positive and negative columns, and give Sts time to complete the gaps.

Get Sts to compare with a partner and then check answers.

[+]	[−]
He **is**	He **isn't**
She **is**	She **isn't**
It **is**	It **isn't**

f (1 22)) (1 23)) (1 24)) Tell Sts to go to **Grammar Bank 1B** on *p.92*.

Focus on the example sentences and play the audio for Sts to listen and repeat. Pause the audio as necessary.

Go through the rules with the class using the expanded information in the **Additional grammar notes** below to help you. You may want to use Sts' L1 here.

Additional grammar notes
Verb *be* (singular): *he, she, it*

- In English *he* is used for a male and *she* for a female. Things in English don't have a gender as they do in many languages. *It* is used for everything which is not a man or a woman, e.g. things, countries, places, buildings, etc. Animals are often *it*, but can also be *he* or *she* if they are yours and you know the sex.

- Remind Sts that in conversations it is more common to use contractions than full forms.

- Point out that *is* is contracted in conversation after question words, e.g. *What's your name? Where's he from?*, but *are* isn't contracted in *Where are you from?*

- The *he | she | it* form of the verb *be* has two possible negations: *he | she | it isn't* and *he's | she's | it's not*. Both forms are common, but we recommend you teach only *he | she | it isn't* so as not to confuse Sts. Only point out the alternative form if Sts ask about it.

Focus on the exercises for **1B** on *p.93* and get Sts to do them individually or in pairs. If they do them individually, get them to compare answers with a partner.

Check answers, getting Sts to read out the full sentences.

a
1 She's	4 It's	7 It's
2 It's	5 He's	8 He's
3 He's	6 She's	

b
1 's, Is, is	4 Is, isn't, 's
2 Is, 's	5 Is, isn't, 's
3 's, 's	

c
1 's, Is, is	3 are, 'm
2 's, Is, isn't, 's, are, 'm	4 's, 's, 're, 'm, 's

Tell Sts to go back to the main lesson **1B**.

Extra support
- If you think Sts need more practice, you may want to give them the Grammar photocopiable activity at this point or leave it for later as consolidation or revision.

3 PRONUNCIATION /ɪ/, /əʊ/, /s/, and /ʃ/

Pronunciation notes
- You may want to highlight some or all of the following sound–spelling rules:

  – /ɪ/ The letter *i* between two consonants is usually pronounced /ɪ/, e.g. *fish*. NB *England* (the *e* = /ɪ/) is irregular.

  – /əʊ/ In English, the sound of the letter *o* in *phone* is a diphthong (literally 'two sounds'), i.e. a combination of the two sounds /ə/ + /ʊ/. It is usually spelt by the letter *o*, or *o* + consonant + *e*.

  – /s/ The letter *s* at the beginning of a word is nearly always pronounced /s/, e.g. *sit, stand*.

  – The letter *c* (before *i*) at the beginning of a word and before consonant + *e* is usually /s/, e.g. *cinema, city*, but the letter *c* is often /k/, e.g. *cat*.

  – /ʃ/ The consonants *sh* are always pronounced /ʃ/, e.g. *she*. The letters *ti* also produce this sound in words that include the syllable *-tion*, e.g. *nationality*. NB *Russia* (the letters *ss* = /ʃ/) is an exception.

! Make sure Sts make a /ʃ/ sound and not an /s/ sound for /ʃ/. It might help to tell Sts that /ʃ/ is the sound of silence by putting your finger to your mouth and saying *shhhhhh*.

- See also **Pronunciation** in the **Introduction**, *p.8*.

a (1 25)) Focus on the four sound pictures *fish, phone, snake*, and *shower*. Remind Sts that they are example words to help them to remember English sounds and that the phonetic symbol in the picture represents the sound.

Read the **Pronunciation notes** and decide how much of the information you want to give your Sts.

Focus on the exercise and play the audio once the whole way through for Sts just to listen.

> (1 25))
> See the words and sounds in the Student's Book on *p.7*

Focus on the sound picture *fish*. Play the audio to model and drill the word and the sound (pause after the sound).

Now focus on the words after *fish*. Remind Sts that the pink letters are the /ɪ/ sound. Play the audio, pausing after each word for Sts to listen and repeat.

Now repeat the same process for *phone* /əʊ/, *snake* /s/, and *shower* /ʃ/.

If these sounds are difficult for your Sts, model them yourself so that Sts can see your mouth position, and get Sts to repeat them a few more times.

Now play the audio again from the beginning, pausing after each group of words for Sts to repeat.

Give further practice as necessary.

Finally, get Sts, in pairs, to practise saying the words.

Extra support

- If you are using an interactive whiteboard, you can focus on each sound individually before moving on to the next one.

b (1 26)) Focus on the exercise and play the audio once the whole way through for Sts just to listen.

> (1 26))
> See the sentences in the Student's Book on *p.7*

Now play the audio again, pausing after each sentence for Sts to repeat.

Then repeat the activity, eliciting responses from individual Sts.

Finally, tell Sts to practise in pairs. Monitor and help with any pronunciation problems.

4 LISTENING & SPEAKING

a (1 27)) This section gives Sts practice in distinguishing aurally between *he* and *she* and then trying to make the distinction themselves. Depending on your Sts' nationality many Sts will find this quite tricky.

Focus on the sentences. Play the audio once the whole way through for Sts to try to hear the difference between the sentences.

> (1 27))
> See the sentences in the Student's Book on *p.7*

Extra support

- Say the sentences to the class, exaggerating slightly the differences in pronunciation.

b (1 28)) Focus on the sentences in **a** again. Explain that Sts are going to hear only one of the sentences for each number and they have to tick the one they hear.

Play the audio, pausing for Sts to tick the sentences.

Play the audio again for Sts to check their answers.

Check answers.

1 b	2 b	3 a	4 b	5 a

> (1 28))
> 1 Is she from Egypt?   4 She's nice.
> 2 He's from Turkey.   5 Where is he?
> 3 Where's he from?

c Focus on the sentences in **a** again and put Sts in pairs.

Get Sts to practise saying them.

Extra challenge

- Put Sts in pairs, **A** and **B**. **A** reads a sentence and **B** says *a* or *b*. Then they swap roles.

d (1 29)) Tell Sts they are going to hear six sentences or questions and they must write them down.

Play the audio once the whole way through for Sts just to listen.

> (1 29))
> 1 He's from Egypt.   4 Is he from Turkey?
> 2 She's from Germany.   5 He isn't from England.
> 3 She isn't from Japan.   6 Is she from Brazil?

Now play the audio again, pausing after each item for Sts to listen and write. Play again as necessary.

Get Sts to compare with a partner and then elicit the answers onto the board.

> See script 1.29

e Focus on the photos and the example speech bubbles. Remind Sts of the difference between *he*, *she*, and *it* (you could do stick drawings on the board).

Remind Sts of the three possible ways of answering the questions (see exercise **1f**):
He | She | It's from…
I think he | she | it's from…
I don't know.

Extra support

- Write the options on the board for reference.

Put Sts in pairs and get them to ask and answer questions. Get a strong pair to demonstrate the activity first.

When Sts have finished, check answers. Don't write these on the board as Sts will be testing each other in the next exercise.

1 It's from Egypt.	6 She's from Russia.
2 He's from Brazil.	7 It's from Japan.
3 He's from Mexico.	8 It's from the USA.
4 She's from Spain.	9 It's from China.
5 It's from England.	10 He's from Italy.

f This exercise practises *yes | no* questions and short answers. Focus on the instructions and the example speech bubbles.

In the same pairs (or in new pairs), Sts now test their partner.

WORDS AND PHRASES TO LEARN

(4 61)) Tell Sts to go to *p.130* and focus on the **Words and phrases to learn** for **1B**. Make sure Sts understand the meaning of each phrase. If necessary, remind them of the context in which the words and phrases came up in the lesson. If you speak your Sts' L1, you might like to elicit a translation for the words / phrases for the Sts to write next to them. Play the audio, pausing after each phrase for Sts to repeat. You may also like to ask Sts to test each other on the phrases.

PRACTICAL ENGLISH
Episode 1 How do you spell it?

Lesson plan

This is the first in a series of six **Practical English** lessons that teach Sts basic functional language to help them survive in an English-speaking environment. Here Sts learn the alphabet and how to spell their names. In Vocabulary, they learn the words for things in the classroom, and useful Classroom language that will help them communicate with the teacher and their classmates in English right from the start.
Sts then learn how to check into a hotel and how to book a table in a restaurant, two contexts which put into practice spelling your name.
The functional dialogues feature two recurring characters: Rob, a British journalist based in London, and Jenny, an American living in New York, who works for the same company as Rob. These two characters reappear in subsequent levels of *English File*.
The lesson ends with a focus on all the useful phrases Sts saw in the lesson.

These sections can be used with *Class DVD*, *iTools*, or *Class Audio* (audio only).

Sts can find all the video content and activities on the *iTutor*.

STUDY LINK
- **Workbook** How do you spell it?
- iTutor
- www.oup.com/elt/englishfile

Extra photocopiable activities

- **Communicative** Who are you? *p.175* (instructions *p.163*)
- **Vocabulary** Classroom language *p.212* (instructions *p.204*)
- **Song** *All Together Now p.228* (instructions *p.226*)

Test and Assessment CD-ROM

- Quick Test 1
- File Test 1
- www.oup.com/elt/teacher/englishfile

Optional lead-in (books open)

- Books open. Focus on the English alphabet at the top of the page. Give Sts a little time to look at it. Ask Sts if it is the same as or different from the alphabet in their first language, e.g. the number of letters, etc.

- Write OK and USA on the board. Ask Sts how to say them. Then elicit the pronunciation of each letter one by one, and model and drill. If you know your Sts' L1, point out that these are examples of how we use letters of the alphabet to communicate.

1 THE ALPHABET

a **1 30)))** Choose a student with a short name and ask *What's your name?* Show that you want to write their name on the board and pretend that you don't know how to spell it. Ask *How do you spell it?* Let Sts try and tell you the letters in English (they may know one or two).

Explain that it's important to learn the English alphabet because you may need to spell your name (especially when you're talking on the phone). Letters of the alphabet are also important for flight numbers, car number plates, email addresses, etc.

Focus on the task and play the audio once the whole way through for Sts just to listen.

> **1 30)))**
> See the alphabet in the Student's Book on *p.8*

Then play the audio again, pausing after every letter for Sts to repeat in chorus. When you finish each group of letters you may want to pause and give extra practice before moving on to the next group. Concentrate especially on the letters which your Sts find particularly difficult to pronounce.

b **1 31)))** This exercise helps Sts to learn the alphabet by dividing letters which share the same vowel sound into three groups. Focus on the task.

Play the audio once the whole way through for Sts to hear the words, sounds, and letters.

> **1 31)))**
> See the chart in the Student's Book on *p.8*

Play the audio again, pausing for Sts to listen and repeat. Model the sounds yourself if necessary showing Sts what position their mouths should be in.

Now try to elicit the whole alphabet round the class, writing the letters on the board to help Sts remember. Give further practice around the class as necessary.

c **1 32)))** This activity is to help Sts distinguish between letters that are sometimes confused. Depending on your Sts' L1 some of these pairs will be more difficult than others.

Play the audio once the whole way through for Sts to hear the difference between the letters. Ask *Can you hear the difference?* If Sts answer 'no', model the letters yourself to help them hear the difference between the sounds. Play the audio again if necessary.

> **1 32)))**
> See the pairs of letters in the Student's Book on *p.8*

PE1

d (**1 33**))) Now tell Sts they're only going to hear <u>one</u> of the letters from each pair in **c**. Explain that they have to circle the letter they think they hear.

Play the audio once for Sts to circle the letter.

1 33)))				
1 A	3 W	5 B	7 J	9 N
2 E	4 I	6 V	8 K	

Get Sts to compare with a partner. Play the audio again if necessary.

Check answers by playing the audio again, pausing after each letter, and eliciting the answer onto the board.

See script 1.33

e (**1 34**))) Focus on the photos and the task. Demonstrate / explain that the letters are abbreviations (you could use MTV as an example = Music Television).

Play the audio once the whole way through for Sts just to listen.

Give Sts time to work out with their partner how to say the abbreviations.

Elicit how you say them one by one, using the audio to confirm the correct pronunciation.

See script 1.34

1 34)))			
1 MTV	3 FBI	5 ATM	7 VW
2 CNN	4 BBC	6 USB	8 EU

To give some extra practice you could call out numbers between 1 and 8 for Sts to say the abbreviation, e.g. **T** *2*   **Sts** *CNN*.

Extra idea

- If your Sts are interested or ask, you could tell them the full form of each abbreviation:
  1 Music Television
  2 Cable News Network
  3 Federal Bureau of Investigation
  4 British Broadcasting Corporation
  5 Automated Teller Machine
  6 Universal Serial Bus
  7 Volkswagen
  8 European Union

Extra support

- You could play the audio again, pausing after each abbreviation for Sts to listen and repeat.

f Put Sts into pairs **A** and **B**. Tell them to go to **Communication** *Game: Hit the ships*, **A** on *p.76* and **B** on *p.80*.

This game is an adapted version of *Battleships*. If the game exists in your Sts' country, they will not have any problems seeing how this activity works. However, if they are not familiar with the original, you may need to use L1 to make it clear.

By playing the game, Sts will practise letters and numbers. The object of the game is to guess where the other person's ships are and to 'hit' them by correctly identifying a square where part of the ship is located.

When all parts of the ship have been hit then it is 'sunk'. The winner is the first person to 'sink' all the other person's ships.

Go through the instructions and make sure Sts understand what they have to do. Quickly elicit the pronunciation of numbers 1–10 and letters A–J. Demonstrate the activity on the board by drawing two small grids and taking the part of **A** or **B**. Show how Sts will use letters and numbers to identify the squares in the grid, e.g. the square in the top left corner is A1 and the bottom right J10. Make sure Sts know what *ship*, *hit*, and *nothing* mean.

Use a gesture to show a ship sinking after being completely hit. Say *It's sunk!* and get Sts to repeat. Write it on the board and model and drill pronunciation.

When Sts have finished find out who won in each pair.

Tell Sts to go back to the main lesson **PE1**.

In later classes try to recycle the alphabet whenever possible, e.g. play *Hangman* (see **Extra idea** below) as a warmer, get Sts to spell words in vocabulary exercises, have spelling quizzes, etc.

Extra idea

- Play *Hangman* to practise the alphabet. Think of a word Sts know, preferably of at least eight letters, e.g. *DICTIONARY*. Write a dash on the board for each letter of the word: _ _ _ _ _ _ _ _ _ _

- Sts call out letters one at a time. Encourage them to start with the five vowels and then move onto consonants. If the letter is in the word (e.g. *A*), fill it in each time it occurs, e.g. _ _ _ _ _ _ _ A _ _. Only accept correctly pronounced letters. If the letter is not in the word, draw the first line of this picture on the board:

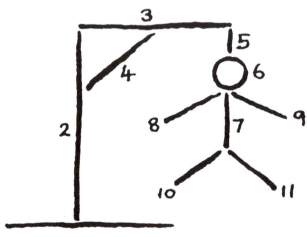

- Write any wrongly-guessed letters under the picture, so Sts don't repeat them. The object of the game is to guess the word before the man is 'hanged'. Sts can make guesses at any time, but each wrong guess is 'punished' by another line being drawn.

- The student who correctly guesses the word comes to the board and chooses a new word.

- Sts can also play on paper in pairs / groups.

2 VOCABULARY the classroom

a (1 35)) Focus on the conversation and the words in the list.

Play the audio once the whole way through for Sts just to listen and read. Tell them <u>not</u> to write at this time.

> (1 35))
> S = student, T = teacher
> S   What's *libro* in English?
> T   Book.
> S   How do you spell it?
> T   B-O-O-K.

Then play the audio again for Sts to listen and write.

Get Sts to compare with a partner and then check answers.

| 1 What | 2 English | 3 Book | 4 spell |

Make sure Sts understand the conversation. Model and drill the pronunciation. You could use the audio to do this. Then get Sts to practise it in pairs, swapping roles.

Extra idea

- You could get Sts to practise the conversation using words from their language which they have already learnt in English, e.g. numbers, days of the week, etc.

b Tell Sts to go to **Vocabulary Bank** *The classroom* on *p.118*. Write the page number on the board.

(1 36)) Look at **1 Things in the classroom** and focus on **a**. Play the audio for Sts to listen and repeat the words in chorus. Pause the audio as necessary. Remind Sts that the stressed syllable is underlined. Highlight the pronunciation of the words Sts find most difficult, e.g. *board, window, coat,* and *dictionary*. Give further practice as necessary, modelling and drilling the pronunciation yourself, or using the audio, and getting choral and individual responses.

> (1 36))
> See the things in the classroom in the Student's Book on *p.118*

Focus on **b**. Ask Sts to cover the words in **a** and look at the picture. Tell them to say the words. They could do this individually or with a partner.

Monitor and help as necessary, correcting any pronunciation errors.

If your Sts ask why some words are preceded by *the* (*the door*) and others *a* (*a window*), explain that we say *a window* because it is one of many, but we say *the door* because there is usually one door in a room. The same is true of *the board*. This difference is focussed on in more detail in **2A**.

Look at **c** and focus attention on the speech bubbles. Model the activity by pointing to something in the classroom and asking *What is it?* Elicit the response *It's a / the* (word).

Put Sts in pairs to continue asking and answering about things in the classroom.

(1 37)) Now look at **2 Classroom language** and focus on **a**. Point out the two sections: phrases Sts will hear you say and phrases they will need in the classroom. Focus on the pictures and the phrases. Elicit / explain the meaning of any words or phrases that Sts don't understand.

Play the audio once the whole way through for Sts just to listen.

> (1 37))
> See the list of phrases in the Student's Book on *p.118*

Then play it again for Sts to listen and repeat the phrases in chorus. Pause the audio as necessary. Give further practice as necessary, modelling and drilling the pronunciation yourself, or using the audio, and getting choral and individual responses.

Focus on **b**. Ask Sts to cover the phrases and look at the pictures. Tell them to say the phrases. They could do this individually or with a partner.

There may be other classroom instructions you use frequently yourself. You could teach them here too.

Tell Sts to go back to the main lesson **PE1**.

Extra support

- If you think Sts need more practice, you may want to give them the Vocabulary photocopiable activity at this point or leave it for later as consolidation or revision.

c (1 38)) Focus on conversations 1–3. Put Sts in pairs and give them time to read the conversations and think about what the missing words are (they could write them in pencil).

Play the audio once the whole way through for Sts just to listen and read at the same time. Tell them <u>not</u> to write at this time.

> (1 38))
> T = teacher, S = student
> 1
> T   Open your books, please. Go to page seven.
> S   Sorry, can you repeat that, please?
> T   Go to page seven.
>
> 2
> S   Excuse me. How do you spell 'birthday'?
> T   B-I-R-T-H-D-A-Y.
>
> 3
> S   Sorry I'm late.
> T   That's OK. Sit down, please.

Then play the audio again for Sts to listen and write.

Get Sts to compare their answers with their partner.

Elicit the answers and write them on the board.

| 1 Open, Go, Sorry, repeat |
| 2 Excuse, How |
| 3 Sorry, down |

The phrases *Excuse me*, *Sorry*, and *Sorry?* are easily confused. Write the three phrases on the board. Demonstrate / elicit the meaning and use of *Excuse me* (for politely attracting someone's attention) by giving an example with one student. Say *Excuse me. Are you* (name)*?* Then elicit the meaning and use of *Sorry* (to apologize) by knocking a student's pencil on the floor.

Finally, elicit the meaning and use of *Sorry?* (to ask for repetition). Say *What's your name?* to a student and pretend not to hear by putting your hand to your ear.

NB You can also say *Pardon?* when you want someone to repeat something. If you personally as a teacher tend to say *Pardon?*, it might be worth teaching it here as well. If so, model and drill the pronunciation /ˈpɑːdən/.

d Put Sts in pairs and get them to practise the conversations in **c**.

Make sure they swap roles. Monitor and help.

You could get a few pairs to perform in front of the class.

e Tell Sts they are going to hear the instructions they have just learnt and they have to do the actions.

Play the audio and pause after each instruction and wait for all the Sts to do each action. If necessary, repeat the phrase yourself.

> **1 39**))
>
> | | | | |
> |---|---|---|---|
> | 1 | Stand up. | 4 | Open your books. |
> | 2 | Close your books. | 5 | Go to page nine. |
> | 3 | Sit down, please. | | |

From now on, make sure you always give these instructions in English.

3 ▶️ CHECKING INTO A HOTEL

a **1 40**)) In this exercise Sts meet, for the first time, a character who will appear in all the **Practical English** lessons.

Focus on the photo of Rob and the task, and make sure Sts understand they will have to circle options **a** or **b** for each question.

Now focus on sentences 1–3. Focus on the UK in 1. If necessary, explain (using a map if you have one) that the UK (the United Kingdom) = England, Scotland, Wales, and Northern Ireland. Also make sure Sts know the meaning of the nouns *an artist* and *a journalist*, as well as the expressions *on holiday* and *for work*.

Play the video or audio once the whole way through for Sts just to listen.

> **1 40**))
>
> (script in Student's Book on *p.86*)
>
> Hello. I'm Rob. I'm from London. I'm a journalist. Today I'm in Poland. I'm not on holiday. I'm here for work.

Now play it again and give Sts time to circle **a** or **b**. Play again as necessary.

Get Sts to compare with a partner and then check answers.

> 1 a   2 b   3 b

Extra support

*   If there's time, you could get Sts to listen again with the script on *p.86*, so they can see exactly what they understood / didn't understand. Translate / explain any new words or phrases.

b **1 41**)) Focus on the **Names** box and go through it with the class.

Extra support

*   To make the distinction clear between *name* and *surname*, write your first name and your surname on the board (or the first name and surname of a well-known celebrity). Elicit which is your first name and which is your surname.

*   Highlight that you can say *name* (or *first name*), and *surname* (or *last name*). When asked *What's your name?* you usually reply with your first name in an informal situation, or your surname or full name in a formal situation, e.g. checking into a hotel.

*   You may want to point out that when we give our full name we always say first name then surname. NB Many people have a *middle name* as well (which is another first name, e.g. Peter / Mary), but this name is rarely used except on official forms.

*   Ask a few Sts *What's your first name?* and *What's your surname?* to practise the difference between the two. Then get Sts to ask each other.

Extra idea

*   You could bring in photos of famous people and show them to the class and ask *What's his / her first name? What's his / her surname?*

Focus on the photo and ask *Where is Rob?* and elicit that he is in a hotel.

Tell Sts to cover the sentences and just listen to Rob checking in. Play the video or audio once the whole way through for Sts just to listen.

> **1 41**))
>
> **Ro = Rob, R = Receptionist**
>
> **Ro** Hello.
> **R** Good afternoon.
> **Ro** My name's Rob Walker. I have a reservation.
> **R** Sorry, what's your surname?
> **Ro** Walker.
> **R** How do you spell it?
> **Ro** W-A-L-K-E-R.
> **R** Sorry?
> **Ro** W-A-L-K-E-R.
> **R** Thank you. OK, Mr Walker. You're in room 321.
> **Ro** Thanks.

Now tell Sts to look at the sentences in **b** and demonstrate / explain that they will hear the dialogue again and this time they need to put the sentences in the right order. Point out that number 1 (*Hello*) and 7 (*W-A-L-K-E-R*) have been done for them.

Play the video or audio again and give Sts time to order the sentences. Play again as necessary.

Check answers by playing the video or audio again and pausing after each line. Elicit / explain the meaning of any new words, e.g. *afternoon* and *reservation*, and model and drill pronunciation.

See script 1.41

Extra challenge

- After playing the video or audio the first time, have Sts uncover the sentences and try to put them in order. Then play the video or audio again for Sts to check their answers and make any corrections necessary.

c (**1** 42))) Play the dialogue again, pausing for Sts to listen and repeat each sentence. Give further practice as necessary.

> (**1** 42)))
> See script 1.41

d Ask Sts to cover their Student Book page and elicit the dialogue in **b** and write it on the board. If necessary, prompt Sts' memory by giving the first letter of a word or phrase.

Underline GOOD AFTERNOON on the board and tell Sts to uncover the page and look at the **Greetings** box. Go through it with the class. Explain the rules to Sts and highlight that these times are very approximate. Write the greetings on the board and elicit the stress. Model and drill the words *morning*, *afternoon*, *evening* as well as the greetings.

! *Good afternoon* and *Good evening* are rather formal in English. People often just say *Hello* when they greet each other. You may also want to teach *Goodnight*, which is used only when saying goodbye at night, e.g. before going to bed.

Now put Sts in pairs, **A** and **B**. Give each student a role (Rob and the receptionist) and ask them to focus on the instructions for the role-play. Make sure Sts understand that they have to use their own names and should use different greetings depending on the time of day.

Clean the board and get Sts to do the role-play.

Make sure Sts swap roles. Monitor and help as needed.

Have one or two pairs present their role-plays to the class.

Extra support

- Leave some words from the dialogue on the board to prompt weaker Sts in the role-play.

4 ◼ BOOKING A TABLE

a (**1** 43))) Tell Sts they are now going to meet the other main character, who will appear in all the **Practical English** lessons. Focus on the photo and tell Sts they are now going to listen to a woman called Jenny. Focus on sentences 1–3 and make sure Sts know the meaning of *birthday*.

Tell Sts to cover the sentences and just listen to Jenny.

Play the video or audio once the whole way through for Sts just to listen.

> (**1** 43)))
> (script in Student's Book on *p.86*)
> Hi. I'm Jenny Zielinski. I'm from New York. Tomorrow's my birthday, and my favourite restaurant in New York is *Locanda Verde*. It's Italian.

Now play it again and give Sts time to circle **a** or **b**. Play again as necessary.

Get Sts to compare with a partner and then check answers.

> 1 a   2 b   3 a

Extra support

- If there's time, you could get Sts to listen again with the script on *p.86*, so they can see exactly what they understood / didn't understand. Translate / explain any new words or phrases.

b (**1** 44))) First, focus on the **Z** box and go through it with the class. Explain that this is the only letter of the alphabet that is different in American English from British English.

Now focus on the task and the information. You might want to quickly revise the days of the week. If there is a table in the classroom, point to it. If not, draw one on the board. Explain / elicit the meaning of the phrase *a table for __ people*. Point to your watch or a clock in your class for *Time*.

Tell Sts Jenny is on the phone to the restaurant. Play the video or audio once the whole way through for Sts just to listen.

> (**1** 44)))
> (script in Student's Book on *p.86*)
> **W = waiter, J = Jenny**
> **W** *Locanda Verde*. Good morning. How can I help you?
> **J** Hello. A table for tomorrow, please.
> **W** Tomorrow... er, Tuesday?
> **J** Yes, that's right.
> **W** How many people?
> **J** Three.
> **W** What time?
> **J** Seven o'clock.
> **W** What's your name, please?
> **J** Jenny Zielinski. That's Z-I-E-L-I-N-S-K-I.
> **W** Thank you, Ms, er, Zielinksi. OK. So, a table for three on Tuesday at seven.
> **J** Great. Thanks. Bye.
> **W** Goodbye, see you tomorrow.

Now play it again and give Sts time to complete the form. Play again as necessary.

Get Sts to compare with a partner and then check answers. Elicit Jenny's surname onto the board.

Day	**Tuesday / tomorrow**
Name	Jenny **ZIELINSKI**
Table for	**three** people
Time	**seven** (o'clock)

Extra challenge

- Ask *What is Ms Zielinski's first name?* to elicit *Jenny*. Ask Sts *How do you spell it?* Then explain that when a word has a double letter, like the *N-N* in *Jenny*, they can say either *N-N* or *double N*. Demonstrate with another name, e.g. *Anna*.

Extra support

- If there's time, you could get Sts to listen again with the script on *p.86*, so they can see exactly what they understood / didn't understand. Translate / explain any new words or phrases.

5 USEFUL PHRASES

1 45)) Focus on the phrases and go through them with the class to make sure they are clear about the meaning. You may want to teach *All right* as a common synonym of *OK*. You may want to point out that nobody knows for sure what the origin is of the expression *OK*.

Play the video or audio once the whole way through for Sts just to listen.

> **1 45))**
> See the phrases in the Student's Book on *p.9*

Now play the video or audio again, pausing after each phrase for Sts to listen and repeat.

Give further practice as necessary, modelling and drilling the pronunciation yourself, or using the video or audio, and getting choral and individual responses.

Extra challenge

- Finally, you could test your Sts' memory of the phrases by writing just the first letters of the words on the board, e.g. I h___ a r_____ (= *I have a reservation*), and seeing if Sts can remember the phrase. Alternatively, you could use L1 translations to prompt the phrases.

6 **4 MP3))** SONG *All Together Now* ♫

For Sts of this level all authentic song lyrics will include language that they don't know. Nevertheless Sts are usually very motivated to try to understand lyrics and if you know your Sts' L1, you can use this to translate unknown words and phrases.

This song was originally recorded by The Beatles in 1967. The song will help Sts remember some of the letters of the alphabet and numbers 1–10. For copyright reasons this is a cover version.

If you want to do this song in class, use the photocopiable activity on *p.228*.

You will find the songs as MP3 files on CD4 of the Class audio CD.

> **4 MP3))**
> ***All Together Now***
> One, two, three, four
> Can I have a little more?
> Five, six, seven, eight, nine, ten
> I love you
>
> A, B, C, D
> Can I bring my friend to tea?
> E, F, G, H, I, J
> I love you
>
> ***Chorus***
> Sail the ship,
> Chop the tree,
> Skip the rope,
> Look at me
>
> All together now... (x4)
>
> Black, white, green, red
> Can I take my friend to bed?
> Pink, brown, yellow, orange and blue
> I love you
>
> All together now... (x8)
>
> ***Chorus***
>
> All together now....(x4)

G verb *be* (plural): *we, you, they*
V nationalities
P /dʒ/, /tʃ/, and /ʃ/

2A We aren't English. We're American.

Lesson plan

In this lesson Sts complete their knowledge of the verb *be*. Here they study the positive, negative, and question forms for *we*, *you*, and *they*.

At the beginning of the lesson Sts learn the nationality adjectives for the countries they learnt in **1B**.

The pronunciation focus is on three new sounds (/dʒ/, /tʃ/, and /ʃ/) as well as nationality words. The grammar is then presented through the context of football fans from different countries. In Reading, Sts read and listen to a conversation between an American and a British couple in a hotel restaurant. The setting provides consolidation of the new language and some useful phrases. Finally, in Speaking Sts practise asking about what nationality different famous people and things are.

STUDY LINK
- Workbook 2A
- iTutor
- www.oup.com/elt/englishfile

Extra photocopiable activities

- **Grammar** verb *be* (plural): *we, you, they p.141*
- **Communicative** Match the sentences *p.176* (instructions *p.164*)
- **Vocabulary** Countries, nationalities, and languages *p.213* (instructions *p.205*)
- www.oup.com/elt/teacher/englishfile

Optional lead-in (books closed)

- Give Sts a quick quiz on capital cities to revise the countries they already know. Tell Sts that you are going to say a capital city, and they have to say the country. You could make this a team game by dividing the class down the middle.

London (England)	Tokyo (Japan)
Brasília (Brazil)	Madrid (Spain)
Cairo (Egypt)	Rome (Italy)
Beijing (China)	Mexico City (Mexico)
Berlin (Germany)	Bern (Switzerland)
Warsaw (Poland)	Moscow (Russia)
Washington DC (the United States)	Ankara (Turkey)

1 VOCABULARY nationalities

a Focus on the instructions and the countries in the list.

Then focus on the first photo and teach the word *plane* /pleɪn/. Model and drill the pronunciation. Ask the class *Where is the plane from?* and point out the example *It's from the UK*. Give Sts time to complete the other sentences with the countries in the list.

Check answers.

2 Switzerland   3 the United States   4 Turkey

b Tell Sts to go to **Vocabulary Bank** *Countries and nationalities* on *p.117*.

1 47)) Look at **2 Nationalities** and focus on **a**. Play the audio and get Sts to repeat the countries and nationalities. Pause the audio as necessary. Give further practice as necessary, modelling and drilling the pronunciation yourself, or using the audio, and getting choral and individual responses.

> **1 47))**
> See the countries and nationalities in the Student's Book on *p.117*

Focus on *the UK / British*. Remind Sts that the UK (the United Kingdom) = England, Scotland, Wales, and Northern Ireland. The official nationality for people from these countries is *British*. If somebody is from England, they may describe themselves as *English* or *British*. *Great Britain* is also often used and technically refers to the island including England, Scotland, and Wales, but not Northern Ireland.

Focus on the **Word stress** box and go through it with the class. You could tell Sts some or all of the following:

- in all multi-syllable English words one syllable is stressed more than the other syllable(s).
- there aren't any firm rules governing word stress, although the majority of two-syllable words are stressed on the first syllable. The number of syllables a word has is determined by the way it is pronounced, not by how it is written, e.g. *nice* = one syllable, not two, because the *e* is not pronounced.
- there are no written accents in English. A dictionary shows which syllable in a word is stressed, e.g. *Brazilian* /brəˈzɪliən/. The syllable after the apostrophe is the stressed one.
- Sts need to be careful with the pronunciation of words which are the same or similar to ones in their language as the stress pattern may be different.

27

Extra support

- Write BRAZIL and BRAZILIAN on the board. Ask Sts how many syllables there are in *Brazil* to check Sts know the meaning of *syllable* (2). Then ask Sts to tell you which syllable is stressed in each word (*the second*). Underline the stressed syllables (BRA<u>ZIL</u>, BRA<u>ZIL</u>IAN).

- Repeat for *China* and *Chinese* (<u>CHI</u>NA, CHI<u>NESE</u>) and elicit that the stress in the words is different.

Focus on **b** and get Sts to cover the words, look at the flags, and to remember and say the countries and nationalities. They could do this individually or with a partner.

Monitor and help. Make a note of any pronunciation problems Sts are having. Write the words on the board and model and drill the ones that Sts find difficult.

Now look at **c**. Teach Sts how to say their nationality if it is not in the list. Give Sts time to complete the gap.

Focus on the **Countries and languages** box and go through it with the class. Highlight that nationality and language words always begin with a capital letter.

Focus on **d**. Give Sts time to answer the question. Ask individual Sts for feedback.

Tell Sts to go back to the main lesson **2A**.

Extra support

- If you think Sts need more practice, you may want to give them the Vocabulary photocopiable activity at this point or leave it for later as consolidation or revision.

2 PRONUNCIATION /dʒ/, /tʃ/, and /ʃ/

Pronunciation notes

- The sounds focussed on in this lesson are all consonant sounds. Sts may find the symbols /dʒ/ and /tʃ/ difficult to remember.

- You may want to highlight the following sound–spelling patterns:

    – /dʒ/ *j* is always pronounced /dʒ/, e.g. *juice*. The letter *g* can also sometimes be /dʒ/, e.g. *German*, *orange*, especially before e, although it is normally /g/, e.g. *goal*.

    – /tʃ/ The consonant clusters *ch* and *tch* are usually pronounced /tʃ/, e.g. *children*, *watch*.

    – /ʃ/ For information on this sound, see the **Pronunciation notes** in **1B**.

- Try to help Sts make these sounds by showing them mouth positions or comparing them to sounds in their L1.

- See also **Pronunciation** in the **Introduction**, *p.8*.

a   (**1** 48)))   Read the **Pronunciation notes** and decide how much of the information you want to give your Sts.

Focus on the exercise and play the audio once the whole way through for Sts just to listen.

> (**1** 48)))
> See the sounds and words in the Student's Book on *p.10*

Focus on the sound picture *jazz*. Play the audio to model and drill the word and sound (pause after the sound).

Now focus on the words after *jazz*. Remind Sts that the pink letters are the /dʒ/ sound. Play the audio, pausing after each word for Sts to listen and repeat.

Focus on the **Sounds** box and go through it with the class.

Now repeat the same process for *chess* /tʃ/ and *shower* /ʃ/.

If these sounds are difficult for your Sts, model them yourself so that Sts can see your mouth position, and get Sts to repeat them a few more times.

Play the audio again from the beginning, pausing after each group of words for Sts to repeat.

Give further practice as necessary.

Finally, get Sts, in pairs, to practise saying the words.

Extra support

- If you are using an interactive whiteboard, you can focus on each sound individually before moving on to the next one.

b   (**1** 49)))   Focus on the sentences and play the audio once the whole way through for Sts just to listen.

> (**1** 49)))
> See the sentences in the Student's Book on *p.10*

Then play the audio again, pausing after each sentence for Sts to listen and repeat.

Finally, get Sts to practise the sentences individually or in pairs.

c   (**1** 50)))   Focus on the instructions and the examples. Explain to Sts that they are going to hear a man or a woman saying *I'm from* + a country, and they have to say the nationality using *he's* if it's a man and *she's* if it's a woman.

Play the two examples, pausing for Sts to say *He's Chinese* and then *She's Spanish* in chorus. Make sure Sts are pronouncing the /ʃ/ sound in *She* correctly. Continue with the rest of the audio, pausing as necessary. Make a note of any mistakes in pronunciation and correct them later on the board.

> (**1** 50)))
> 1   I'm from China. (*pause*) He's Chinese.
> 2   I'm from Spain. (*pause*) She's Spanish.
> 3   I'm from Japan. (*pause*) He's Japanese.
> 4   I'm from Switzerland. (*pause*) She's Swiss.
> 5   I'm from the USA. (*pause*) He's American.
> 6   I'm from Italy. (*pause*) She's Italian.
> 7   I'm from Germany. (*pause*) He's German.
> 8   I'm from Mexico. (*pause*) She's Mexican.
> 9   I'm from England. (*pause*) He's English.
> 10   I'm from Turkey. (*pause*) She's Turkish.
> 11   I'm from Poland. (*pause*) He's Polish.
> 12   I'm from Egypt. (*pause*) She's Egyptian.
> 13   I'm from Brazil. (*pause*) He's Brazilian.
> 14   I'm from France. (*pause*) She's French.
> 15   I'm from Russia. (*pause*) He's Russian.
> 16   I'm from the UK. (*pause*) She's British.

Then repeat the activity, eliciting responses from individual Sts.

3 GRAMMAR verb be (plural): we, you, they

a Focus on the pictures and get Sts to complete the three gaps with nationalities.

b (1 51)) Now play the audio for Sts to listen and check.

Check answers by eliciting the nationalities onto the board. Correct any spelling errors and pronunciation.

See script 1.51

(1 51))
1 We're Japanese. Hi. Hi.
2 Are you German?
3 They're English.

Now focus on the chart and make sure Sts know what *plural* means.

Give Sts time to complete the chart.

Get Sts to compare with a partner and then check answers. Make sure that Sts are clear what the pronouns *we*, *you*, and *they* mean. You can demonstrate this or use L1 if you know it.

+	−
We are	We aren't
You **are**	You **aren't**
They **are**	They **aren't**

c (1 52)) (1 53)) (1 54)) Tell Sts to go to **Grammar Bank 2A** on *p.94*.

Focus on the example sentences and play the audio for Sts to listen and repeat. Pause the audio as necessary.

Go through the rules with the class using the expanded information in the **Additional grammar notes** below to help you. You may want to use Sts' L1 here.

Additional grammar notes
verb be (plural): we, you, they

* *We*, *you*, and *they* are plural pronouns.

* *We* and *you* can be used for men or women or both.

* The pronoun *you* and the verb form after it is the same in the singular and the plural.

* *They* can be used for people or things.

* Remind Sts that people normally use contractions after pronouns in conversation, e.g. *We're from Texas.*

* Contractions are <u>not</u> used in positive short answers, e.g. *Yes, they are.* NOT ~~Yes, they're.~~

! For *we | you | they* there are two possible negations – *we | you | they aren't* and *we're | you're | they're not* – but we recommend you teach only *we | you | they aren't* so as not to confuse Sts.

Focus on the exercises for **2A** on *p.95* and get Sts to do them individually or in pairs. If they do them individually, get them to compare answers with a partner.

Check answers, getting Sts to read the full sentences.

a
1 We	4 she	7 You
2 It	5 They	8 We
3 they	6 He	9 They

b
1 We aren't Mexican.
2 You're / You are in class 4.
3 Are they English?
4 Are we in class 4?
5 You aren't in class 4.
6 We're / We are on holiday.

c
1 Are, aren't, 're	6 Are, are, 's
2 Are, are, 're	7 'm not
3 isn't	8 aren't
4 aren't	9 's, Is, is
5 Is, isn't, 's	

Tell Sts to go back to the main lesson **2A**.

Extra support
* If you think Sts need more practice, you may want to give them the Grammar photocopiable activity at this point or leave it for later as consolidation or revision.

d (1 55)) Focus on the instructions and the examples in the speech bubbles. Make sure Sts remember the meaning of *late* (as in *Sorry I'm late*). Then play the audio, pausing after the first sentence for Sts to say *Are you Chinese?* in chorus. Do the same for the second example.

Play the rest of the audio, pausing if necessary after each sentence to give Sts time to say the question in chorus.

(1 55))
1 You're Chinese. (*pause*) Are you Chinese?
2 We're late. (*pause*) Are we late?
3 They're in class two. (*pause*) Are they in class two?
4 You're Italian. (*pause*) Are you Italian?
5 They're English. (*pause*) Are they English?
6 We're in room five. (*pause*) Are we in room five?
7 They're Japanese. (*pause*) Are they Japanese?

You could repeat the activity, eliciting responses from individual Sts.

Extra support
* Play the audio, pausing after each sentence, to give Sts time to write the sentence they heard. Then ask them to transform it into a question. Check answers as you go along.

4 READING

a (1 56))) Focus on the three pictures and ask Sts *Where are they?* to elicit *in a hotel restaurant.*

Now play the audio once the whole way through for Sts to listen and read at the same time.

Then focus on the instructions and give Sts time to read 1–5. Make sure Sts understand all the lexis, e.g. *free, too,* and *children.*

Play the audio again for Sts to listen and answer the questions.

Get Sts to compare with a partner and then check answers.

1 They're from Texas / the United States.
2 No, they aren't. They're English / British.
3 Yes, they are.
4 No, they aren't. They're on business.
5 Yes, they are.

> (1 56)))
> See the conversations in the Student's Book on *p.11*

b (1 57))) Focus on the instructions and the phrases.

Give Sts a few minutes to see if they can remember any of the missing words.

Play the audio for Sts to listen and complete the task.

Get Sts to compare with a partner and then check answers.

1	Excuse	3	We're	5	late
2	holiday	4	Look	6	day

> (1 57)))
> 1 Excuse me. Are they free?   4 Look at the time!
> 2 Are you on holiday?   5 We're late.
> 3 We're on business.   6 Have a nice day!

c Put Sts in groups of four and have them act out the conversation. If possible, set up seats in the classroom to mimic the seats in a restaurant.

5 SPEAKING

a In this speaking activity Sts practise nationality adjectives and the third-person singular and plural of the verb *be*. Focus on the instructions and four questions. Make sure Sts understand what they have to do. You could do the first one with the class.

Put Sts in pairs and give them a few minutes to answer the questions.

Monitor and help, encouraging Sts to guess if they don't know the right answer.

Check answers by getting one student to ask another the questions.

1 No, he isn't. He's Spanish.
2 No, they aren't. They're Japanese.
3 No, it isn't. It's Swiss.
4 Yes, she is.

b Put Sts in pairs, **A** and **B**, and tell them to go to **Communication** *Is dim sum Japanese?*, **A** on *p.76* and **B** on *p.80.*

Go through the instructions and speech bubbles. Sts must take turns asking their partner questions about every other photo.

When Sts have asked and answered about all the photos, you could ask the whole class some of the questions to round up the activity.

Extra support

*   Before Sts ask and answer the questions, put **A**s and **B**s together to complete the questions with *Is* or *Are.* Write the two options on the board for reference.

Extra idea

*   Have Sts make up their own questions about people and things they know to ask their classmates.

WORDS AND PHRASES TO LEARN

(4 61))) Tell Sts to go to *p.130* and focus on the **Words and phrases to learn** for **2A**. Make sure Sts understand the meaning of each phrase. If necessary, remind them of the context in which the words and phrases came up in the lesson. If you speak your Sts' L1, you might like to elicit a translation for the words / phrases for the Sts to write next to them. Play the audio, pausing after each phrase for Sts to repeat. You may also like to ask Sts to test each other on the phrases.

G *Wh-* and *How* questions with *be*
V phone numbers; numbers 11–100
P sentence rhythm

2B What's your phone number?

Lesson plan

The topic of this lesson is personal information.

The lesson starts with Sts listening to two conversations providing the context for learning how to introduce other people and to ask how people are. This is followed by a grammar focus on question words and word order in questions. The vocabulary focus is on phone numbers and numbers from 11–100. In Listening, Sts try to distinguish between pairs of numbers that sound similar, e.g. 13 and 30. In Writing, Sts focus on words related to personal information, e.g. *address*, *postcode*, *married*, etc., and practise giving their own personal information by filling in a form. We have avoided forcing Sts to ask what may be sensitive questions, e.g. *How old are you?*, *Are you married?*, as these questions are practised in the final speaking exercise using invented information.

STUDY LINK
- Workbook 2B
- iTutor
- iChecker on iTutor
- www.oup.com/elt/englishfile

Extra photocopiable activities

- **Grammar** *Wh-* and *How* questions with *be p.142*
- **Communicative** What's the answer? *p.177* (instructions *p.164*)
- **Vocabulary** Numbers dictation *p.214* (instructions *p.205*)
- **www.oup.com/elt/teacher/englishfile**

Optional lead-in (books closed)

- Draw a picture on the board of a real or imaginary friend of yours. Then write some personal information in note form under it, e.g. phone number, address, single or married, and age.

- Tell Sts *This is my friend* (name). Then ask questions such as *What's his / her phone number? How old is he / she? Is he / she married?* etc. Elicit answers by pointing to the relevant information on the board.

1 READING & LISTENING

a (**1 58**)) Books open. Focus on the instructions and make sure Sts know the word *online*.

Now focus on the photo and introduce the listening using very simple language. Point to the people in the photo and say their names.

Play the audio once the whole way through for Sts to read and listen at the same time. Help Sts to understand the new lexis in the messages, e.g. *brother*, *Wow*, *How old is he?*

Now focus on the chart and help with vocabulary, e.g. *age*. Give Sts time to complete it. You could play the audio again.

Get Sts to compare with a partner and then check answers.

> Name: Adam
> Age: 26
> Single ✓

> (**1 58**))
> See the online conversation in the Student's Book on *p.12*

b (**1 59**)) Focus on the photo and ask Sts who is in the photo and where they are (Sally, Amy, and Adam; in a café).

Tell Sts to cover the conversation and play the audio once the whole way through for them just to listen.

Now tell them to uncover the conversation and give them time to think about what the missing words are, but tell them <u>not</u> to write them yet.

Play the audio again for Sts to listen and complete the task.

Get Sts to compare with a partner and then check answers. Help Sts understand the new words and phrases in the conversation. You could teach that (*I'm*) *Very well* (*thanks*) is a common alternative to (*I'm*) *fine* (*thanks*). You might want to point out to Sts the exclamation *Oh* as Amy uses it to introduce something she has just thought of – Amy and Adam don't know each other, so she needs to introduce them – and Adam uses it to express disappointment that he has to leave.

> 1 She's   4 I'm sorry   7 phone number
> 2 Nice   5 meet
> 3 Look   6 See

(1 59)))

A = Adam, S = Sally, Am = Amy

A   Hi Sally. How are you?
S   Hello, Adam! I'm fine. Oh, this is Amy. She's a friend from work.
A   Hi Amy. Nice to meet you.
Am Hi.
***
A   Oh no. Look at the time. I'm sorry. I'm late for work. Nice to meet you, Amy. See you later, Sally.
Am Goodbye.
A   Er, Amy, what's your phone number?

c **(1 60)))** Play the audio, pausing after each sentence for Sts to listen and repeat.

(1 60)))
See script 1.59

Now put Sts in pairs, **A** and **B**. Tell the **B**s to read Adam's and Amy's lines.

Make sure Sts swap roles. Monitor and help as needed.

Extra idea

• You could divide the class into two and practise this exchange across the class:

  A *How are you?*
  B *I'm fine. How are you?*
  A *Very well, thanks.*

• Then get Sts to practise the conversations in pairs, swapping roles.

2 GRAMMAR Wh- and *How* questions with *be*

a Focus on the instructions and the example.

Get Sts to complete the second question. Elicit the question *How are you?*

Give Sts time to complete the other questions.

Get Sts to compare with a partner.

b **(1 61)))** Play the audio for Sts to listen and check.

Check answers.

2 How	4 What	6 What
3 Who	5 How	

(1 61)))

1	A Where are you from?	B	I'm from Dublin.
2	A How are you?	B	Fine, thanks.
3	A Who is he?	B	He's a friend.
4	A What's your name?	B	Molly.
5	A How old are you?	B	26.
6	A What's your phone number?	B	Nine six oh eight three six.

c **(1 62)))** Tell Sts to go to **Grammar Bank 2B** on *p.94*.

Focus on the example sentences and play the audio for Sts to listen and repeat. Pause the audio as necessary.

Go through the rules with the class using the expanded information in the **Additional grammar notes** in the next column to help you. You may want to use Sts' L1 here.

Additional grammar notes
Wh- and *How* questions with *be*

• In English statements with *be*, the subject comes before the verb. The pattern is S + V.

• In questions, the order of the subject and verb is reversed. The pattern is V + S.

• When a question begins with a *Wh-* word or *How*, the pattern is *Wh-* (*How*) + V + S.

• In questions with question words, the verb *is* is often contracted, e.g. *What's, Where's, Who's*. This is especially the case when the subject is a noun, e.g. *What's your name? Where's the toilet?* It is often not contracted when the subject is a pronoun. *Are* is not contracted after a *Wh-* word: *Where are the students?* NOT *Where're the students?*

Focus on the exercises for **2B** on *p.95* and get Sts to do them individually or in pairs. If they do them individually, get them to compare answers with a partner.

Check answers, getting Sts to read the full sentences. For **b**, you could also elicit the contracted forms (see the answers in brackets).

a
1   When, Where
2   What
3   Who, Where
4   What
5   Who, How old

b
1   Who is she? (Who's she?)
2   What is your phone number? (What's your phone number?)
3   Where is room 4? (Where's room 4?)
4   Is Marta married?
5   When is your English class? (When's your English class?)
6   Is your phone number 0151 496 0362?
7   What is his email? (What's his email?)
8   How old is Pedro?

c
1   Where are you from?
2   Where's Monterrey?
3   What's your email?
4   What's your phone number?
5   How old are you?

Tell Sts to go back to the main lesson **2B**.

Extra support

• If you think Sts need more practice, you may want to give them the Grammar photocopiable activity at this point or leave it for later as consolidation or revision.

3 VOCABULARY phone numbers; numbers 11–100

a **(1 63)))** Focus on the **Phone numbers** box and go through it with the class. Model and drill the word *double* /'dʌbl/.

Now focus on the instructions and play the audio once the whole way through for Sts just to listen.

Then play the audio again and get Sts to listen and complete the phone number.

Check answers.

03069 990 **375**

> **1 63))**
> oh three oh six nine double nine oh three seven five

Highlight that:
– when saying phone numbers, we give the individual digits, (usually in blocks of three or four), so that *3074128* is said as *three oh seven, four one two eight*. We <u>don't</u> say *thirty, seventy-four, a hundred and twenty-eight* as in some languages.
– many native speakers use *double*. However, it is also acceptable to just say the number twice, so don't over-correct your Sts if they don't always remember to use *double*.

Finally, play the audio again and get Sts to listen and repeat the phone number.

b **1 64))** Focus on the first phone number. Ask a student to say it, and write what he / she says on the board for the class to check.

Put Sts in pairs and get them to tell each other the other two phone numbers.

Play the audio for Sts to listen and check.

> **1 64))**
> 1 oh two eight nine oh one eight oh three six one
> 2 oh double seven double oh nine double oh six four nine
> 3 oh one three one four nine six oh six three eight

Play the audio again, pausing after each phone number and get Sts to repeat it. Give further practice as necessary.

c Focus on the instructions and speech bubble. Put Sts in pairs and get them to ask and answer the question.

! Some Sts may not be happy about using their own phone number, so you could suggest that they invent a number, but with a normal number of digits from the area where they live.

Monitor and help, encouraging Sts to break the phone number up into blocks, so it sounds more natural.

Get some feedback by eliciting some numbers onto the board.

Extra support
• You could ask Sts to write their phone number (or invented phone number) on a piece of paper to help them say it in English.

Extra idea
• You could get Sts to mingle as a whole class to ask each other's phone number.

d Tell Sts to go to the **Vocabulary Bank** *Numbers and days* on *p.116*.

1 65)) Look at **3 11–100** and focus on **a**. Play the audio and get Sts to repeat numbers 11 to 20 in chorus. Remind Sts that the underlined syllables are stressed more strongly. Give further practice as necessary, modelling and drilling the pronunciation yourself, or using the audio, and getting choral and individual responses.

> **1 65))**
> See numbers 11–20 in the Student's Book on *p.116*

Now focus on **b**. Ask Sts to cover the words and say the numbers. They could do this individually or with a partner.

1 66)) Now focus on **c**. Play the audio and get Sts to repeat numbers 21 to 100 in chorus. Give further practice as necessary, modelling and drilling the pronunciation yourself, or using the audio, and getting choral and individual responses.

> **1 66))**
> See numbers 21–100 in the Student's Book on *p.116*

Explain that both *a hundred* and *one hundred* are acceptable.

Focus on the **Word stress** box and go through it with the class. Give some practice of this by writing up pairs of numbers on the board, e.g. 15 / 50, 18 / 80, and getting Sts to say them.

Now focus on **d**. Ask Sts to cover the words and say the numbers. They could do this individually or with a partner.

Monitor and help. Make a note of any pronunciation problems they are having. Write the words on the board and model and drill the ones that Sts find difficult.

Tell Sts to go back to the main lesson **2B**.

Extra support
• If you think Sts need more practice, you may want to give them the Vocabulary photocopiable activity at this point or leave it for later as consolidation or revision.

e Put Sts in small groups or pairs and get them to say the numbers to each other.

Elicit the numbers from the whole class.

Extra support
• Put Sts in pairs, **A** and **B**. **A** has his / her book open at *p.13* and **B** has his/her book open at the **Vocabulary Bank** on *p.116*. **B** can give **A** hints if he / she is struggling.

f **1 67))** Focus on the instructions and the example.

Play the audio, pausing after each number to give Sts time to write. Play again as necessary.

Get Sts to compare with a partner and then elicit the numbers onto the board.

1 15	4 100	7 16	10 78
2 97	5 40	8 62	11 34
3 11	6 29	9 56	12 81

> **1 67))**
> 1 fifteen   7 sixteen
> 2 ninety-seven   8 sixty-two
> 3 eleven   9 fifty-six
> 4 a hundred   10 seventy-eight
> 5 forty   11 thirty-four
> 6 twenty-nine   12 eighty-one

g Tell Sts that *Buzz* is the name of a number game.

Get Sts to sit or stand in a circle and count out loud. When they come to a number that contains three (e.g. 13) or a multiple of three (three, six, nine, etc.) they have to say *buzz* instead of the number.

If a student makes a mistake, either saying the number instead of *buzz* or simply saying the wrong number, he / she is out. The next player has to say correctly what the player who is out should have said.

Continue until there is only one student left, or until the class reaches, for example, 30.

Note: You can use any number between three and nine as the 'buzz' number.

Extra idea

• Another number game you may like to play now or when you want to practise numbers is *Two-digit number chains*.

• Write three two-digit numbers on the board, e.g. 27 71 13.

• Elicit the numbers from your Sts. Then show them that the second number begins with seven, because the previous one ended with seven, and the third number begins with one because the second number ended with one. Then ask Sts what the fourth number could be and elicit a number, e.g. 32, and then another, e.g. 26, and write the numbers up on the board.

• Tell Sts that the numbers can't have a zero, e.g. not 20, 30, etc.

• Now make a chain round the class. Say the first number, and then elicit the second from the first student on your left and continue around the class.

• Finally, get Sts to make 'chains' in pairs, where **A** says one number, **B** says another, **A** says a third, etc.

4 LISTENING

a (**1** 68))) Remind Sts of the rule about stress on numbers like *thir<u>teen</u>* and *<u>thir</u>ty*.

Focus on the activity and play the audio once the whole way through for Sts just to listen to the difference between the pairs of numbers. Pause and play again as necessary.

> (**1** 68)))
> See the numbers in the Student's Book on *p.13*

b (**1** 69))) Focus on the instructions and play the audio once for Sts to circle **a** or **b**. Play again as necessary.

Play the audio again to check the answers.

1 a	3 b	5 b	7 a
2 b	4 a	6 a	

> (**1** 69)))
> | | | | | |
> |---|---|---|---|---|
> | 1 | thirteen | 4 | sixteen | 7 nineteen |
> | 2 | forty | 5 | seventy | |
> | 3 | fifty | 6 | eighteen | |

Get Sts to practise saying the numbers in pairs.

Monitor and help. Make a note of any pronunciation problems Sts are having. Write on the board any numbers that they are finding it difficult to say and model and drill the pronunciation, underlining the stressed syllable.

Extra idea

• Put Sts in pairs, **A** and **B**. **A** reads one of the numbers from each pair in **a** and **B** must say *a* or *b*. Then they swap roles.

c (**1** 70))) Focus on the instructions and the four questions.

Play the audio and pause after the first conversation. Ask Sts *Which question is it?* Elicit that the question in the conversation is *What's your phone number?* Get Sts to write number one next to the question.

Play the rest of the audio for Sts to listen and write the numbers.

Check answers.

> 2 What's your address?
> 3 How old are you?
> 4 What's your email?

> (**1** 70)))
> (script in Student's Book on *p.86*)
> 1 A Great. OK, see you on Tuesday.
>   B Yes. Oh, what's your phone number?
>   A It's, er, oh two oh seven nine four six oh four one five.
> 2 A Thank you. What's your address, please?
>   B It's fifty-seven King Street. Very near here…
> 3 A Come in, sit down. You're Martin Blunt, right?
>   B Yes.
>   A And how old are you Mr Blunt?
>   B I'm thirty-nine…
> 4 A Thank you very much. Er, one more thing. What's your email?
>   B It's James one six oh at uk mail dot com.

d Focus on the instructions and make sure Sts understand that they must only write the numbers they hear.

Play the audio, pausing after each conversation to give Sts time to write. Play again as necessary.

Get Sts to compare with a partner and then check answers.

> 1 ☎ 020 7946 0415
> 2 57 King Street
> 3 Age: 39
> 4 james160@ukmail.com

5 WRITING

completing a form

This is the first time Sts are sent to the **Writing** at the back of the Student's Book. In this section Sts will find model texts with exercises and language notes, and then a writing task. We suggest that you go through the model and do the exercise(s) and set the actual writing (the last activity) in class, except maybe for Writing 5, which could be set for homework.

Tell Sts to go to **Writing Completing a form** on *p.84*.

a Focus on the form and explain / elicit the meaning of the word *form*. Go through the form line by line and check the meaning and pronunciation of any new words, e.g. *divorced*, *separated*, *postcode*, *home*, and *mobile*.

Focus on the **Titles** box and go through it with the class. Highlight that *Ms* and *Mrs* are both used for women. *Ms* can be for either a married or single woman, but *Mrs* always indicates that the woman is married.

Note that there is no question for the 'title' line. This is because people would not normally ask *What is your title?*

Now focus on the instructions for **a**. Point out that the questions correspond to the spaces in the form. The first item *What's your name?* (question f) has been completed as an example.

Give Sts time to match each question with a part of the form.

Get Sts to compare with a partner and then check answers.

2 d		3 a		4 h		5 c		6 e		7 b		8 g

Extra challenge

• Get Sts to cover the questions and just look at the form. Elicit the questions from individual Sts or from the class.

Focus on the **Capital letters** box and go through it with the class.

b Focus on the instructions and give Sts a few minutes to complete the form for themselves. Tell Sts to invent the information if they want to.

Monitor and check that they are doing it correctly. Help as needed.

Tell Sts to go back to the main lesson **2B**.

6 PRONUNCIATION & SPEAKING

sentence rhythm

Pronunciation notes

• Tell Sts that in English the words that carry the important information are said more strongly than others, e.g. in *What's your name? What* and *name* are stressed more strongly than *your*.

• Generally speaking, question words, nouns, verbs, adjectives, etc., are usually stressed whereas small words like articles, pronouns and prepositions are not. It is this mixture of stressed and unstressed words which gives English its characteristic rhythm.

• Even at this low level it is good to help Sts, through these exercises, to begin to get a feel for English sentence rhythm.

• As well as helping their spoken English, an awareness of the fact that important words are stressed more strongly will also help with Sts' understanding. They can be encouraged to listen out for the stressed words in a sentence and deduce overall meaning from them. Unstressed words are hardly heard at all.

• See also **Pronunciation** in the **Introduction**, *p.8*.

a **1 71)))** Focus on questions 1 to 7. Tell Sts that the words in bigger font are the ones which are stressed (because they carry the important information) and that the underlined syllables in the multi-syllable words are stressed more.

Play the audio once the whole way through for Sts just to listen.

> **1 71)))**
> See the questions in the Student's Book on *p.13*

Then play the audio again, pausing after each question for Sts to listen and repeat in chorus, encouraging them to try and copy the rhythm on the audio by stressing the bigger words in bold more strongly and by saying the others more lightly and quickly. Give further practice as necessary using choral and individual repetition.

b Put Sts in pairs, **A** and **B**, and tell them to go to **Communication** *Personal information*, **A** on *p.77* and **B** on *p.81*.

Go through the instructions with Sts carefully. Focus on the **Email addresses** box and go through it with the class.

Sit **A** and **B** face-to-face if possible. **A** starts by interviewing **B** and writing the information in the form.

Monitor and help. Encourage Sts to use sentence rhythm when asking the questions.

B then interviews **A** and completes his / her form.

When they have finished, get them to compare forms.

WORDS AND PHRASES TO LEARN

4 61))) Tell Sts to go to *p.130* and focus on the **Words and phrases to learn** for **2B.** Make sure Sts understand the meaning of each phrase. If necessary, remind them of the context in which the words and phrases came up in the lesson. If you speak your Sts' L1, you might like to elicit a translation for the words / phrases for the Sts to write next to them. Play the audio, pausing after each phrase for Sts to repeat. You may also like to ask Sts to test each other on the phrases.

There are two pages of revision and consolidation after every two Files.

The first section revises the grammar, vocabulary, and pronunciation of the two Files. These exercises can be done individually or in pairs, in class or at home, depending on the needs of your Sts and the class time available. The pronunciation exercises revise sentence stress and individual sounds Sts have learnt. In the sounds exercises students are referred to the **Sound Bank** on *pages 133-135*, which helps students to see the many clear sound-spelling patterns that *do* exist in English and gives common examples of them. The **Sound Bank** audio is available on both the *Class audio CD* and on the *iTutor*. See also **Pronunciation** in the **Introduction**, *p.8*.

The second section presents Sts with a series of skills-based challenges. First, there is a reading text, which is of a slightly higher level than those in the File, but which revises grammar and vocabulary Sts have already learnt. Then Sts can watch or listen to five unscripted street interviews, where people are asked questions related to the topics in the File. You can find these on the *Class DVD*, *iTools*, and *Class Audio* (audio only). Finally, there is a speaking challenge which measures Sts' ability to use the language of the File orally. We suggest that you use some or all of these activities according to the needs of your class.

In addition, there is a short documentary film available on the *Class DVD* and *iTools* on a subject related to one of the topics of the Files. This is aimed at giving Sts enjoyable extra listening practice and showing them how much they are now able to understand. Sts can find all the video content and activities on the *iTutor*.

STUDY LINK
- iTutor

Test and Assessment CD-ROM

- **Quick Test 2**
- **File Test 2**

GRAMMAR

1	a	6	a	11	a
2	b	7	b	12	b
3	b	8	a	13	a
4	a	9	a	14	b
5	b	10	b	15	b

VOCABULARY

a	1 Turkish	3 American		5 Egypt	
	2 Switzerland	4 England		6 Japanese	
b	1 two	3 thirteen		5 Thursday	
	2 seven	4 twenty-one		6 Sunday	
c	1 Open	3 know		5 number, email	
	2 Sorry, down	4 me, what's, repeat			
d	1 the board	3 a chair			
	2 the door	4 a pen			

PRONUNCIATION

a	1 Chi<u>nese</u>	3 fif<u>teen</u>	5 <u>German</u>
	2 <u>fifty</u>	4 to<u>mo</u>rrow	

b	/iː/ tree	/ɪ/ fish	/h/ house
	/əʊ/ phone	/ʃ/ shower	

CAN YOU UNDERSTAND THIS TEXT?

Mark	**Davis**	28	**American**
Bianca	**Costa**	16	**Brazilian**
Lucas	**Brauer**	40	**German**

▶ CAN YOU UNDERSTAND THESE PEOPLE?

1 72)) 1 c   2 a   3 b   4 a   5 b

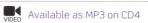

1 72))
See the script in the Student's Book on *p.86*

Remind Sts that they can watch the short film on *iTutor*.

▶ **VIDEO** *Available as MP3 on CD4*

Short film: Meet the Students

Hello, I'm Alicia. Today I'm in Brighton.
Brighton is in the south of England. It's on the coast. It's a fantastic town and it's famous for the Royal Pavilion, the pier, and the beach. But I'm not on holiday. I'm here to visit an English Language School.
This is the school. It's a big school with about 350 students. Rike and Hyeongwoo are students at the school.
Hyeongwoo is 23 years old. He's from Korea. He is a beginner student. His class is small, with only six students. His teacher is Stephen. He's English. He's very friendly and he's a very good teacher.
Rike is 19 years old. She's from Germany. She's an intermediate student and her class is big, with 11 students. Her teacher is Laura. She's English. She's really nice and she's a very good teacher, too.
When Rike and Hyeongwoo aren't in class they're in the computer room ...or here in the canteen. In the evening they're at home. Rike and Hyeongwoo live in a student house. It's near the school. It's a big house with five bedrooms, a kitchen, and a beautiful garden. Brighton is great for students like Rike and Hyeongwoo. The people are friendly and the town is exciting and fun!

G singular and plural nouns; *a* / *an*
V small things
P /z/ and /s/; plural endings

3A What's in your bag?

Lesson plan

This lesson is about things that people normally carry around with them, and how to use singular and plural nouns.

In Vocabulary Sts learn the words for common small objects. Then, real information about objects most commonly left on planes provides the context for learning plural nouns in Grammar. Sts also learn the difference between *a* and *an*, although the concept of articles has already been introduced in **Vocabulary Bank** *The classroom* in **1 Things in the classroom** in **Practical English 1**. The pronunciation focus is first on the two sounds /z/ and /s/, and then on plural endings – /z/, /s/, and /ɪz/. In a short listening activity Sts listen for objects in some announcements and conversations. In the speaking activity Sts try to identify mystery objects photographed from a strange angle and then they talk about what they have in their pocket or bag.

STUDY LINK
- Workbook 3A
- iTutor
- www.oup.com/elt/englishfile

Extra photocopiable activities
- **Grammar** singular and plural nouns; *a* / *an* *p.143*
- **Communicative** The same or different? *p.178* (instructions *p.164*)
- **Vocabulary** Things in a classroom *p.215* (instructions *p.205*)
- www.oup.com/elt/teacher/englishfile

Optional lead-in (books closed)
- To revise vocabulary and spelling play *Hangman* with a word from **Vocabulary Bank** *The classroom* in **1 Things in the classroom** on *p.118*, e.g. *laptop* (See *p.22* for instructions on how to play *Hangman*).

1 VOCABULARY small things

a Books open. Focus on the task.

Give Sts time to write the words for the four objects.

Check answers by eliciting the missing letters onto the board.

> 1 book   2 laptop   3 phone   4 photo

b Tell Sts to go to **Vocabulary Bank** *Small things* on *p.119*.

1 74))) Focus on the title, *Small things*, tell Sts to quickly look at the pictures, and guess what the title means.

Focus on the instructions for **a**. Play the audio and get Sts to repeat the words in chorus. Pause the audio as necessary. Give further practice of words which your Sts find most difficult.

1 74)))
See the list of small things in the Student's Book on *p.119*

Point out that we only use *a* or *an* with singular nouns. *Glasses* is a plural noun (although it is one object). For this reason we <u>don't</u> say *a glasses*.

Focus on the *a* / *an* and *ph* boxes and go through them with the class. Elicit / explain that we use *an* in front of a noun when it starts with a vowel sound, e.g. *an umbrella*, *an ID card*.

Focus on **b** and get Sts to cover the words, look at the photo, and say the words. They could do this individually or with a partner. Remind Sts to use *a* or *an* with all of the nouns except *glasses*.

Monitor and help. Make a note of any pronunciation problems they are having. Write the words on the board and model and drill the ones that Sts find difficult.

Tell Sts to go back to the main lesson **3A**.

Extra support
- If you think Sts need more practice, you may want to give them the Vocabulary photocopiable activity at this point or leave it for later as consolidation or revision.

2 GRAMMAR singular and plural nouns; *a* / *an*

a Focus on the instructions and the photo. Read the title and the first line of the text. You could use Sts' L1 or a simple mime to elicit the meaning of *leave something on a plane*. Make sure Sts know what all the things are, e.g. *magazines*, *iPods or MP3 players*, and *jackets*. Make it clear that the things are not in order.

Give Sts a minute or so to read the list and then, in pairs, guess what the top three things (in order) are that are often left on planes. Tell them not to write anything in the boxes yet.

Elicit some ideas from Sts and write them on the board.

b **1 75)))** Play the audio, pausing after each number for Sts to listen and number the things in **a** 1–10.

Play again as necessary.

Get Sts to compare with a partner and then check answers.

Find out if any Sts guessed all top three correctly.

> 10 keys (house and car)   5 jackets and coats
> 9 books and magazines   4 laptops and tablets
> 8 cameras   3 mobile phones
> 7 iPods and MP3 players   2 glasses
> 6 wallets and purses   1 passports

1 75))

(script in Student's Book on *p.86*)

And at number ten of the top things people leave on planes, it's...
keys. House keys and car keys.
At number nine, books and magazines.
At number eight, cameras.
At number seven, iPods and MP3 players.
At number six, wallets and purses.
At number five, coats and jackets.
At number four, laptops and tablets.
And now for the top three.
At number three... mobile phones,
And at number two glasses – reading glasses and sunglasses
And at number one –, yes, that's right – passports.
So next time you're on a plane, be careful not to leave anything
     behind.

c   Remind Sts of the concept of singular and plural by
showing Sts a pen and saying *a pen*. Then show the
class three pens and say *pens*. Write on the board:
SINGULAR = (A) PEN   PLURAL = PENS

Focus on the chart and make sure Sts know what each
item is. Then model and drill their pronunciation. Point
out that the first one has been done for them.

Now give Sts time to complete the chart.

Check answers.

> 1   four pencils
> 2   a notebook, three notebooks
> 3   an umbrella, two umbrellas

d   **1 76)) 1 77))** Tell Sts to go to **Grammar Bank 3A**
on *p.96*.

Focus first on the rules for **Singular nouns; *a | an***.
Play the audio for Sts to listen and repeat the sentences.

Go through the rules with the class using the expanded
information in the **Additional grammar notes** to
help you. You may want to use Sts' L1 here. At this
point, use only the notes that deal with singular nouns
and the articles *a | an*.

Now focus on the rules for **Plural nouns**. Play the
audio and get Sts to listen and repeat the example
sentences.

Go through the rules, using the expanded information
in the **Additional grammar notes**. Focus on the
notes that deal with plural forms.

Now focus on the box about ***the*** and go through it with
the class.

Go through the rules, using the expanded information
in the **Additional grammar notes**. Focus on the
notes that deal with the article *the*.

> **Additional grammar notes**
> **singular nouns; *a | an***
>
> • You may want to point out to Sts that not all words
>   that begin with vowels begin with a vowel sound,
>   for example several words which begin with *u* are
>   pronounced /juː/, e.g. *university*, so it's *a university*
>   (NOT *an university*).
>   Also sometimes a word that starts with a vowel
>   **sound** has the consonant *h* as the first letter. For
>   now, the only word Sts will encounter soon is the
>   word *hour*. The *h* is silent and we write and say
>   *an hour*.

plural nouns

• Irregular plurals are dealt with in **4A**.

• Regular nouns form the plural by adding an *s*.
  The only problem is the pronunciation as the
  final *s* is sometimes pronounced /z/, e.g. *keys*, and
  sometimes /s/, e.g. *books*. This will be dealt with in
  Pronunciation.

• *-es* is added to nouns ending in: *-ch*, *-sh*, *-ss*, and *-x*
  (e.g. *watch – watches*). This is because it would be
  impossible to pronounce the word if only an **s** were
  added to the words. (NOT *watchs*)

• With words ending in consonant + *y*, the *y* changes
  to *i* and *-es* is added.

• With compound nouns, e.g. *credit card*, *identity
  card*, only the second noun adds an *s* when plural.

• These rules for forming plural nouns are
  important because they are also true for verbs in
  the third person in the present simple.

the

• Explain that we use *the* to refer to something
  specific, e.g. *look at the board*, *open the door*, *close
  the windows*. We can use *the* with singular and
  plural nouns.

• Articles are easy for some nationalities and more
  difficult for others depending on their L1. If articles
  are a problem for your Sts, give more examples
  to highlight the difference between *a | an* and *the*,
  e.g. *What is it? It's a door* (explaining what it is) and
  *Open **the** door* (talking about a specific door, e.g.
  the door of the classroom).

Focus on the exercises for **3A** on *p.97* and get Sts to do
them individually or in pairs. If they do them individually,
get them to compare answers with a partner.

Check answers, getting Sts to read the full sentences.

> a
> 1   It's a phone.   6   They're cities.
> 2   They're watches.   7   It's an email.
> 3   It's an umbrella.   8   They're passports.
> 4   They're dictionaries.   9   It's a tablet.
> 5   They're brushes.
>
> b
> 1   What are they? They're books.
> 2   What is it? It's a bag.
> 3   What are they? They're glasses.
> 4   What is it? It's a camera.
> 5   What is it? It's an ID card.

Tell Sts to go back to the main lesson **3A**.

Extra support

• If you think Sts need more practice, you may want to
  give them the Grammar photocopiable activity at this
  point or leave it for later as consolidation or revision.

e   Tell Sts to go to **Communication** *Memory game*
on *p.79*.

Put Sts in pairs. Tell them that they have 30 seconds to
look at the photo. Make sure nobody is taking notes or
writing.

Give Sts exactly 30 seconds. Then tell them to close
their books.

Get each pair to write down as many things as they remember.

Call on pairs to read their lists to see if any pair remembered all the items. Reporting Sts should use *a* or *an* when there was only one of an item, e.g. *an umbrella*.

> a camera, dictionaries, an umbrella, glasses (one pair), watches, a wallet, a credit card, keys, a mobile phone, a bag, photos, pencils, a notebook, a tablet, a brush, passports

Tell Sts to go back to the main lesson **3A**.

3 PRONUNCIATION /z/ and /s/; plural endings

Pronunciation notes
/z/ **and** /s/

- For these sounds the phonetic symbols are the same as the alphabet letters.
- The letter *z* is always pronounced /z/, e.g. *zero, magazine*. This is a voiced* sound.
- The letter *s* at the beginning of a word is nearly always pronounced /s/. This is an unvoiced* sound.
- NB Sts will learn the exceptions *sure* and *sugar*, where *s* is pronounced /ʃ/, later in the course.
- The letter *s* in the middle or at the end of a word can be pronounced /s/ or /z/:
  – in the middle of a word it can be /s/, e.g. *glasses*, or /z/, e.g. *music*.
  – at the end of a word, for example in plurals, it can be pronounced /s/, e.g. *thanks*, or /z/, e.g. *is*.

plural endings

- When plural nouns end in *s* the *s* is either pronounced /s/ or /z/ depending on the previous sound.
- The *s* ending on most plural nouns is pronounced /z/ when it is added to voiced sounds, e.g. *mobiles*, *doors*, *keys*.
- The *s* ending is pronounced /s/ after the voiced sounds /f/, /k/, /p/, /t/, e.g. *books*, *wallets*.
- /ɪz/ -*es* is pronounced /ɪz/ when it is added after *ch*, *sh*, *s*, *z*, and *x*, e.g. *addresses*, *watches*. This adds one more syllable to the word. Show Sts that after these sounds it is very difficult to add only an /s/ sound. This is why the extra syllable is added.
- -*ies* is always pronounced /iːz/, e.g. *countries*.
- ! The difference between /s/ and /z/ is small and not easy for Sts to notice or produce at this level. However, it is useful to make Sts aware that *s* can be /s/ or /z/ and to point out which sound it is on new words that have an *s* in them.
- See also **Pronunciation** in the **Introduction**, *p.8*.

> *** Voiced and unvoiced consonants**
>
> - **Voiced** consonant sounds are made in the throat by vibrating the vocal chords, e.g. /b/, /l/, /m/, /v/, /z/. **Unvoiced** consonant sounds are made in the mouth without vibration in the vocal chords, e.g. /f/, /k/, /p/, /t/, /s/, etc.
> - You can demonstrate this to Sts by getting them to hold their hands against their throats. For voiced sounds they should feel a vibration, but not for unvoiced sounds.

a (**1** 78))) Read the **Pronunciation notes** and decide how much of the information you want to give your Sts.

Focus on the exercise and play the audio once the whole way through for Sts just to listen.

> (**1** 78)))
> See the words and sounds in the Student's Book on *p.17*

Focus on the sound picture *zebra*. Play the audio to model and drill the word and sound (pause after the sound).

Now focus on the words after *zebra*. Remind Sts that the pink letters are the /z/ sound. Play the audio, pausing after each word for Sts to listen and repeat.

Now repeat the same process for *snake* /s/.

If these sounds are difficult for your Sts, model them yourself so that Sts can see your mouth position, and get Sts to repeat them a few more times.

Play the audio again from the beginning, pausing after each group of words for Sts to repeat.

Give further practice as necessary.

Finally, get Sts, in pairs, to practise saying the words.

Extra support

- You could tell Sts that /s/ is the sound made by a snake ('sssss') and /z/ is the sound made by a bee or mosquito ('zzzzz').

Extra support

- If you are using an interactive whiteboard, you can focus on each sound individually before moving on to the next one.

b (**1** 79))) Focus on the **Saying plural nouns** box and go through it with the class. Highlight that the -*es* ending is pronounced /ɪz/ after certain combinations of letters, e.g. *watches*, and go over the spelling rules in the **Pronunciation notes**.

Explain to Sts that the plural *s* is usually pronounced /z/, e.g. *bags*, but can also be /s/, e.g. *books* (see the **Pronunciation notes**).

Play the audio once the whole way through for Sts just to listen.

> (**1** 79)))
> See the sounds and words in the Student's Book on *p.17*

Then play it again, pausing after each group of words for Sts to listen and repeat.

Give further practice as necessary using choral and individual repetition.

c (1 80))) Focus on the task and the example. Play the audio and pause after *It's a photo* for Sts to say *They're photos* in chorus. You could also demonstrate by saying a sentence yourself and eliciting the plural from the class, e.g. *It's a bag* (*They're bags*).

Then play the audio and pause after the second sentence *It's a key*. Ask Sts what the plural is (*keys*). Make sure Sts understand fully what they have to do before continuing.

Play the rest of the audio and give Sts time to say the plural in chorus. Correct pronunciation as necessary.

(1 80)))
1   It's a photo. (*pause*) They're photos.
2   It's a key. (*pause*) They're keys.
3   It's a passport. (*pause*) They're passports.
4   It's a phone. (*pause*) They're phones.
5   It's a watch. (*pause*) They're watches.
6   It's a pencil. (*pause*) They're pencils.
7   It's a book. (*pause*) They're books.
8   It's a purse. (*pause*) They're purses.
9   It's a credit card. (*pause*) They're credit cards.
10 It's a brush. (*pause*) They're brushes.

Finally, repeat the activity, eliciting responses from individual Sts.

4   LISTENING

(1 81))) Focus on the instructions. Stress that each short situation mentions a small thing or things that Sts have learnt in the **Vocabulary Bank**. They just have to listen for the thing mentioned and write the number in the correct box.
NB The conversations are linked and feature the same person who is travelling. Situation 1 is in airport security, 2 and 3 are on a plane, 4 and 5 in the reception of a hotel.

Before playing the audio, you could elicit what the things are (clockwise: *a passport, mobiles / phones, laptops, a key, a bag*).

Play the audio once the whole way through for Sts just to listen. You could at this point elicit where the person is in each situation.

Now play the first situation twice and elicit the answer (*laptops*). Make sure Sts write 1 in the correct box.

Then play the other four situations.

Check answers by playing the audio again. Stop after the relevant word in each situation.

2 phones   3 bag   4 passport   5 key

(1 81)))
(script in Student's Book on *p.86*)
1   Please take out your laptops. All laptops out of cases, please.
2   Please switch off all mobile phones and electronic devices.
3   A   Excuse me – is this your bag?
    B   Oh yes! Thanks very much!
4   A   Hi. My name's Sam Smith. I have a reservation.
    B   Can I see your passport, please?
    A   Sure, here you are.
5   A   OK, Mr Smith, you're in room 315. Here's your key.
    B   Thank you very much. Er, where's the lift?

Extra support

• If there's time, you could play the audio again while Sts read the script on *p.86*, so they can see what they understood / didn't understand. Translate / explain any new words or phrases.

5   SPEAKING

a   Focus on the photos and the three speech bubbles. Demonstrate by focussing on photo 1 and elicit the answer *They're books*.

Put Sts in pairs and give them time to try to work out what the photos are.

Monitor and help with pronunciation.

Check answers by asking individual Sts.

---

2 They're wallets.	8 They're pieces of paper.
3 It's a watch.	9 It's a camera.
4 They're keys.	10 They're pens.
5 They're credit cards.	11 It's a laptop.
6 It's a brush.	12 It's an ID card.
7 It's a (mobile) phone.	

---

b   Focus on the instructions and make sure Sts know the meaning of *pocket*. Demonstrate the activity by showing Sts what's in your bag / pocket and saying *In my bag, I have…* and taking out any of the things mentioned that you have.

Now give Sts time to see what they have in their bag / pocket.

Ask them to tick (✓) the things they have.

c   Focus on the instructions and the speech bubble.

Put Sts in pairs and get them to tell their partner about the things they ticked in **b**.

d   This exercise gives Sts the opportunity to name other things they have in their bag / pocket. Encourage them to ask you the question (*How do you say … in English? How do you spell it?*) and spell the words to them.

Finally, write all the new words on the board.

WORDS AND PHRASES TO LEARN

(4 61))) Tell Sts to go to *p.130* and focus on the **Words and phrases to learn** for **3A**. Make sure Sts understand the meaning of each phrase. If necessary, remind them of the context in which the words and phrases came up in the lesson. If you speak your Sts' L1, you might like to elicit a translation for the words / phrases for the Sts to write next to them. Play the audio, pausing after each phrase for Sts to repeat. You may also like to ask Sts to test each other on the phrases.

G *this / that / these / those*
V souvenirs
P /ð/ and /ə/

3B   Is that a hat?

Lesson plan

The topic of this lesson is buying souvenirs.

First, a picture of a souvenir stall in London is used to teach Sts the vocabulary for more objects. Then three dialogues with a tourist and the stallholder provide the context for introducing the grammar of demonstrative pronouns *this*, *that*, *these*, and *those*.

In Pronunciation, Sts practise the voiced *th* sound /ð/ used in the demonstrative pronouns and the vowel sound /ə/. These topics are brought together in the final speaking activity in which Sts practise asking and answering questions about a variety of objects.

STUDY LINK
- Workbook 3B
- iTutor
- iChecker on iTutor
- www.oup.com/elt/englishfile

Extra photocopiable activities
- **Grammar** *this / that / these / those p.144*
- **Communicative** What's this? What's that? *p.179* (instructions *p.165*)
- www.oup.com/elt/teacher/englishfile

Optional lead-in (books closed)
- To revise vocabulary for small things, put Sts in pairs or small groups. Give them one minute exactly to write down as many small things as they can.
- When the time is up ask Sts how many words they have. Get the pair with the most words to spell them to you as you write them on the board. They get a point for each correct answer.
- Finally, tell Sts that in this lesson they are now going to learn vocabulary for souvenirs.

1 VOCABULARY souvenirs

a (1 82)) Books open. Focus on the picture of the souvenir stall and make sure Sts understand the meaning of the word *souvenir*. Model and drill pronunciation /suːvəˈnɪə/. Ask Sts where the people are (*London*) and elicit that the woman is probably a tourist.

Focus on the instructions. Point out that Sts have already learnt the words for all the items.

Get Sts to match the words.

Play the audio and then check answers.

See script 1.82

> **(1 82))**
> 1 a picture   2 a flag   3 a bag   4 an umbrella

b (1 83)) Focus on the instructions and give Sts time to look at the items in the photo. Make sure Sts understand what each one is.

Play the audio for Sts to listen and repeat each item.

> **(1 83))**
> See the words in the Student's Book on *p.18*

c Do this as an open-class activity. Write any new words on the board, and model and drill their pronunciation.

2 LISTENING

a (1 84)) Focus on the instructions and elicit / explain the meaning of the verb *buy*. Model and drill pronunciation. Now get Sts to cover the dialogues with a piece of paper and focus on the picture.

Play the audio once the whole way through for Sts to listen to the dialogues and answer the question.

Check the answer.

Sts should circle a **key ring** (9).

> **(1 84))**
> 1 **A** Excuse me, what are those?
>   **B** They're T-shirts.
>   **A** And is that a hat?
>   **B** Yes, it is.
>   **A** Ah. It's very nice.
> 2 **A** How much are these key rings?
>   **B** They're ten pounds.
>   **A** Oh! That's expensive! I'm sorry. Bye.
> 3 **A** Excuse me, miss! Is this your bag?
>   **B** Oh, yes, it is. Thank you!
>   **A** You're welcome. A key ring? Only ten pounds.
>   **B** OK!

b Focus on the instructions and get Sts to uncover the dialogues.

Give Sts time to read the dialogues and think about what the missing words are, but tell them <u>not</u> to write them yet.

Play the audio, pausing after each dialogue to give Sts time to write. Play again as necessary.

Get Sts to compare with a partner and then check answers.

1 what	4 ten	7 Thank
2 nice	5 sorry	8 ten
3 key rings	6 Excuse	9 OK

Go through the dialogues and explain / elicit the following:
- *Ah* and *Oh* are not words, just noises we make when we react to something that someone has said.
- *nice* here means *good*.
- the question *How much are these key rings?* is used to ask about the price. The currency in the UK is the pound.
- the expression *That's expensive* means the price is too high, and that the tourist says *I'm sorry* because she has decided that she doesn't want to buy a key ring.
- *You're welcome* is a common response to *Thanks* or *Thank you*.

c (1 85))) Play the audio again and get Sts to repeat each line in chorus.

> (1 85)))
> See script 1.84

Extra challenge
- Divide the class in half. One half takes the role of the woman. The other half is the stallholder. Write the first part of the conversation on the board. Have Sts repeat the conversation going back and forth between the woman and 'stallholder' groups. Then delete the last part of each sentence and repeat the activity with Sts relying on memory to finish each line. Finally, delete the whole conversation and have Sts repeat it from memory.

Now put Sts in pairs and get them to practise the dialogues.

3 GRAMMAR *this / that / these / those*

a Focus on the instructions. Give Sts a few minutes to complete the gaps.

Check answers by getting Sts to read the full questions.

1 this	2 these	3 that	4 those

b Focus on the chart and elicit the meaning of *singular* and *plural*. Elicit / demonstrate the difference between *here* and *there*.

Get Sts to complete the chart.

Check answers.

	here	there
singular	*this*	**that**
plural	**these**	**those**

c (1 86))) Tell Sts to go to **Grammar Bank 3B** on *p.96*.

Focus on the example sentences and play the audio for Sts to listen and repeat. Pause the audio as necessary.

Go through the rules with the class using the expanded information in the **Additional grammar notes** to help you. You may want to use Sts' L1 here.

Additional grammar notes
this | that | these | those

- The words *this* and *these* are used for things within reach of or near the speaker. *That* and *those* are for things that are out of reach or farther away.

- The best way to explain the words is to demonstrate. Touch something that is close to you and say, e.g. *This is a book* or *These are pencils*. Then point at something across the room and say, e.g. *That's a board* or *Those are bags*.

- *This | these* are often used with the word *here*, e.g. *Is this your book here? That | those* are often used with *there | over there*, e.g. *Is that your bag (over) there?*

- *That is* is often contracted as *That's*. However, there are no contracted forms for *this is* or *these | those are*.

Focus on the exercises for **3B** on *p.97* and get Sts to do them individually or in pairs. If they do them individually, get them to compare answers with a partner.

Check answers, getting Sts to read the full sentences.

a					
1 This	3 These	5 these			
2 those	4 that	6 that			
b					
1 It's	3 They're	5 they are	7 is that
2 these	4 those	6 this	8 It's

Tell Sts to go back to the main lesson **3B**.

Extra support
- If you think Sts need more practice, you may want to give them the Grammar photocopiable activity at this point or leave it for later as consolidation or revision.

4 PRONUNCIATION /ð/ and /ə/

Pronunciation notes

/ð/ and /ə/

- The letters *th* can be pronounced two ways in English, /θ/ or /ð/. Sts have already been exposed to both sounds, /θ/ in *three, thirteen, Thursday, thank you*, etc. and /ð/ in *they, the,* and *brother.*

- Here the focus is on the /ð/ sound, which occurs in *this, that, these,* and *those.*

- Sts may have problems with this sound as it may not exist in their language.

- Show Sts the correct position of the mouth with the tongue behind the teeth and moving forward between the teeth as the /ð/ sound is made. Model the sound and have Sts put their hands on their throats to feel the vibration of the voiced sound.

- /ə/ This is the most common vowel sound in English. It is called the schwa. Many unstressed syllables have this sound, e.g. the **bold** syllables in Br**a**zil, **A**meric**a**, pap**er**, dict**io**nary.

- These two sounds are **voiced** sounds.

- It is worth making Sts aware that *th* can be pronounced in two different ways, but at this stage it may not be helpful to compare them too much.

Sentence rhythm

- For information on **Sentence rhythm**, see the **Pronunciation notes** in **2B**.

- See also **Pronunciation** in the **Introduction**, *p.8*.

a (1 87)) Read the **Pronunciation notes** and decide how much of the information you want to give your Sts.

Focus on the exercise and play the audio once the whole way through for Sts just to listen.

> (1 87))
> See the words and sounds in the Student's Book on *p.19*

Focus on the sound picture *mother*. Play the audio to model and drill the word and sound (pause after the sound).

Now focus on the words after *mother*. Remind Sts that the pink letters are the /ð/ sound. Play the audio, pausing after each word for Sts to listen and repeat.

Now repeat the same process for *computer* /ə/.

If these sounds are difficult for your Sts, model them yourself so that Sts can see your mouth position, and get Sts to repeat them a few more times.

Play the audio again from the beginning, pausing after each group of words for Sts to repeat.

Give further practice as necessary.

Finally, get Sts, in pairs, to practise saying the words.

Extra support

- If you are using an interactive whiteboard, you can focus on each sound individually before moving on to the next one.

b (1 88)) This exercise focusses on sentence rhythm. Focus on the questions and answers, and play the audio once the whole way through for Sts just to listen and pay attention to sentence rhythm. Point out to Sts that the words in bigger bold print are the important words and they are stressed. You could also point out that in the questions *What are these?* and *What are those? are* is pronounced /ə/ because it is unstressed.

> (1 88))
> See the questions and answers in the Student's Book on *p.19*

Now play the audio again, pausing once after each question for Sts to listen and repeat, and then again after each answer for Sts to repeat that, too.

Finally, put Sts in pairs and get one to ask the questions and the other to answer. Monitor and help with pronunciation and sentence rhythm.

Then get Sts to swap roles.

5 SPEAKING

a Focus on the instructions and the picture.

Give Sts time to write what souvenirs 1–10 are.

Check answers by eliciting the words and getting Sts to spell them.

1	a T-shirt	7	watches
2	hats	8	a mug
3	umbrellas	9	a map
4	a picture	10	key rings
5	a bag	11	postcards
6	sunglasses	12	a flag

b Put Sts in pairs, **A** and **B**, and tell them to go to **Communication** *How much are these watches?*, **A** on *p.77* and **B** on *p.81*.

Go over the instructions and speech bubbles, and make sure Sts are clear about what they have to do. They must take turns asking their partner questions about the items with blank price tags. They need to use *this / these* for things which are in touching distance at the front of the stall and *that / those* for things which are at the back of the stall out of reach.

When Sts have asked and answered about all the items, get some feedback from the class, e.g. *The mugs are £13.*

Extra support

- For reference write the following on the board: *How much is...?, How much are...?, It's..., They're...*

WORDS AND PHRASES TO LEARN

(4 61)) Tell Sts to go to *p.130* and focus on the **Words and phrases to learn** for **3B**. Make sure Sts understand the meaning of each phrase. If necessary, remind them of the context in which the words and phrases came up in the lesson. If you speak your Sts' L1, you might like to elicit a translation for the words / phrases for the Sts to write next to them. Play the audio, pausing after each phrase for Sts to repeat. You may also like to ask Sts to test each other on the phrases.

Saying and understanding prices
Buying lunch
/ʊə/, /s/, and /k/

PRACTICAL ENGLISH
Episode 2 Can I have an orange juice, please?

Lesson plan

In this lesson Sts learn how to ask for food and drink in a restaurant, café or pub and how to say prices in pounds, dollars and euros. They also revise asking how much something is, which they learnt in the previous lesson. At this level, Sts need more practice in understanding prices than in saying them, as they are likely to have to understand prices if they travel. There is a pronunciation focus on the /ʊə/, /s/, and /k/ sounds, which they need to get right in order to pronounce the currencies correctly. Language for buying something to eat and drink is presented through Rob buying lunch in a pub. Sts then go on to practise buying a drink and something to eat from the same menu.
The language is further consolidated through listening to Jenny and her friend buying lunch in a New York deli. Sts then focus on the useful phrases from the lesson, and finally they listen to the song, *That's How Much*.

STUDY LINK
- **Workbook** Can I have an orange juice, please?
- iTutor
- www.oup.com/elt/englishfile

Extra photocopiable activities

- **Communicative** Can I have an orange juice, please? *p.180* (instructions *p.165*)
- **Song** *That's How Much p.229* (instructions *p.226*)

Test and Assessment CD-ROM

- Quick Test 3
- File Test 3
- www.oup.com/elt/teacher/englishfile

Optional lead-in (books closed)

- Revise numbers 11–99 by giving Sts a dictation. Dictate ten numbers and ask Sts to write them down. Make sure you write the numbers down as you say them. Get them to compare with a partner and then check answers.

- Now tell Sts to choose five numbers of their own and to write them on a piece of paper. Put Sts in pairs, **A** and **B**, and ask **A** to dictate their numbers for **B** to write them down. Then get Sts to swap roles. Monitor and make a note of any problems.

- Ask Sts to check answers by comparing the numbers they wrote with the numbers their partner wrote.

- Correct any mistakes on the board.

1 UNDERSTANDING PRICES

a **1 89))** Books open. Focus on the three money pictures and elicit where they are from (Britain, the EU [the European Union], and the United States). You may want to point out that not all countries in the EU use the euro.

Play the audio once the whole way through for Sts just to listen. Highlight that *pence* can be shortened to *p* /piː/.

> **1 89))**
> See the prices in the Student's Book on *p.20*

Now play the audio again for Sts to listen and repeat. Give further practice as necessary.

b Draw the symbols for pounds, dollars, and euros on the board and elicit what currency they refer to.

Focus on the instructions and the example.

Get Sts to continue matching the prices and words. Monitor and deal with any problems.

Get Sts to compare with a partner.

c **1 90))** Play the audio once for Sts to listen and check.

Check answers.

2	D	5	A	8	I
3	F	6	G	9	E
4	C	7	J	10	B

> **1 90))**
> 1 H twelve pounds seventy-five
> 2 D fifteen euros ninety-nine
> 3 F fifty dollars and nineteen cents
> 4 C five pounds thirty-five
> 5 A thirteen dollars and twenty-five cents
> 6 G three euros twenty
> 7 J twenty-five cents
> 8 I one pound fifty
> 9 E sixty p
> 10 B eighty cents

Now play the audio again, pausing after each price for Sts to listen and repeat.

Highlight that we don't use *and* between pounds and pence or between euros and cents in British English (e.g. NOT ~~two pounds and twenty~~), and that we normally only use the word *pence* / *cents* for an amount that is less than a pound / euro (e.g. *fifty cents*).

d Tell Sts to cover the words A–J and look at the prices 1–10.

Give them time to practise saying the prices. Monitor and correct any mistakes.

Then with the prices in words still covered elicit the prices one by one from the class.

e (**1 91**)) Focus on the four items and the prices, and elicit them from the class.

Play the audio, repeating each dialogue twice for Sts to listen and circle the right price. Play again as necessary.

Get Sts to compare with a partner and then check answers.

1 $1.25	2 €15	3 $9.49	4 £30.20

> (**1 91**))
> (script in Student's Book on p.86)
> **M = man, W = woman**
> 1
> W *The New York Times*, please.
> M Here you are.
> W How much is it?
> M It's one dollar twenty-five.
> 2
> M A phone card, please.
> W For how much?
> M Fifteen euros, please.
> W Here you are.
> M Thanks.
> 3
> M1 A memory card, please.
> M2 Two gigs or four?
> M1 Two, please. How much is it?
> M2 Nine dollars forty-nine.
> M1 Is a credit card OK?
> M2 Sure.
> 4
> W A one-way ticket to Oxford, please.
> M Thirty pounds twenty p, please.
> W Here you are.
> M Thank you.

Extra support

• If there's time, you could play the audio again while Sts read the script on p.86, so they can see what they understood / didn't understand. Translate / explain any new words or phrases.

2 PRONUNCIATION /ʊə/, /s/, and /k/

Pronunciation notes

• The /ʊə/ sound is not a very common sound in English. You might like to point out that the sound is a diphthong, i.e. two sounds (a combination of /ʊ/ and /ə/).

• *eu* is usually pronounced /ʊə/ and three of the most common words with *eu* are *euro*, *Europe*, and *European*.

• The aim of the section on /s/ and /k/ is to help Sts with two pronunciations of the letter *c*.

• You might like to highlight the following sound–spelling rules:

– the letter *c* is pronounced /s/ before the vowels *e* and *i*, e.g. *centre*, *city*, *nice*, *piece*, *pencil*.

– the letter *c* is pronounced /k/ before consonants and before the letters *a*, *o*, and *u*, e.g. *class*, *cat*, *computer*, *coat*, *picture*.

(**1 92**)) Read the **Pronunciation notes** and decide how much of the information you want to give your Sts.

Focus on the exercise and play the audio once the whole way through for Sts just to listen.

> (**1 92**))
> See the words and sounds in the Student's Book on p.20

Focus on the sound picture *tourist*. Play the audio to model and drill the word and the sound (pause after the sound).

Now focus on the words after *tourist*. Remind Sts that the pink letters are the /ʊə/ sound. Play the audio, pausing after each word for Sts to listen and repeat.

Now repeat the same process for *snake* /s/ and *key* /k/.

If these sounds are difficult for your Sts, model them yourself so that Sts can see your mouth position, and get Sts to repeat them a few more times.

Play the audio again from the beginning, pausing after each group of words for Sts to repeat.

Give further practice as necessary.

Finally, get Sts, in pairs, to practise saying the words.

Extra support

• If you are using an interactive whiteboard, you can focus on each sound individually before moving on to the next one.

Focus on the **The letter *c*** box and go through it with the class.

Extra idea

• Write these sentences on the board:

1 IN EUROPE A LOT OF COUNTRIES USE THE EURO.

2 THE CINEMA TICKET IS SIX EUROS AND SIXTY CENTS.

3 CAN I HAVE A COFFEE, PLEASE?

• Model the first sentence. Repeat the sentence and get Sts to repeat it. Do the same with sentences 2 and 3. Then put Sts in pairs and get them to practise saying the sentences. Get a few Sts to say the sentences in front of the class.

3 ◼️ BUYING LUNCH

a (**1 93**)) Focus on the title and explain / elicit the meaning of *Buying lunch*. Model and drill pronunciation.

Now focus on the menu and answer any questions about vocabulary. If possible, show pictures of the different foods and drinks, e.g. *pie*, *cheese*, *tuna*, *mineral water*, etc. If Sts don't recognize the word *burger*, write HAMBURGER on the board and strike through HAM. You might also want to point out that *Coca-Cola* is the real name for *Coke*, but nobody uses it nowadays.

Give Sts time to read the menu.

Now play the video or audio for Sts to listen and repeat the food, drinks, and prices.

> (**1 93**))
> See the menu in the Student's Book on p.20

You could help Sts by writing the multi-syllable words on the board and underlining the stressed syllables (<u>bur</u>ger, <u>sand</u>wiches, <u>tu</u>na, <u>sal</u>ad, <u>chick</u>en, <u>min</u>eral water, <u>or</u>ange juice, <u>cof</u>fee) or you could ask them to listen again and underline the stressed syllables.

Then drill the words in chorus and individually.

Extra challenge
- In pairs or as a class, get Sts to tell you the prices of each item on the menu before they listen to the audio.

b Put Sts in pairs and focus on the task and the example. Model and drill the question.

Highlight that Sts should use a singular question for all the items, even ones which are plural on the menu (e.g. *How much is a pie | a sandwich?*). Quickly elicit the questions from the class and then demonstrate a couple of questions and answers with a good student. Remind Sts to use *an* not *a* with *orange juice*.

Now get Sts to practise in pairs. Monitor and help.

Make sure they swap roles.

c (**1** 94))) Focus on the photo and ask Sts who the man on the right is (*Rob*). Ask Sts what they can remember about him from the previous **Practical English** lesson. Ask Sts where he is now (in a pub). Elicit that the other man is a barman, and model and drill pronunciation.

Focus on the menu. Explain that they have to tick the items that Rob asks for.

Play the video or audio once or twice for Sts to do the task.

Get Sts to compare with a partner and then check answers.

> Sts should tick a cheese sandwich and a Coke.

> (**1** 94)))
> B = barman, R = Rob
> B Who's next?
> R Can I have a cheese sandwich, please?
> B Anything else?
> R And a Coke, please.
> B Ice and lemon?
> R No, thanks.
> B There you go.
> R Thanks. How much is it?
> B Six pounds seventy-five.
> R Here you are.
> B Thanks. Here's your change.

d Focus on the instructions and the dialogue.

Then play the video or audio again for Sts to listen and complete the task. Play again as necessary.

Check answers by playing the video or audio again and pausing after each answer.

| 1 | cheese | 3 | No | 5 | are |
| 2 | Coke | 4 | £6.75 | | |

Go through the dialogue line by line, eliciting / explaining any words or phrases Sts don't know. Highlight that *Can I have…?* is a polite way of ordering food or drink, usually with *please* at the end of the question.

Highlight also that *There you go* and *Here you are* are the two common phrases that people use when they give something to somebody. *There you go* is more informal than *Here you are*.

e (**1** 95))) Play the audio for Sts to listen and repeat, encouraging them to copy the rhythm on the audio. Give further practice as necessary.

> (**1** 95)))
> See script 1.94

Put Sts in pairs and assign roles. Give Sts time to practise the dialogue. Monitor and correct any pronunciation mistakes.

Make sure Sts swap roles.

f Focus on the instructions. Sts role-play a dialogue using the food items on the menu. Demonstrate the activity with a strong student. The student is the barman and you order a different food item and a different drink.

Put Sts in pairs and assign roles. Give them time to role-play the dialogue ordering different food items and drinks. Monitor and help.

Make sure Sts swap roles.

Get some pairs to act out the role-play in front of the class.

g (**1** 96))) Focus on the photos in **g** and **h** and ask Sts who is in both photos (*Jenny*). Ask Sts what they can remember about her from the previous **Practical English** lesson. Ask who they think the other women might be (the other woman in the first photo is the deli assistant and in the second a friend of Jenny's called Amy.)

Now focus on the instructions and the question. Highlight that the prices are going to be in dollars.

Play the video or audio once the whole way through for Sts to listen and find out how much Jenny's lunch cost.

Check the answer.

> Jenny's lunch is $9.70.

> (**1** 96)))
> (script in Student's Book on *p.86*)
> A = assistant, J = Jenny, Am = Amy
> A Hi. How can I help you?
> J Hi. How much is this tuna salad?
> A It's seven twenty.
> J OK fine. And this mineral water, please.
> A That's nine dollars seventy cents.
> J Here you are.
> A Thank you. Have a nice day.
> ***
> Am Jenny!
> J Amy! Hi, how are you?
> Am I'm fine. How are you?
> J I'm fine, too.
> Am What's that?
> J Oh, just a salad and some water.
> Am You are good! Look, wait for me. We can have lunch together in the park.
> J Sure! Great idea.
> Am Can I have a cheese sandwich, a cappuccino, and a brownie, please?

h Focus on the chart and tell Sts they need to listen and find out what Jenny and Amy have for lunch.

Play the video or audio again for Sts to listen and complete the chart.

Get Sts to compare with a partner and check answers.

Jenny	a tuna salad and mineral water
Amy	a cheese sandwich, a cappuccino, and a brownie

Extra support

- If there's time, you could play the audio again while Sts read the script on *p.86*, so they can see what they understood / didn't understand. Translate / explain any new words or phrases.

4 ◼️ USEFUL PHRASES
VIDEO

1 97)) Focus on the phrases and make sure Sts understand what each one means.

Play the video or audio once the whole way through for Sts just to listen.

> **1 97))**
> See the phrases in the Student's Book on *p.21*

Now play the video or audio again, pausing after each phrase for Sts to listen and repeat.

Give further practice as necessary, modelling and drilling the pronunciation yourself, or using the video or audio, and getting choral and individual responses.

5 **4 MP3))** SONG *That's How Much* 🎵

For Sts of this level all authentic song lyrics will include language that they don't know.

This song was recorded by the American singer Brian Hyland in 1960. For copyright reasons this is a cover version.

If you want to do this song in class, use the photocopiable activity on *p.229*.

You will find the songs as MP3 files on CD4 of the Class audio CD.

> **4 MP3))**
> *That's How Much*
> **Chorus**
> That's how much
> That's how much uh, huh, uh huh, uh huh,
> Yeah, yeah, yeah
> That's how much
> I love you
> (Yeah, I love you)
>
> Pick a number from one to ten
> Double it and add a million
>
> **Chorus**
>
> Count the miles from here to Mars
> Triple it and add a trillion
>
> **Chorus**
>
> Although I'm not a mathematical genius
> At least I know the score
> Who cares how far to Venus
> When you live right next door
> Oh, count the pebbles on every beach
> Triple it and add a trillion
>
> **Chorus**
>
> Who cares how far to Venus
> When you live right next door
> (Yeah, yeah, yeah)
> (Right next door)
> Count the pebbles on every beach
> Triple it and add a trillion
>
> **Chorus**

G possessive adjectives; possessive 's
V people and family
P /ʌ/, /æ/, and the /ə/ sound

4A Family and friends

Lesson plan

The topic of this lesson is the family.

Sts start by learning the words for people and family members in the **Vocabulary Bank** and also some irregular plurals. Then the new vocabulary is supported by the pronunciation section, which highlights common sounds in the new words. In Grammar possessive adjectives and the possessive 's are presented through a conversation where Sarah, a babysitter, arrives at a couple's house and is introduced to the family.

In the second half of the lesson Sts listen to a man describing some people in photos to a friend. The lesson ends with Sts talking and writing about their own family.

STUDY LINK
- Workbook 4A
- iTutor
- www.oup.com/elt/englishfile

Extra photocopiable activities

- **Grammar** possessive adjectives; possessive 's *p.145*
- **Communicative** Happy families *p.181* (instructions *p.165*)
- **Vocabulary** People and family *p.216* (instructions *p.206*)
- www.oup.com/elt/teacher/englishfile

Optional lead-in (books closed)

- Show Sts a photo of your family, projected onto the board or use a large printed photo. Point to the people in the photo and talk about them like this, e.g. *This is my brother. His name's Dermot. He's 24*, etc.
- Then write the family words for the people you introduced on the board, e.g. *father, brother*, etc. and model and drill the pronunciation.

1 VOCABULARY people and family

a Books open. Focus on the instructions and the four words.

Give Sts time to complete the gaps. Even complete beginners will probably recognize at least two of these words, but if some Sts don't, then you can elicit suggestions from the whole class.

b **(2 2)))** Now play the audio for Sts to listen and check.

Check answers and make sure Sts are clear about the meaning of *boy, girl, woman*, and *man*. Model and drill the pronunciation, especially *woman* /ˈwʊmən/.

1 girl	2 boy	3 woman	4 man

(2 2)))
1 It's a photo of a girl.   3 It's a photo of a woman.
2 It's a photo of a boy.   4 It's a photo of a man.

c Tell Sts to go to **Vocabulary Bank** *People and family* on *p.120*.

(2 3))) Look at **1 People** and focus on **a**. Play the audio and get Sts to repeat the words in chorus. Pause the audio as necessary. Remind Sts that the underlined syllables are stressed more strongly. Give extra practice as necessary, modelling the words yourself or using the audio, especially for the words which your Sts find difficult.

(2 3)))
See the words in the Student's Book on *p.120*

Now focus on **b**. Get Sts to cover the words and then look at the photos and say the family members. They could do this individually or with a partner.

Monitor and help. Make a note of any pronunciation problems they are having. Write the words on the board and model and drill the ones that Sts find difficult.

(2 4))) Focus on the **Irregular plurals** box in **c** and go through it with the class. Explain that these four words have irregular plurals. Play the audio and get Sts to listen and repeat the plural words in chorus and individually. Highlight how the pronunciation changes in *child / children* and *woman / women*. Pause and play again as necessary. Model and drill any words that are difficult for your Sts and give extra practice as necessary.

(2 4)))
See the words in the Student's Book on *p.120*

Extra support

- Get Sts to look at the words in **a** and elicit which are plural (*children* and *friends*).

Focus on **d**. Get Sts to cover the plural words and say them. They could do this individually or with a partner.

Monitor and help. Make a note of any pronunciation problems Sts are having. Write these words on the board, and model and drill them.

(2 5))) Now look at **2 Family** and focus on **a**. Play the audio and get Sts to repeat the words in chorus and individually. Give extra practice as necessary, modelling the words yourself or using the audio, especially for the words which your Sts find difficult.

(2 5)))
See the words in the Student's Book on *p.120*

You may also want to teach the word *partner*, which is very common nowadays to describe the person you are either married to or in a relationship with. Highlight that this word is also used to describe the person you work with in class.

Extra challenge

- You could teach Sts a few other family words such as *grandmother* / *grandfather*, but don't overload them with too much new lexis.

Now focus on **b**. Get Sts to cover the words and look at the photos. Tell them to say the words. They could do this individually or with a partner.

Extra idea

- Put Sts in pairs **A** and **B**. Get the **A**s (books open) to ask the **B**s (books closed) to spell five words. **A** chooses the words and reads them for **B** to spell, e.g. *How do you spell 'husband'?* Demonstrate with a pair of Sts.
- When Sts have finished, tell them to swap roles.

Tell Sts to go back to the main lesson **4A**.

Extra support

- If you think Sts need more practice, you may want to give them the Vocabulary photocopiable activity at this point or leave it for later as consolidation or revision.

2 PRONUNCIATION /ʌ/, /æ/, and the /ə/ sound

Pronunciation notes

- Sts may have problems with the first two sounds /ʌ/ and /æ/ as they may not have exactly the same vowel sounds in their language.
- You may want to highlight the following sound–spelling patterns:

– /ʌ/ The letter u is usually pronounced /ʌ/, especially between consonants, e.g. *husband*, *Russia*. The letter *o* is sometimes pronounced /ʌ/, e.g. *mother*.

– /æ/ *a* between consonants is often pronounced /æ/, e.g. *man*, *thanks*.

– /ə/ For information on this sound, see the **Pronunciation notes** in **3B**.

- See also **Pronunciation** in the **Introduction**, *p.8*.

a **(2 6)))** Read the **Pronunciation notes** and decide how much of the information you want to give your Sts.

Focus on the exercise and play the audio once the whole way through for Sts just to listen.

> **(2 6)))**
> See the words and sounds in the Student's Book on *p.22*

Focus on the sound picture *up*. Play the audio to model and drill the word and sound (pause after the sound).

Now focus on the words after *up*. Remind Sts that the pink letters are the /ʌ/ sound. Play the audio, pausing after each word for Sts to listen and repeat.

Now repeat the same process for *cat* /æ/ and *computer* /ə/. If these sounds are difficult for your Sts, model them yourself so that Sts can see your mouth position, and get Sts to repeat them a few more times.
Play the audio again from the beginning, pausing after each group of words for Sts to repeat.
Give further practice as necessary.
Get Sts, in pairs, to practise saying the words.

Extra support

- If you are using an interactive whiteboard, you can focus on each sound individually before moving on to the next one.

Finally, focus on the /ə/ box and go through it with the class. Give some other examples of words Sts already know which have the /ə/ sound, e.g. *Saturday*, *tomorrow*, *children*, *camera*, *woman*, *sister*, etc. Highlight that this very common sound often occurs <u>after</u> (and sometimes <u>before</u>) an unstressed syllable. Final letters *-er* (e.g. *brother*, *mother*, *teacher*) are always pronounced /ə/.

b **(2 7)))** Focus on the sentences and play the audio once the whole way through for Sts just to listen.

> **(2 7)))**
> See the sentences in the Student's Book on *p.22*

Play the audio, pausing after each sentence for Sts to listen and repeat.

Finally, put Sts in pairs and get them to practise saying the sentences.

3 GRAMMAR possessive adjectives;
possessive 's

a Focus on the first photo on the right. Do the question as an open-class activity to try to elicit that they are the people from **1a**. The man and the woman are husband and wife, and the boy and the girl are their children. Ask Sts who they think the older girl is and elicit / teach that she is a babysitter.

b **(2 8)))** Focus on the instructions and the conversation on *p.23*.

Play the audio once the whole way through for Sts to listen and read.

Then get them to point to the people and say their names.

> **(2 8)))**
> See the conversation in the Student's Book on *p.23*

c Play the audio again and go through the conversation with Sts line by line. Elicit / explain / demonstrate any new words, e.g. *welcome* and *house*.

! Remind Sts that animals are usually *it*. However, if you know whether an animal is male or female, for example, because it is a pet, you can say *he* or *she*. (Sts might be interested to know that about 45 per cent of all UK households have a pet, usually a fish, a cat, or a dog.)

Focus on the instructions and give Sts a few minutes to complete the chart.

Check answers, writing the missing words on the board. You could also ask Sts to spell the words to review spelling.

you	your number
he	his name
she	her name
it	its name
you	your number
they	their names

d Explain / elicit the use of the possessive *'s*. Pick up something that belongs to a student, e.g. a book. Ask *What is it?* (It's a book.) Then say *It's* (name)*'s book*, e.g. *It's Mary's book*. Write the words (NAME)'S BOOK on the board and explain that in this case the *'s* shows possession.

Focus on the instructions. Tell Sts to look for the two examples of the *'s* ending in the second part of the conversation. Then get Sts to complete the sentences.

Check answers.

1 Mario's   2 husband's

e (2 9))) Focus on the question and play the audio once the whole way through for Sts to listen.

Elicit opinions.

(2 9)))

M = Maria, C = children, S = Sarah, E = Emma
M Now, children. Sarah is your babysitter. Be good.
C OK, Mum.
M Goodbye, Sarah.
S Bye, Mrs Taylor.
***
S OK, let's order pizza and watch TV.
E My mother says no pizza and no TV.
S Well your mother isn't here, is she?

---

f (2 10))) (2 11))) Tell Sts to go to **Grammar Bank 4A** on *p.98*.

Focus on **Possessive adjectives**. Play the audio and ask Sts to listen and repeat the sentences. Pause the audio as necessary.

Now focus on the **Possessive *'s*** and have Sts listen and repeat the sentences. Pause the audio as necessary.

Go through the rules for using possessive adjectives and possessive *'s* with the class using the expanded information in the **Additional grammar notes** below to help you. You may want to use L1 here.

Additional grammar notes
Possessive adjectives

- Some languages use the same possessive adjective for *he*, *she*, and *it*. Highlight that in English we use three different possessive adjectives, i.e. *his* for *he*, *her* for *she*, and *its* for *it*.

- In English, the possessive adjective agrees with the <u>person</u> who possesses something, not the noun that follows it, e.g. *Sam's key = his key* and *Ann's keys = her keys*.

- Remind Sts that *your* is used for singular and plural, formal and informal.

! Point out that the possessive adjective *its* has no apostrophe. Sts may confuse this with *it's = it is*.

Possessive *'s*

- Highlight that we use *'s* with words for people, e.g. *girl, boy, husband*, and names, e.g. *Jack's car, my husband's keys*, to show possession, and as an alternative to a possessive adjective. We do <u>not</u> usually use *'s* with things, e.g. *the pages of the book* NOT ~~the book's pages~~.

- For plural nouns, the apostrophe goes <u>after</u> the *s*, e.g. *the students' books*.

- NB For irregular plurals, use *'s*, e.g. *the children's toys*. This isn't focussed on in the lesson, but Sts may ask you about this.

- The pronunciation of the possessive *'s* follows the same rules as those for the pronunciation of plurals formed with *s*.

Focus on the exercises for **4A** on *p.99* and get Sts to do them individually or in pairs. If they do them individually, get them to compare answers with a partner.

Check answers, getting Sts to read the full sentences.

a
1 Their	4 its	7 Her	10 our
2 your	5 Their	8 their	11 my
3 His	6 Its	9 your	12 Our

b
1 Peter is Karen's father.
2 Diana is Sam's mother.
3 Karen is Peter's daughter.
4 Peter is Diana's husband.
5 Sam is Peter's son.
6 Diana is Peter's wife.
7 Sam is Karen's brother.

Tell Sts to go back to the main lesson **4A**.

Extra support
- If you think Sts need more practice, you may want to give them the Grammar photocopiable activity at this point or leave it for later as consolidation or revision.

g Focus on the instructions and demonstrate the activity, which is to consolidate the difference between *his* and *her*. Point to one student and ask another student *What's his / her name?* Elicit *His / Her name is _____*. Repeat with a different student.

You might want to teach the expression *I don't remember*.

Put Sts in pairs and give them a few minutes to ask and answer questions about the other Sts' names.

Monitor and help with any pronunciation problems.

h Focus on the instructions. Put Sts in pairs and get them to ask and answer questions about the photos in 1a. Monitor and help.

4 LISTENING

a (2 12))) Focus on the photo. Ask a couple of questions about it, e.g. *Who are these people?* (a family) *Where are they?* (in a garden or park).

Point to Eric, the man in the centre at the back. Tell Sts that they are going to hear Eric talking about the people in the photo.

Make sure Sts understand that they have to complete each gap with one or more words.

Play the audio and pause after Eric says *Yes, she is French*. Ask *Which person is Eric talking about?* (1). *Who is she?* (his mother). Get Sts to write *mother* in the gap in 1.

When you are sure Sts understand the task, continue playing the audio, pausing after each part of the conversation to give Sts time to write the missing word(s).

Check answers.

> 2 is Eric's sister.
> 3 and 4 are Eric's sister's children.

Ask about the other man in the photo – the man on the left: *Is he in Eric's family?* (No) *Who is he?* (We don't know. He is a person who got into the photo as a joke).

---

2 12))
(script in Student's Book on *p.87*)

E = Eric, W = woman
E   Look, this is a photo of my family.
W Is that woman there your mother?
E   Yes. She's French.
W Really? Who is that? Is she your wife?
E   No, she isn't. She's my sister. Her name's Sophie.
W She's very pretty. And are they your sister's children?
E   Yes.
W How old are they?
E   Her daughter's four and her son's seven.
W And who's that? Is he your sister's husband?
E   No, he isn't.
W Oh. Who is he?
E   I don't know! He isn't in our family.

---

b Give Sts some time to read questions 1–3.

Play the audio again, pausing after each question to give Sts time to write. Tell Sts to write full sentences.

Get Sts to compare with a partner and then check answers.

> 1   She's from France.
> 2   Her name's Sophie.
> 3   They are four and seven.

In the first part of the conversation the woman says *Really?* As this is a high frequency word, you might want to tell Sts that this expression is used to show interest in or surprise at what somebody is saying. In the second part of the conversation point out the adjective *pretty* /ˈprɪti/. Model and drill pronunciation.

Extra support

- If there's time, you could play the audio again while Sts read the script on *p.87*, so they can see what they understood / didn't understand. Translate / explain any new words or phrases.

c Focus on the instructions and the speech bubble.

Put Sts in pairs and get them to tell each other about the people in the photo. They need to say everything they can remember about each person.

Get some feedback from the class.

5   SPEAKING & WRITING

a Put Sts in pairs, **A** and **B**. Tell Sts that they should each write the names of six people they know (people in their family or their friends) on a piece of paper. Give Sts one or two minutes to do this.

Read the instructions and the example with the whole class. Model the activity by looking at a list from a strong student and asking about the first name on the list. *Who's* (name)? Elicit the response *He | She's my* (e.g. *brother*). Encourage Sts to describe family members using the possessive *'s*.

Sts continue asking and answering in pairs.

b Tell Sts to go to **Writing** *Posting a photo: your family* on *p.84*.

Focus on the title and make sure Sts understand it.

Now focus on **a**. Look at the photo and read the instructions. Give Sts time to read the text and write the numbers of the people in the correct place on the photo. Point out that the first one has been done for them.

Check answers. Now ask *Who's Henri?* (to elicit Alice's father) and do the same with the other people.

A 2 (Henri – father)		**D** 4 (Alice)	
B 3 (Cécile – mother)		**E** 5 (Olivier – brother)	
C 1 (Pauline – sister)		**F** 6 (Toto – dog)	

Focus on **b** and the **Punctuation** box and go through it with the class.

Finally, focus on **c** and tell Sts they are going to write about their families. Explain that they should follow the model in **a**.

Write the sentence stems MY NAME IS ____ . I'M FROM ____ on the board to show Sts how to begin.

Give Sts time to write their paragraph. Monitor and help with grammar, spelling, and vocabulary. If you don't have enough time, you could set the writing for homework and ask Sts to attach a photo.

Get Sts to exchange pieces of paper.

Extra challenge

- You could get Sts to draw a family tree and tell their partners about their family from memory.

WORDS AND PHRASES TO LEARN

4 61)) Tell Sts to go to *p.130* and focus on the **Words and phrases to learn** for **4A**. Make sure Sts understand the meaning of each phrase. If necessary, remind them of the context in which the words and phrases came up in the lesson. If you speak your Sts' L1, you might like to elicit a translation for the words / phrases for the Sts to write next to them. Play the audio, pausing after each phrase for Sts to repeat. You may also like to ask Sts to test each other on the phrases.

G adjectives
V colours and common adjectives
P /uː/, /ɑː/, and /ɔː/; linking

4B Big cars or small cars?

Lesson plan

This lesson uses the context of a woman buying a car for Sts to learn some common adjectives and how to use them. The vocabulary load at the beginning of the lesson is quite high as it includes both colours and adjectives, although some beginners may already know some of these words. Students then move on to the grammar of adjectives, which is relatively straightforward. Pronunciation focusses on the sounds /uː/, /ɑː/, and /ɔː/, and on linking. The lesson ends with Sts using adjectives in a speaking activity where they talk about their preferences.

STUDY LINK
- Workbook 4B
- iTutor
- iChecker on iTutor
- www.oup.com/elt/englishfile

Extra photocopiable activities
- **Grammar** adjectives *p.146*
- **Communicative** What is it? *p.182* (instructions *p.166*)
- **Vocabulary** Colours and common adjectives *p.217* (instructions *p.206*)
- www.oup.com/elt/teacher/englishfile

Optional lead-in (books closed)
- Show Sts some photos of new cars or write the name of some popular cars on the board, e.g. VW GOLF. Elicit the names of other cars.
- Then elicit from the class the nationality of each car, e.g. VW Golf = German.
- Finally, ask Sts which cars are popular in their country.

1 LISTENING & VOCABULARY colours and common adjectives

a (2 13)) Books open. Focus on the photo and the task.

Give Sts time to match the nationalities with the cars.

Play the audio for Sts to listen and check their answers.

1	British	3	German	5	Japanese
2	French	4	American	6	Italian

> (2 13))
> (script in Student's Book on *p.87*)
> 4 It's American. It's a Ford.
> 1 It's British. It's a Mini.
> 2 It's French. It's a Renault.
> 3 It's German. It's an Audi.
> 6 It's Italian. It's a Fiat.
> 5 It's Japanese. It's a Honda.

Extra idea
- If your Sts are interested, you could now elicit what models the cars are that are featured on this page. Point to the first car and ask *What car is it?* (It's a Mini.), then ask *What model is it?* (Clubman). Write the information on the board (2 = RENAULT ZOE, 3 = AUDI TT, 4 = FORD FOCUS, 5 = HONDA JAZZ, 6 = FIAT 500).

b (2 14)) Focus on the instructions and get Sts to cover the dialogue with a piece of paper. Before playing the audio you might want to tell Sts that the woman in the audio is buying a second-hand car from a car salesman.

Play the audio once the whole way through for Sts to listen and try to answer the question.

Check the answer.

> the (red) Audi TT

> (2 14))
> See the conversation in the Student's Book on *p.24*

Teach / elicit the meaning of *thousand* and highlight that it doesn't have an *s* on the end.

c Focus on the instructions and get Sts to uncover the dialogue. Play the audio again for Sts to listen and read at the same time.

Then focus on the first highlighted word and ask Sts *What's 'good'?* Elicit the meaning and tell Sts that the highlighted words are all colours or adjectives.

Tell Sts that they are going to work out the meaning of the highlighted words. Tell them not to worry if there are some words they can't work out. The photo will help them for two of the words.

Get Sts to work with a partner.

Check answers by asking individual pairs for their ideas. Explain the meaning of any words Sts couldn't work out.

d (**2 15**))) Play the audio, pausing after each phrase for Sts to listen and repeat. Encourage Sts to copy the rhythm and intonation on the audio. Give further practice as necessary using choral and individual repetition.

> (**2 15**)))
> See the conversation in the Student's Book on *p.24*

Put Sts in pairs, **A** and **B**. Assign roles and get them to practise the dialogue.

Monitor and help, encouraging Sts to use the intonation they heard on the audio.

You could get some pairs to act out the dialogue for the class.

e Tell Sts to go to **Vocabulary Bank** *Adjectives* on *p.121*.

(**2 16**))) Look at **1 Colours** and focus on **a**. Play the audio and get Sts to repeat the colours in chorus. Pause the audio as necessary. Give extra practice of words which your Sts find difficult.

> (**2 16**)))
> See the colours in the Student's Book on *p.121*

Now focus on **b**. Ask Sts to cover the words, look at the photos, and ask and answer about the colours in pairs.

Monitor and help. Make a note of any pronunciation problems. Write the words on the board. Model and drill difficult ones, e.g. *orange* and *yellow*.

Extra idea
• You could point to different objects in the classroom and say *What colour is it?* to practise the ten colours in the **Vocabulary Bank**.

Extra challenge
• Sts may ask for the words for other colours, e.g. *purple, beige*. Write them on the board, and model and drill pronunciation.

(**2 17**))) Look at **2 Common adjectives** and focus on **a**. Play the audio and get Sts to repeat the adjectives in chorus. Pause the audio as necessary. Give extra practice of words which your Sts find most difficult.

> (**2 17**)))
> See the common adjectives in the Student's Book on *p.121*

Explain that we normally use *beautiful* for a woman (not a man) or an animal, place, piece of music, etc. You could remind Sts that they saw *pretty* in **4A** and say that it is normally used for a woman or child and also a place. You could also elicit *good-looking*, which Sts saw in **2B**, and tell them that it is used for both men and women.

Now focus on **b**. Ask Sts to cover the words, look at the photos, and say the adjectives. They could do this individually or with a partner.

Now focus on **c**. Model and drill the question *What's the opposite of 'new'?* and elicit / explain the meaning of *the opposite*.

Put Sts in pairs and give them a few minutes to test each other on the adjectives.

Monitor and correct any pronunciation mistakes on the board.

(**2 18**))) Focus on the **Positive and negative adjectives** box in **d** and go through it with the class. Then play the audio for Sts to listen and repeat the adjectives. Point out that *very* can be used with any adjective, e.g. *very big*, *very expensive*, etc., apart from adjectives that already have an extreme meaning, e.g. *great | fantastic | terrible*.

> (**2 18**)))
> See the positive and negative adjectives in the Student's Book on *p.121*

Tell Sts to go back to the main lesson **4B**.

Extra support
• If you think Sts need more practice, you may want to give them the Vocabulary photocopiable activity at this point or leave it for later as consolidation or revision.

f Focus on the instructions and the example. Give Sts a few minutes to think of at least two adjectives for each car.

Put Sts in pairs and get them to tell each other about the cars.

Monitor and help.

Get some feedback about each car.

Extra support
• Sts could write a sentence with two adjectives about each car, e.g. *The Renault is small and cheap.*

g Focus on the instructions and the example. Give Sts a few minutes to think of adjectives to describe their own car or their family's car.

Put Sts in pairs or small groups and get them to tell each other about their cars.

Monitor and help.

Get some feedback from various Sts. You could find out if any Sts have the same car and if they have used the same adjectives to describe it.

2 GRAMMAR adjectives

a Focus on the sentences and give Sts time to circle the correct one for 1 and 2. Sts should be able to do this from examples of this grammar point that they saw in the conversation between the salesman and the woman, e.g. *a good car*.

Get Sts to compare with a partner and then check answers.

> 1 a   2 b

b (**2 19**))) Tell Sts to go to **Grammar Bank 4B** on *p.98*.

Focus on the example sentences and play the audio for Sts to listen and repeat. Pause the audio as necessary.

Go through the rules with the class using the expanded information in the **Additional grammar notes** on the next page to help you. You may want to use Sts' L1 here.

Additional grammar notes

adjectives

- In English, an adjective can go after the verb *be*, but when it is with a noun it always goes BEFORE the noun, e.g. *My car is fast. It's a fast car.*

- Adjectives are the same for singular and plural nouns, so you never add an *s* to an adjective. This is different from many other languages where adjectives have to 'agree' with nouns.

- Adjectives have no masculine or feminine form.

very

- *very* is often used before an adjective to intensify it, e.g. *very fast.*

Focus on the exercises for **4B** on *p.99* and get Sts to do them individually or in pairs. If they do them individually, get them to compare answers with a partner.

Check answers, getting Sts to read the full sentences.

a
1 It's an old car.
2 They're black coats.
3 It's a new phone.
4 They're big houses.
5 They're expensive glasses.
6 It's a good book.
b
1 It's a beautiful day.
2 Amy's husband is very nice.
3 They're very difficult questions.
4 This is a cheap phone.
5 It's a terrible photo.
6 Maria is a very tall girl.
7 Our cat is very old.
8 This isn't a very good restaurant.
9 It's a very long exercise.
10 Their dog is very ugly.
11 Italian bags are very expensive.
12 This is a very small room.

Tell Sts to go back to the main lesson **4B**.

Extra support
- If you think Sts need more practice, you may want to give them the Grammar photocopiable activity at this point or leave it for later as consolidation or revision.

c Focus on the instructions. Now tell Sts to go back to **Vocabulary Bank** *Adjectives* on *p.121*. Focus on the photo of the mobile phone, and elicit *It's a pink mobile phone*. Do the same with *It's a big house.*

Put Sts in pairs and get Sts to make ten sentences about the photos.

Get some feedback from various pairs.

Extra support
- Put Sts in pairs and get them to write their ten sentences.

Tell Sts to go back to the main lesson **4B**.

d (2 20)))) Focus on the instructions and example. Explain to Sts that they are going to hear a phrase in the singular, and they have to say the plural form.

Play the example, *an American car*, pausing for Sts to say *American cars* in chorus.

Play the audio, pausing after each item, for Sts to listen and say the plural.

(2 20)))
1 an American car (*pause*) American cars
2 an expensive watch (*pause*) expensive watches
3 a big house (*pause*) big houses
4 a tall man (*pause*) tall men
5 a long book (*pause*) long books
6 a new phone (*pause*) new phones
7 a good friend (*pause*) good friends
8 a beautiful woman (*pause*) beautiful women
9 a small child (*pause*) small children

Now repeat the activity, eliciting responses from individual Sts.

3 PRONUNCIATION /uː/, /ɑː/, and /ɔː/; linking

Pronunciation notes

/uː/, /ɑː/, and /ɔː/

- Remind Sts that the two dots in the symbols mean that they are long sounds.

- You may want to highlight the following sound–spelling patterns:

– /uː/ The letters *oo* are often pronounced /uː/, e.g. *food*, but not always, e.g. *book*, *look* /ʊ/.

– /ɑː/ The letters *ar* are usually pronounced /ɑː/, e.g. *car*, *are*. In American English and in some regions of Britain words like *fast* and *glasses* are pronounced /fæst/ and /ˈɡlæsɪz/. If this is the way you pronounce them, you may want to explain this to Sts, and teach them your pronunciation rather than the pronunciation on the audio.

– /ɔː/ The letters *all* usually have an /ɔː/ sound, e.g. *call*. The letters *or* are sometimes pronounced /ɔː/, e.g. *short*, but sometimes /ɜː/, e.g. *world*.

Linking

- It is very common in English to link words together, especially when one word finishes with a consonant sound and the next word begins with a vowel sound, e.g. *an old umbrella*. Being aware of this will not only help Sts pronounce better, but also help them to 'separate' words in their head when people speak to them.

- See also **Pronunciation** in the **Introduction**, *p.8*.

a (2 21))) Read the **Pronunciation notes** and decide how much of the information you want to give your Sts.

Focus on the exercise and play the audio once the whole way through for Sts just to listen.

(2 21)))
See the words and sounds in the Student's Book on *p.25*

Focus on the sound picture *boot*. Play the audio to model and drill the word and the sound (pause after the sound).

Now focus on the words after *boot*. Remind Sts that the pink letters are the /uː/ sound. Play the audio, pausing after each word for Sts to listen and repeat.

Now repeat the same process for *car* /ɑː/ and *horse* /ɔː/.

If these sounds are difficult for your Sts, model them yourself so that Sts can see your mouth position, and get Sts to repeat them a few more times.

Play the audio again from the beginning, pausing after each group of words for Sts to repeat.

Give further practice as necessary.

Finally, get Sts, in pairs, to practise saying the words.

Extra support
- If you are using an interactive whiteboard, you can focus on each sound individually before moving on to the next one.

b (**2 22**)) Focus on the word *linking* in the title and tell Sts that when one word ends with a consonant, e.g. *old*, and the next word begins with a vowel, e.g. *umbrella*, we link the two words: *old umbrella*. For more information see the **Pronunciation notes**.

Now focus on the phrases and make sure Sts know what an *egg* is as this may be a new word for them. Remind Sts that the words in bigger font are the ones which are stressed (because they carry the important information). Also remind them that the underlined syllables in the multi-syllable words are stressed more.

Play the audio once the whole way through for Sts just to listen.

> (**2 22**))
> See the phrases in the Student's Book on *p.25*

Now play the audio, pausing after each phrase for Sts to listen and repeat.

Then repeat the activity, eliciting responses from individual Sts.

Finally, get Sts, in pairs, to practise saying the phrases.

c (**2 23**)) Focus on the instructions.

Play the audio once the whole way through for Sts just to listen. Tell them not to write yet.

> (**2 23**))
> 1 an ugly house   4 good evening
> 2 an easy exercise   5 an American friend
> 3 my old ID card

Now play it again, pausing after each phrase to give Sts time to write it down.

Check answers by eliciting each phrase onto the board.

Extra idea
- Put Sts in pairs and get them to practise saying the phrases.

4 SPEAKING

Focus on the nine items and make sure Sts know what they are.

Now focus on the phrase *I prefer* and demonstrate / elicit its meaning.

Focus on the three example speech bubbles and explain that the person saying *Me, too* agrees with the first person.

Get a good pair to demonstrate the activity to the class.

Put Sts in small groups of three or four and get them to discuss each item.

Get some feedback from individual Sts.

WORDS AND PHRASES TO LEARN

(**4 61**)) Tell Sts to go to *p.130* and focus on the **Words and phrases to learn** for **4B**. Make sure Sts understand the meaning of each phrase. If necessary, remind them of the context in which the words and phrases came up in the lesson. If you speak your Sts' L1, you might like to elicit a translation for the words / phrases for the Sts to write next to them. Play the audio, pausing after each phrase for Sts to repeat. You may also like to ask Sts to test each other on the phrases.

3&4 Revise and Check

For instructions on how to use these pages see *p.36*.

STUDY **LINK**
- iTutor

Test and Assessment CD-ROM

- Quick Test 4
- File Test 4

GRAMMAR

1	a	6	a	11	b
2	b	7	b	12	b
3	b	8	b	13	a
4	b	9	a	14	b
5	a	10	a	15	a

VOCABULARY

a
1 an umbrella   3 a key   5 a hat
2 a credit card 4 a map

b
1 mother   3 daughter   5 girlfriend
2 husband   4 brother

c
1 women   3 men
2 children   4 people

d
1 blue   3 red   5 black
2 green   4 yellow   6 pink

e
1 small   3 short   5 beautiful
2 cheap   4 old

PRONUNCIATION

a
1 <u>wo</u>man   3 <u>o</u>range   5 <u>s</u>ister
2 <u>fa</u>mily   4 ex<u>pe</u>nsive

b /uː/boot   /ɔː/ horse   /ð/ mother
   /ʌ/ up   /z/ zebra

CAN YOU UNDERSTAND THIS TEXT?

a   Photo 1: 1 Jeremy   3 Matthew
              2 Anna   4 Susanna
    Photo 2: 1 Louise   2 Claire   3 Anne

b
1 Fisher   5 French
2 Liverpool / the UK 6 her sister
3 tall   7 No, she isn't.
4 19   8 31

VIDEO CAN YOU UNDERSTAND THESE PEOPLE?

(2 24))) 1 c   2 a   3 b   4 a   5 b

> **(2 24)))**
> See the script in the Student's Book on *p.87*)

Remind Sts that they can watch the short film on *iTutor*.

> **VIDEO** Available as MP3 on CD4
>
> **Short film: National Motor Museum, Beaulieu**
>
> Hi! I'm Louise and today I'm in Beaulieu. Beaulieu is a small village. It's in England, but Beaulieu is a French word. In English we say 'Bjuli', but in French it's 'Beau' 'Lieu' – beautiful place. And it really is beautiful! Beaulieu is in the New Forest. It's famous for its big house, old church, and fantastic motor museum.
>
> The National Motor Museum in Beaulieu is 62 years old. It's a very interesting place, with lots and lots of cars. Let's go and see!
>
> These are some of the cars. These are old, vintage cars. These are fast, modern cars. This is a very small car.
>
> This is my favourite car. It's British and its name is Bluebird. It's 55 years old and it's very, very fast!

G present simple + and −: *I, you, we, they*
V food and drink
P word stress; /tʃ/, /dʒ/, and /g/

5A Breakfast around the world

Lesson plan

The context of this lesson is what people in different parts of the world have for breakfast.

Sts begin by learning the vocabulary for basic food items, e.g. *fruit* (later in the lesson, they learn the words for other meals – *lunch* and *dinner*). After reading about different breakfasts, Sts learn the *I, you, we,* and *they* forms in the present simple. Sts then listen to four people talking about their favourite meal of the day, where they have it, and what they have. In Pronunciation, Sts have more practice in word stress and pronouncing consonant sounds. The lesson builds up to a speaking activity, where Sts talk about their eating habits and what people eat in their country. Finally, Sts write a paragraph about their typical breakfast.

STUDY LINK
- Workbook 5A
- iTutor
- www.oup.com/elt/englishfile

Extra photocopiable activities

- **Grammar** present simple + and −: *I, you, we, they* p.147
- **Communicative** Talk about food p.183 (instructions p.166)
- **Vocabulary** Food and drink p.218 (instructions p.206)
- www.oup.com/elt/teacher/englishfile

Optional lead-in (books closed)

- Write the names of some 'international' food words on the board, e.g. *pasta, pizza, sushi, burgers, croissants,* etc. If possible, choose words that are the same or very similar in your Sts' L1. You might be able to elicit more words from the class. Model and drill pronunciation.

- Ask Sts *Where are these foods from?* and elicit, e.g. *Pasta and pizza are from Italy,* etc.

1 VOCABULARY food and drink

a **2 26))** Books open. Focus on the title of the lesson, *Breakfast around the world,* and elicit / teach the meaning. Elicit / explain that *breakfast* is what people eat in the morning. Elicit the word *lunch,* which Sts saw in **Practical English 2**. Now focus on the photo and ask Sts *Where is Dominic from?* (Bath / the UK).

Focus on the task and then play the audio once the whole way through for Sts to read and listen at the same time.

> **2 26))**
> See the text in the Student's Book on *p.28*

Now give Sts time to write the highlighted words on the photo. The first one (cereal) has been done for them.

Check answers. Model and drill the pronunciation of the food and drink words: *orange juice* /ˈɒrɪndʒ dʒuːs/, *milk* /mɪlk/, *fruit* /fruːt/, *coffee* /ˈkɒfi/, *yoghurt* /ˈjɒgət/, *cereal* /ˈsɪəriəl/.

1 orange juice	3 cereal	5 yoghurt
2 hot milk	4 coffee	

Go through the text and focus on any other new words, e.g. *at home, drink, healthy,* etc. Model and drill the pronunciation.

b Tell Sts to go to **Vocabulary Bank** *Food and drink* on *p.122*. There is quite a heavy vocabulary load, so you may need to spend longer on the drilling stage here.

2 27)) Focus on **a**. Play the audio and get Sts to repeat the words in chorus and individually as necessary. Model and drill any words which are difficult for your Sts and give further practice. Remind Sts that the underlined syllables are stressed more strongly.

> **2 27))**
> See the list of food and drink in the Student's Book on *p.122*

You may want to highlight that:

- *ea* is pronounced /iː/ in *tea* and *meat,* but /e/ in *bread* and *breakfast,* and /ɪə/ in *cereal.*
- *vegetables* and *chocolate* both have a syllable which is not pronounced.
- the *d* in *sandwich* /ˈsænwɪtʃ/ is not usually pronounced.
- the *s* in *sugar* is pronounced /ʃ/.

Focus on the **Meals** box and go through it with the class. Remind Sts that *breakfast* is a meal in the morning. Elicit / explain that *lunch* is in the early afternoon, and *dinner* is usually in the evening (although in some parts of the UK, some people call the midday meal *dinner* if it is their main meal of the day).

! Highlight that the verbs *eat* and *drink* describe the general actions, e.g. *I eat a lot of bread. I don't drink coffee.* However, we usually use *have* with meals, e.g. *have breakfast,* and to describe what we eat / drink at a particular meal, e.g. *I have toast and tea for breakfast.*

Now focus on **b**. Ask Sts to cover the words with a piece of paper, look only at the photos (they do this for each row of photos), and say the words. They could do this individually or with a partner.

Monitor and help. Make a note of any pronunciation problems they are still having to focus on at the end of the activity.

Tell Sts go back to the main lesson **5A**.

Extra support

- If you think Sts need more practice, you may want to give them the Vocabulary photocopiable activity at this point or leave it for later as consolidation or revision.

2 READING

a Focus on the instructions and the two photos of breakfasts, and elicit the food words which Sts already know, e.g. *eggs*, *potatoes*, etc. Don't teach the new words (*sausage*, *toast*, *soup*, *green tea*) as Sts will focus on these in **b**.

> Sts should be able to identify eggs, potatoes, orange juice, coffee, rice, fish, and tea. (These are on the lists in the **Vocabulary Bank**.)

b Focus on the highlighted words. Sts then write the highlighted words on the photos.

Check answers.

7 toast	9 soup
8 sausages	10 green tea

c (2 28)) Now focus on the two texts. Play the audio for Sts to read and listen at the same time.

Give Sts time to complete the chart. They can do this in their notebooks or on a separate sheet of paper.

Get Sts to compare with a partner and then check answers.

Louisa	Drink: orange juice, coffee Food: eggs, potatoes, sausages, toast
Ken	Drink: green tea Food: rice, fish, soup

> (2 28))
See the texts in the Student's Book on *p.28*

Other lexis Sts may ask about are *typical*, *only*, *traditional*, *different*, and *a lot of*. If Sts ask what *miso* is, tell them it is a substance made from beans used in Japanese cooking.

In **4A** Sts saw *Really?* to express interest in something someone is saying; here they see the word *really* ('But I *really* like my breakfast on Saturdays!') to emphasize an opinion being given (= I like it a lot).

d Focus on the two questions. Give Sts time to look at all three breakfasts again and then with a show of hands find out which breakfast is the most popular.

Now focus on the second question and tell Sts what you have for breakfast. Give them time to think of what they have.

Put Sts in pairs and give them time to ask and answer the question. Monitor and help.

Get feedback by asking some Sts to tell the class what their partner has for breakfast.

3 GRAMMAR present simple ⊞ and ⊟:
I, you, we, they

a Focus on the instructions and give Sts time to complete the sentences.

Check answers and write them on the board.

1 have	3 have	5 don't have
2 drink	4 don't have	6 don't drink

b (2 29)) Tell Sts to go to **Grammar Bank 5A** on *p.100*.

Focus on the example sentences and play the audio for Sts to listen and repeat. Pause the audio as necessary.

Go through the rules with the class using the expanded information in the **Additional grammar notes** below to help you. You may want to use Sts' L1 here.

> **Additional grammar notes**
> **present simple ⊞ and ⊟: *I, you, we, they***
>
> - The *I*, *we*, *you*, and *they* forms of the present simple are the same, e.g. *I live, you live, we live, they live*. The verb endings don't change, unlike in many languages. Highlight that it is the subject pronoun *I | you | we | they* that changes, not the verb (*live*). For this reason it is essential to always use the pronouns. Otherwise, it wouldn't be clear which person you were talking about.
>
> - In the present simple, for *I*, *we*, *you*, and *they*, we use *don't* before the infinitive form of the verb to form negatives. *Don't* is the contraction of *do not*. *Do* and *don't* are called auxiliary verbs. They are used to form negatives and questions. Remind Sts that native speakers nearly always use the contracted form *don't* in spoken English.

Focus on the exercises for **5A** on *p.101* and get Sts to do them individually or in pairs. If they do them individually, get them to compare answers with a partner.

Check answers, getting Sts to read the full sentences.

a
1 I have eggs for breakfast.
2 We don't drink coffee in the evening.
3 They like chocolate.
4 You eat meat.
5 We eat rice in the evening.
6 I don't have sugar in my coffee.
7 You don't like cheese.
8 The children eat vegetables.
b
1 don't have, have	3 drink, don't drink
2 don't eat, eat	4 don't go, go

Tell Sts to go back to the main lesson **5A**.

Extra support
- If you think Sts need more practice, you may want to give them the Grammar photocopiable activity at this point or leave it for later as consolidation or revision.

c Focus on the emoticons in the instructions and the two speech bubbles. Model and drill the examples.

Now tell Sts to go to **Vocabulary Bank** *Food and drink* on *p.122*.

Put Sts in pairs and get them to tell each other what they like and dislike.

Get some feedback from the class.

Extra support
- Write I LIKE and I DON'T LIKE on the board for reference. Demonstrate first by telling Sts about foods you like and don't like.

Tell Sts to go back to the main lesson **5A**.

4 LISTENING

a (2 30))) Focus on the instructions and the question *What's their favourite meal of the day?* Tell Sts they are going to listen to four people talking about their favourite meal and the first time they listen they just have to answer this one question. If you know your Sts' L1, you may want to pre-teach the adverbs of frequency *usually*, *always*, and *never*, which come up in these recordings.

Play the audio once the whole way through for Sts to listen and do the task. Play again as necessary.

Check answers.

Chris	breakfast	**Jackie**	lunch
Josh	dinner	**Steve**	breakfast

(2 30)))
(script in Student's Book on *p.87*)

1 **Chris**
My favourite meal of the day is breakfast. I'm always hungry then. I have breakfast at home. I usually start with fruit juice or fruit salad, then coffee and toast, and then more coffee.

2 **Josh**
My favourite meal of the day is dinner. I usually have dinner at home, and I have soup or pasta. I love eating my dinner sitting on the sofa and watching a DVD.

3 **Jackie**
My favourite meal is Sunday lunch. I always have it at a friend's house with our families. We usually have chicken soup, then meat and lots of vegetables.

4 **Steve**
My favourite meal is breakfast on Saturday and Sunday. I have it at home, in the kitchen. I don't always have the same thing, but I always have eggs.

---

b Now focus on columns two and three of the chart. Make sure Sts understand what the columns *Where* and *Food and drink* refer to.

Play the audio again, pausing after each speaker to give Sts time to write. Play again as necessary.

Get Sts to compare with a partner and then check answers.

Chris	2	at home
	3	fruit juice or fruit salad, coffee, toast
Josh	2	at home
	3	soup or pasta
Jackie	2	at a friend's house
	3	chicken soup, meat and vegetables
Steve	2	at home
	3	eggs

Extra support

• If there's time, you could play the audio again while Sts read the script on *p.87*, so they can see what they understood / didn't understand. Translate / explain any new words or phrases.

c Focus on the question and give Sts a few minutes to think about their answers.

Put Sts in pairs or small groups and get them to tell each other what their favourite meal is.

Get some feedback from the class. With a show of hands you could find out which is the class's favourite meal.

5 PRONUNCIATION word stress; /tʃ/, /dʒ/, and /g/

Pronunciation notes
Word stress

• Several of the new food words have quite a tricky stress pattern, e.g. *vegetables*, and the exercise here focusses on these.

/tʃ/, /dʒ/, and /g/

• The sounds in this lesson are all consonant sounds.

• For information on /dʒ/ and /tʃ/ see the **Pronunciation notes** in **2A**.

• You might want to highlight the following sound–spelling rules:

– /g/ This sound only occurs where there is the letter *g*.

• You could remind Sts that the letter *g* is always pronounced /g/ when it comes after a vowel at the end of a word, e.g. *bag*, *dog*, and often at the beginning and in the middle of a word, e.g. *glasses*, *sugar*. However, before *e* and *i* the letter *g* is often pronounced /dʒ/, e.g. *German*, *orange*.

• See also **Pronunciation** in the **Introduction**, *p.8*.

a (2 31))) Focus on the instructions. Demonstrate the activity by doing an example with the class. Write COFFEE on the board and ask *How many syllables?* (two – co ffee). Now ask *Where's the stress?* (on syllable one). Underline the first syllable: COFFEE.

Put Sts in pairs and get them to underline the stressed syllables in the words. Tell Sts that this exercise is easier if they say the words aloud quietly to each other, so they can hear where the stress is. Monitor and help.

Play the audio for Sts to listen and check their answers.

Check answers by writing the words on the board and eliciting the stressed syllable.

vegetables	potatoes	butter	sugar	salad
cereal	chocolate	yoghurt		

(2 31)))
See the words in the Student's Book on *p.29*

! The word *vegetables* has only three syllables, and *chocolate* only two syllables, because they contain silent letters. Write the words on the board, say them and ask *Which letter is silent?* (the second *e* in *vegetables*, the second *o* in *chocolate*). Cross out these letters, i.e. *vegetables*, *chocolate*, and drill the two words in chorus and individually.

Now play the audio for Sts to listen and repeat the words.

b (2 32))) Read the **Pronunciation notes** and decide how much of the information you want to give your Sts.

Now focus the exercise and play the audio once the whole way through for Sts just to listen.

(2 32)))
See the sounds and words in the Student's Book on *p.29*

Now focus on the sound picture *chess*. Play the audio to model and drill the word and the sound (pause after the sound).

Now focus on the words after *chess*. Remind Sts that the pink letters are the /tʃ/ sound. Play the audio, pausing after each word for Sts to listen and repeat.

Now repeat the same process for *jazz* /dʒ/ and *girl* /g/.

If these sounds are difficult for your Sts, model them yourself so that Sts can see your mouth position, and get Sts to repeat them a few more times.

Play the audio again from the beginning, pausing after each group of words for Sts to repeat.

Give further practice as necessary.

Finally, get Sts, in pairs, to practise saying the words.

Extra support
• If you are using an interactive whiteboard, you can focus on each sound individually before moving on to the next one.

c (2 33)) Focus on the sentences and play the audio once the whole way through for Sts just to listen.

> (2 33))
> See the sentences in the Student's Book on *p.29*

Then play the audio again, pausing after each sentence, for Sts to listen and repeat.

Finally, put Sts in pairs and get them to practise saying the sentences. Monitor and help.

Get individual Sts to say the sentences to the class.

6 SPEAKING

a Focus on the questionnaire and make sure Sts understand all the statements and the question *Is it true?* As well as food words, note other words or phrases that may be new for Sts, e.g. *school*, *fast food*, etc.

Give Sts time to think about their answers and tick the sentences that are true for them, or true about their country.

b Focus on the speech bubble, and say if the first statement in the **About you** section is true for you or not. If you are not from your Sts' country, you could also focus on the first sentence in the **About your country** section and say if it's true about people from your country.

Then put Sts in pairs and give them time to talk about each statement. Monitor and help, and encourage Sts to correct the statements that are not true for them.

Get some feedback from individual students.

! If your Sts are all from the same country, you could do the **About your country** section as an open-class activity as Sts may not always agree on these.

7 WRITING

Posting a comment

Tell Sts to go to **Writing *Posting a comment*** on *p.84*.

a Focus on the title, *Posting a comment*, and make sure Sts understand it.

Focus on the instructions and then give Sts time to read Marco's comment.

Before eliciting Sts' opinions on whether they like Marco's breakfast, elicit each item he has and check Sts know the meaning: *papaya, mango, bread, butter, jam.* Model and drill pronunciation.

If you didn't focus on the word *healthy* in Dominic's text in **1**, then focus on it here. If you did, check Sts can remember what it means.

Now tell Sts if you like or don't like Marco's breakfast, and then ask *What about you?* With a show of hands you could find out how many Sts like his breakfast.

b Focus on the instructions and give Sts time to look at the highlighted words and then complete sentences 1–3.

Check answers.

1 or	2 and	3 but

Check Sts know the meaning of the three words.

Extra support
• Write the following sentences on the board to help Sts understand how to use *and, or, but*.

 I LIKE TEA. I LIKE COFFEE. → I LIKE TEA *AND* COFFEE.

 SOME DAYS I DRINK TEA AND SOME DAYS I DRINK COFFEE. → I DRINK TEA *OR* COFFEE.

 I LIKE CEREAL. I DON'T LIKE TOAST. → I LIKE CEREAL *BUT* I DON'T LIKE TOAST.

c Give Sts time to write their own comments. Tell them to use Marco's comment as a model. They can begin with *For breakfast I have…* Give Sts about 6–8 minutes to write about 50 words for this task.

Go around the room to monitor and help as Sts are writing. However, don't make a lot of corrections at this time. Allow Sts to focus on putting their ideas down on paper.

Extra idea
• You could get Sts to post their comments around the classroom. Then Sts can circulate around the room and read about their classmates' breakfasts. (Check to make sure that comments don't have too many errors before Sts put them up.)

WORDS AND PHRASES TO LEARN

(4 61)) Tell Sts to go to *p.130* and focus on the **Words and phrases to learn** for **5A**. Make sure Sts understand the meaning of each phrase. If necessary, remind them of the context in which the words and phrases came up in the lesson. If you speak your Sts' L1, you might like to elicit a translation for the words / phrases for the Sts to write next to them. Play the audio, pausing after each phrase for Sts to repeat. You may also like to ask Sts to test each other on the phrases.

G present simple ?: *I, you, we, they*
V common verb phrases 1
P /w/, /v/, and /ɒ/; sentence rhythm and linking

5B A very long flight

Lesson plan

The focus of this lesson is on forming questions in the present simple with some common verbs.

A conversation between two women travelling on a plane provides the context for Sts to revise positive and negative forms of *I, we, you,* and *they* in the present simple and it also introduces the grammar of question formation. After the grammar presentation and practice, Sts go to the **Vocabulary Bank** to learn a group of common verb phrases, which are then recycled in the listening (the two women from the first activity meet again on the return flight). In Pronunciation, Sts focus on two consonant sounds, /w/ and /v/, one vowel sound, /ɒ/, and they practise linking words together as well as sentence rhythm. Finally, all the language is brought together in the speaking activity where Sts ask and answer questions about lifestyle before writing a few sentences about themselves.

STUDY LINK
- Workbook 5B
- iTutor
- iChecker on iTutor
- www.oup.com/elt/englishfile

Extra photocopiable activities

- **Grammar** present simple ?: *I, you, we, and they p.148*
- **Communicative** Do you...? *p.184* (instructions *p.166*)
- **Vocabulary** Common verb phrases *p.219* (instructions *p.207*)
- www.oup.com/elt/teacher/englishfile

Optional lead-in (books closed)

- Revise present simple + and − sentences by writing the following on the board:

	FOOTBALL
	DOGS
	PIZZA
I LIKE	TEA
I DON'T LIKE	BURGERS
	CATS
	TENNIS

- Model and drill pronunciation of the nouns and then of *I like / don't like.*

- Put Sts in pairs and demonstrate the activity yourself by making true sentences using *I like / I don't like....* Point out that you don't use *the* before the nouns NOT ~~I like the football~~ (because you are making general statements).

- Students practise in pairs taking it in turns to say what they like / don't like.

1 LISTENING & READING

a **2 34))** Books open. Get Sts to cover the conversation and focus on the instructions and the pictures. Make sure Sts understand the word *flight.*

Play the audio once the whole way through for Sts to listen and number the pictures. Make it clear to Sts that, at this stage, they are not expected to understand the conversation, just to get a rough idea of what is being said. Sts will get help here from the sound effects and from words they already know. Pause and play again as necessary.

Get Sts to compare with a partner and then play the audio again to check answers.

> 1 D 2 B 3 A 4 C

> **2 34))**
> E = Eve, W = Wendy, FA = flight attendant
> **1**
> E Do you like the book?
> W Yes, I do. It's very good.
> E She's my favourite writer. I love her books.
> **2**
> E Do you live in New York?
> W No, I don't. I live in London. My husband and I work for a British company.
> E Oh! Do you have children?
> W No, we don't.
> E I have two sons and a daughter. David and Andrew are at university, and Carla's at school. Look. Here are some photos, That's my David ... This is a photo of our holiday in Barbados.
>   Do you know Barbados?
> W No, I don't.
> **3**
> FA Do you want meat, fish, or pasta?
> E Oh, er, fish, please.
> W Pasta for me, please.
>   ***
> E Is your pasta nice?
> W It's OK.
> E This fish isn't very good. Excuse me, I don't like this fish. Can I have the pasta, please?
> FA I'm sorry, madam. The pasta is finished.
> **4**
> E Oh, I need to go to the toilet. Oops, sorry.
> W Excuse me. What time do we arrive?
> FA In twenty-five minutes, madam.
> W That's good!

b Get Sts to uncover the conversation and focus on the instructions. Sts have seen all the words in the list in previous lessons, but you might want to quickly check that they can remember what they mean.

There is quite a lot of new vocabulary in the conversation, so Sts will need to use the pictures as a guide.

Give Sts time to read the conversation and think about what the missing words are, but tell them <u>not</u> to write them in yet.

Play the audio once the whole way through for Sts to listen and complete the gaps.

c Play the audio for Sts to listen and check. Pause after each gap and elicit the answers onto the board.

1 favourite	4 meat	7 twenty-five
2 children	5 OK	
3 holiday	6 Excuse	

Go through the conversation with Sts line by line. Elicit / explain any words or phrases that Sts don't understand, e.g. *writer, Do you know…?, Do you want…?*, etc. Highlight that *Oops* (dialogue 4) is an exclamation word that we sometimes use when someone has a small accident or does something by mistake. Here Eve knocks Wendy as she gets out of her seat.

! Sts may ask about the meaning of *do* here. Explain that we use *do* to make a question. This will be explained later in the grammar section.

! The question *Do you have children?* can also be asked as *Do you have **any** children?* However, at this level, we think it is easier to teach the question without *any*.

Elicit a reaction from the class, using L1 if necessary, by asking *Is the American woman happy that it's almost the end of the flight? Why?*

Extra idea
• Get Sts to practise the conversation in pairs.

2 GRAMMAR present simple ?: *I, you, we, they*

a Focus on the instructions and give Sts time to complete the chart. Emphasize that they can find the answers in the conversation in **1**.

Check answers and write them on the board. Explain that the chart shows them all forms of the present simple for *I, you, we,* and *they.*

⊟	**I don't** live in New York.
?	**Do** you live in London?
✓	Yes, I **do.** ✗ No, I **don't.**

b (2 35)) Tell Sts to go to **Grammar Bank 5B** on *p.100.*

Focus on the example sentences and play the audio for Sts to listen and repeat. Pause the audio as necessary.

Go through the rules with the class using the expanded information in the **Additional grammar notes** below to help you. You may want to use Sts' L1 here.

Additional grammar notes
present simple ?: *I, you, we, they*

• We use the verb *do* + the infinitive form of the verb to form questions. *Do* in this context cannot be translated. It simply indicates to the other person that you are going to ask a question in the present tense.

• Highlight the use of the short answers *Yes, I do* and *No, I don't,* which can be used as an alternative to just answering *Yes* or *No.* You might add that a simple *Yes* or *No* can sound too abrupt to an English speaker.

Focus on the exercises for **5B** on *p.101* and get Sts to do them individually or in pairs. If they do them individually, get them to compare answers with a partner.

Check answers, getting Sts to read the full sentences.

a			
1 Do, don't		6 do, don't
2 don't		7 Do, don't, don't
3 Do, don't		8 Do, do
4 don't		9 Do, don't
5 Do, don't		10 Do, do, don't

b	
1	I don't know.
2	Do you live near here?
3	I don't like football.
4	Do you want a coffee?
5	They work in the city centre.
6	I have two sisters.
7	Do you speak French?
8	I don't need a big car.
9	Do you go to German classes?
10	I don't have a watch.
11	Do you listen to music in the car?
12	I don't work on Saturdays.

Tell Sts to go back to the main lesson **5B**.

Extra support
• If you think Sts need more practice, you may want to give them the Grammar photocopiable activity at this point or leave it for later as consolidation or revision.

3 VOCABULARY common verb phrases 1

a Focus on the instructions and point out that the first one has been done for them.

Give Sts a few minutes to match the phrases.

Check answers.

2 c	3 a	4 d	5 b

b Tell Sts to go to **Vocabulary Bank** *Common verb phrases 1* on *p.123.*

(2 36)) Focus on the instructions for **a**. Play the audio and get Sts to repeat the phrases in chorus and individually as necessary. Make sure Sts understand the meaning of each phrase.

> (2 36))
> See the common verb phrases in the Student's Book on *p.123*

Highlight the irregular pronunciation of the verb *live* /lɪv/. Sts might expect /laɪv/, especially as *like* /laɪk/ is taught here, too. You could tell Sts that *i* + consonant + *e* is usually /aɪ/.

Highlight also the use of the preposition *to* in *listen to the radio,* but remind Sts that if there is no object after *listen,* you don't use *to.* Compare *Please listen!* and *Listen to me.*

(2 37)) Now focus on **b**. Focus on the example and then demonstrate the activity by saying part of a phrase, omitting the verb, and eliciting the complete phrase from the class, e.g. *tea* (drink tea).

Play the audio and pause after the first prompt (*in a flat*) and elicit the phrase (*live in a flat*) from the class. Make sure Sts are clear what they have to do before continuing.

Play the rest of the audio and give Sts time to say the phrases in chorus.

2 37))

Common verb phrases 1b

1 in a flat (*pause*) live in a flat
2 breakfast (*pause*) have breakfast
3 TV (*pause*) watch TV
4 to the radio (*pause*) listen to the radio
5 the newspaper (*pause*) read the newspaper
6 fast food (*pause*) eat fast food
7 tea (*pause*) drink tea
8 English (*pause*) speak English
9 a coffee (*pause*) want a coffee
10 a dog (*pause*) have a dog
11 cats (*pause*) like cats
12 in a bank (*pause*) work in a bank
13 Spanish (*pause*) study Spanish
14 to English classes (*pause*) go to English classes
15 a new car (*pause*) need a new car

Then repeat the activity, eliciting responses from individual Sts.

Now focus on **c** and the example. Put Sts in pairs and get them to ask and answer questions.

Get some pairs to ask and answer in front of the class.

Tell Sts to go back to the main lesson **5B**.

Extra support

• If you think Sts need more practice, you may want to give them the Vocabulary photocopiable activity at this point or leave it for later as consolidation or revision.

4 LISTENING

a **2 38**)) Focus on the picture and establish the context for the listening by asking questions like these:
Who is she? (She's Eve, the woman from the flight)
Where is she? (She's in a taxi).

Focus on the instructions and check that Sts understand *end* and *back to the airport*.

Play the audio once the whole way through for Sts to listen and answer the question.

Check the answer.

Because Wendy, the American woman, is on the same flight.

2 38))

(script in Student's Book on *p.87*)
T = Taxi driver, E = Eve, FA = flight attendant, W = Wendy

T Where to, ma'am?
E Hello. To the airport, please.
T JFK or Newark?
E JFK, please.
***
E Oh dear. The traffic is bad this morning.
T Yes. It's terrible. Where are you from?
E I'm from Manchester, but I live in London. Are you from New York?
T No, ma'am, I'm from Puerto Rico.
E Oh, do you like New York?
T It's a great city, but it's very expensive.
E London is very expensive, too. Do you have children?
T I have two daughters.
E Oh really? I have two sons and a daughter. David and Andrew are at university and Carla's at school...
***

T OK. Here we are.
E How much is that?
T That's $87.50.
E Here's $100. Keep the change.
T Thanks. Have a good flight.
E I need to hurry. I'm late!

This is the final call for flight BA 641 to London Heathrow. Would all passengers please procedd to Gate B5.

E I'm late!
FA1 Can I see your passport and boarding pass, please?
E Here you are.
***
FA2 Good afternoon madam. Your boarding pass please. Seat 3D. This way please.
E Oh, what a nice surprise. We meet again!
W Hi! Yes, what a nice surprise!

b Focus on the options in sentences 1–10. Give Sts time to read them and ask you about any words they don't understand, e.g. *traffic, gate*.

Play the audio for Sts to circle the right option. You could pause after each question and give Sts time to choose the right answer. Play the audio again as necessary.

Get Sts to compare with a partner and then check answers. For 8, you could ask Sts if they can remember a similar expression to *Have a good day!*, which they saw in **2A** (*Have a nice day!*).

1 b	3 b	5 b	7 a	9 a
2 a	4 a	6 b	8 b	10 a

Ask Sts *Is the American woman happy to see the British woman again?*

5 PRONUNCIATION /w/, /v/, and /ɒ/; sentence rhythm and linking

Pronunciation notes
/w/, /v/, and /ɒ/

• The /w/ and /v/ sounds are often confused because in several languages *w* is pronounced /v/.

• You may want to highlight to Sts the following sound–spelling patterns:

– /w/ The letter *w* (without *h*) is always pronounced /w/ at the beginning of a word, e.g. *watch*. The letters *wh* are usually pronounced /w/, e.g. *what*, *where*, but there are some exceptions, e.g. *who* /huː/.

– /v/ The letter *v* is always pronounced /v/, e.g. *live*.

– /ɒ/ This sound is sometimes the letter *o*, e.g. *coffee*, *not*, but can exceptionally be the letter *a*, especially after *w*, e.g. *want*, *watch*, *what*. However, you may want to remind Sts to be careful with the letters *o* and *a* as they have several other pronunciations depending on the word.

Sentence rhythm and linking

• For information on **Sentence rhythm**, see the **Pronunciation** notes in **2B**.

• For information on **Linking**, see the **Pronunciation notes** in **4B**.

• See also **Pronunciation** in the **Introduction**, *p.8*.

a **2 39**)) Read the **Pronunciation notes** and decide how much of the information you want to give your Sts.

Focus on the exercise and play the audio once the whole way through for Sts just to listen.

> **2 39))**
> See the words and sounds in the Student's Book on *p.31*

Focus on the sound picture *witch*. Play the audio to model and drill the word and the sound (pause after the sound).

Now focus on the words after *witch*. Remind Sts that the pink letters are the /w/ sound. Play the audio, pausing after each word for Sts to listen and repeat.

Now repeat the same process for *vase* /v/ and *clock* /ɒ/.

If these sounds are difficult for your Sts, model them yourself so that Sts can see your mouth position, and get Sts to repeat them a few more times.

Play the audio again from the beginning, pausing after each group of words for Sts to repeat.

Give further practice as necessary.

Finally, get Sts, in pairs, to practise saying the words.

Extra support
- If you are using an interactive whiteboard, you can focus on each sound individually before moving on to the next one.

b **2 40))** Focus on the sentences and remind Sts that the words in bigger font are the ones which are stressed (because they carry the important information). Also remind them that the underlined syllables in the multi-syllable words are stressed more.

Play the audio once the whole way through for Sts just to listen.

Highlight the linked phrases, e.g. *want a coffee*, *an espresso*, and model and drill the pronunciation.

> **2 40))**
> See the sentences in the Student's Book on *p.31*

Now play the audio, pausing after each sentence for Sts to listen and repeat chorally.

Then repeat the activity, eliciting responses from individual Sts.

6 SPEAKING & WRITING

a Focus on the instructions and the example. Elicit / explain the meaning of *near*. Model and drill pronunciation.

Go through the other nine sentences checking Sts know the meaning of all the lexis, e.g. *a gym*. Model and drill any words you think Sts might have problems with.

Give Sts time to complete 2–10 with the verbs from the list.

Check answers by asking individual Sts to read the two phrases aloud (they should include the verb with each phrase, e.g. *live near here, live in a house*).

2 have	5 read	8 speak
3 watch	6 eat	9 need
4 listen	7 drink	10 go

Highlight that *have* has two meanings, *have* = possession as in *have a dog*, and *have* = eat as in *have breakfast*.

b Focus on the instructions and speech bubbles. Remind Sts we use *do* to make questions in the present simple. Elicit the possible answers (*Yes* or *Yes, I do* | *No* or *No, I don't*.).

Model and drill some or all of the questions. Encourage Sts to use the correct sentence rhythm and not to overstress *Do you…?*

Demonstrate the activity by getting the class to interview you first, asking you some or all of the questions. Give true answers and, where possible, try to give some extra information, but use language within the Sts' range.

Put Sts in pairs and get them to take turns asking and answering questions with the phrases. Encourage them to give extra information in their answers.

Monitor and help with pronunciation and sentence stress. Correct any mistakes on the board.

c Focus on the instructions and the examples.

Give Sts time to write their four true sentences.

Get some feedback from the class.

WORDS AND PHRASES TO LEARN

4 61)) Tell Sts to go to *p.130* and focus on the **Words and phrases to learn** for **5B**. Make sure Sts understand the meaning of each phrase. If necessary, remind them of the context in which the words and phrases came up in the lesson. If you speak your Sts' L1, you might like to elicit a translation for the words / phrases for the Sts to write next to them. Play the audio, pausing after each phrase for Sts to repeat. You may also like to ask Sts to test each other on the phrases.

Telling the time
Saying how you feel, e.g. *I'm tired, hungry*, etc.
Silent consonants

PRACTICAL ENGLISH
Episode 3 What time is it?

Lesson plan

In this lesson, Sts learn how to tell the time. In most languages there are two possible ways of telling the time: digital (hour + minutes), e.g. *seven forty, six twenty*, and analogue (minutes before (*to*) or after (*past*) the hour), e.g. *twenty to six, twenty past six*. Sts will hear both if they travel to an English-speaking country. To avoid confusing Sts with two forms, the focus here is on the more common analogue time. Teachers may want to point out the alternative (digital time) to Sts, so they will recognize it if they hear it, and can use it if they find it easier. After Sts have learnt and practised telling the time, they focus on words with silent consonants, such as *half* and *Wednesday*. The next vocabulary focus is on a few adjectives describing how you feel. After listening to Jenny and her friend, Amy, on a night out, Sts practise some useful phrases. The lesson ends with the song *Stop the Clock*.

STUDY LINK
- **Workbook** What time is it?
- **iTutor**
- www.oup.com/elt/englishfile

Extra photocopiable activities
- **Communicative** Time bingo *p.185* (instructions *p.167*)
- **Song** *Stop the Clock p.230* (instructions *p.226*)

Test and Assessment CD-ROM
- **Quick Test 5**
- **File Test 5**
- www.oup.com/elt/teacher/englishfile

Optional lead-in (books closed)
- Revise numbers 1–30. Get Sts to count around the class, first normally, then in twos (*2, 4, 6*, etc.), in threes (*3, 6, 9*, etc.), and finally with fives (*5, 10, 15*, etc.).

1 ◼◄ TELLING THE TIME

a (2 41))) Books closed. Show Sts your watch or a picture of a watch and ask *What is it?* (a watch). Then point to the clock in the classroom (or draw one on the board) and ask *What is it?* (a clock). Say *What time is it?* and then look at your watch or at your mobile. Now model and drill the question and write it on the board.

Books open. Focus on the instructions and ask Sts to cover the conversations with a piece of paper.

Play the video or audio for Sts to listen and match the conversations and photos. Play again as necessary.

Check answers.

1 A   2 C   3 B

(2 41)))
See the conversations in the Student's Book on *p.32*

Now tell Sts to uncover the conversations. Play the video or audio again while Sts listen and read at the same time.

Explain / elicit new vocabulary as you go, e.g. *tired, hurry*. Sts will be able to understand the times (*eleven o'clock, a quarter to eight*, etc.) because of the clocks in the photos. Highlight that *seven forty-seven* is digital time, but Sts should have no problem with this.

Finally, ask *Is Rob usually early or late for things?* and elicit that he's usually late.

b (2 42))) Focus on the **need** box and go through it with the class. You may want to tell Sts that *to* + verb = the infinitive and that is the form of the verb we use after *need*.

Play the audio again for Sts to listen and repeat. Make sure Sts pronounce *quarter* as /ˈkwɔːtə/ and *half* as /haːf/ (pointing out the silent *l*). You could pause the audio after each line and get individual Sts to repeat. Give further practice of any phrases Sts found difficult.

(2 42)))
See script 2.41

Then get Sts to practise the conversations in pairs.

! There are two common ways of asking the time: *What's the time?* and *What time is it?* Here *What time is it?* is taught as it is easier for Sts to move from this to questions with the present like *What time do you finish work?*

c Focus on the instructions and either get Sts to do it in pairs or do it as an open-class activity. Tell Sts to look at the clock in photo A and ask *What time is it?* (It's 11 o'clock). Do the same for photo B. (It's a quarter to seven) and photo C (It's half past ten).

2 VOCABULARY the time

a (2 43))) Give Sts a minute to look at the clocks and read the times.

Then play the audio and get Sts to listen and repeat the times in chorus. Pause the audio as necessary. Give further practice of words which your Sts find difficult.

(2 43)))
See the times in the Student's Book on *p.32*

Focus on *o'clock* and explain that we sometimes use the word *o'clock* when we are just saying the hour, as in *It's one o'clock* or *It's six o'clock*, but you can also say *It's six*. We don't use *o'clock* when including minutes in the time, e.g. *It's twenty past four* NOT ~~It's twenty past four o'clock~~.

Remind Sts of the pronunciation of *half* and *quarter*. You might also mention that some people don't put *a* in front of *quarter*, e.g. *It's quarter past three.* Both are correct.

b Tell Sts to cover the times and look at the clocks. Give them time to practise saying the times to themselves.

Monitor and help, correcting pronunciation as necessary. Note any general problems and focus on them on the board at the end.

With the first line of sentences covered, ask individuals *Clock one. What time is it?* Do the same for all the clocks, calling on Sts at random. Sts could also practise this in pairs.

c (2 44)) Focus on the instructions. Draw a clock on the board like the ones in the Student's Book, with no hands. Play the audio and pause after the first time. Ask a student to come to the board and draw the time. Then get the Sts to draw the time (*twenty to nine*) on the first clock in their books.

Play the rest of the audio, pausing after each item to give Sts time to draw the hands on their clocks.

Get Sts to compare with a partner and then check answers by writing the times on the board or by getting individual Sts to come to the board to draw the time on each clock.

See script 2.44

(2 44))

1 It's twenty to nine.
2 It's a quarter past seven.
3 It's five past two.
4 It's twelve o'clock.
5 It's half past eight.
6 It's a quarter past eleven.

---

d Put Sts in pairs to practise asking and answering about the clocks.

Monitor and help as needed. Note any problems and write these on the board.

Finally, focus on **The time** box and go through it with the class. Highlight that you can always use digital time and this has become more common with digital watches and mobile phone use. However, the analogue use of telling the time is still widely used by native speakers.

e Put Sts in pairs, **A** and **B**. Tell them to go to **Communication** *What time is it?*, **A** on *p.77* and **B** on *p.81*.

Sts each have ten clocks, five of which are complete and five of which have no clock hands. Sts share information and draw the missing clock hands.

Go through the instructions with Sts and get a good pair to demonstrate. Monitor and help.

When Sts have finished, get them to compare their clocks and check the times.

Tell Sts to go back to the main lesson **PE3**.

3 PRONUNCIATION silent consonants

Pronunciation notes
- English words frequently have consonants that are not pronounced, i.e. that are 'silent'. It is important for Sts to realize that in English, spelling and pronunciation do not always go together.
- Encourage Sts to cross out silent letters when they learn new words, e.g. lis~~t~~en.
- It is also common for English words to be pronounced with fewer syllables than appear in the written word, e.g. *Wednesday* /ˈwenzdeɪ/ and *interesting* /ˈɪntrəstɪŋ/.

a (2 45)) Write the word HALF on the board and say it /hɑːf/. Ask *Which letter is not pronounced?* Elicit that the letter *l* is not pronounced. It is silent.

Focus on the **silent letters** box and go through it with the class.

Now focus on the instructions. Play the audio once the whole way through for Sts just to listen. Highlight that the letters with a pink strikethrough line are silent.

Now play the audio again for Sts to listen and repeat.

! Highlight that *Wednesday* looks like it has three syllables, but in fact it is pronounced as a two-syllable word /ˈwenzdeɪ/. The first *d* and the second *e* are both silent.

(2 45))
See the words in the Student's Book on *p.33*

Finally, put Sts in pairs and get them to practise saying the words.

Get a few individual Sts to say the words.

b (2 46)) Give Sts a minute to look at the conversations and note the words with silent letters.

Play the audio once the whole way through for Sts just to listen.

(2 46))
See the conversations in the Student's Book on *p.33*

Put Sts in pairs and get them to practise the conversations.

Ask two or three pairs to practise each conversation for the class.

Extra support
- Before Sts practise in pairs, play the audio, pausing after each line for Sts to listen and repeat.

4 VOCABULARY saying how you feel

a (2 47)) Pretend to be for example *very hot*, by miming. Write this on the board: I'M HOT = I FEEL HOT. Focus on the title, *saying how you feel* and explain / elicit its meaning.

Now focus on sentences 1–5 and make sure Sts understand what they mean.

Play the audio once the whole way through for Sts just to listen.

2 47))
See the sentences in the Student's Book on *p.33*

Now play the audio again, pausing after each sentence for Sts to listen and repeat. Give extra practice as necessary focussing on the words which Sts find most difficult.

b Focus on the instructions and give Sts a few minutes to match 1–5 in **a** with a–e.

Get Sts to compare with a partner.

c **2 48**)) Play the audio for Sts to listen and check.

Check answers.

1 d	2 c	3 b	4 e	5 a

2 48))
1	**A** I'm hot.	d	**B** It's 35 degrees!
2	**A** I'm cold.	c	**B** It's five degrees this morning.
3	**A** I'm hungry.	b	**B** Time for lunch.
4	**A** I'm thirsty.	e	**B** I need a glass of water.
5	**A** I'm tired.	a	**B** Time for bed.

Highlight that we use *be*, not *have*, with *hot*, *cold*, *hungry*, etc. because they are adjectives. Many languages express these feelings using *have* + noun.

Now either put Sts in pairs and get them to ask and answer the question *How do you feel at the moment?* or do it as an open-class activity.

5 ◼◀ A NIGHT OUT
VIDEO

a **2 49**)) Focus on the instructions and the five places in the list. Make sure Sts know what they mean. Model and drill their pronunciation.

Play the video or audio once the whole way through for Sts to listen and tick the two places Jenny and Amy go to.

Check answers.

Sts should tick *a restaurant* and *a theatre*.

2 49))
(script in Student's Book on *p.87*)
A = Amy, J = Jenny

A Hi. Sorry I'm late. What time's the show?
J Don't worry. It's at eight o'clock.
A What time is it now?
J It's OK. It's only twenty to eight.
***
A What a great show!
J Yes, fantastic. I'm hungry. Do you want a pizza?
A What time is it?
J Quarter to eleven.
A It's late and I'm tired.
J Oh, come on. I know a really good Italian restaurant near here.
A Oh, OK. Let's go.

Extra challenge

• You could play the video or audio again and write these questions on the board:
  WHO IS LATE, AMY OR JENNY?
  IS THE SHOW GOOD?   WHO IS TIRED?
  WHAT RESTAURANT DO THEY GO TO?
  WHAT DO THEY EAT?

Extra support

• If there's time, you could play the audio again while Sts read the script on *p.87*, so they can see what they understood / didn't understand. Translate / explain any new words or phrases.

b Focus on the instructions and give Sts time to read 1–3. Make sure they understand what they mean.

Play the video or audio for Sts to listen and complete the sentences with the times. Play again as necessary.

Get Sts to compare with a partner and then check answers.

1 eight o'clock
2 twenty to eight
3 a quarter to eleven

6 ◼◀ USEFUL PHRASES
VIDEO

2 50)) Focus on the phrases and make sure Sts understand what each one means.

Play the video or audio once the whole way through for Sts just to listen.

2 50))
See the phrases in the Student's Book on *p.33*

Now play the video or audio again, pausing after each phrase for Sts to listen and repeat.

Give further practice as necessary, modelling and drilling the pronunciation yourself, or using the video or audio, and getting choral and individual responses.

7 **4 MP3**)) **SONG** *Stop the Clock* ♫

For Sts of this level all song lyrics will include language that they don't know.

This song was recorded by the American singer-songwriter Fats Domino in 1962. For copyright reasons this is a cover version.

If you want to do this song in class, use the photocopiable activity on *p.230*.

You will find the songs as MP3 files on CD4 of the Class audio CD.

4 MP3))
Stop the Clock

Tick-tock, stop the clock (x2)
Time keeps moving on
Soon my baby will be gone
Away, poor me
Tick-tock, stop the clock (x2)
She's gonna catch the train at three
That'll be the end of me
Tick-tock, stop the clock (x3)
For my baby would be mine
If I could just turn back the time
Tick-tock, stop the clock

Tick-tock, stop the clock (x2)
Time keeps moving on
Soon my baby will be gone
Tick-tock, stop the clock (x3)
For my baby would be mine
If I could just turn back the time
Tick-tock, stop the clock

G present simple: *he, she, it*
V jobs and places of work
P third person *-s*; /ɜː/; sentence rhythm

6A She works for Armani

Lesson plan

This lesson introduces the third person singular (*he, she, it*) of the present simple. This is the only verb form in the present tense that is different as there is a change to the verb ending (+ *-s* or *-es*, e.g. *works, teaches*) and where a different auxiliary is used (*does / doesn't*) to form questions and negatives. For this reason, a whole lesson has been devoted to this point and beginners will need time to assimilate it.

The context of this lesson is people at work. The new grammar point is presented through a conversation between a boss and her assistant at a fashion magazine's Christmas party. This conversation is inspired by a similar scene in the Meryl Streep film *The Devil Wears Prada*, but the names of the characters have been changed. This leads into Pronunciation where Sts practise the three possible third person *-s* sounds, /z/, /s/, and /ɪz/. This is followed by Vocabulary where Sts learn the words for some common jobs and places of work (e.g. *in an office*). Then Sts read about people who use English in their work, e.g. a Spanish waiter serving tourists in Madrid. There is a second pronunciation focus in this lesson – Sts focus on the /ɜː/ sound, which is quite common in job names, e.g. *nurse*, and sentence rhythm. Sts talk about the jobs of two people they know and whether they use English at work. Finally, Sts write a couple of paragraphs about the two people they spoke about.

STUDY LINK
- Workbook 6A
- iTutor
- www.oup.com/elt/englishfile

Extra photocopiable activities
- **Grammar** present simple: *he, she, it* p.149
- **Communicative** What do they do? Where do they work? p.186 (instructions p.167)
- **Vocabulary** Jobs and places of work p.220 (instructions p.207)
- www.oup.com/elt/teacher/englishfile

Optional lead-in (books closed)
- Write seven dashes on the board and play *Hangman* with the word TEACHER (see *p.22* for how to play *Hangman*). Tell Sts that the word is a job, making sure Sts know what *job* means.
- When the word has been guessed ask Sts if they know any other English words for jobs, e.g. *doctor*, and write them on the board.

1 GRAMMAR present simple: *he, she, it*

a Books open. Focus on the lesson title, *She works for Armani*, and read the text on the photo. Ask Sts where the women are (at a party). Model and drill *party*. Explain / elicit the meaning of *boss, assistant*, and *guest*. Elicit who the boss is (the woman with grey hair).

Ask the class if they know the actresses (Anne Hathaway on the left and Meryl Streep on the right) and if they know the title of the film (*The Devil Wears Prada*). Find out if any Sts have seen it.

b **2 52))** Focus on the task and give Sts time to read 1–4.

Now get Sts to cover the conversation and play the audio once the whole way through for Sts just to listen.

Play the audio again and give Sts time to do the task.

Find out with a show of hands how many Sts have put T or F for each item, but <u>don't</u> give the right answers at this point as Sts will check their own answers in **c**.

> **2 52))**
> See the conversation in the Student's Book on *p.34*.

c Tell Sts to uncover the conversation and play the audio again for Sts to listen and read at the same time. Get Sts to check their answers to **b**.

Check answers.

1 F	2 T	3 F	4 F

Extra challenge
- Get the Sts to correct the F ones:
  1 Anna Crawley works for **Armani**.
  3 He works for **Hello** magazine.
  4 Kim is Andrew's **friend**.

Now go through the conversation line by line, dealing with any vocabulary problems that arose.

d Focus on the instructions and give Sts time to read the conversation again and to complete the chart.

Check answers and write them on the board. Highlight the changes from first person singular to third person.

+	He **works** at *Hello* magazine.
−	He **doesn't have** a wife.
?	**Does** she work for our magazine?
✗	No, she **doesn't**.
Wh	Where **does** he work?

e **2 53))** Tell Sts to go to **Grammar Bank 6A** on *p.102*.

Focus on the example sentences and play the audio for Sts to listen and repeat. Pause the audio as necessary. You may want to point out that the sentences *It works. / It doesn't work* are a different meaning of the verb *work* = It isn't broken. / It's broken.

Go through the rules with the class using the expanded information in the **Additional grammar notes** below to help you. You may want to use Sts' L1 here.

Additional grammar notes
present simple: *he, she, it*

- The *he, she*, and *it* forms of the present simple are different from the other forms. The positive form of the verb always finishes with an *-s* (or *-es*). At this low level Sts will find it difficult to remember to add the *-s* / *-es* and will need constant reminding.

- Highlight that we form negatives by putting *doesn't* /'dʌznt/ (NOT ~~don't~~) before the infinitive form. Emphasize that there is no *s* on the main verb in these sentences. Typical mistake: *He doesn't works here.*

- *Doesn't* is the contracted form of *does not*. Remind Sts that native speakers usually use contractions in spoken English.

- Highlight that we use *does* (NOT ~~don't~~) with *he, she*, or *it* and the infinitive to make questions, e.g. *Does she work for our magazine?*

! If Sts ask about the meaning of *does*, tell them that, like *do*, it is a word we need in the present simple to help make negatives and questions and it cannot be translated.

Spelling rules third person *-s*

- Highlight that most verbs make the *he / she / it* form by adding *-s*, e.g. *eats, drinks.*

- Verbs ending in *-ch, -sh, -s, -z, -ss, -zz*, and *-x* make the *he / she / it* form by adding *-es*, e.g. *watches, finishes, kisses.*

- Verbs ending in a consonant + *y* make the *he / she / it* form by changing the *y* to *i* and adding *-es*, e.g. *studies.* This change does not occur when the verb ends in a vowel + *y*, e.g. *plays.*

- Point out that spelling rules for verbs in the third person singular are the same as those for plural nouns (see Student's Book p.96, **3A**, and **Pronunciation notes** below).

- The verbs *have, do* and *go* are irregular in the *he / she / it* form and change to *has, does*, and *goes*. Highlight that *goes* /gəʊz/ and *does* /dʌz/ are pronounced differently.

Focus on the exercises for **6A** on *p.103* and get Sts to do them individually or in pairs. If they do them individually, get them to compare answers with a partner.

Check answers, getting Sts to read the full sentences.

a
1 He reads magazines.
2 My sister studies Italian.
3 Does he speak English?
4 My brother doesn't eat fish.
5 Where does your wife work?
6 Tom doesn't speak Italian.
7 Does she like cats?
8 Andrew has two brothers.
9 What does he eat for lunch?
10 My mother watches a lot of TV.
11 What does your son do?
12 Maria doesn't need a new car.

b
1	listens	7	don't watch
2	goes	8	Do…want
3	don't work	9	do…go
4	Does…live	10	doesn't eat
5	finishes	11	Does…like
6	has	12	doesn't have

Tell Sts to go back to the main lesson **6A**.

Extra support
- If you think Sts need more practice, you may want to give them the Grammar photocopiable activity at this point or leave it for later as consolidation or revision.

2 PRONUNCIATION third person -s

Pronunciation notes
- The rules for pronouncing the third person *-s* are the same as those for pronouncing the *s* of plural nouns (See **Pronunciation notes** in **3A** on *p.39*).

- The difference between the /s/ and /z/ endings is small and you may not wish to focus too much on this at this level.

- We suggest you highlight the /ɪz/ pronunciation of the *-es* ending in verbs that end in *-sh* and *-ch*, e.g. *watches, teaches*. Stress that this adds an extra syllable to the word: *watch* = one syllable; *watches* = two syllables. Write examples on the board showing the stressed syllables, e.g. <u>watch</u>es, <u>teach</u>es.

- See also **Pronunciation** in the **Introduction**, *p.8*.

a  **2 54**)) Focus on the aim, *third person -s*, and tell Sts the endings of present simple verbs with *he, she, it* have the same pronunciation rules as plural nouns, e.g. *books* /s/, *bags* /z/, *watches* /ɪz/.

Focus on the exercise and play the audio once the whole way through for Sts just to listen.

> **2 54**))
> See the words and sounds in the Student's Book on *p.34*

Now focus on the sound picture *zebra*. Play the audio to model and drill the word and the sound (pause after the sound).

Now focus on the words after *zebra*. Remind Sts that the pink letters are the /z/ sound. Play the audio, pausing after each word for Sts to listen and repeat.

Now repeat the same process for *snake* /s/ and /ɪz/.

If these sounds are difficult for your Sts, model them yourself so that Sts can see your mouth position, and get Sts to repeat them a few more times.

Play the audio again from the beginning, pausing after each group of words for Sts to repeat.

Give further practice as necessary.

Finally, get Sts, in pairs, to practise saying the words.

Extra support

- If you are using an interactive whiteboard, you can focus on each sound individually before moving on to the next one.

b **2 55))** Focus on the instructions and then play the audio for Sts to listen and repeat.

> **2 55))**
> See the conversation in **1c** in the Student's Book on *p.34*

Now put Sts in groups of three or four and get them to practise the conversation. If Sts are in groups of three, one student should play Anna and Andrew.

Get a group to perform the conversation for the class.

c **2 56))** Focus on the instructions. Focus on the example and tell Sts they will hear a sentence with *I* and then they will hear either *he, she, it,* a name, or a family member. They have to say the sentence again beginning with the word(s) they just heard.

Play the example, pausing for Sts to say *He lives in New York* in chorus. Make sure Sts understand what they have to do before continuing.

Play the rest of the audio and give Sts time to say the third person forms in chorus.

> **2 56))**
> 1 I live in New York. He (*pause*) He lives in New York.
> 2 I speak Japanese. She (*pause*) She speaks Japanese.
> 3 I work in Mexico. My brother (*pause*) My brother works in Mexico.
> 4 I watch CNN. She (*pause*) She watches CNN.
> 5 I want a sandwich. He (*pause*) He wants a sandwich.
> 6 I have a new car. John (*pause*) John has a new car.
> 7 I don't eat meat. My sister (*pause*) My sister doesn't eat meat.
> 8 I don't read newspapers. My husband (*pause*) My husband doesn't read newspapers.
> 9 Do you work? He (*pause*) Does he work?
> 10 Do you drink coffee? She (*pause*) Does she drink coffee?

Then repeat the activity, eliciting responses from individual Sts.

3 VOCABULARY jobs and places of work

a Focus on the questions and explain / elicit that the question *What does Alice do?* = *What's her job?*

Elicit the answers.

> Alice is the boss of a fashion magazine.
> Melanie is Alice's assistant. / Melanie works for a fashion magazine.
> Anna works for Armani.
> Andrew works for *Hello* magazine / Andrew is a journalist.

b Tell Sts to go to **Vocabulary Bank *Jobs and places of work*** on *p.124.*

2 57)) Look at **1 What do they do?** and focus on **a**. Play the audio and get Sts to repeat the words in chorus and individually as necessary. Model and drill any words which are difficult for your Sts and give further practice. Remind Sts that the underlined syllables are stressed more strongly.

> **2 57))**
> See the jobs in the Student's Book on *p.124*

Highlight:

- that in English after *He's, She's,* etc., we always use *a* or *an* before jobs, e.g. *He's a teacher, She's an actress.*
- *waiter* is used for a man and *waitress* for a woman.
- an *assistant* is someone who helps others do their job. For example, a shop assistant helps customers in shops and serves them.

Now focus on **b**. Get Sts to cover the words and look at the questions in the speech bubbles, *What does she / he do?* Model and drill the examples in chorus and individually.

Put Sts in pairs and give them time to ask and answer questions about the photos. Monitor and help, correcting pronunciation where necessary.

2 58)) Now focus on **c**. Play the audio for Sts to listen and repeat the sentences.

> **2 58))**
> See the sentences in the Student's Book on *p.124*

Highlight that we say work **for** a company, **at** school / university. Elicit / explain the meaning of *unemployed* and *retired*.

Now focus on **d**. If Sts are working, check that they know how to say their own job and get them to write it on the line. Write any new jobs on the board. Get Sts to underline the stress in these words.

If Sts are not working, get them to write what is true for them, e.g. *I'm at school. / I'm a student. / I'm unemployed. / I'm retired.*

2 59)) Look at **2 Where do they work?** and focus on **a**. Play the audio and get Sts to repeat the words in chorus and individually as necessary. Model and drill any words which are difficult for your Sts and give further practice.

> **2 59))**
> See the phrases in the Student's Book on *p.124*

Highlight that we use usually say work **in** a place, but with *home* we use the preposition *at*, i.e. *at home*.

Now focus on **b** and get Sts to cover the phrases, look at the photos, and say the phrases. they could do this individually or with a partner.

Now focus on **c**. Model and drill the example question and answer in chorus and individually.

Then get Sts to ask and answer questions about the jobs in pairs. Monitor and help, correcting pronunciation where necessary.

Finally, focus on **d**. Get Sts to write a sentence with their place of work or study. Write any new places on the board.

Tell Sts to go back to the main lesson **6A**.

Extra support

• If you think Sts need more practice, you may want to give them the Vocabulary photocopiable activity at this point or leave it for later as consolidation or revision.

c Focus on the instructions and elicit the meaning of *favourite*. Make sure Sts choose a job in the **Vocabulary Bank** and <u>not</u> their ideal job.

Give Sts time to choose their favourite job from the **Vocabulary Bank** on *p.124*.

Tell Sts to stand up and mingle and ask at least five other Sts the two questions.

Get some feedback from various Sts.

4 READING

a Focus on the question and elicit answers from the class.

b Focus on the article and read the introduction together (as far as *Write and tell us.*). Make sure Sts understand the phrase *have in common*.

Tell Sts to read the rest of the article and complete the two gaps with jobs from the **Vocabulary Bank** *Jobs and places of work* on *p.124*.

Get Sts to compare with a partner.

c (2 60)) Play the audio for Sts to listen and read at the same time.

Check answers.

1 waiter	2 receptionist

> (2 60))
> See the article in the Student's Book on *p.35*

d Focus on the **Why...? Because...** box and go through it with the class. Model and drill the pronunciation of the two words.

Now focus on the instructions and give Sts time to read questions 1–5.

Give Sts time to read the article again.

Put Sts in pairs and get them to do the task.

Check answers.

> 1 Because he needs to help tourists.
> 2 He helps customers with the menu and he says what the special dishes are.
> 3 She works for a multinational company.
> 4 She welcomes people and she answers the phone.
> 5 Because it's the language of the company.

e Focus on the highlighted words and get Sts to guess their meaning with a partner. The word *barman* has already appeared in **PE 2**.

Get Sts to check words they couldn't guess in a dictionary or if dictionaries are not available, elicit / explain the meanings. Do this in English if possible, perhaps by giving an example, e.g. *Toyota is a **multinational company**. It has offices in many different countries.*

Deal with any other vocabulary problems that arose.

5 PRONUNCIATION /ɜː/ sentence rhythm

Pronunciation notes

/ɜː/

• Remind Sts that the two dots in /ɜː/ mean that this sound is long.

• Point out that this sound is a longer version of the /ə/ sound that Sts focussed on in **3B** and **4A**.

• *er*, *ir*, and *ur* are usually pronounced /ɜː/, e.g. *verb*, *first*, *nurse*.

• *or* is usually pronounced /ɜː/ after the letter *w* and the most common examples are *work*, *word*, and *world*. However, note that *or* after other letters is usually pronounced /ɔː/, e.g. *forty*, *airport*.

• You could also remind Sts that when *er* and *or* are unstressed, e.g. at the end of many job words, they are pronounced /ə/ (the schwa), e.g. *waiter*, *doctor*.

Sentence rhythm

• For information on **Sentence rhythm**, see the **Pronunciation notes** in **2B**.

• See also **Pronunciation** in the **Introduction**, *p.8*.

a (2 61)) Read the **Pronunciation notes** and decide how much of the information you want to give your Sts.

Focus on the exercise and play the audio once the whole way through for Sts just to listen.

> (2 61))
> See the words and sound in the Student's Book on *p.35*

Focus on the sound picture *bird*. Play the audio to model and drill the word and the sound (pause after the sound).

Now focus on the words after *bird*. Remind Sts that the pink letters are the /ɜː/ sound. Play the audio, pausing after each word for Sts to listen and repeat.

If this sound is difficult for your Sts, model it yourself so that Sts can see your mouth position, and get Sts to repeat it a few more times.

Play the audio again from the beginning, pausing at the end of the group of words for Sts to repeat.

Give further practice as necessary.

Finally, get Sts, in pairs, to practise saying the words.

Extra support

• If you are using an interactive whiteboard, you can focus on each word individually before moving on to the next one.

b (2 62)) Focus on the instructions and the conversation. Remind Sts that the words in bigger font are the ones which are stressed (because they carry the important information). Also remind them that the underlined syllables in the multi-syllable words are stressed more.

Play the audio once the whole way through for Sts just to listen.

> (2 62))
> See the conversation in the Student's Book on *p.35*

Now play the audio again, pausing after each line, for Sts to listen and repeat, encouraging them to try and copy the rhythm on the audio by stressing the bigger words in bold more strongly and by saying the others more lightly and quickly.

Extra support

• Put Sts in pairs and get them to practise the conversation. Make sure they swap roles.

6 SPEAKING & WRITING

a Focus on the instructions and tell Sts they are going to have a similar conversation about their two people as in **5b**.

Focus on the question prompts and the example. Elicit the other questions Sts will need to ask using the prompts:
Where does she work?
Does she speak English at work?
Does she like her job?

Model and drill the questions. Then put Sts in pairs, **A** and **B**. Get **A** to tell **B** who his / her first person is. **B** then asks the four questions.

Then **B** tells **A** who his / her first person is. **A** then asks the four questions.

They then repeat for their second person. Monitor and help with vocabulary.

Get feedback and find out about some of the Sts' friends' or relatives' jobs. If some Sts discuss jobs not on the vocabulary list, write these on the board and encourage Sts to add these to their notebooks.

Extra support

• Demonstrate the activity by getting Sts to ask you first about a friend's or a relative's job.

Extra idea

• If most of your class have jobs, elicit all the questions, i.e. *What do you do? Where do you work? Do you speak English at work? Do you like your job?* Then get them to ask each other the questions.

b Focus on the instructions and ask Sts to read the model paragraph. Point out that the sentences are the answers to the questions in **a**.

Give Sts time to write about their two people. Monitor and help. Correct any mistakes on the board.

Finally, get Sts to swap their writing.

WORDS AND PHRASES TO LEARN

(4 61)) Tell Sts to go to *p.130* and focus on the **Words and phrases to learn** for **6A**. Make sure Sts understand the meaning of each phrase. If necessary, remind them of the context in which the words and phrases came up in the lesson. If you speak your Sts' L1, you might like to elicit a translation for the words / phrases for the Sts to write next to them. Play the audio, pausing after each phrase for Sts to repeat. You may also like to ask Sts to test each other on the phrases.

G adverbs of frequency
V a typical day
P /j/; sentence rhythm

6B A day in my life

Lesson plan

This lesson begins with the context of a questionnaire, *Are you a morning person?*, about typical morning activities. This leads into learning the vocabulary to talk about daily routines. Pronunciation focusses on the /j/ sound, e.g. *usually*, and on sentence rhythm. The grammar focus is on using adverbs of frequency. We have deliberately limited the choice of adverbs to the four most common ones – *always*, *never*, *usually*, and *sometimes*. The focus is on their position with the present simple (other adverbs of frequency, and their position after *be*, are taught in *English File* Elementary). Sts consolidate the grammar and vocabulary by reading an adapted magazine article about a day in the life of Russian ballet dancer Ivan Vasiliev. The lesson builds up to a speaking and writing activity where Sts first talk about their typical evening and then write about their typical morning.

STUDY LINK
- Workbook 6B
- iTutor
- iChecker on iTutor
- www.oup.com/elt/englishfile

Extra photocopiable activities
- **Grammar** adverbs of frequency *p.150*
- **Communicative** What do you usually do? *p.187* (instructions *p.167*)
- **Vocabulary** What's the word? *p.221* (instructions *p.208*)
- www.oup.com/elt/teacher/englishfile

Optional lead-in (books closed)
- Write the following questions on the board:
  ARE YOU A 'MORNING PERSON'?
  ARE YOU A 'NIGHT PERSON'?
- Elicit / explain the meaning of the two phrases. (A 'morning person' is very awake and energetic in the morning, but is usually tired at night. A night person is the opposite.)
- With a show of hands get Sts to vote for what they are to see what the majority of the class consider themselves to be.

1 LISTENING & SPEAKING

a Books open. Focus on the two pictures and do the question as an open-class activity (She doesn't like mornings, but he does).

b **2 63))** Focus on the questionnaire *Are you a morning person?* and if you didn't do the **Optional lead-in**, elicit / explain what it means. Give Sts time to read the questions. Then go through them making sure Sts understand each one.

Tell Sts that they are going to hear Sue, a teacher, answering the seven questions in the questionnaire, and the first time they listen they only need to find out if Sue likes mornings.

Play the audio once the whole way through for Sts to listen and answer the question.

Check the answer.

Yes, she does.

2 63))
(script in Student's Book on *p.87*)
I = interviewer, S = Sue
I What time do you usually get up?
S I get up at six.
I Do you have a shower or a bath in the morning?
S I have a shower in the evening, before I go to bed.
I Where do you have breakfast?
S I have it in bed. It's my favourite meal of the day!
I What do you have for breakfast?
S I have orange juice, toast, and hot chocolate.
I What time do you go to work?
S At seven, because I have a class at eight.
I Do you need to hurry in the morning?
S No. I'm very organized and I prepare everything the night before.
I Do you like mornings?
S Yes. Very much.
I Why?
S Because I love breakfast, and because I love going to work on my bike in the morning – the streets are empty and it's really quiet.

c Play the audio again for Sts to answer the seven questions in the questionnaire. They can write the question number and a short answer on a piece of paper. Play the audio again as necessary.

Check answers by playing the audio again and pausing after Sue answers each question.

Check answers.

1 six
2 no
3 in bed
4 orange juice, toast, and hot chocolate
5 seven
6 no
7 yes (because she loves breakfast and she loves going to work on her bike in the morning)

Highlight any new useful lexis, e.g. *organized*, *empty*, *quiet*, etc. You might also want to point out the use of *really* in the conversation ('…it's really quiet') meaning *very*.

Extra support

- If there's time, you could play the audio again while Sts read the script on *p.87*, so they can see what they understood / didn't understand. Translate / explain any new words or phrases.

d (2 64)) Tell Sts they are now going to listen and repeat the seven questions in **a**.

Play the audio for Sts to listen and repeat, encouraging them to copy the rhythm.

Give further practice as necessary.

> (2 64))
> See the questions in the Student's Book on *p.36*

e Tell Sts they are now going to interview each other. Demonstrate the activity by getting Sts to ask you some or all of the questions in the questionnaire. Give simple answers that Sts can understand.

Put Sts in pairs, **A** and **B**. Ask the **B**s to close their books. Tell **A** to ask **B** the questions and to write down his / her answers on a piece of paper.

Then they swap roles. Monitor and help.

When Sts have finished, get some feedback. Ask a few Sts to tell you some things about their partner, e.g. *Lina gets up at 7.30. I get up at 7.00.*

Extra challenge

- You could get Sts to change pairs and tell another student what they know about their first partner, e.g. *Amy gets up at 7.30, she has a shower*, etc.

2 VOCABULARY a typical day

a Tell Sts to go to **Vocabulary Bank *A typical day*** on *p.125*.

(2 65)) Focus on **a**. Play the audio and get Sts to repeat the phrases in chorus and individually as necessary. Model and drill any words / phrases which are difficult for your Sts and give further practice.

> (2 65))
> See the phrases in the Student's Book on *p.125*

Focus on **make** and **do** in the box and go through it with the class.

! Stress that *housework* means doing things to take care of a house like cooking and cleaning. Sts may confuse this with *homework* (= work a teacher gives you to do at home).

Focus on **go with *to* and *the*** in the box and go through it with the class.

(2 66)) Focus on the instructions for **b**. Demonstrate the activity by playing the first two sentences and asking Sts to point to the pictures. Each time ask them *What number is the picture?*

Now play the audio from the beginning, pausing after each sentence for Sts to listen and point to the picture.

> (2 66))
> She has lunch at one o'clock.
> She finishes work at six o'clock.
> She goes to the gym.
> She watches TV.
> She goes shopping.
> She goes to work.
> She does housework.
> She gets up at a quarter to seven.
> She goes to bed at half past eleven.
> She makes dinner.
> She has a coffee.
> She has dinner at half past eight.

Focus on the instructions for **c**. Elicit the first five sentences, i.e. *In the morning She gets up at a quarter to seven; She has breakfast; She has a shower;* etc.

Then get Sts to continue in pairs. Remind them to use the third person *-s*. Monitor and help. Make a note of any mistakes and correct them on the board later.

Finally, elicit Lisa's day from the whole class, picture by picture.

Tell Sts to go back to the main lesson **6B**.

Extra support

- If you think Sts need more practice, you may want to give them the Vocabulary photocopiable activity at this point or leave it for later as consolidation or revision.

b Focus on the instructions and demonstrate the activity or get a good student to demonstrate.

Put Sts in pairs and get them to continue miming or drawing.

Monitor and help. Correct any mistakes on the board.

Extra support

- Let Sts refer to **Vocabulary Bank *A typical day*** on *p.125* if they can't remember all the verb phrases.

3 PRONUNCIATION /j/; sentence rhythm

> **Pronunciation notes**
> **/j/**
> - You might like to highlight the following sound–spelling pattern:
>
> – /j/ The letter y at the beginning of a word is pronounced /j/, e.g. *yes*. The letter u is sometimes pronounced /juː/, e.g. *music, student, university*.
>
> – Highlight that the sound /j/ is **not** pronounced the same as the letter *j*.
>
> **Sentence rhythm**
> - For information on **Sentence rhythm**, see the **Pronunciation notes** in **2B**.
> - See also **Pronunciation** in the **Introduction**, *p.8*.

a (2 67)) Read the **Pronunciation notes** and decide how much of the information you want to give your Sts.

Focus on the exercise and play the audio once the whole way through for Sts just to listen.

2 67)))
See the words and sound in the Student's Book on *p.36*

Focus on the sound picture *yacht*. Play the audio to model and drill the word and the sound (pause after the sound).

Now focus on the words after *yacht*. Remind Sts that the pink letters are the /j/ sound. Play the audio, pausing after each word for Sts to listen and repeat.

If this sound is difficult for your Sts, model it yourself so that Sts can see your mouth position, and get Sts to repeat it a few more times.

Play the audio again from the beginning, pausing at the end of the group of words for Sts to repeat.

Give further practice as necessary.

Finally, get Sts, in pairs, to practise saying the words.

Extra support
• If you are using an interactive whiteboard, you can focus on each word individually before moving on to the next one.

b **2 68**))) Focus on the conversation and play the audio once the whole way through for Sts just to listen. Remind Sts that the words in bigger font are the ones which are stressed (because they carry the important information). Also remind them that the underlined syllables in the multi-syllable words are stressed more.

2 68)))
See the conversation in the Student's Book on *p.36*

Now play the audio again for Sts to listen and repeat, encouraging them to try to copy the rhythm on the audio by stressing the bigger bold words more strongly and by saying the others more lightly and quickly. Pause and play again as necessary.

Extra idea
• Put Sts in pairs and get them to practise the conversation. Make sure they swap roles.

c Now tell Sts they are going to ask and answer the questions in **b** about a typical weekday. Demonstrate the activity by getting Sts to ask you the questions and answering them. Try to use *about* in one of your answers, e.g. *I go to bed at about 9.30* and write the sentence on the board. Highlight that *about* = more or less, approximately.

Put Sts in pairs and get them to ask and answer the questions, paying special attention to sentence stress. Monitor and help. You could expand this activity by writing a few more verb prompts on the board, e.g. *get up, have breakfast.*

Make a note of any general problems Sts are having and deal with these on the board at the end.

Get some feedback from various Sts.

4 GRAMMAR adverbs of frequency

a Focus on the chart and elicit the days of the week from the letters at the top of the chart.

Then elicit the meaning of the highlighted words by looking at the ticks and crosses and asking *How many days?* (*always* = five days, *never* = no days, *usually* = four days, *sometimes* = two days).

If you speak your Sts' L1, you may want to elicit a translation of these words.

Focus on the matching task. Tell Sts that 1–4 are the first halves of a sentence and a–d are the second halves. Tell Sts they have to read the sentences and match the two parts. Focus on the example.

Give Sts time to complete the task.

Get Sts to compare with a partner and then check answers by asking individual Sts to read out the complete sentence.

2 d	3 a	4 b

b **2 69**))) Tell Sts to go to **Grammar Bank 6B** on *p.102.*

Focus on the example sentences and play the audio for Sts to listen and repeat. Pause the audio as necessary.

Go through the rules with the class using the expanded information in the **Additional grammar notes** below to help you. You may want to use Sts' L1 here.

Additional grammar notes
adverbs of frequency

• With all verbs except *be*, adverbs of frequency go before the main verb. At this level we have not focussed on adverbs of frequency with *be*. This is taught in *English File* Elementary.

• In positive sentences they usually go between the pronoun and the verb, e.g. *I always have coffee for breakfast.*

! *Sometimes* and *usually* can also be used at the beginning of a sentence, but it is probably best to just give Sts a simple rule at this level.

• You may want to tell Sts that in a negative sentence they go between *don't | doesn't* and the main verb, e.g. *I don't usually have breakfast.* However, this is not practised in the exercises.

• Highlight that we always use a positive verb with *never*, e.g. *I never eat meat.* NOT ~~I never don't eat meat.~~

Focus on the exercises for **6B** on *p.103* and get Sts to do them individually or in pairs. If they do them individually, get them to compare answers with a partner.

Check answers, getting Sts to read the full sentences.

a
1 My husband sometimes goes to the gym.
2 I always have a shower in the morning.
3 We usually have breakfast at home.
4 I never go to bed before 12.00.
5 They always go to work by bus.
6 He sometimes has a sandwich for lunch.
7 The restaurant usually closes late.
8 She never goes shopping after work.
9 I usually do my homework at the weekend.
10 I sometimes make fish for dinner.

b
1 Alex **sometimes goes** to bed very late.
2 We **always do** housework at the weekend.
3 We **usually have** lunch at home at the weekend.
4 I **never drink** coffee in the evening.
5 My sister **always gets** up early.
6 I **never speak** English at work.
7 We **sometimes watch** TV after dinner.
8 My husband **usually finishes** work at 7.30 p.m.
9 I **never have** a bath, I **always have** a shower.
10 We **sometimes drink** tea with milk, but I prefer it with lemon.

Tell Sts to go back to the main lesson **6B**.

Extra support

• If you think Sts need more practice, you may want to give them the Grammar photocopiable activity at this point or leave it for later as consolidation or revision.

c Focus on the instructions and make sure Sts understand all the lexis, e.g. *outside class*. Demonstrate the activity by telling Sts about yourself, e.g. *I always listen to the radio in the car. I never read a newspaper in the morning*, or read the speech bubble. Encourage Sts to add a bit of extra information (e.g. *I listen to Kiss FM*) or a reason.

Ask a few Sts to make a true sentence with the first prompt. If they use *always* or *usually*, you could ask them *Which radio station?*

Now put Sts in pairs and tell them to make true sentences.

Monitor and help. Make a note of any general problems and deal with them at the end.

Get some feedback from various Sts.

Extra support

• You could ask Sts to write the sentences and then read them out to a partner.

Extra challenge

• At the end you could get Sts to tell the class a sentence about their partner, e.g. *Ivan always drinks espresso after lunch.*

5 READING

a Focus on the photos and the title. Ask *What does he do?* and elicit / teach *He's a ballet dancer.* Elicit / teach the verb *to dance* and the noun *a dancer.* Model and drill pronunciation. Ask Sts if they know the dancers in the photos or any other famous ballet dancers.

Now ask the second question, making sure Sts understand the adverb *hard*, and elicit some opinions.

b ◯ **2 70**))) Tell Sts that this article is adapted from a newspaper, so it will have some words they don't know. Remind them that when they read they should try to focus on the words they know and try to guess the meaning of new words.

Before Sts read the article, go through the **Glossary** to make sure they understand all the new words.

Now play the audio for Sts to read and listen at the same time to find out the answer to the question *Do you think he works hard?* in **a**.

Elicit opinions.

Yes, he does.

2 70)))
See the article in the Student's Book on *p.37*

c Focus on questions 1–10 and make sure Sts understand all the lexis.

Now set a time limit for Sts to read the article again.

Put Sts in pairs and get them to answer the questions orally with a partner or to write short answers.

Monitor and help.

Check answers.

1 St Petersburg
2 at about nine
3 eggs and sausages
4 10.30
5 no
6 a big steak
7 He sometimes goes out.
8 Because his clothes don't look good.
9 yes, sometimes
10 No because he has a lot of things in his head.

Extra challenge

• You could ask the class more comprehension questions on the article, e.g. *Does he like staying in hotels?* (Yes, he does) *How many eggs does he sometimes eat?* (five), etc.

d Focus on the highlighted words in the article and point out that they all refer to time. Put Sts in pairs to guess their meaning.

Get Sts to check in a dictionary words they couldn't guess or, if dictionaries are not available, elicit / explain the meanings. To show *before* and *after* write a time on the board, e.g. 5.30. Then ask *Is 4.00 o'clock before or after this time?* (before) *What about 6.00 o'clock?* (after). Highlight that *often* can be pronounced in two ways, either /ˈɒftən/ or /ˈɒfn/ where the *t* is silent.

e Focus on the instructions and ask Sts to complete each sentence with one of the highlighted words. Sts could do this activity in pairs or individually.

f (**2** 71))) Play the audio for Sts to listen and check.

Check answers.

1	Then	3	until	5	after
2	often	4	before	6	about

> (**2** 71)))
>
> 1 I get up at seven. Then I have breakfast.
> 2 I often go to the cinema at the weekend.
> 3 Gina doesn't finish work until seven in the evening.
> 4 I never drink coffee before I go to bed.
> 5 My wife always has a bath or shower after she gets up in the morning.
> 6 We usually go to bed at about eleven.

Deal with any other new vocabulary.

g Focus on the question. Write on the board HE'S A TYPICAL CELEBRITY BECAUSE… and HE ISN'T A TYPICAL CELEBRITY BECAUSE…

Elicit ideas from the class and write them on the board, e.g. *He's a typical celebrity because he stays in hotels. | He likes expensive watches. He isn't a typical celebrity because he lives in a flat. | He isn't interested in clothes*, etc.

Finally, ask Sts if they think he has a nice day.

6 SPEAKING & WRITING

a Tell Sts they are going to use the pictures in the **Vocabulary Bank *A typical day*** to tell a partner about their typical evening. Focus on the example and elicit more example sentences from two or three Sts, e.g. *I usually have dinner at about half past six. Then I watch TV…*

Tell Sts to go to **Vocabulary Bank *A typical day*** on *p.125*.

Put Sts in pairs and get them to continue describing their typical weekday evening, and to use adverbs of frequency whenever appropriate.

Get feedback from some Sts.

Extra challenge

• Get fast finishers to talk about their typical Saturday or Sunday.

Tell Sts to go back to the main lesson **6B**.

b Write on the board: MY TYPICAL MORNING AND AFTERNOON, and write a sentence with the first expression (*get up*) on the board, e.g. *I usually get up at seven o'clock*.

Ask Sts to copy the title and write a sentence saying what time they get up in the morning. Check to make sure Sts understand the task.

Then tell Sts to refer back to the **Vocabulary Bank** on *p.125* for the phrases they need to write about their typical morning and afternoon (during the week). Remind them to use adverbs of frequency and time words.

Monitor and help while they do so.

Get Sts to exchange papers with a partner and read each other's text. If you are short of time, you could get Sts to do this for homework.

WORDS AND PHRASES TO LEARN

(**4** 61))) Tell Sts to go to *p.130* and focus on the **Words and phrases to learn** for **6B**. Make sure Sts understand the meaning of each phrase. If necessary, remind them of the context in which the words and phrases came up in the lesson. If you speak your Sts' L1, you might like to elicit a translation for the words / phrases for the Sts to write next to them. Play the audio, pausing after each phrase for Sts to repeat. You may also like to ask Sts to test each other on the phrases.

5&6 Revise and Check

For instructions on how to use these pages, see *p.36*.

STUDY LINK
• iTutor

Test and Assessment CD-ROM

• Quick Test 6
• File Test 6
• Progress Test 1-6

GRAMMAR

1	a	6	a	11	b
2	a	7	b	12	b
3	b	8	a	13	a
4	a	9	b	14	b
5	b	10	a	15	b

VOCABULARY

a
1	water	3	milk	5	orange juice
2	sugar	4	cheese		

b
1	read	6	watch
2	listen	7	do
3	go	8	speak
4	live	9	have
5	get	10	drink

c
1	unemployed	3	retired	5	journalist
2	waiter	4	nurse		

d
1 a quarter to eight / seven forty-five
2 ten past nine
3 twenty-five past five / five twenty-five
4 half past three / three thirty
5 five to seven / six fifty-five

PRONUNCIATION

a
1	po<u>ta</u>toes	3	<u>a</u>lways	5	<u>ce</u>real
2	po<u>li</u>ceman	4	<u>u</u>sually		

b
/tʃ/	chess	/w/	witch	/g/	girl
/dʒ/	jazz	/v/	vase		

CAN YOU UNDERSTAND THIS TEXT?

a
2	meat	7	hamburgers
3	vegetables	8	every
4	good	9	coffee
5	potatoes	10	small
6	Don't	11	Stop

◼◂ CAN YOU UNDERSTAND THESE PEOPLE?

2 72)) 1 c 2 a 3 b 4 c 5 b

2 72))
See the script in the Student's Book on *p.88*

Remind Sts that they can watch the short film on *iTutor*.

> ◼◂ VIDEO Available as MP3 on CD4
>
> **Short film: A day in the Life of a Tour Guide**
>
> **N = narrator, P = Peter**
>
> **N** Hi! I'm in New York. I'm from England, but I'm here to learn about the life of a tour guide.
> Peter Greenwald is a New York tour guide. He lives in a small apartment in Brooklyn. He usually gets up at eight o'clock. Peter has a big breakfast. He usually has fruit and cereal, and sometimes he has an omelette. He leaves the house at nine o'clock.
> Peter works for a company called Real New York Tours. His tours always begin in Times Square. Every morning he goes there by subway. Peter usually arrives at about 9.45. He meets his group and tells them about the tour. At ten o'clock the tour begins.
> **P** OK, guys, let's go!
> **N** Peter takes them to places of interest all around Manhattan.
> **P** Central Park is over 150 years old.
> **N** They have lunch in Greenwich Village. Peter usually has a real New York pizza.
> The tour ends in Wall Street.
> **P** Wall Street is a very old street. The New York Stock Exchange is here.
> **N** After work, Peter takes the subway back to Brooklyn. Then he relaxes. He usually reads a book magazines. Sometimes, he watches TV. He goes to bed at about 11 o'clock. He needs to sleep. Every day he walks about six miles!
> Peter is an excellent tour guide: he loves his job and he loves New York.

G word order in questions: *be* and present simple
V sports; common verb phrases 2: free time
P /w/, /h/, /eə/, and /aʊ/; sentence rhythm

7A What do you do in your free time?

Lesson plan

The topic of this lesson is sport and other free time activities.

The lesson begins with an article about the most popular sport in five different countries around the world. This is followed by an interview with a professional handball player, who plays for a Danish handball team. She talks about how much she trains and what she does in her spare time. In Grammar, the focus is on word order in questions (both with the verb *be* and the present simple of other verbs). Then in Vocabulary, Sts learn some more common verb phrases to describe free time activities.
The pronunciation focus is on four more sounds, /w/, /h/, /eə/, and /aʊ/ followed by sentence rhythm. The lesson builds up to a speaking activity where Sts use the grammar and vocabulary to talk about what they do in their free time.

STUDY LINK
- Workbook 7A
- iTutor
- www.oup.com/elt/englishfile

Extra photocopiable activities

- **Grammar** word order in questions: *be* and present simple *p.151*
- **Communicative** Free time questionnaire *p.188* (instructions *p.167*)
- **Vocabulary** Common verb phrases 2: free time *p.222* (instructions *p.208*)
- www.oup.com/elt/teacher/englishfile

Optional lead-in (books closed)

- Write the question on the board and makes sure Sts understand it:

  WHAT ARE THE TOP FIVE POPULAR SPORTS IN YOUR COUNTRY?

- Elicit ideas from the class and help them with the English words for the sports. Write the sports on the board. Try to get consensus as to which five sports are the most popular and number them from 1–5.

- Model and drill pronunciation of the sports.

1 READING

a Books open. Focus on the photos and the sports in the list. Point out the underlined stressed syllables. Give Sts time to match the photos with the sports.

a **3 2))** Play the audio for Sts to listen and check.

Check answers. Model and drill pronunciation of the sports using the audio.

A rugby	C archery	E table tennis
B ice hockey	D handball	

3 2))

C archery	E table tennis	A rugby
B ice hockey	D handball	

Do the question as an open-class activity. If you aren't from the same country as your Sts, tell them which sports are popular in your country.

c Focus on the title of the article and elicit what it means (other sports are also popular, not just football).

Now focus on the five countries in the article and make sure Sts know where they are. Ask Sts if they can guess which sports might be popular there. Don't tell Sts if they are right or not.

Extra idea

- If you have a map in class, get Sts to find each country.

Tell Sts to read the article and to complete the gaps with the sports in **a**.

Get Sts to compare with a partner.

d **3 3))** Play the audio for Sts to listen, read, and check their answers to **c**.

Check answers.

1 handball	3 table tennis	5 archery
2 rugby	4 ice hockey	

3 3))

Football isn't the only sport
Football is probably the top sport in the world, but in some countries other sports are the number one...

Iceland
Here, the national sport is handball, and they're very good at it. The population is only 300,000, but their men's team is one of the top teams in the world. This sport is also very popular in Denmark, Norway, and Sweden.

Samoa
In this very small Pacific island, rugby is the number one sport and their team usually plays in the World Cup finals. People from this country also often play in Australia, New Zealand, and the UK.

China
Table tennis, or ping-pong, is the national sport here and they have the top five men and women players in the world. Other countries that are very good at this sport are Japan, Korea, and Germany.

Canada
Here people love all winter sports, and they always win medals in the Winter Olympics. The favourite sport to watch and to play here is ice hockey.

Bhutan
In this small country in the Himalayas, archery is the national sport. In competitions, the men play in teams. During a match the players' wives sing and dance. They want to distract the other teams!

Deal with any other new vocabulary, e.g. *team*, *player*, *win*, *medal*, *match*. You might want to teach / elicit the four seasons (*winter*, *spring*, *summer*, *autumn*) as Sts see *winter* here.

d Put Sts in pairs or small groups to answer the questions.

Get some feedback from the class.

Extra support

• Answer the questions first and make sure the distinction between watching and doing a sport is clear.

2 LISTENING

a Focus on the instructions and the photo.

Then give Sts time to read the information about Verónica Cuadrado and answer questions 1–3.

Check answers. Explain / elicit that *Danish* is both the nationality and language of the people who come from Denmark.

> 1 Santander / Spain
> 2 Denmark
> 3 She plays (professional) handball.

Extra support

• Read the information about Verónica Cuadrado to the class and do the questions as an open-class activity.

b (3 4)) Focus on the instructions and make sure Sts understand them. Go through the questions, dealing with any new vocabulary, e.g. mime the meanings of *relax* and *train* (verb). Also check Sts understand the phrase *free time*.

Point out to Sts that the first question has been numbered for them.

Now tell Sts to listen to the interview and write 2–8 in the boxes next to the questions.

Play the audio once the whole way through for Sts to complete the task. Then play the audio again as necessary.

Get Sts to compare with a partner and then check answers.

> 2 How often do you train?
> 3 How many hours do you train?
> 4 What do you do in your free time?
> 5 Do you do any other sport or exercise?
> 6 What do you do at the weekend?
> 7 How do you relax before a match?
> 8 What do you do in the holidays?

> (3 4))
> (script in Student's Book on *p.88*)
> **I = interviewer, V = Verónica**
> 1
> I What time do you usually get up?
> V During the week I usually get up at about eight.
> 2
> I How often do you train?
> V We have one training session every day, and some days two.
> 3
> I How many hours do you train?
> V We train for two hours.
> 4
> I What do you do in your free time?
> V In my free time I go to Danish lessons, I go shopping, or I meet friends. I also talk online to my family and friends in Spain nearly every day.
> 5
> I Do you do any other sport or exercise?
> V I often go to the gym, but I don't do other sports. I don't have time. But I often watch sport on TV. Handball of course, football, tennis. I like most sports.
> 6
> I What do you do at the weekend?
> V At the weekend I always have a match. When it's a home match I have some free time, but when it's an away match I don't have any. I travel to the match, play the match, and then travel back home.
> 7
> I How do you relax before a match?
> V I go and sit down somewhere quiet. I need to be alone, and think about the match.
> 8
> I What do you do in the holidays?
> V In the holidays I always want to go to a hot place and relax. Denmark is usually cold, and the winters are very long. I dream of the sun!

c You might want to pre-teach some new vocabulary, e.g. *training session*, *home match*, *away match*, *somewhere quiet*, etc., or you may prefer to focus on this afterwards.

Tell Sts to listen again and this time to make notes of Verónica's answers.

Play the audio, pausing after Verónica answers each question to give Sts time to write. Play again as necessary.

Get Sts to compare with a partner and then check answers.

> 1 (She gets up) at about eight.
> 2 (She has) one or two training sessions a day
> 3 (She trains for) two hours
> 4 She goes to Danish lessons, shopping, or meets friends. She also talks online to her family and friends in Spain.
> 5 She goes go to the gym.
> 6 She always has a match.
> 7 She sits (in a quiet place) and thinks about the match.
> 8 She goes to a hot place and relaxes.

Extra support

• If there's time, you could play the audio again while Sts read the script on *p.88*, so they can see what they understood / didn't understand. Translate / explain any new words or phrases.

3 GRAMMAR word order in questions: *be* and present simple

a Focus on the task. Elicit the first question and write it on the board (WHERE IS VERÓNICA FROM?)

Give Sts a few minutes to write the other three questions.

Check answers and write them on the board.

> 2 Is Bhutan a big country?
> 3 When does Canada win Olympic medals?
> 4 Does Verónica do other sports?

Elicit the answers from individual Sts.

> 1 Santander / Spain   3 in the Winter Olympics
> 2 No, it isn't.   4 No, she doesn't.

b (3 5)) (3 6)) Tell Sts to go to **Grammar Bank 7A** on *p.104*.

Focus on the example sentences and play the audio for Sts to listen and repeat. Pause the audio as necessary.

Go through the rules with the class using the expanded information in the **Additional grammar notes** below to help you. You may want to use Sts' L1 here.

Additional grammar notes
Word order in questions

Questions with *be*

- Remind Sts that to make a question with the verb *be*, you simply invert the subject and the verb, so *They are American* becomes *Are they American?* and *This is your coat* becomes *Is this your coat?* It's important to highlight again that questions with *be* do not use the auxiliaries *do* or *does*.

- In questions with *be* Sts sometimes forget to invert the subject and verb. Typical mistakes include: *Ana's a student? What they're doing?*

Questions with other verbs

- Remind Sts that with other main verbs in the present simple, you need to first use the auxiliary *do* or *does*, then the subject, and then the main verb in the infinitive, so *She lives in London* becomes *Does she live in London?*

- If a question has a question word, e.g. *What* or *Where*, etc. then the question word always comes first.

- The acronyms **ASI** (**A**uxiliary verb + **S**ubject + **I**nfinitive) and **QuASI** (**Qu**estion word + **A**uxiliary verb + **S**ubject + **I**nfinitive) will help Sts remember the correct word order in questions in the present simple (with verbs other than *be*).

- In questions with the auxiliaries *do* or *does* Sts may leave out the auxiliary or get the word order wrong. Typical mistakes include: *You live with your parents? How you do spell it?*

Focus on the exercises for **7A** on *p.105* and get Sts to do them individually or in pairs. If they do them individually, get them to compare answers with a partner.

Check answers, getting Sts to read the full sentences.

```
a
1  What       5  When
2  How        6  How
3  What       7  Where
4  Who        8  Where
b
1  Where do your brothers work?
2  Is this your phone?
3  What time does the film start?
4  Does your husband speak Spanish?
5  How is your family?
6  Are we late for class?
7  Do your children like sushi?
8  What time does your wife finish work?
```

```
c
1  Is      4  Are     7  is
2  do      5  do      8  does
3  are     6  Does    9  Do
```

Tell Sts to go back to the main lesson **7A**.

Extra support
- If you think Sts need more practice, you may want to give them the Grammar photocopiable activity at this point or leave it for later as consolidation or revision.

4 VOCABULARY common verb phrases 2: free time

a This exercise revises verb-noun collocations Sts already know. Focus on the instructions and give Sts a few minutes to complete the sentences.

b (3 7)) Play the audio for Sts to listen and check.

Check answers.

```
1  go, go, meet        2  travel, play, travel
```

> (3 7))
> 1 In my free time I go to Danish lessons, I go shopping, or I meet friends.
> 2 I travel to the match, play the match, and then travel back home.

c Tell Sts to go to **Vocabulary Bank *Common verb phrases 2*** on *p.126*.

(3 8)) Look at **1 Free time** and focus on **a**. Play the audio and get Sts to repeat the verbs and verb phrases in chorus and individually as necessary. Model and drill any words which are difficult for your Sts and give further practice.

> (3 8))
> See 1 Free time in the Student's Book on *p.126*

You might want to highlight that:
- we use *play* + names of ball and racket sports, e.g. *golf, football, tennis*, etc.
- we use *play* with musical instruments, e.g. *play the piano*. With musical instruments we use *the* (*play **the** piano*), but not with sports (*play football*).
- we say *do sport* (in general).

Now focus on **b**. Ask Sts to cover the words, look at the photos, and say the verbs or verb phrases. They could do this individually or with a partner.

Monitor and help. Make a note of any pronunciation problems.

Focus on the ***meet*** box and go through it with the class.

Now focus on **c**. Write SOMETIMES and NEVER on the board. Demonstrate the activity by making sentences about yourself, e.g. *I sometimes go to the beach, I never play the piano*. Elicit sentences with *sometimes* and *never* from two or three Sts and then ask Sts to continue in pairs.

Monitor and help. Make a note of any common mistakes and deal with them afterwards on the board.

Tell Sts to go back to the main lesson **7A**.

Extra support

- If you think Sts need more practice, you may want to give them the Vocabulary photocopiable activity at this point or leave it for later as consolidation or revision.

5 PRONUNCIATION /w/, /h/, /eə/, and /aʊ/

Pronunciation notes

/w/, /h/, /eə/, and /aʊ/

- You may want to highlight the following sound–spelling patterns:

– /w/ For information on this sound, see the **Pronunciation notes** in **5B**. Note that most question words, e.g. *What, Where, Why*, are pronounced /w/. The common exceptions are *Who* and *How*, which are pronounced /h/.

– /h/ For information on this sound, see the **Pronunciation notes** in **1A**.

– The letters *ere* are sometimes pronounced /eə/, e.g. *where*, but can also be /ɪə/ as in *here*.

– /aʊ/ *ou* and *ow* are often pronounced /aʊ/, e.g. *house, brown*. NB *ow* can also be /əʊ/ as in *window*.

Sentence rhythm

- For information on **Sentence rhythm**, see the **Pronunciation notes** in **2B**.

- See also **Pronunciation** in the **Introduction**, *p.8*.

a **3 9))** Read the **Pronunciation notes** and decide how much of the information you want to give your Sts.

Focus on the exercise and play the audio once the whole way through for Sts just to listen.

> **3 9))**
> See the sounds and words in the Student's Book on *p.41*

Focus on the sound picture *witch*. Play the audio to model and drill the word and the sound (pause after the sound).

Now focus on the words after *witch*. Remind Sts that the pink letters are the /w/ sound. Play the audio, pausing after each word for Sts to listen and repeat.

Now repeat the same process for *house* /h/, *chair* /eə/, and *owl* /aʊ/.

If these sounds are difficult for your Sts, model them yourself so that Sts can see your mouth position, and get Sts to repeat them a few more times.

Play the audio again from the beginning, pausing after each group of words for Sts to repeat.

Give further practice as necessary.

Finally, get Sts, in pairs, to practise saying the words.

Extra support

- If you are using an interactive whiteboard, you can focus on each sound individually before moving on to the next one.

b **3 10))** Focus on the sentences and play the audio once the whole way through for Sts just to listen. Remind Sts that the words in bigger font are the ones

which are stressed (because they carry the important information). Also remind them that the underlined syllables in the multi-syllable words are stressed more.

> **3 10))**
> See the sentences in the Student's Book on *p.41*

Now play the audio again, pausing after each question and answer for Sts to listen and repeat.

Finally, give Sts time in pairs to practise the activity asking and answering the questions. Make sure they swap roles.

6 SPEAKING

Tell Sts to go to **Communication** *Weekdays and weekends* on *p.83*.

Focus on **a** and give Sts time to look at the questions. Make sure the meaning of *During the week* and *At the weekend* is clear. Explain that later they will have to make the questions, but now they just have to answer them. Demonstrate the activity by asking a few Sts the first question *What time do you finish work | school?*

Get Sts to continue working individually to write answers that are true for them in the **You** column.

When Sts have written their answers in the **You** column, focus on the questions and elicit what the missing words are (shown by |). Elicit that in *During the week* what is missing is *do you* in all the questions except 7 where what is missing is *Are you*, and that in *At the weekend* the missing words are all *do you* except for 7 (also *Are you*). Check Sts are making the questions correctly by getting them to ask you all of them.

Now focus on **b** and put Sts in pairs, **A** and **B**, to ask and answer the questions and write their partner's answers.

Monitor and help.

Extra challenge

Encourage Sts to add extra information.

Now focus on **c** and the example. Get Sts to find new partners. With their new partners, they ask and answer questions about their first partner's week and weekend. Remind them to use *does* in non-*be* questions and to use the correct pronouns and possessive forms (*he, she, his, her*). For both questions 7 they will need to ask *Is he | she…?*

Monitor and help. Make notes of any problems and revise these at the end.

WORDS AND PHRASES TO LEARN

4 61)) Tell Sts to go to *p.130* and focus on the **Words and phrases to learn** for **7A**. Make sure Sts understand the meaning of each phrase. If necessary, remind them of the context in which the words and phrases came up in the lesson. If you speak your Sts' L1, you might like to elicit a translation for the words | phrases for the Sts to write next to them. Play the audio, pausing after each phrase for Sts to repeat. You may also like to ask Sts to test each other on the phrases.

G imperatives; object pronouns: *me, him,* etc.
V kinds of films
P sentence rhythm and intonation

7B Lights, camera, action!

Lesson plan

In this lesson, actors on a film set provide the context for introducing imperatives and object pronouns.

The lesson starts with a dialogue in which two actors are acting a scene in a film and the film director is giving them instructions. This allows Sts to see the new grammar in context before going to the Grammar Bank to practise it. In Vocabulary, Sts learn words for different film genres, e.g. *a comedy, a drama,* etc. Then Sts listen to two people expressing their opinions about certain actors and film genres using adjectives like *fantastic* and verbs, e.g. *like, love.* This leads into Pronunciation where Sts practise rhythm and intonation in a conversation similar to the listening. The lesson ends with Sts giving their own opinions about actors and kinds of films.

STUDY LINK
- Workbook 7B
- iTutor
- iChecker on iTutor
- www.oup.com/elt/englishfile

Extra photocopiable activities
- **Grammar** imperatives; object pronouns: *me, him,* etc. *p.152*
- **Communicative** What do you think of...? *p.189* (instructions *p.168*)
- www.oup.com/elt/teacher/englishfile

Optional lead-in (books closed)
- Write the names of some actors, actresses, and film directors on the board.
- Then ask Sts *What does he / she do?* and elicit *He's an actor. / She's an actress. / He's a film director.*, etc.
- Then ask Sts if they know any more film directors and if they think they are good.

1 GRAMMAR imperatives; object pronouns: *me, him,* etc.

a **3 11)))** Books open. Focus on the instructions and questions. Tell Sts to put their pens / pencils down and <u>not</u> to write anything the first time they listen.

Play the audio once the whole way through for Sts to read and listen at the same time, and answer the questions.

Extra challenge
- Get Sts to cover the dialogue and just listen.

Check answers.

> She doesn't know.
> No, she doesn't love Rupert.

---

3 11)))

D = director, S = Scarlett, Sa = Sam

D OK. Be quiet, please. Scene one, take one. Lights, camera, ... action!
S Hello, Sam.
Sa Hello, Scarlett.
S Come in. Sit down. We need to talk.
Sa Talk? What about?
S Us. You and me.
Sa Listen to me, Scarlett. I love you! Do you love me?
S I don't know, Sam. I need time.
Sa And Rupert? Do you love him?
S Don't talk about Rupert. Yes, I like Rupert, but I don't love him. You don't understand.
Sa Don't cry, Scarlett. Please don't cry.
D Cut! Great! I like it.
***
D OK, scene two. This is a big scene. Scarlett, go to the windows. Open them. Sam, go to Scarlett. Stand next to her. Scarlett, look at him. That's great. Don't move.
Sa What do I say to her? I don't remember.
D Nothing. Don't say anything. Kiss her.

---

b Now play the audio again and get Sts to complete the gaps.

Get Sts to compare with a partner and then check answers.

2	Come	5	Don't	8	Stand
3	Listen	6	go	9	look
4	talk	7	Open	10	say

c Tell Sts to cover the dialogue and to look at sentences 1–6 and the words in the list. Point out that number 1 has been done for them. You could tell them that the gaps are all object pronouns and explain that a subject pronoun is used for a person who <u>does</u> an action, and an object pronoun is for the person who <u>receives</u> the action.

Give Sts time to complete the task.

d **3 12)))** Play the audio for Sts to listen and check.

Check answers, getting Sts to read the sentences in full. Highlight that although the word *them* is pronounced /ðem/ when said in isolation, it is usually pronounced /ðəm/ when it follows other words, e.g. *Open them* /ðəm/.

2	me	4	him	6	them
3	you, me	5	it		

---

3 12)))

1 S We need to talk.
  Sa Talk? What about?
  S Us. You and me.
2 Listen to me, Scarlett.
3 I love you! Do you love me?
4 I like Rupert, but I don't love him.
5 Great! I like it.
6 Go to the windows. Open them.

83

e (3 13)) (3 14)) Tell Sts to go to **Grammar Bank 7B** on *p.104*.

Focus on the example sentences and play the audio for Sts to listen and repeat. Pause the audio as necessary.

Go through the rules with the class using the expanded information in the **Additional grammar notes** below to help you. You may want to use Sts' L1 here.

Additional grammar notes
Imperatives

- Highlight the simplicity of imperatives in English. There are only two forms – positive and negative, e.g. *Wait, Don't wait*. Elicit / give a few more examples of imperatives, encouraging Sts to give the negative forms, e.g. *Sit down, Look, Listen, Don't write, Don't look*, etc.

Object pronouns

- Like subject pronouns, object pronouns are used to refer to people and things when we don't want to repeat a noun, e.g. *Rachel likes **Jim**, but she doesn't love **him***.

- Highlight that *it* is used for things, *him* for a man or boy, and *her* for a woman or girl. You may want to remind Sts that *her* is also the possessive adjective for a woman. The plural form *them* is used for both people and things.

- Highlight that the object pronouns for *it* and *you* are the same as the subject pronouns.

Focus on the exercises for **7B** on *p.105* and get Sts to do them individually or in pairs. If they do them individually, get them to compare answers with a partner.

Check answers, getting Sts to read the full sentences.

a					
1	Close	4	Speak	7	Sit, open
2	Don't eat	5	Go	8	Don't read
3	Don't play	6	Don't make	9	Don't worry
b					
1	it	4	her	7	us
2	him	5	them	8	you
3	them	6	me		

Tell Sts to go back to the main lesson **7B**.

Extra support

- If you think Sts need more practice, you may want to give them the Grammar photocopiable activity at this point or leave it for later as consolidation or revision.

f (3 15)) Focus on the example and explain to Sts that they will hear someone say a subject pronoun and they should say the object pronoun.

Play the example, pausing after the speaker says *I* for Sts to say *me* in chorus.

Continue playing the audio, pausing after each item for Sts to respond in chorus.

(3 15))			
1	I (*pause*) me	5	it (*pause*) it
2	you (*pause*) you	6	we (*pause*) us
3	he (*pause*) him	7	they (*pause*) them
4	she (*pause*) her		

Then repeat the activity, eliciting responses from individual Sts.

Extra support

- Write all the object pronouns on the board for Sts to look at whilst listening.

g (3 16)) Focus on the instructions and example. Ask why the new sentence uses *her* and elicit that it is because Scarlett is a woman.

Play the audio, pausing after each item for Sts to respond in chorus.

(3 16))
1 I love Scarlett. (*pause*) I love her.
2 I don't like dogs. (*pause*) I don't like them.
3 I like your house. (*pause*) I like it.
4 Wait for Daniel. (*pause*) Wait for him.
5 Read the book. (*pause*) Read it.
6 I love cats. (*pause*) I love them.
7 Speak to your mother. (*pause*) Speak to her.
8 I don't like Johnny Depp. (*pause*) I don't like him.

Then repeat the activity, eliciting responses from individual Sts.

Extra support

- Write HIM, HER, IT, THEM on the board as a reminder for Sts.

h Put Sts in groups of three and get them to act out the dialogue in **a**.

Monitor and help. Make sure they swap roles.

You could get a group to perform the role-play for the class.

2 VOCABULARY kinds of films

a Focus on the instructions and photos. You could ask Sts if they know any of the films in the stills (1 *Kung Fu Panda*, 2 *Dumb and Dumber*, 3 *Carrie*, 4 *12 Years a Slave*, 5 *Skyfall*, 6 *Django Unchained*).

Put Sts in pairs and give them time to match the kinds of films with the photos.

b (3 17)) Play the audio for Sts to listen and check.

Check answers.

1	an animation	4	a drama
2	a comedy	5	an action film
3	a horror film	6	a western

(3 17))			
5	an action film	1	an animation
2	a comedy	6	a western
4	a drama	3	a horror film

Play the audio again for Sts to listen and repeat. Give further practice as necessary, modelling and drilling the pronunciation yourself, or using the audio, and getting choral and individual responses.

Extra idea

- You could write each kind of film on the board and elicit from the class titles of recent films or films everyone knows for each category.

3 LISTENING

a Focus on the instructions and the two photos. Make sure Sts know the meaning of *actor*. You might want to tell them that *actor* can be used for both men and women, but *actress* is also quite common for women.

Do the questions as an open-class activity.

> The photo on the left is Daniel Craig. His films include the James Bond films, *The Girl with the Dragon Tattoo*, and *The Golden Compass*.
> The photo on the right is Gwyneth Paltrow. Her films include the *Iron Man* films and *Contagion*.

b **3 18**)) Focus on the instructions and the chart. Make sure Sts understand that the first time they listen they just need to tick the appropriate column depending on whether the speakers like the actor or not and whether they like comedies.

Play the audio once the whole way through for Sts to listen and tick the columns.

Get Sts to compare with a partner then check answers.

	Jessica		Callum	
	☺	☹	☺	☹
Daniel Craig		✓	✓	
Gwyneth Paltrow	✓			✓
comedies	✓			✓

> **3 18**))
> (script in Student's Book on *p.88*)
> **C = Callum, J = Jessica**
>
> **C** The new James Bond film is on next week. Do you want to see it?
> **J** Not especially, I don't like Daniel Craig. He's very attractive, but he isn't a very good James Bond. Do you like him?
> **C** Yes, I do. I think he's a really good actor.
> **J** There's a film I really want to see with Gwyneth Paltrow. I think she's a fantastic actress. Do you like her?
> **C** She's OK. What kind of film is it?
> **J** It's a comedy.
> **C** Sorry. I don't like comedies, especially American comedies. They're usually very silly.
> **J** Oh, I love comedies.

You could highlight the meaning of *really* (= *very* or *very much*) and this use of *love* (= *like very much*).

c Focus on the instructions and make sure Sts know what an *adjective* is. If necessary, remind them of the **Vocabulary Bank** *Adjectives* on *p.121*.

Play the audio again the whole way through for Sts to listen and do the task. Play the audio again as necessary.

Get Sts to compare with a partner and then check answers.

	Jessica	Callum
	adjectives	adjectives
Daniel Craig	attractive, (not very) good	good
Gwyneth Paltrow	fantastic	OK
comedies		American, silly

Extra support
- If there's time, you could play the audio again while Sts read the script on p.88, so they can see what they understood / didn't understand.

d Do this as an open-class activity. You could get Sts to vote with a show of hands.

4 PRONUNCIATION & SPEAKING
sentence rhythm and intonation

Pronunciation notes
Sentence rhythm
- For information on **Sentence rhythm**, see the **Pronunciation notes** in **2B**

Intonation
- Intonation is the way in which we say something in English, using a rise or fall in the movement of our voice. Through our intonation we can 'sound' polite, rude, happy, angry, interested, bored, etc. You can make Sts appreciate the importance of intonation by speaking like a robot, i.e. with no intonation. Encourage Sts to develop a friendly and interested intonation by copying the audio.

a **3 19**)) Focus on the task and the conversation. Ask Sts if they know the actors in the three photos.

Play the audio once the whole way through for Sts just to listen.

> **3 19**))
> See the conversation in the Student's Book on *p.43*

Now play the audio again, pausing after each question and answer for Sts to listen and repeat. Encourage them to copy the rhythm and intonation.

b Put Sts in pairs and get them to practise the conversation in **a**.

c Focus on the instructions and the chart.

Give Sts time to complete their chart with films / people that they like (or don't like). Make sure they write the kinds of films in the plural, e.g. *action films*.

d Focus on the instructions. Explain that the questions should all start with *Do you like…* and encourage Sts to use *Yes, I like him | her | them* (*a lot*) or *No, I don't like him | her | them* in their answers. Tell Sts to use *What about you?* to ask the question back to their partner. Encourage them to use adjectives too, e.g. *very | really good, fantastic, great, terrible*, etc. You could write these on the board to remind Sts to use them.

Put Sts in pairs and get them to ask and answer about the information in their chart in **c**.

Get some feedback from various pairs by asking, e.g. *What actors do you like? What kinds of films do you like?*

WORDS AND PHRASES TO LEARN

4 61)) Tell Sts to go to *p.131* and focus on the **Words and phrases to learn** for **7B**. Make sure Sts understand the meaning of each phrase. If necessary, remind them of the context in which the words and phrases came up in the lesson. If you speak your Sts' L1, you might like to elicit a translation for the words / phrases for the Sts to write next to them. Play the audio, pausing after each phrase for Sts to repeat. You may also like to ask Sts to test each other on the phrases.

PRACTICAL ENGLISH
Episode 4 What's the date?

Lesson plan

In this lesson, Sts learn how to say the date in English. This involves first teaching Sts the months of the year. Sts then learn ordinal numbers, which are presented through a general knowledge quiz, and, finally, they learn how to say the date. As this is the Beginner level Sts are just taught one way of saying the date, i.e. *the first of May* (as opposed to *May the first*). They are <u>not</u> taught how to say the year as this is introduced in *English File* Elementary. Sts then listen to a telephone conversation between Rob and Jenny, which involves them understanding various dates, and they learn some useful phrases. The lesson finishes with the song *Calendar Girl*, which recycles the months of the year.

STUDY LINK
- **Workbook** What's the date?
- iTutor
- www.oup.com/elt/englishfile

Extra photocopiable activities

- **Communicative** Famous birthdays *p.190* (instructions *p.168*)
- **Vocabulary** Months and ordinal numbers *p.223* (instructions *p.208*)
- **Song** *Calendar Girl p.231* (instructions *p.226*)

Test and Assessment CD-ROM

- Quick Test 7
- File Test 7
- www.oup.com/elt/teacher/englishfile

Optional lead-in (books closed)

- Play the number game *Buzz*. For instructions, see **2B**, **3 Vocabulary**, exercise **g** on *p.34*.

1 MONTHS

a Books open. Focus on the instructions. Explain / elicit what *special* means.

Focus on the names of the special days. Ask Sts which of these special days are celebrated in their country. If Sts are not familiar with a holiday, explain it without saying which month it is in.

Focus on the months *January, October, December* and model and drill the pronunciation. Sts may have difficulty with *January* /'dʒænjuəri/.

Now get Sts to match the special days with the months. Tell them to guess if they are not sure.

Check answers.

1 C	2 A	3 B

- **Christmas Day:** The day when Christians celebrate the birth of Christ. It is celebrated on 25th December.
- **New Year's Day:** The first day of the new year, in most countries 1st January.
- **Halloween:** A holiday celebrated on 31st October in which children dress up and go around the neighbourhood calling out *Trick or treat?*. People then give them sweets or other 'treats'.

b Tell Sts to go to **Vocabulary Bank** *Months and ordinal numbers* on *p.127*.

3 20)) Look at **1 Months** and focus on **a**. Give Sts time to read the list of months. Now play the audio and get Sts to repeat the words in chorus and individually as necessary. Model and drill any words which are difficult for your Sts and give further practice.

> **3 20))**
> See the months in the Student's Book on *p.127*

Focus on the information box and explain that in English months begin with a capital letter. If appropriate, compare this with Sts' L1.

Now focus on **b**. Get Sts to cover the months and focus on the abbreviations. Get them to remember and say the months individually or with a partner.

Extra idea

- Test Sts by telling them to close their books. Write the abbreviations for the months on the board in order (numbered 1–12), e.g. JAN, FEB, MAR, and elicit the month from the class.

Extra idea

- Get Sts to test each other in **A** / **B** pairs. **A** says a number, e.g. *five*, and **B** then says the month (*May*).

Tell Sts to go back to the main lesson **PE 4**.

c Put Sts in small groups of three or four and get them to answer questions 1–4.

Check answers.

1 February
2 May
3 January, June, July
4 September, October, November, December

2 ORDINAL NUMBERS

a Focus on the quiz and go through the nine questions making sure Sts understand them and the three options.

Now focus on the words in red (*first*, *second*, etc.) and elicit / explain that these are 'ordinal numbers' so called because they tell us the order of something.

Now put Sts in pairs and give them time to circle the answers. Tell them to guess if they are not sure of an answer. Monitor and help with any vocabulary problems.

b (3 21))) Play the audio, pausing after each number for Sts to listen and check.

Check answers and elicit more information for each question, e.g. *Where is Messi from? What medal do they get if they come first?*, etc. Find out who got the most correct answers.

1 a 2 b 3 c 4 c 5 b 6 a 7 b 8 c 9 b

(3 21)))
1 The famous Argentinian footballer Messi's first name is Lionel, or Leo.
2 People who come second in the Olympics win a silver medal.
3 The author of the novel *The Third Man* is the British writer Graham Greene.
4 The fourth of July is Independence Day, an important holiday in the USA.
5 The famous shopping street Fifth Avenue is in New York.
6 The sixth letter of the alphabet is F.
7 The seventh month of the year is July.
8 King Henry the eighth of England is famous for his six wives.
9 Beethoven's ninth symphony is called *The Choral Symphony*.

Finally, tell Sts to cover the quiz. Write the number *1* on the board and ask *What's the number?* (one) *What's the ordinal?* (first). Do the same for 2 and 3. Finally, write number 4 on the board and see if the class can remember *fourth*.

c Tell Sts to go to **Vocabulary Bank *Months and ordinal numbers*** on *p.127*.

(3 22))) Look at **2 Ordinal numbers** and focus on **a**. Play the audio and get Sts to repeat the ordinal numbers in chorus and individually as necessary. Model and drill any words which are difficult for your Sts and give further practice. Remind Sts that the underlined syllables are stressed more strongly. You may want to model and drill some of the trickier ones yourself, e.g. *fifth* /fɪfθ/, *eighth* /eɪtθ/, and twelfth /twelfθ/.

(3 22)))
See the ordinal numbers in the Student's Book on *p.127*

Highlight that:
– we put the two small letters after the number to distinguish it from a normal (cardinal) number. Remind Sts again that the two letters are the last two letters of the ordinal number, e.g. *first → 1st*.
– *first*, *second*, and *third* are irregular in that they are completely different in form from the cardinal numbers *one*, *two*, and *three*.
– all the other ordinals are formed by adding *th* to the cardinal number, pronounced /θ/.
– the following ordinals are slightly irregular in their full written form:
fifth /fɪfθ/ (compare with ordinal, *five*)
eighth /eɪtθ/ (compare with ordinal, *eight*)
ninth /naɪnθ/ (compare with ordinal, *nine*)
twelfth /twelfθ/ (compare with ordinal, *twelve*)

(3 23))) Now focus on **b**. Point out that we say *twenty-first*, *twenty-second*, *twenty-third* NOT ~~twenty-oneth~~, ~~twenty-twoth~~, ~~twenty-threeth~~. Play the audio and get Sts to repeat the ordinal numbers in chorus and individually as necessary. Model and drill any words which are difficult for your Sts and give further practice.

Give Sts time to practise saying the ordinal numbers. Monitor and help. Make a note of any general problems they are having and focus on these when Sts finish.

(3 23)))
See the ordinal numbers in the Student's Book on *p.127*

Tell Sts to go back to the main lesson **PE4**.

Extra support
• If you think Sts need more practice, you may want to give them the Vocabulary photocopiable activity at this point or leave it for later as consolidation or revision.

Pronunciation notes
• The letters *th* can only be pronounced in two ways – /θ/ as in *thumb* /θʌm/ or /ð/ as in *mother* /ˈmʌðə/ and there are no easy rules to give Sts. They have already focussed on this voiced* sound /ð/ in **3B**. The /θ/ sound in *thumb* is **unvoiced***.

  * For an explanation of **voiced** and **unvoiced** sounds, see the **Pronunciation notes** in **3A** on *p.39*.

• It is hard for many Sts to produce the /θ/ sound and so the aim here should be for intelligibility and helping Sts to at least make a reasonable approximation of the sound.

d (3 24))) Read the **Pronunciation notes** and decide how much of the information you want to give your Sts.

Focus on the exercise and play the audio once the whole way through for Sts just to listen.

(3 24)))
See the sound and words in the Student's Book on *p.44*

Focus on the sound picture *thumb*. Play the audio to model and drill the word and the sound (pause after the sound).

Now focus on the words after *thumb*. Remind Sts that the pink letters are the /θ/ sound. Play the audio, pausing after each word for Sts to listen and repeat.

If this sound is difficult for your Sts, model it yourself so that Sts can see your mouth position, and get Sts to repeat it a few more times.

Play the audio again from the beginning, pausing after the group of words for Sts to repeat.

Give further practice as necessary.

Finally, get Sts, in pairs, to practise saying the words.

Extra support
• If you are using an interactive whiteboard, you can focus on each word individually before moving on to the next one.

e (3 25)) Focus on the instructions and the example.

Play the example, pausing after *one* for Sts to say *first* in chorus.

Play the audio and pause after the next number (*three*). Ask Sts what the ordinal number is (*third*). Play the audio, so Sts can hear the correct answer. Make sure Sts are clear what they have to do before continuing.

Play the rest of the audio and give Sts time to say the ordinal numbers in chorus.

(3 25))

Number 1	one (*pause*) first
Number 2	three (*pause*) third
Number 3	five (*pause*) fifth
Number 4	nine (*pause*) ninth
Number 5	twelve (*pause*) twelfth
Number 6	sixteen (*pause*) sixteenth
Number 7	twenty (*pause*) twentieth
Number 8	twenty-two (*pause*) twenty-second
Number 9	twenty-seven (*pause*) twenty-seventh
Number 10	thirty-one (*pause*) thirty-first

Then repeat the activity, eliciting responses from individual Sts.

3 ◼ SAYING THE DATE

a (3 26)) Focus on the title, *Saying the date*, and explain / elicit the meaning of *date*.

Now focus on the instructions and the conversation. Highlight that most of the missing words in the spaces are ordinal numbers.

Play the video or audio once the whole way through for Sts just to listen.

Now play it again and get Sts to complete the task.

Check answers. You might want to point out to Sts that *dad* is an informal way of saying *father*.

---

1 2nd	2 1st	3 2nd	4 birthday

(3 26))

R = Rob, A = Alan

R What's the date today?
A I think it's the second of June.
R Are you sure? Isn't it the first?
A No, definitely the second.
R Oh no! It's my dad's birthday.

---

b Focus on the instructions. Play the video or audio again, pausing after each line for Sts to listen and repeat.

Put Sts in pairs and get them to practise the conversation.

Make sure they swap roles. Monitor and help.

Get some pairs to perform the role-play for the class.

c (3 27)) Focus on the instructions and give Sts time to read questions 1–3.

Play the video or audio for Sts to listen and complete the task. Play again as necessary. NB *wine* (answer 2) is a new word for Sts although some may already know it.

Check answers.

---

1 Rob goes to see his father. / to his father's house.
2 wine
3 His father's birthday is on the second of July.

(3 27))

(script in Student's Book on *p.88*)
R = Rob, H = Henry

R Dad!
H Rob, hi!
R Hi. This is for you.
H For me? It's my favourite wine. Thanks, Rob. But why?
R For your birthday of course! Happy birthday!
H Rob, it isn't my birthday today! My birthday's on the second of July! Today's the second of June.
R Oh no!
H Don't worry. Come in! Have a glass of wine...

Now focus on the **Saying the date** box and go through it with the class.

Highlight that the British convention for saying dates is to say, for example *the fourth of May*. You can also say *May the fourth*; however, this is less common. At this level it is better for Sts to just learn one way.

Explain that although we don't have to use an ordinal when writing a date (see the three different ways of writing it), we <u>always</u> use the ordinal when *saying* the date: *the fourth of May*, NOT ~~four May~~.

Highlight that we *say*, but don't write, *the* and *of*, e.g. (*the*) 4th (*of*) *June*.

! You may want to point out that the American English convention for writing dates is to give the month first and then the day, e.g. *8/12 = 12th August*.

d (3 28)) Focus on the instructions and the dates.

Play the audio for Sts to listen and repeat. Give further practice as necessary.

(3 28))

See the dates in the Student's Book on *p.45*

Focus on the first date again. Elicit how to say it (*the first of January*) and write it on the board.

Put Sts in pairs and give them time to practise saying the dates. Note any problems and focus on them at the end.

Finally, ask individual Sts to say each of the dates.

e Focus on the instructions and make sure Sts know the word *tomorrow*. Put Sts in pairs to answer the questions.

Check answers.

> 3 Christmas Day is on the twenty-fifth of December.
> New Year's Day is on the first of January.
> Halloween is on the thirty-first of October.

f Focus on the instructions. Model and drill *When's your birthday?* Elicit an answer (month and day, <u>not year</u>) from a student.

Get Sts to stand up and ask other Sts *When's your birthday?* Tell them to make a list of names and dates.

! If your class is very large, tell them just to choose ten Sts.

Put Sts in pairs or small groups to compare lists. Get them to make a list with the number of birthdays in each month. Which month has the most birthdays?

If Sts see they are missing a birthday on their lists, they should ask *When is* (name)*'s birthday?*

g Focus on the instructions and the speech bubble. Demonstrate the activity yourself by writing down three birthdays on the board as in the example and telling Sts whose birthdays they are, e.g. *My mother's birthday is on the fourth of October.*

Give Sts a few minutes to write down their three important birthdays. Monitor and help as needed.

Put Sts in pairs and get them to tell each other about their important birthdays.

Get some feedback from the class.

4 ▶ TALKING ON THE PHONE

a (3 29))) Focus on the photo and ask Sts to describe it (Jenny is on the phone).

Focus on the two questions and then play the video or audio once the whole way through for Sts to listen and answer the questions. You may want to pre-teach the words *trip* and *Thanksgiving* before Sts listen. Thanksgiving is a public holiday celebrated in the USA on the fourth Thursday in November. It is a time when families usually get together and eat a big meal.

Check answers.

> 1 To talk about her trip to London (in March).
> 2 Because she is with her family.

> (3 29)))
> (script in Student's Book on *p.88*)
> **J = Jenny, R = Rob, JM = Jenny's mum**
> J Hello?
> R Hello. Is that Jennifer Zielinski?
> J Yes. Who's that?
> R This is Rob Walker.
> J I'm sorry, who?
> R Er, Rob Walker. I work for *London24seven*. Er... we need to talk about your trip to London in March. Er... you arrive on the 12th of March and you leave on the 19th, is that right?
> J I'm really sorry, Mr Walker...er Rob, but I'm not at work. Today is a holiday here.
> R A holiday?
> J Yes, er you know, it's Thanksgiving. I'm at my parents' house, with my family.

> R Thanksgiving. Of course. Sorry. We don't have Thanksgiving in England.
> J No problem. Listen, call me on Monday at work. No, not Monday, Tuesday.
> R Tuesday the third of December?
> J Yes.
> JM Jenny! Hurry up!
> J Er, talk to you on Tuesday. Thanks for calling.
> R Bye.
> J Bye.

You might want to point out to Sts that both Rob and Jenny use time fillers in this conversation, such as *er* and *ah*, to give themselves time to think.

b Focus on the instructions and give Sts time to read sentences 1–5.

Play the video or audio again for Sts to mark the sentences T (true) or F (false). Play again as necessary.

Get Sts to compare with a partner and then check answers.

> 1 F   2 F   3 T   4 F   5 F

Extra challenge

- Get Sts to correct the F ones:
  1 Jenny arrives in London on **12th March**.
  2 She leaves on the **19th**.
  4 Jenny is with her **family**.
  5 Rob needs to call Jenny on Tuesday **3rd** December.

Extra support

- If there's time, you could play the audio again while Sts read the script on *p.88*, so they can see what they understood / didn't understand. Translate / explain any new words or phrases.

5 ▶ USEFUL PHRASES

(3 30))) Focus on the phrases and make sure Sts understand what each one means.

Play the video or audio once the whole way through for Sts just to listen.

> (3 30)))
> See the phrases in the Student's Book on *p.45*

Now play the video or audio again, pausing after each phrase for Sts to listen and repeat.

Give further practice as necessary, modelling and drilling the pronunciation yourself, or using the video or audio, and getting choral and individual responses.

Extra challenge

- Put Sts in pairs and ask them to write a short conversation, using some of the **Useful phrases** and including at least two dates. When they have finished, get a few pairs to act out their role-play for the class. The others should listen and make a note of the dates.

6   (4 MP3))) **SONG** *Calendar Girl* ♫

For Sts of this level all song lyrics will include language that they don't know. Nevertheless Sts are usually motivated to try to understand lyrics and if you know your Sts' L1, you can use this to translate unknown words and phrases.

The activity for this song focusses on rhyming words.

This is one of the best-known songs by American singer Neil Sedaka in 1961. For copyright reasons this is a cover version.

If you want to do this song in class, use the photocopiable activity on *p.231*.

You will find the songs as MP3 files on CD4 of the Class audio CD.

(4 MP3)))

Calendar Girl

I love, I love, I love my calendar girl
Yeah, sweet calendar girl
I love, I love, I love my calendar girl
Each and every day of the year

(January)
You start the year all fine
(February)
You're my little Valentine
(March)
I'm gonna march you down the aisle
(April)
You're the Easter bunny
When you smile

Chorus
Yeah, yeah
My heart's in a whirl
I love, I love, I love my little calendar girl
Every day (every day)
Every day (every day)
Of the year (every day of the year)

(May)
Maybe if I ask your dad and mom
(June)
They'd let me take you to the junior prom
(July)
Like a firecracker
I'm aglow
(August)
When you're on the beach you steal the show

Chorus

Whoo!

Chorus

(September)
I light the candles at your sweet sixteen
(October)
Romeo and Juliet on Halloween
(November)
I'll give thanks that you belong to me
(December)
You're the present 'neath my Christmas tree

Chorus

I love, I love, I love my calendar girl
Yeah, sweet calendar girl
I love, I love, I love my calendar girl
Yeah, sweet calendar girl

G can / can't
V more verb phrases
P /æ/, /ɑː/, and /ɔ/; sentence rhythm

8A Can you start the car, please?

Lesson plan

Can is a very versatile verb in English and is used to express ability, possibility, permission, and to make requests. This lesson focusses on two of the most common uses: permission and possibility. *Can* for ability is taught in *English File* Elementary.

The lesson begins with a young British woman learning to drive, which provides the context for presenting *can / can't* for permission and possibility. Then there is a pronunciation focus on *can / can't* (particularly the difference between the positive and negative forms) and on sentence rhythm. The vocabulary focus is on more verb phrases, especially those used in the context of permission / possibility, e.g. *pay*, *park*.

Finally, Sts role-play conversations between tourists and locals about what people can / can't do in their town, and then they write a few sentences to give tourists useful information.

STUDY **LINK**
- Workbook 8A
- iTutor
- www.oup.com/elt/englishfile

Extra photocopiable activities
- **Grammar** can / can't *p.153*
- **Communicative** What's missing? *p.191* (instructions *p.168*)
- www.oup.com/elt/teacher/englishfile

Optional lead-in (books closed)
- Write on the board _____ A CAR.
- Use mime to elicit *drive* a car, *start* a car, *stop* a car, and *park* a car.
- Write them on the board. model and drill pronunciation.

1 GRAMMAR *can / can't*

a Books open. This exercise pre-teaches lexis that will be used in **b** and **c**. Focus on the instructions and make sure Sts know the meaning of *sign*. If you have any on the classroom wall, you could point to them.

Give Sts time to match the words with the pictures.

Check answers.

| A No parking | B Motorway | C Traffic lights |

b (3 32)) Focus on the instructions and if you didn't do the **Optional lead-in**, make sure Sts know the verb *drive*. Model and drill pronunciation.

You could tell Sts that if you want to drive a car or ride a motorcycle in the UK at 17, you need to pass the driving theory test first. You can do this on the internet. You also need to pass a practical driving test and you can take driving lessons with an instructor.

You phone to book lessons and the instructor comes to pick you up from your house. When you think you are ready and have passed the theory test, you can take the practical test, which you do with an examiner.

Play the audio once the whole way through for Sts to read and listen at the same time.

Give Sts time to number the pictures.

Check answers. You could explain the meaning of *book lessons* and elicit / explain what you need to do to get a driving licence (i.e. pass a theory exam and pass a practical test).

| 1 C | 2 A | 3 B |

(3 32))
See the dialogues in the Student's Book on *p.46*

c (3 33)) Focus on the question and make sure Sts understand *to pass* (a test).

Play the audio once the whole way through for Sts to listen and answer the question. Play again as necessary.

Check the answer. You could try to elicit why she doesn't pass. (Because she turns left not right / She doesn't stop at a red traffic light / She doesn't see that it is no parking). You could also try to elicit what the instructor says to her (*You need more lessons*).

No, she doesn't.

(3 33))
E = examiner, A = Anna
E OK. Turn right. Right, not left.
A Sorry!
E The traffic lights are red! Stop!... OK, can you park the car, please?
A Can I park here?
E No, you can't. Look, it's no parking. Park over there.
A Sorry. I'm very nervous.
I Well, Ms Taylor, I'm sorry, but you need more lessons.

d Tell Sts to look at dialogues 1 and 2 and to complete the chart.

Check answers.

⊟	I **can't** answer this question.
?	**Can** you come on Monday at 8.30?
✓	Yes, I **can**.
✗	No, I **can't**.

e (3 34)) Tell Sts to go to **Grammar Bank 8A** on *p.106*.

Focus on the example sentences and play the audio for Sts to listen and repeat. Pause the audio as necessary.

Go through the rules with the class using the expanded information in the **Additional grammar notes** on the next page to help you. You may want to use Sts' L1 here.

Additional grammar notes

can | can't

- *Can | can't* are used to talk about permission (*you can park there* = it is permitted) and possibility (*Can I book some driving lessons?* = Is it possible for me to book some lessons?).NB *Can* for ability is taught in *English File* Elementary.

- There are only two possible forms, *can* or *can't* (there is no change for the third person).

- The negative *can't* is a contraction of *cannot*. *Can't* is almost always used in both conversation and informal writing.

- Questions with *can* are formed by inverting the subject and the auxiliary *can*, not with *do*.

- The verb after *can* is the infinitive, e.g. *You can park here* NOT *to* + infinitive ~~You can to park here~~.

Focus on the exercises for **8A** on *p.107* and get Sts to do them individually or in pairs. If they do them individually, get them to compare answers with a partner.

Check answers, getting Sts to read the full sentences.

```
a
1  Can we sit here?
2  You can't start classes until next week.
3  James can help us tomorrow.
4  Can you come to lunch on Sunday?
5  You can use my phone if you like.
6  We can't park here.
7  Can we watch TV after dinner?
8  He can't go to the cinema tonight.
b
1  can't drive          5  can...go
2  Can...pay            6  can watch
3  Can...swim           7  Can...come
4  can walk             8  can't listen
```

Tell Sts to go back to the main lesson **8A**.

Extra support

- If you think Sts need more practice, you may want to give them the Grammar photocopiable activity at this point or leave it for later as consolidation or revision.

2 PRONUNCIATION /æ/, /ɑː/, and /ə/; sentence rhythm

Pronunciation notes

- There are two main pronunciation problems related to *can | can't*:

1 – *can* is usually unstressed = /kən/ in positive sentences, e.g. *You can take photos.* Your Sts may find this difficult to hear and to say. However, getting the stress right is vital because if they stress *can*, the listener may think they are saying a negative sentence.

  – *Can* in *Can I park here?* can be stressed /kæn/ or unstressed /kən/ depending on how fast you are speaking. It is always in positive short answers, e.g. *Yes, I can.* However, *can* is usually unstressed in questions with a question word, e.g. *Where can we park?*

2 The negative *can't* is always stressed. Not stressing it can cause a communication problem (the listener may understand *can* instead of *can't*). The pronunciation of *can't* varies among different groups of native English speakers, e.g. in standard American English it is usually pronounced /kænt/. In standard British English, it is usually pronounced /kɑːnt/, but there are regional variations. If your own pronunciation of *can't* is different from what is on the audio, you may want to model the sentences yourself. The important thing is for Sts to make sure that they stress *can't* strongly and, as ever, the aim in pronunciation is intelligibility rather than perfection.

a (3 35))) Read the **Pronunciation notes** and decide how much of the information you want to give your Sts.

Focus on the exercise and play the audio once the whole way through for Sts just to listen.

> (3 35)))
> See the sounds and sentences in the Student's Book on *p.47*

Focus on the sound picture *cat*. Play the audio to model and drill the word and the sound (pause after the sound).

Now focus on the question and answer after *cat*. Remind Sts that the pink letters are the /æ/ sound, and that the words in bigger font are stressed. Play the audio, pausing after each sentence for Sts to repeat, encouraging them to copy the rhythm.

Now repeat the same process for *car* /ɑː/ and *computer* /ə/.

If the sounds are difficult for your Sts, model them yourself so that Sts can see your mouth position, and get Sts to repeat them a few more times.

Play the audio again from the beginning, pausing after each question and answer for Sts to repeat.

Give further practice as necessary.

Finally, repeat the activity, eliciting responses from individual Sts.

Extra support

- If you are using an interactive whiteboard, you can focus on each sound individually before moving on to the next one.

b (3 36))) This section gives Sts practice in distinguishing between *can* and *can't*. Focus on the sentences and give Sts time to read them.

Play the audio once the whole way through for Sts to hear the difference between the sentences. Try to elicit what the difference is – the negative *can't* /kɑːnt/ is longer and is stressed compared to the shorter and unstressed *can* /kən/.

> (3 36)))
> See the sentences in the Student's Book on *p.47*

c (3 37)) Now tell Sts that they are going to hear only <u>one</u> of the sentences (**a** or **b**) and they have to circle the letter of the one they hear.

Play the audio, pausing for Sts to circle **a** or **b**.

Play the audio again for Sts to listen and check.

Check answers, getting Sts to read out the letter **a** or **b** and the full sentence.

1 a   2 b   3 b   4 a

> (3 37))
> 1 We can park here.   3 You can't sit here.
> 2 I can't help you.   4 Mark can go with me.

Extra challenge

• Put Sts in pairs, **A** and **B**. Get Sts **A** to say either sentence **a** or **b** for sentences 1–4 to **B**, who listens and says **a** or **b** depending on which sentence he / she understands. **A** says *yes* or *no*. Then they swap roles.

d Focus on the dialogues in **1b**. Put Sts in pairs and assign roles (Anna and the instructor / examiner). Tell Sts to practise the dialogues and then swap roles.

Monitor and make a note of any pronunciation problems. Correct any mistakes on the board.

You could get some pairs to perform the role-play for the class.

3 VOCABULARY more verb phrases

a Focus on the instructions and the signs. Tell Sts they need to complete each sentence with *can* or *can't* and a verb from the list. Go through the list of verbs and make sure Sts know what they all mean.

Focus on the example and elicit / explain the use of the impersonal form of *you* in the sentence *You can't swim here* (*you* = people in general).

Give Sts time to complete the sentences and then get them to compare with a partner.

b (3 38)) Play the audio for Sts to listen and check.

Check answers, getting Sts to read full sentences.

See script 3.38

> (3 38))
> 1   You can't swim here.
> 2   You can pay by credit card here.
> 3   You can't use your mobile phone here.
> 4   You can park here.
> 5   You can have a coffee here.
> 6   You can use the internet here.
> 7   You can't take photos here.
> 8   You can't play football here.
> 9   You can change money here.
> 10 You can't drive fast here.

c Ask Sts to cover sentences 1–10 with a piece of paper and look at the signs. Put Sts in pairs, **A** and **B**. Tell the **A**s to say the *can / can't* sentences for 1–5 and the **B**s for 6–10. Then they should swap roles.

Monitor and make a note of any pronunciation problems and drill any sentences that Sts are mispronouncing.

4 SPEAKING & WRITING

a Focus on the instructions and the questions. Give Sts time to read through them and check they understand them. Deal with any new vocabulary, e .g. *museum*. Model and drill pronunciation.

! If your Sts are all from the same town, encourage Sts **A** to pretend that he / she doesn't know anything about the town. If all the Sts are from different countries or towns / cities, get them to do the activity about their hometown, so, e.g. if a **B** student is from Lima, he / she should answer (and later write) about Lima.

Tell Sts they are going to do a role-play, where **A** is a tourist and **B** lives in the town **A** is visiting.

Put Sts in pairs, **A** and **B**. Demonstrate the activity by getting a student **A** to ask **B** the first question in each of the two sections (*Where can I have a good, cheap meal? | Can I take photos in museums?*) and encourage **B**, the local person, to give a clear answer, e.g. *You can have a good, cheap meal in X* (name of restaurant or part of town) and, if possible to add some extra information, e.g. *It's a very nice restaurant*. For the second question encourage **B** to use a short answer (*Yes, you can | No, you can't*).

Give Sts **A** time to ask their questions. Monitor and help.

Extra support

• Give Sts time to read the questions they will be asked and to think of their answers.

b Get Sts to swap roles, so **B** is now the tourist. Monitor and help.

If there's time, get one or two pairs to perform their role-play for the class.

c Focus on the instructions and the example. Make sure Sts write about their hometown.

Elicit a couple more examples from Sts and write them on the board (*You can go to good concerts*; *You can't smoke in restaurants…*).

Give Sts time to write their four sentences. Monitor and help.

Get some general feedback from the class. If all the Sts are from the same town, see if they agree with sentences that other Sts have written.

WORDS AND PHRASES TO LEARN

(4 61)) Tell Sts to go to *p.131* and focus on the **Words and phrases to learn** for **8A**. Make sure Sts understand the meaning of each phrase. If necessary, remind them of the context in which the words and phrases came up in the lesson. If you speak your Sts' L1, you might like to elicit a translation for the words / phrases for the Sts to write next to them. Play the audio, pausing after each phrase for Sts to repeat. You may also like to ask Sts to test each other on the phrases.

G like / love / hate + verb + -ing
V activities
P /ʊ/, /uː/, and /ŋ/; sentence rhythm

8B What do you like doing?

Lesson plan

This lesson focusses on free-time activities.

After learning some common free-time activities in Vocabulary, e.g. *camping, travelling*, the grammar (*like / love / hate* + verb + *-ing*) is presented through the context of a dating website. In Pronunciation, Sts practise the short and long vowel sounds /ʊ/ and /uː/, and the /ŋ/ sound, as well as sentence rhythm. They then say whether they like the activities in the Vocabulary section. Finally, Sts read various tweets where people around the world say what they like doing when they have two free hours and then write their own tweet.

STUDY LINK
- Workbook 8B
- iTutor
- iChecker on iTutor
- www.oup.com/elt/englishfile

Extra photocopiable activities

- **Grammar** *like, love, hate* + verb + *-ing p.154*
- **Communicative** What do you like doing? *p.192* (instructions *p.169*)
- www.oup.com/elt/teacher/englishfile

Optional lead-in (books closed)

- Write FREE TIME on the board and elicit the meaning (Sts saw this phrase in **7A**).

- Ask Sts *What do you do when you have free time?* and elicit verbs onto the board, e.g. *I read, I watch TV*, etc.

- Now show Sts that if you add *-ing* to the verbs, you have the word for the activity (grammatically a noun), e.g. *reading, watching TV*, etc. Show how you can change *I read, I watch TV*, etc. to *I like reading, I like watching* TV, etc.

1 VOCABULARY activities

a Books open. Focus on the task and on photo 1. Ask *What's the activity?* and elicit *travelling*. Don't ask *What's he doing?* as this grammar is not taught until **9A**.

Put Sts in pairs and give them a few minutes to match the rest of the activities with the photos.

b (3 39)) Play the audio for Sts to listen and check.

Check answers.

1	travelling	7	going to the cinema
2	reading	8	cycling
3	cooking	9	watching DVDs
4	running	10	camping
5	swimming	11	painting
6	buying clothes	12	flying

(3 39))			
10	camping	2	reading
6	buying clothes	4	running
3	cooking	5	swimming
8	cycling	11	painting
12	flying	1	travelling
7	going to the cinema	9	watching DVDs

Make sure Sts are clear about the meaning of all the activities.

Play the audio again, pausing for Sts to repeat the activities. Remind Sts that the underlined syllables are the ones that they have to stress. Highlight that the *-ing* ending is not stressed. Give further practice as necessary, modelling and drilling the pronunciation yourself, or using the audio, and getting choral and individual responses.

c Focus on the instructions. Ask Sts to cover the activities and give them time to look at the photos and remember and say the activities. They could do this individually or with a partner.

Monitor and correct any mistakes in pronunciation while Sts do this.

Then, with Sts looking only at the photos, elicit all the activities from the class, helping them with pronunciation.

2 GRAMMAR like / love / hate + verb + -ing

a Focus on the instructions. Tell Sts they are going to read information on a dating website (a website where people can find a new partner).

Focus on the website and on the verbs *love* and *hate*. Remind Sts that in English we use *love* to say, e.g. *I love you*, but we also use *love* to mean we like something very much, e.g. *I love playing the piano*. Explain / elicit that hate in I hate shopping is a stronger way of saying I don't like...

Give Sts time to read the information about the six people and deal with any vocabulary problems. Highlight the difference between *shopping* and *buying*: *shopping* = going to (usually several) shops to buy food, clothes, etc. and *buying* = giving money in exchange for something. We always put a noun (a thing) after buying, e.g. *buying CDs*, etc., but not after *shopping*.

Now ask Sts to read the information again and, in pairs, match the men and women. Explain that Sts need to complete sentences 1–3 with the name of the most suitable man.

Focus on the gapped sentence and encourage Sts to say why they think the two people are a good 'match'.

Get feedback by asking pairs to explain their choices. Encourage them to begin *We think…* and then ask the rest of the class if they agree.

1 Isabella and William because she loves playing the piano and he likes classical music, she likes doing sport and he loves running and cycling, and she doesn't like travelling and he hates flying.
2 Angie and Luke because she loves buying clothes and he loves shopping, and she likes the cinema and he likes watching DVDs.
3 Adriana and Daniel because she loves walking in the mountains and he likes camping, and she likes good food and he loves cooking.

Extra idea
• You could ask Sts if they think internet dating is a good way to find a partner, and if they know anyone who met their partner through a dating website.

b (3 40)》 Tell Sts to go to **Grammar Bank 8B** on *p.106*.

Focus on the example sentences and play the audio for Sts to listen and repeat. Pause the audio as necessary.

Go through the rules with the class using the expanded information in the **Additional grammar notes** below to help you. You may want to use Sts' L1 here.

Additional grammar notes
like / love / hate + verb + *-ing*

• When another verb follows *love*, *like*, or *don't like*, the *-ing* form is normally used, e.g. *camping*, *cooking*, not the infinitive, e.g. NOT ~~I like camp~~.

• *to* + the infinitive after *like* and *love* is sometimes used (especially in US English), e.g. *I like to swim*, but it is easier for Sts at this level to learn the most common form.

• Highlight that *I hate getting up early* is a stronger way of saying that you don't like getting up early.

Spelling rules
– most verbs simply add *-ing* to the infinitive to make the *-ing* form, e.g. *reading*, *watching*.
– verbs ending in *y* don't change from *y* to an *i* (as they do in 3rd person singular, present tense), e.g. *fly – flying* NOT ~~fliing~~.
– verbs ending in *e* drop the *e* before adding *-ing*, e.g. *cycle – cycling*.
– verbs ending in consonant + one vowel + consonant: double the final consonant and add *-ing*, e.g. *running*, *swimming*.

Focus on the exercises for **8B** on *p.107* and get Sts to do them individually or in pairs. If they do them individually, get them to compare answers with a partner.

Check answers. For **a**, get Sts to write the answers on the board or elicit how to spell each verb. For **b**, get Sts to read the full sentences.

a
1 meeting   5 crying
2 stopping   6 writing
3 buying   7 running
4 going   8 cycling

b
1 She likes cooking.
2 Do you like travelling?
3 I love shopping for presents.
4 They don't like watching TV.
5 Does your father like playing chess?
6 I don't like doing exercise.
7 My mother loves reading detective novels.
8 We don't like going to bed late.

Tell Sts to go back to the main lesson **8B**.

Extra support
• If you think Sts need more practice, you may want to give them the Grammar photocopiable activity at this point or leave it for later as consolidation or revision.

3 PRONUNCIATION & SPEAKING /ʊ/, /uː/, and /ŋ/; sentence rhythm

Pronunciation notes
/ʊ/, /uː/, and /ŋ/

• Remind Sts that the two dots in the symbol /uː/ mean that it's a long sound.

• You may want to highlight the following sound–spelling rules:
  – the most common pronunciation of *oo* is the long sound /uː/, e.g. *food*, *school*, *soon*. However, *oo* is sometimes pronounced using the short /ʊ/, e.g. *good*, *book*, *look*.
  – the letters *-ng* at the end of a word (and without an *e* after them) are always pronounced /ŋ/ in English, e.g. *thing*, *wrong*. However, *-nge* is usually pronounced /ndʒ/, e.g. *change*.

Sentence rhythm
• For information on **Sentence rhythm**, see the **Pronunciation notes** in 2B.

a (3 41)》 Read the **Pronunciation notes** and decide how much of the information you want to give your Sts.

Focus on the exercise and play the audio once the whole way through for Sts just to listen.

(3 41)》
See the words and sounds in the Student's Book on *p.49*

Focus on the sound picture *bull*. Play the audio to model and drill the word and the sound (pause after the sound).

Now focus on the words after *bull*. Remind Sts that the pink letters are the /ʊ/ sound. Play the audio, pausing after each word for Sts to listen and repeat.

Now repeat the same process for *boot* /uː/ and *singer* /ŋ/.

If these sounds are difficult for your Sts, model them yourself so that Sts can see your mouth position, and get Sts to repeat them a few more times.

Play the audio again from the beginning, pausing after each group of words for Sts to repeat.

Give further practice as necessary.

Finally, get Sts, in pairs, to practise saying the words.

Extra support

* If you are using an interactive whiteboard, you can focus on each sound individually before moving on to the next one.

b Focus on the conversation. Remind Sts that the words in bigger font are the ones which are stressed (because they carry the important information). Also remind them that the underlined syllables in the multi-syllable words are stressed more. Play the audio once the whole way through for Sts to read and listen at the same time. Make sure they understand it all.

> (3 42)))
> See the conversation in the Student's Book on *p.49*

Now play the audio again, pausing after each sentence or question for Sts to repeat. Encourage them to copy the rhythm on the audio by stressing the bigger words in bold more strongly and by saying the others more lightly and quickly.

Now get Sts to read the conversation in pairs. Then get them to swap roles.

c Focus on the instructions, the example, and the photos in **1a**. In the examples highlight the use of *What about you?* to return the question and the use of *Me, too!* in the answer.

You could demonstrate the activity by telling Sts whether you like / love or don't like / hate the first three or four activities.

Put Sts in pairs and give them a few minutes to talk about the rest of the photos. Monitor and make a note of any difficulties Sts are having.

Highlight any general mistakes on the board.

Get some feedback from various Sts.

4 READING & WRITING

a Focus on the title and introduction, and read it with the class. Make sure Sts understand *tweets* (= posts on the social media site Twitter) and *all over the world*.

Now focus on the tweets and the **Glossary**. Model and drill the phrases in the glossary.

Play the audio for Sts to read and listen to the tweets. Then go through them and elicit / explain any new vocabulary e.g. *dry, from cover to cover, the country, garden, a series*, etc.

> (3 43)))
> See the tweets in the Student's Book on *p.49*

Finally, tell Sts to tick two tweets where they really like the activities, too. NB Some of the people like doing two different things, but Sts can tick the person even if they only like doing one of the things.

b Put Sts in pairs and get them to compare their answers.

Get feedback first by finding out if any pairs ticked exactly the same two people, then by asking individual Sts who they ticked and why, e.g. *David – because I like going for a run* (too).

c Focus on the title again. Tell Sts to write their own answer to the question on a piece of paper, but not to put their name on it. Monitor and help with vocabulary and spelling.

Collect the answers and shuffle them. Read out each answer in turn and then ask the class *Who do you think it is?* Elicit from the class the name of the student who wrote it.

Extra idea

* With a small class you could number the answers and pin them on the wall for Sts to read and guess the name of the student who wrote each one. Then check answers to find out who guessed the most correctly.

WORDS AND PHRASES TO LEARN

(4 61))) Tell Sts to go to *p.131* and focus on the **Words and phrases to learn** for **8B**. Make sure Sts understand the meaning of each phrase. If necessary, remind them of the context in which the words and phrases came up in the lesson. If you speak your Sts' L1, you might like to elicit a translation for the words / phrases for the Sts to write next to them. Play the audio, pausing after each phrase for Sts to repeat. You may also like to ask Sts to test each other on the phrases.

For instructions on how to use these pages see *p.36*.

STUDY LINK
• iTutor

Test and Assessment CD-ROM

• **Quick Test 8**
• **File Test 8**

GRAMMAR

1	a	6	a	11	a
2	b	7	b	12	a
3	a	8	b	13	b
4	b	9	a	14	b
5	a	10	b	15	a

VOCABULARY

a 1 play
  2 pay
  3 walk, ski
  4 meet, go
  5 go, swim
  6 do, play

b 1 seventh
  2 twelfth
  3 twentieth
  4 thirty-first
  5 March
  6 May
  7 July
  8 November

c 1 cooking
  2 camping
  3 travelling
  4 flying
  5 painting
  6 running
  7 buying clothes

PRONUNCIATION

a 1 <u>thir</u>tieth
  2 <u>Jan</u>uary
  3 <u>Ju</u>ly
  4 seven<u>teenth</u>
  5 <u>sin</u>gle

b /aʊ/ owl   /æ/ cat   /ʊ/ bull
  /θ/ thumb   /ɑː/ car

CAN YOU UNDERSTAND THIS TEXT?

a Sts should tick 2, 5, and 7.

b 1 St George's Market
  2 The *Titanic* museum
  3 World class golf

VIDEO CAN YOU UNDERSTAND THESE PEOPLE?

3 44))) 1 b   2 c   3 a   4 c   5 b

3 44)))
See the script in the Student's Book on *p.88*.

Remind Sts that they can watch the short film on *iTutor*.

VIDEO Available as MP3 on CD4

Short film: I love London

Hi, I'm Helen. I'm from Newcastle in the north of England. Now I live in London.

I study here at UCL in Bloomsbury. I love Bloomsbury. It has a lot of great places to eat and drink. My favourite coffee shop is 'TAP coffee' in Tottenham Court Road. It's a very friendly coffee shop. The atmosphere is really relaxing. I think it has the best coffee in London.

There are a lot of great cafés and restaurants in Bloomsbury, too. This is 'Planet Organic'. It's my favourite place to eat. And it has a supermarket. But I don't always have the money to go here. So, I often come to the food market in Goodge Street for lunch. I can get a great meal for about £5. That's really cheap for London! The food is delicious, too. You can eat food from all over the world.

Bloomsbury is also famous for the British Museum. I sometimes come here in my free time. There are often great exhibitions. At the moment you can see Vikings and Ancient Egyptian mummies.

A lot of famous writers lived in Bloomsbury. It was the home of Virginia Woolf and Charles Dickens.

My favourite shop is the Oxfam Bloomsbury Bookshop. You can buy a lot of books here. They're all very cheap!

Bloomsbury is also near Covent Garden, where there are a lot of great clothes shops.

In this one small area I'm just minutes away from lots of interesting places.

Now, it's time for another coffee. See you later!

G present continuous
V common verb phrases 2: travelling
P sentence rhythm

9A What are they doing?

Lesson plan

In this lesson, Sts learn a new verb form, the present continuous used to talk about actions happening now.

The lesson begins with a presentation of the new grammar through a series of telephone calls between a woman who is travelling and her boyfriend, who wants to talk to her quite urgently. Then, in Pronunciation Sts practise sentence rhythm in present continuous sentences. In Vocabulary Sts learn common verb phrases related to travel and then they listen to some short travel-related conversations and do two comprehension tasks. In Reading Sts read and match phone messages sent between two people trying to meet in front of a cinema. The lesson ends with Sts describing photos to each other and talking about what they think members of their family are doing at the moment.

STUDY **LINK**
- Workbook 9A
- iTutor
- www.oup.com/elt/englishfile

Extra photocopiable activities

- **Grammar** present continuous *p.155*
- **Communicative** Guess what I'm doing! *p.193* (instructions *p.169*)
- **Vocabulary** Common verb phrases 2: travelling *p.224* (instructions *p.209*)
- www.oup.com/elt/teacher/englishfile

Optional lead-in (books closed)

- Write these phrases on the board and the list of verbs underneath:
  1 _____ THE DOOR
  2 _____ TO THE AIRPORT
  3 _____ AT PASSPORT CONTROL
  4 _____ ME LATER
  5 _____ A HOTEL
  CALL, CHECK INTO, CLOSE, DRIVE, WAIT

- Then get Sts to complete the phrases with the correct verb.

  1 **close** the door
  2 **drive** to the airport
  3 **wait** at passport control
  4 **call** me later
  5 **check** into a hotel

- Make sure Sts understand the meaning of all the phrases. Model and drill pronunciation and then get Sts to open their Student Book's and do the presentation.

1 GRAMMAR present continuous

a (3 46)) Focus on the pictures, the phone calls, and the instructions, making sure Sts know what *a phone call* is. You might also want to remind Sts of the meaning of the verb *to call*. Elicit where Mia is in each picture (at passport control, in her car, on the plane, at the hotel). If Sts ask why we use the different prepositions *in*, *on*, and *at*, tell them they will focus on this later in **10B** and for the moment just to learn the phrases.

Get Sts to cover the phone calls and play the audio once the whole way through for them to listen and number the pictures.

Check answers.

1 B	2 C	3 A	4 D

> (3 46))
> See the phone calls in the Student's Book on *p.52*

Tell Sts to uncover the phone calls and play the audio again, so they can read and listen again.

Deal with any vocabulary problems that arose.

b (3 47)) Focus on the question and do this as an open-class activity. Don't tell Sts if they are right or not.

Play the audio for Sts to listen and check their ideas.

Check the answer, making Sts know what *to leave someone* means.

> (3 47))
> *Twenty minutes later*
> **Simon** Hello?
> **Mia**   Hello? Simon? I can talk now.
> **Simon** OK. Listen, Mia. I don't know how to say this...
> **Mia**   What is it?
> **Simon** I'm sorry, but... I'm leaving you.

c Focus on the instructions. Give Sts time to read all the highlighted words in the phone calls and then circle **a** or **b**.

Check the answer.

> b (now)

d (3 48)) Tell Sts to go to **Grammar Bank 9A** on *p.108*.

Focus on the example sentences and play the audio for Sts to listen and repeat. Pause the audio as necessary.

Go through the rules with the class using the expanded information in the **Additional grammar notes** on the next page to help you. You may want to use Sts' L1 here.

Additional grammar notes
present continuous (*be* + verb + *-ing*)

* Highlight that when we talk about activities we are doing right now, we need to use the present continuous, <u>not</u> the present simple, e.g. *I'm watching TV now*. NOT ~~I watch TV now~~.

* Other typical mistakes Sts make are in word order, e.g. *You're working now? What you are doing?*, or leaving out the verb *be*, e.g. *I working now*.

* ! You may want to point out to Sts that some verbs, e.g. *like* and *love*, are not usually used in the present continuous. They are normally used in the present simple, e.g. *I like this music*, NOT ~~I'm liking this music~~.

Spelling rules

* Highlight that the spelling rules for the *-ing* form in the present continuous are the same as those Sts learnt for activities, e.g. *camping, travelling*, in **8B** (See the **Additional grammar notes** in **8B** on *p.98*).

Focus on the exercises for **9A** on *p.109* and get Sts to do them individually or in pairs. If they do them individually, get them to compare answers with a partner.

Check answers, getting Sts to read the full sentences.

a
1	'm driving	4	's playing
2	're doing	5	're studying
3	's working	6	're swimming

b
1 're sitting
2 isn't watching, 's sleeping
3 are...doing, 'm shopping
4 'm going, 'm not working
5 Is...doing, 's playing
6 'm not reading, 'm watching
7 's talking
8 Are...having, 're having
9 's visiting, 'm calling
10 Are...getting

Tell Sts to go back to the main lesson **9A**.

Extra support

* If you think Sts need more practice, you may want to give them the Grammar photocopiable activity at this point or leave it for later as consolidation or revision.

e (3 49))) Explain to Sts that they are going to hear some sounds that represent things that Mia is doing. They have to use the present continuous to describe the actions.

Play the audio for the sound effects for 1, then pause the audio and focus on the example.

Now play each sound effect and then pause the audio to give Sts time to write their answers.

Get Sts to compare with a partner, then play the audio again, pausing after each sound effect, and elicit answers.

2 She's crying.
3 She's having a drink. / She's drinking something.
4 She's eating chocolate / something.
5 She's watching TV.
6 She's phoning a friend.
7 She's having a shower.
8 She's getting a taxi.
9 She's dancing.

(3 49)))
(Sound effects)
1 *Mia opening door to hotel room*
2 *Mia crying*
3 *Mia pouring something into a glass and drinking it*
4 *Mia unwrapping and eating some chocolate*
5 *Mia turning on the TV*
6 *Mia phoning a friend* 'Hi Louise. It's me. Mia... Yes I'm in Paris. Are you free this evening?'
7 *Mia having a shower*
8 *Mia getting a taxi, greeting taxi driver in French and asking for a nightclub*
9 'Come on, let's dance!' *Mia and Louise dancing*

---

2 PRONUNCIATION sentence rhythm

Pronunciation notes

* Remind Sts that words that carry the important information are said more strongly than others, e.g. in <u>What</u> are you <u>doing</u>?, I'm <u>making</u> the <u>dinner</u>. (The underlined words are the ones which communicate the message.)

* To pronounce well, with a good rhythm, Sts need to stress these words more strongly and pronounce unstressed words as lightly as possible. Obviously the ability to do this will improve with time and is not something Sts can pick up immediately.

* Being aware of the way important words are stressed in English will also help Sts with understanding English as these are the words they need to listen out for when listening.

a (3 50))) Focus on the conversation and remind Sts that the words in bigger bold print are stressed.

Play the audio once the whole way through for Sts just to listen.

(3 50)))
See the conversation in the Student's Book on *p.53*

Now play it again, pausing after each question or sentence for Sts to listen and repeat. Encourage them to copy the rhythm. on the audio by stressing the bigger words in bold more strongly and by saying the others more lightly and quickly.

b Put Sts in pairs and get them to practise the phone calls between Mia and Simon in **1a**.

Make sure they swap roles. Monitor and help.

You could get some pairs to perform the phone calls for the class.

Extra challenge

* Get Sts to improvise the last phone call where Simon says he is leaving Mia.

c Focus on the instructions and the two speech bubbles with the questions.

Put Sts in pairs, **A** and **B**. Get Sts **A** to ask **B** about photos 1–3 and Sts **B** to ask **A** about photos 4–6.

Check by getting different pairs to ask and answer about each photo.

3 VOCABULARY common verb phrases 2: travelling

a Focus on the instructions and elicit answers from the class.

> In picture D Mia is checking into a hotel. Simon is calling her.

b Tell Sts to go to **Vocabulary Bank** *Common verb phrases* **2** on *p.126*.

3 51)) Look at **2 Travelling** and focus on **a**. Play the audio and get Sts to repeat the verbs and verb phrases in chorus and individually as necessary. Model and drill any words which are difficult for your Sts and give further practice.

> **3 51))**
> See the common verb phrases in the Student's Book on *p.126*

Now focus on **b**. Get Sts to cover the words, look at the photos, and say the verbs or verb phrases. They could do this individually or with a partner.

Now focus on **c**. Get Sts to cover the words and look at the questions *What's she / he doing?* Model and drill the questions in chorus and individually.

Put Sts in pairs and give them time to ask and answer questions about the photos. Monitor and help, correcting pronunciation where necessary.

Tell Sts to go back to the main lesson **9A**.

Extra support

• If you think Sts need more practice, you may want to give them the Vocabulary photocopiable activity at this point or leave it for later as consolidation or revision.

4 LISTENING

a **3 52))** Focus on the instructions and 1–4. You could point out that in 1 and 2 the auxiliary is already there for Sts.

Play the audio once the whole way through for Sts just to listen.

> **3 52))**
> (script in Student's Book on *p.89*)
> **W = woman, M = man**
> 1
> **W** Oh look! An Inter Milan football shirt. It's perfect for Johnny!
> **M** Yes, good idea. Oh...it's very expensive.
> **W** Football shirts are always expensive. OK. What can we get for Jessica?
> **M** She likes football, too.
> **W** Yes, but she never wears football shirts. What about this bag?
> **M** I don't know. Does she like bags?
> **W** All girls like bags...

> 2
> **W** Tom, do we need swimming things?
> **M** Yes, the hotel has a swimming pool. Can you see my camera?
> **W** Yes, here it is. Do you want me to put the camera in the suitcase or in your bag?
> **M** In the suitcase, please. My bag isn't very big and it's quite full.
> **W** OK.
> 3
> **W** Good morning. How can I help you?
> **M** I need a car for three days.
> **W** What kind of car are you looking for?
> **M** A small car. It's just for me.
> **W** Automatic or manual?
> **M** Manual, please.
> **W** Can I see your driving licence?
> **M** Yes, here you are.
> 4
> **M** Is that a number 13?
> **W** Yes. I think it is. No, it's a 23.
> **M** Another 23? I don't believe it! That's the third one. And no 13...
> **W** Another one's coming now. Let's see. Yes. That's a 13.
> **M** At last!

Now play it again, pausing after each conversation to give Sts time to write. Tell Sts they should use verb phrases they have just learnt in the **Vocabulary Bank** *Common verb phrases 2: travelling*.

Get Sts to compare with a partner and then check answers.

> 1 The man and the woman are **buying presents**.
> 2 The woman is **packing** (the suitcase).
> 3 The man **is renting a car**.
> 4 The man and the woman **are waiting for a bus**.

b Focus on sentences 1–4. Put Sts in pairs and give them time to think about what the correct words are, but tell them <u>not</u> to write them yet.

Play the audio again, pausing after each conversation to give Sts time to circle the answer.

Get Sts to compare with a partner and then check answers.

> 1 They buy **a football shirt** for Johnny and **a bag** for Jessica.
> 2 They need **swimming** things and the man wants to take his **camera**.
> 3 The man wants a **small**, manual car for **three** days.
> 4 The first bus that comes is a number **23**. They want a number **13**.

Extra support

• If there's time, you could play the audio again while Sts read the script on *p.89*, so they can see what they understood / didn't understand. Translate / explain any new words or phrases.

5 READING

a Focus on the instructions and make sure Sts understand the situation. Tell Sts that Mike and Lina are friends who are going to the cinema, but they are not together now, so they are texting / messaging each other.

Make it clear that Mike's messages are in the correct order and that Lina answers each one of the messages, so Sts should write 1 next to Lina's response to Mike's first message. Give Sts time to read Mike's messages and then number Lina's messages.

Get Sts to compare with a partner.

b (3 53))) Play the audio for Sts to listen and check.

Check answers.

> 1 Me, too. I'm walking to the bus stop. Are you getting the bus, too?
> 2 Yes, see you.
> 3 Sorry, we're in a lot of traffic. There in five minutes.
> 4 I'm arriving at the cinema now. Where are you?
> 5 Yes! Can you see me? I'm walking towards you now!

(3 53)))

M = Mike, L = Lina

1
M Hi. I'm just leaving the house now.
L Me, too. I'm walking to the bus stop. Are you getting the bus, too?

2
M No, I'm not. I'm cycling. See you in twenty minutes?
L Yes, see you.

3
M Where are you? I'm at the cinema, but I can't see you. I'm waiting outside.
L Sorry, we're in a lot of traffic. There in five minutes.

4
M It's really cold outside. I'm going in.
L I'm arriving at the cinema now. Where are you?

5
M I'm standing near the box office. I'm wearing a black jacket. Can you see me?
L Yes! Can you see me? I'm walking towards you now!

---

c Focus on the instructions and give Sts time to find the word or phrase for definitions 1–6.

Get Sts to compare with a partner.

d (3 54))) Play the audio for Sts to listen and check.

Check answers.

See script 3.54

(3 54)))
1 bus stop
2 box office
3 jacket
4 towards
5 traffic
6 outside

Deal with any vocabulary problems that arose.

6 SPEAKING

a Put Sts in pairs, **A** and **B**, and get them to sit face-to-face if possible.

Tell them to go to **Communication** *The same or different?*, **A** on *p.78* and **B** on *p.82*.

Go over the instructions and make sure Sts understand what they have to do.

When they have finished, get them to describe some of the pictures.

Tell Sts to go back to the main lesson **9A**.

b Focus on the instructions and example. Get Sts to write the names of people in their family and as they write the names, tell them to think about what the people are doing now. If they don't know, tell them to guess.

Put Sts in pairs and get them to tell their partner about the people on their lists.

Get some feedback from various Sts and find out if any of the people are doing the same thing.

Extra idea

- Sts can do this by asking and answering questions with their partner. Model a conversation like this one and write it on the board for Sts to refer to.
  A (looking at **B**'s list of names) *Who's Maria?*
  B *She's my mother.*
  A *What do you think she's doing now?*
  B *I think she's working.*

WORDS AND PHRASES TO LEARN

(4 61))) Tell Sts to go to *p.131* and focus on the **Words and phrases to learn** for 9A. Make sure Sts understand the meaning of each phrase. If necessary, remind them of the context in which the words and phrases came up in the lesson. If you speak your Sts' L1, you might like to elicit a translation for the words / phrases for the Sts to write next to them. Play the audio, pausing after each phrase for Sts to repeat. You may also like to ask Sts to test each other on the phrases.

G present continuous or present simple?
V clothes
P /ɜː/, /iː/, /e/, and /eə/

9B Working undercover

Lesson plan

This lesson helps Sts understand the difference between the present continuous and the present simple.

The lesson begins with a presentation of the grammar based on an episode of the TV programme *Undercover Boss* (where a boss works 'undercover' to check on his workers). This leads into a reading activity where Sts find out more about what happens to the undercover boss. In Vocabulary Sts learn some common items of clothing. They then listen to a student who is doing work experience in a clothes shop. In Pronunciation, Sts practise four more vowel sounds: /ɜː/, /iː/, /e/, and /eə/. Finally, the new grammar and vocabulary is pulled together in a speaking activity where Sts talk about clothes they are wearing at the moment as compared to clothes they wear in different seasons and for particular occasions.

STUDY LINK
- Workbook 9B
- iTutor
- iChecker on iTutor
- www.oup.com/elt/englishfile

Extra photocopiable activities
- **Grammar** present continuous or present simple? *p.156*
- **Communicative** A board game *p.194* (instructions *p.169*)
- www.oup.com/elt/teacher/englishfile

Optional lead-in (books closed)
- Write on the board JOBS IN A HOTEL.
- Elicit from Sts different jobs and write them on the board, e.g. receptionist, waiter / waitress, chef, cleaner, etc.
- Then ask what the word is for the person in charge of the hotel and elicit *the manager*. Model and drill pronunciation of all the jobs.

1 GRAMMAR present continuous or present simple?

a **3 55** Focus on the title, *Undercover Boss*, and tell Sts this is a TV show. Explain / elicit the meaning of the title and ask Sts if this programme is also on TV in their country. Highlight that *boss* is an informal way of saying the person who is in charge of a group of workers or an organization.

! Don't ask Sts their opinion of this kind of show as they will do this later in the lesson.

Play the audio once the whole way through for Sts to read and listen at the same time.

Give Sts time to answer the question.

Check the answer. You might want to explain what a *hotel chain* is.

> He wants to know more about his workers and about the problems in his hotels.

> **3 55**
> See *Undercover Boss* in the Student's Book on *p.54*

b Before Sts do the exercise focus on the words *bedroom* and *kitchen* in the **Glossary** on *p.55* and make sure Sts understand their meanings. Model and drill pronunciation.

Now focus on the instructions and the three verbs in the list. Tell Sts to read all four bullet points in the text first as this will help them when completing the gaps. You could explain / elicit the meaning of the noun *a suit* /suːt/ and the phrase *to wash dishes*. Model and drill pronunciation.

Give Sts time to complete the sentences with the verbs in either the present simple or the present continuous.

Play the audio again for Sts to listen and check.

Check answers and elicit which verb form is used in each one and why.

> 1 's wearing (present continuous because it's just today, not usually)
> 2 has (present simple because it's usually)
> 3 's working (present continuous because it's just today, not usually)

c Focus on the instructions. Tell Sts to look at the four completed bullet points in the text to help them.

Check answers.

> Use the present simple to talk about **every day**.
> Use the present continuous to talk about **today** / **now**.

d (3 56)) Tell Sts to go to **Grammar Bank 9B** on *p.108*.

Focus on the example sentences and play the audio for Sts to listen and repeat. Pause the audio as necessary.

Go through the rules with the class using the expanded information in the **Additional grammar notes** below to help you. You may want to use Sts' L1 here.

> **Additional grammar notes**
> **present continuous or present simple?**
>
> • It is important to make clear that there is a definite distinction in the use of the two present forms in English, which may (or may not) exist in your Sts' own language(s).
>
> • In English you have to use the present continuous (not the present simple) to talk about things which are happening at the moment of speaking, e.g. *Hello! What are you doing?* NOT *Hello! What do you do?*
>
> • You have to use the present simple (not the present continuous) for habitual actions, e.g. *I live in Berlin.* NOT *I'm living in Berlin.*
>
> • If you know your Sts' L1, you might want to make some comparisons.
>
> • NB The use of the present continuous with a future meaning is taught in **12B**.

Focus on the exercises for **9B** on *p.109* and get Sts to do them individually or in pairs. If they do them individually, get them to compare answers with a partner. Tell Sts to refer to the spelling rules if they are not sure how to spell the *-ing* forms.

Check answers, getting Sts to read out the full sentences.

> a
> 1 I'm working
> 2 Are you doing, I'm playing
> 3 She works
> 4 We're staying
> 5 are you driving, I'm not driving, I'm talking
> 6 rains
> 7 have, I'm having
> b
> 1 is raining
> 2 have
> 3 're skiing
> 4 Are...watching, 'm doing
> 5 get up, have
> 6 is travelling
> 7 do...go
> 8 's wearing
> 9 are...going, go

Tell Sts to go back to the main lesson **9B**.

Extra support

• If you think Sts need more practice, you may want to give them the Grammar photocopiable activity at this point or leave it for later as consolidation or revision.

2 READING

a (3 57)) Focus on the photos and elicit that the man is David, the 'undercover boss'.

Now focus on the instructions. Make sure Sts know the meaning of *summary* and point out the **Glossary**.

Give Sts time to read sentences 1–8 and make sure they understand them.

Now play the audio once the whole way through for Sts to read and listen at the same time.

Give Sts time to read the text again if necessary and mark 1–9 T (true) or F (false).

Get Sts to compare with a partner and then check answers.

> 1 T 2 F 3 T 4 T 5 F 6 F 7 F 8 T 9 F

> (3 57))
> See *Undercover Boss: Episode 1 Summary* in the Student's Book on *pp.54–55*

Extra challenge

• Get Sts to correct the false sentences:
  2 On Monday David is **washing the dishes** in the kitchen.
  5 David is **serving** breakfast.
  6 The workers only have **15 minutes / a quarter of an hour** to clean the rooms.
  7 David **thinks** cleaning is hard work.
  9 The **good** workers get more money.

b Focus on the highlighted words and phrases and get Sts to guess their meaning with a partner.

Get feedback. Get Sts to check words they couldn't guess in a dictionary or if dictionaries are not available, elicit / explain the meanings. Do this in English if possible, or mime, or use the board.

c Do this as an open-class activity.

3 VOCABULARY clothes

a Focus on the topic and model and drill the word *clothes* /kləʊðz/.

Now focus on the instructions and point out that the first one has been done for them. You could do this as an open-class activity or put Sts in pairs. If you know your Sts' L1, you could let them translate the words. If not, Sts could point to the clothes in the class or draw a picture.

If Sts worked in pairs, check answers.

> Sts should underline: jeans, T-shirt, uniform, jacket, hat.

b **3 58**))) Focus on the instructions and give Sts time to match the words with the pictures.

Get Sts to compare with a partner.

Now play the audio for Sts to listen and check.

Check answers.

1	jeans	6	shoes
2	sweater	7	dress
3	jacket	8	T-shirt
4	skirt	9	suit
5	trousers	10	shirt

> **3 58**)))
> | | | | |
> |---|---|---|---|
> | 7 | dress | 2 | sweater |
> | 4 | skirt | 10 | shirt |
> | 3 | jacket | 8 | T-shirt |
> | 9 | suit | 6 | shoes |
> | 1 | jeans | 5 | trousers |

4 LISTENING

a **3 59**))) Focus on the instructions. You could tell Sts in their L1 that the expression *work experience* is widely used to mean volunteer work that is commonly intended for young people – often students – to get a feel for professional working environments. Most students go out on work experience for one or two weeks in a year and do not get paid. Make sure Sts understand the task.

Play the audio once the whole way through for Sts to listen.

Check the answer.

> She is positive.

> **3 59**)))
> (script in Student's Book on *p.89*)
> **I = interviewer, S = Sandra**
> **I** Hi, Sandra. Tell us a bit about your experience. Where are you working?
> **S** I'm working in a clothes shop called *fat face*.
> **I** What kind of clothes does *fat face* have?
> **S** Er, well, clothes for men and women, informal clothes, trousers, T-shirts, sweaters, things like that.
> **I** What do you do every day?
> **S** Well, er, I help the customers to find the clothes that they're looking for. It's a big shop and it has a lot of things. People sometimes can't see the things that they want.
> **I** Do you like working there?
> **S** Yes, I love it. The people are really nice to me. I'm making a lot of new friends.
> **I** Is there anything you don't like?
> **S** Well, we can't sit down, we're standing up all the time. So that's quite hard.
> **I** But in general you're happy?
> **S** Oh yes. And when my two weeks finish they say I can work here on Saturdays! That's great for me. I really like working in a clothes shop.
> **I** Do you wear a uniform?
> **S** No, we don't. We wear clothes from the shop.
> **I** Are the clothes that you're wearing today from *fat face*?
> **S** Yes, they are!

b Focus on the instructions and questions 1–7. Give Sts time to read them.

Now play the audio again for Sts to listen and answer the questions. Play again as necessary.

Get Sts to compare with a partner and then check answers.

> 1 clothes for men and women, informal clothes, trousers, T-shirts, sweaters, things like that
> 2 She helps the customers find the clothes that they're looking for.
> 3 The people are really nice to her. She's making a lot of new friends.
> 4 She can't sit down.
> 5 She can work at the shop on Saturdays.
> 6 No, she doesn't.
> 7 from the shop / *fat face*

Extra support

- If there's time, you could play the audio again while Sts read the script on *p.89*, so they can see what they understood / didn't understand. Translate / explain any new words or phrases.

c Put Sts in pairs or small groups and get them to discuss the question.

Get some feedback from various pairs or groups.

Extra support

- Do this as an open-class activity.

5 PRONUNCIATION & SPEAKING /ɜː/, /iː/, /e/, and /eə/

Pronunciation notes

- /ɜː/ For information on this sound, see the **Pronunciation notes** in **6A**.

- /iː/ For information on this sound, see the **Pronunciation notes** in **1A**.

- /e/ A single letter *e* is <u>usually</u> pronounced /e/, e.g. *ten*. Sometimes the vowels *ea* also have this sound, e.g. *breakfast*.

- /eə/ For information on this sound, see the **Pronunciation notes** in **7A**.

a **3 60**))) Read the **Pronunciation notes** and decide how much of the information you want to give your Sts.

Focus on the exercise and play the audio once the whole way through for Sts just to listen.

> **3 60**)))
> See the words and sounds in the Student's Book on *p.55*

Focus on the sound picture *bird*. Play the audio to model and drill the word and the sound (pause after the sound).

Now focus on the words after *bird*. Remind Sts that the pink letters are the /ɜː/ sound. Play the audio, pausing after each word for Sts to listen and repeat.

Now repeat the same process for *tree* /iː/, *egg* /e/, and *chair* /eə/.

If these sounds are difficult for your Sts, model them yourself so that Sts can see your mouth position, and get Sts to repeat them a few more times.

Play the audio again from the beginning, pausing after each group of words for Sts to repeat.

Give further practice as necessary.

Finally, get Sts, in pairs, to practise saying the words.

b **3 61**))) Focus on the three sentences and play the audio
once the whole way through for Sts just to listen.

> **3 61**)))
> See the sentences in the Student's Book on *p.55*

Now play the audio again, pausing after each sentence
for Sts to listen and repeat.

Put Sts in pairs and get them to practise saying the
sentences.

c Go through questions 1–3 with the class, checking Sts
understand the lexis, e.g. *summer*.

Put Sts in pairs and get them to discuss the questions,
giving as much information as possible.

Get some feedback from the class.

d Do this as an open-class activity. Sts could start by
saying what you are wearing and what you usually
wear.

WORDS AND PHRASES TO LEARN

4 61))) Tell Sts to go to *p.131* and focus on the
Words and phrases to learn for **9B**. Make sure Sts
understand the meaning of each phrase. If necessary,
remind them of the context in which the words and
phrases came up in the lesson. If you speak your Sts'
L1, you might like to elicit a translation for the words /
phrases for the Sts to write next to them. Play the
audio, pausing after each phrase for Sts to repeat.
You may also like to ask Sts to test each other on the
phrases.

PRACTICAL ENGLISH
Episode 5 Would you like to come?

Lesson plan

In this **Practical English** lesson, Sts learn to make invitations and offers using *Would you...?*, and to accept or decline these politely. These skills are presented in the context of informal social conversations in which Rob invites a friend to a football match and once there offers to buy food and a drink. In Pronunciation, Sts practise making invitations and offers using *Would you like...?*, with a focus on sentence rhythm and linking. Continuing the theme of invitations, Sts then watch or listen to Jenny meeting an ex-boyfriend in the street. In Speaking & Writing, Sts practise inviting each other to a party, as well as accepting and declining an invitation – they do this first orally and then in writing. Finally, the song at the end of the lesson is *Song I'd Like to Sing*.

STUDY LINK
- **Workbook** Would you like to come?
- **iTutor**
- www.oup.com/elt/englishfile

Extra photocopiable activities

- **Communicative** Would you like to...? *p.195* (instructions *p.170*)
- **Song** *Song I'd Like to Sing p.232* (instructions *p.227*)

Test and Assessment CD-ROM

- Quick Test 9
- File Test 9
- www.oup.com/elt/teacher/englishfile

Optional lead-in (books closed)

- Pretend to have two tickets for something that you think many of your Sts would like to do (e.g. a football match or a concert involving a well-known singer or group).

- Invite individual Sts using *Would you like to (come with me to a X concert) on Saturday night?* and teach the answers *I'd love to. Thanks. | I'm sorry I can't. I'm busy on Saturday night.*

- Write these on the board and model and drill pronunciation.

- Finally, when you have invited several people, write the question on the board, and model and drill pronunciation.

1 ◼◢ INVITING AND OFFERING

a (3 62)) Books open. Focus on the task and get Sts to cover the conversations and focus on the photos.

Play the video or audio once the whole way through for Sts to listen and number the photos.

Check answers.

1 B		2 A		3 C		

> (3 62))
> R = Rob, A = Alan, B = Barman
> **1**
> R Hey, Alan. Would you like to come to the match with me on Sunday? It's Norwich against Chelsea, and I have two tickets.
> A Wow! What time's the match?
> R It's at four o'clock.
> A Yeah, I'd love to. Thanks.
> R Would you like to meet for lunch first?
> A Sorry, I can't. It's my mum's birthday, and I need to have lunch with her. But I can meet you there.
> R Great. Let's meet at half past three at the entrance to the Tube station.
> A Fine. See you there.
> **2**
> A They are playing really badly. I hope the second half is better.
> R Me, too. I know they can win. Would you like a burger?
> A No, thanks. I'm not very hungry.
> R How about a coffee?
> A Yeah, great.
> ***
> R Um, a burger and a water, please.
> A And I'd like a coffee.
> B Milk and sugar?
> A Yes, please.
> R Oh! Come on!

b Get Sts to uncover the conversations. Go through the definition for *the entrance* with the class and explain / elicit that *the Tube* is the informal name for the London Underground.

Tell Sts to read the conversations and as they read they should think about what the missing words might be.

Now play the video or audio again for Sts to listen and complete the gaps. Pause after each conversation to give Sts time to write.

Check answers.

1	match	6	3.30	11	water
2	Saturday	7	know	12	coffee
3	four o'clock	8	burger	13	Milk
4	lunch	9	hungry		
5	birthday	10	coffee		

Go through the conversations line by line and focus on any new or unfamiliar expressions, e.g. *It's Norwich against Chelsea*, etc. You may want to point out that the *w* is silent in *Norwich*.

Remind Sts of the use of *Wow!* to express surprise or happiness.

Point out to Sts that native speakers often use *yeah* instead of *yes*, e.g. when Alan accepts the invitation he says *Yeah, I'd love to*. You could also point out the sound um that Rob makes before ordering (*Um, a burger, please.*) and explain / elicit that we sometimes use it when we are giving ourselves time to think.

c Focus on the question and do it as an open-class activity.

Now focus on the **Would you like…?** box and go through it with the class.

2 PRONUNCIATION sentence rhythm

Pronunciation notes

- Good sentence rhythm depends on stressing the important words in a sentence and linking some words together. Here Sts get intensive practice of asking *Would you like…?* questions with good rhythm and intonation.

a (3 63))) Focus on the two questions and tell Sts that they are going to 'build' them bit by bit.

Play the audio once the whole way through for Sts just to listen. Remind Sts that the words in bold are stressed pronounced more strongly.

Explain that when saying *Would you*, the *d* of *would* is linked or connected to the *y* of *you* and that this creates a /dʒ/ sound.

> (3 63)))
> See the words in the Student's Book on *p.57*

Now play the audio, pausing at the end of each line for Sts to listen and repeat. Check that Sts are linking *would* and *you*. If Sts are having problems, model the words yourself for them to repeat.

b Focus on the instructions and speech bubbles. Elicit the eight questions from the class. Then model and drill them.

Now ask one of the questions with *Would you like a…?* to elicit the two possible answers *Yes, please. | No, thank you.*

Then ask one of the questions with *Would you like to go to…?* to elicit the two possible answers *Yes, I'd love to. | Sorry, I can't.*

Put Sts in pairs, **A** and **B**. Tell the **A**s to ask about the first photos in each group. Sts then take turns asking each other about the things in the photos and responding.

Monitor and help.

Get some pairs to perform for the class.

c Put Sts in pairs and get them to practise the conversations in **1b**. The person playing Rob should read the barman's line.

Make sure they swap roles.

You could get a pair to perform the conversations for the class.

3 ▶ MEETING AN OLD FRIEND

a (3 64))) Focus on the instructions and questions, and make sure Sts understand *ex-boyfriend*.

Play the video or audio once the whole way through for Sts to listen and answer the questions. Play again as necessary.

Get Sts to compare with a partner and check answers.

> He invites her to have a cup of coffee.
> He invites her to a Picasso exhibition. He also invites her to have dinner or to see a show.

> (3 64)))
> (script in Student's Book on *p.89*)
> **S = Steve, J = Jenny**
>
> S Hi, Jenny. What a surprise!
> J Hi, Steve.
> S How are you? You're looking great.
> J Thanks. I'm well. How about you?
> S I'm OK. Hey, it's starting to rain. Would you like a coffee?
> J Oh, thanks, Steve, but I have a meeting in an hour.
> S Oh, come on Jenny. I'd like to talk to you.
> J OK. A quick coffee.
> ***
> S Jenny, I'd like to ask you something.
> J Yes?
> S There's an exhibition of Picasso at the MOMA next week. I know you love Picasso. Would you like to come with me?
> J Ah, listen, Steve. I'm really busy at work at the moment. Next week isn't a good week for me.
> S Sure. No problem. Maybe we can meet one evening – when you have more time – and have dinner or see a show?
> J Listen, Steve. I don't think it's a good idea. But thanks. Oh, look at the time! I need to go. Let's ask for the check.

b Focus on the instructions and give Sts time to read sentences 1–5. Make sure they understand all the lexis in the options.

Play the video or audio again for Sts to listen and circle the right answer.

Get Sts to compare with a partner and then check answers.

> 1 well
> 2 starting to rain
> 3 an hour
> 4 can't
> 5 isn't

Extra support

- If there's time, you could play the audio again while Sts read the script on *p.89*, so they can see what they understood / didn't understand. Translate / explain any new words or phrases.

4 🎥 USEFUL PHRASES

3 65))) Focus on the phrases and make sure Sts understand what each one means.

Play the video or audio once the whole way through for Sts just to listen.

> **3 65)))**
> See the phrases in the Student's Book on *p.57*

Now play the video or audio again, pausing after each phrase for Sts to listen and repeat.

Give further practice as necessary, modelling and drilling the pronunciation yourself, or using the video or audio, and getting choral and individual responses.

Extra challenge

- Put Sts in pairs and ask them to write a short conversation, using some of the **Useful phrases**. When they have finished, get a few pairs to act out their role-play for the class.

5 SPEAKING & WRITING

a **3 66)))** Focus on the instructions. Before you play the audio, you might want to check Sts know the meaning of *busy*. Model and drill its pronunciation.

Play the audio once the whole way through for Sts just to listen.

> **3 66)))**
> See the conversations in the Student's Book on *p.57*

Now play the audio again, pausing after each line for Sts to listen and repeat.

Then put them in pairs and get them to practise the conversations. Make sure they swap roles.

b Focus on the instructions. Highlight that Sts should use the conversation in **1a** as a model to role-play a conversation using their own ideas.

Put Sts in pairs, **A** and **B**, and get them to role-play their own conversations. Monitor and help as needed.

Make sure they swap roles.

c Tell Sts they need to invite their friends to their party. When they accept an invitation, tell them to make sure they make a note of whose party they are going to and when, so they don't accept two invitations on the same day.

Now get Sts to stand up and move around the classroom inviting as many people as possible to their party.

Monitor and help as needed.

Ask a few Sts when their party is and how many people are coming.

d Ask Sts to go to **Writing** *An email* on *p.85*.

Focus on **a** and get Sts to read the email and answer the question.

Check the answer.

> Lucy invites Kate to her house (for dinner).

Now focus on **b** and get Sts to read Kate's email and choose the right phrases.

Check answers.

> I'm sorry, but I can't come.
> Maybe see you at the weekend?

Focus on the **Emails** box in **c** and go through it with the class.

Focus on the instructions for **d** and put Sts in pairs. Highlight that the invitations have to include the date and time.

Sts write their emails inviting their partner. Monitor and help as needed. Make sure Sts are including all of the information.

Now focus on **e** and get Sts to exchange their invitation with their partner. When Sts have read the invitation they should write a reply, accepting or declining the invitation.

Now focus on **f** and get Sts to give their reply to their partner.

Get some feedback from various pairs and find out what kind of invitations Sts made (i.e. to the cinema, to a party, for coffee, etc.) and what kind of excuses they used if they declined.

Tell Sts to go back to the main lesson **PE5**.

6 🎵 SONG *Song I'd Like to Sing* 🎵

For Sts of this level all song lyrics will include language that they don't know.

This song was recorded by American singers Kris Kristofferson and Rita Coolidge in 1973. For copyright reasons this is a cover version.

If you want to do this song in class, use the photocopiable activity on *p.232*.

You will find the songs as MP3 files on CD4 of the Class audio CD.

> **4 MP3)))**
> *Song I'd Like to Sing*
>
> There's a song I'd like to sing
> Do you know the song I mean?
> It don't always sound the same
> But it's always good to sing.
>
> Anyone can say the words
> Anyone can sing the tune
> If you have a little time,
> I can teach this song to you.
>
> And we can get to know each other
> Like a sister and a brother
> Like a father and a mother
> Like a woman and a man.
>
> And we can sing along together
> Just enjoy until it's over
> It don't need to last forever
> If we want it to it can.
>
> Maybe it don't mean a thing
> It's a pretty little tune.
> It's a song I like to sing
> That I'd love to sing with you.
> (la la la la la la la)

G *there's a... / there are some...*
V hotels; *in, on, under*
P /eə/ and /ɪə/

10A Is there really a monster?

Lesson plan

The topic of this lesson is hotels.

At the start of the lesson Sts learn vocabulary related to hotels and hotel rooms. Then the new grammar (*there's a* and *there are some*) is presented through a conversation between a couple of tourists and a hotel receptionist. The receptionist is showing the couple their room in a hotel (whose website Sts can visit) that looks onto Loch Ness in Scotland. They discuss the things that there are or aren't in the hotel and area, and they enquire about the famous monster. In Pronunciation, Sts practise the sounds /eə/ and /ɪə/.

In the second half of the lesson, a hotel room provides a context for Sts to learn the prepositions *in, on,* and *under*. Then there is a speaking activity in which Sts use prepositions to describe the location of common objects.

STUDY LINK
- Workbook 10A
- iTutor
- www.oup.com/elt/englishfile

Extra photocopiable activities

- **Grammar** *there's a... / there are some... p.157*
- **Communicative** My hotel *p.196 (instructions p.170)*
- **Vocabulary** Draw it! *p.225 (instructions p.209)*
- www.oup.com/elt/teacher/englishfile

Optional lead-in (books closed)

- Write on the board A HOTEL ROOM and give Sts three minutes, in pairs, to brainstorm words for things you might find in a hotel room, e.g. *table, chair, bed, bathroom, shower, bath, phone, mini bar, door, window,* etc.

- Write the words they say on the board. Model and drill pronunciation.

1 VOCABULARY hotels

a Books open. Focus on the instructions and give Sts time to read the information. Elicit / explain that an *inn* is a small hotel. Make sure Sts understand *friendly* and *views*. You could put Sts in pairs to answer the questions or do it as an open-class activity.

Elicit opinions. Also ask if Sts have heard of Loch Ness. You could tell them that *loch* is the Scottish word for *lake*. Ask *What is Loch Ness famous for?* and elicit / teach the word *monster*.

b Get Sts to look at the photo of the bedroom and match the words with the items in the room.

Check answers.

1 a window	3 a picture	5 the floor
2 a bed	4 a lamp	

c Tell Sts to go to **Vocabulary Bank** *Hotels* on *p.128*.

4 2)) Look at **1 In a hotel room** and focus on **a**. Play the audio and get Sts to repeat the words in chorus and individually as necessary. Model and drill any words which are difficult for your Sts and give further practice.

> **4 2))**
> See the hotel room words in the Student's Book on *p.128*

Highlight that:
– the letter *h* in *hotel*, as with most words beginning with *h*, is pronounced /h/ (it is not silent as in some languages).
– the letters *ow* are pronounced /aʊ/ in *towel*, but /əʊ/ in *pillow*.
– the *p* in *cupboard* is silent.

Remind Sts that we usually use *the* with *bedroom, bathroom,* and *floor* because it is clear which one you are talking about.

Focus on **b** and get Sts to cover the words, look at the picture, and say the words. They could do this individually or with a partner. Remind Sts to use *a* or *the* with all of the nouns.

Monitor and help. Make a note of any pronunciation problems Sts are having. Write the words on the board and model and drill the ones that they find difficult.

4 3)) Look at **2 In a hotel** and focus on **a**. Play the audio and get Sts to repeat the words in chorus and individually as necessary. Model and drill any words which are difficult for your Sts and give further practice.

> **4 3))**
> See the hotel words in the Student's Book on *p.128*

Highlight pronunciation, especially the /ɑː/ sound in *spa, bar, garden,* and *car park*.

Focus on **b** and get Sts to cover the words, look at the picture, and say the words. They could do this individually or with a partner.

Focus on the *ground floor* box and go through it with the class. In some countries, e.g. the USA, people refer to the ground floor of a building as the *first floor*.

Highlight that *floor* has two different meanings – the part of the room below your feet and the different levels in a building.

Finally, focus on **c** and the speech bubbles. Look at the drawing of the hotel and highlight that we use ordinal numbers to talk about the floors of a hotel. Model and drill *the ground floor, the first floor, the second floor*, etc. in chorus and individually. Highlight that we use the preposition *on* to talk about the floors of a building.

Demonstrate the activity by asking a student *Where's the bar?* (It's on the first floor). Elicit a question from the same student and answer the question yourself.

Put Sts in pairs and give them a few minutes to ask and answer questions about the hotel. Monitor and help. Make a note of any problems they are having and correct any mistakes on the board.

Tell Sts to go back to the main lesson **10A**.

Extra support

• If you think Sts need more practice, you may want to give them the Vocabulary photocopiable activity at this point or leave it for later as consolidation or revision.

2 GRAMMAR *there's a… / there are some…*

a **4 4**))) F ocus on the lesson title, *Is there really a monster?*, and elicit / explain the meaning (= Is it true that there is a monster?).

Now focus on the instructions. Get Sts to cover the conversation and focus on the list of items. Model and drill pronunciation of *Wi-fi* /ˈwaɪ faɪ/. Point out that the first one has been done for them.

Play the audio once the whole way through for Sts to listen and complete the task. Play again as necessary. You may want to point out to your Sts that the receptionist speaks with a Scottish accent.

Check answers by asking *Is there (a TV)? | Are there (shops near)?* and getting Sts to just say *Yes* or *No*.

✓ TV	✓ Wi-fi	✗ a restaurant
✓ a bar	✓ a good view	✗ shops near

Deal with any vocabulary problems that arose. You could point out that *cases*, in line 6, is an abbreviation of *suitcases*, which they saw in the **Vocabulary Bank** *Common verb phrases 2: travelling*.

4 4)))

E = Eric, R = receptionist, L = Louisa
E Hello. Do you have a room for tonight?
R Let's see. eR, Yes, there's a room on the second floor.
L Great. Can we see it?
R Of course. Come with me.
E Is there a lift?
R I'm sorry, no, there isn't. But I can help you with your cases.
***
R This is the room.
L Ah! It's beautiful. I love it.
E Yes, and there's a great view of Loch Ness.
R The remote control for the TV is on the table.
E Is there Wi-fi?
R Yes, there is. There's Wi-fi in every room in the hotel. This is the bathroom. There's a bath and a shower.
E Is there a restaurant? We're very hungry.
R No, there isn't a restaurant, sir. But you can have dinner in the bar or there are some pubs in the village.
L Are there any shops near here?
R No, madam, there aren't any shops near the hotel.
E OK, thanks. I have one more question.
R Yes, sir?
E Is there a monster in the loch?
R Well, some people say there is and some people say there isn't. Enjoy your stay. Breakfast is at eight.

b Focus on the instructions and get Sts to uncover the conversation.

Play the audio again for Sts to read and listen at the same time.

Give Sts time to look at 1–3 and circle the right words. If you know your Sts' L1, you may want to elicit a translation of *There's | There are* at this point.

Check answers.

1 a (singular)
2 b (plural)
3 b (negative sentences) and questions

c **4 5**))) Focus on the task and play the audio once the whole way through for Sts to listen and answer the first two questions.

Check answers to the first two questions.

They see something in Loch Ness.
Louisa takes photos with her phone.

4 5)))

(script in Student's Book on *p.89*)
E Louisa, time to get up.
L OK. What time is it?
E It's half past seven. Breakfast is at eight.
L Is it a nice day?
E Let's see. Ahh! Louisa, quick! Come here! Look at that!
L What is it?
E Look. Over there.
L Where?
E There. In the loch. There! Can't you see? There's something in the loch. It's moving. Can you see it now?
L Yes. What is it?
E I don't know. Quick, take a photo with your phone.
L I can't see it now. Can you?
E No. I can't. I can't see anything now. Let's see those photos, Louisa. Wow! I don't believe it. Look at that…

Do the final question as an open-class activity.

You could find out with a show of hands how many Sts believe in the Loch Ness monster.

d (4 6))) Tell Sts to go to **Grammar Bank 10A** on *p.110*.

Focus on the example sentences and play the audio for Sts to listen and repeat. Pause the audio as necessary.

Go through the rules with the class using the expanded information in the **Additional grammar notes** below to help you. You may want to use Sts' L1 here.

Additional grammar notes

there's a… | there are some…

- Sts may have trouble remembering that *there is* is used with singular nouns and *there are* with plural nouns.

- Highlight that:
  - *there is* contracts to *there's*, but we write *there are* NOT ~~there're~~.
  - *there is* isn't contracted in short answers, i.e. *Yes, there is.* NOT ~~Yes, there's.~~
  - negative sentences are formed with the negative of *be*, i.e. *isn't* and *aren't*.
  - questions are formed by inverting *there* and *is | are*, e.g. *There is → Is there…?* and *There are → Are there…?*

- When giving a list of things we use *There is* if the first word in the list is singular, e.g. *There's a bed, a table, and two chairs.*

some and any

- Highlight that we use *some* in positive plural sentences, e.g. *There are some pictures.* We use *any* in negative plural sentences and questions, e.g. *There aren't any towels, Are there any pillows?*

- NB The use of *some* and *any* with uncountable nouns, e.g. *There's some bread*, is not taught here. This grammar point is taught in *English File Elementary*.

Focus on the exercises for **10A** on *p.111* and get Sts to do them individually or in pairs. If they do them individually, get them to compare answers with a partner.

Check answers, getting Sts to read the full sentences.

a			
1	any	6	a
2	some	7	any
3	a	8	some
4	any	9	some
5	a	10	any
b			
1	Are there	6	There are
2	There aren't	7	Is there
3	There's	8	There are
4	Is there	9	There isn't
5	There isn't	10	Are there

Tell Sts to go back to the main lesson **10A**.

Extra support

- If you think Sts need more practice, you may want to give them the Grammar photocopiable activity at this point or leave it for later as consolidation or revision.

3 PRONUNCIATION /eə/ and /ɪə/

Pronunciation notes

- You could point out that /eə/ and /ɪə/ are diphthongs, i.e. two sounds, if you think this will help Sts.

- /eə/ For information on this sound, see the **Pronunciation notes** in **7A**.

- /ɪə/ The letters *eer* are always pronounced /ɪə/, e.g. *beer*.
  The letters *ere* and *ear* are sometimes pronounced /ɪə/, e.g. *here, near*, but are also sometimes pronounced /eə/, e.g. *there, wear*. Sts need to learn these common examples by heart.

a (4 7))) Read the **Pronunciation notes** and decide how much of the information you want to give your Sts.

Focus on the exercise and play the audio once the whole way through for Sts just to listen.

> (4 7)))
> See the words and sounds in the Student's Book on *p.59*

Focus on the sound picture *chair*. Play the audio to model and drill the word and the sound (pause after the sound).

Now focus on the words after *chair*. Remind Sts that the pink letters are the /eə/ sound. Play the audio, pausing after each word for Sts to listen and repeat.

Now repeat the same process for *ear* /ɪə/.

If these sounds are difficult for your Sts, model them yourself so that Sts can see your mouth position, and get Sts to repeat them a few more times.

Play the audio again from the beginning, pausing after each group of words for Sts to repeat.

Give further practice as necessary.

Finally, get Sts, in pairs, to practise saying the words.

Extra support

- If you are using an interactive whiteboard, you can focus on each sound individually before moving on to the next one.

Focus on the *ear* box and go through it with the class. There is no easy rule here, so Sts will have to learn and remember how these words are pronounced.

b (4 8))) Play the audio once the whole way through for Sts just to listen.

> (4 8)))
> See the sentences in the Student's Book on *p.59*

Then play it again for Sts to listen and repeat.

Then repeat the activity, eliciting responses from individual Sts.

c Put Sts in pairs and tell them to practise the conversation in **2b** on p.58. The person playing Eric should read Louisa's lines.

Make sure they swap roles.

You could get some pairs to perform the role-play for the class.

d Focus on the instructions, the two categories and words, and the example.

Put Sts in pairs and get a good pair to demonstrate the activity. Then get Sts to make a ⊞ or ⊟ sentence with *there's a… | there are some…* for each noun. Monitor, correcting pronunciation.

Elicit some sentences from individual Sts.

Extra support

- Get Sts to write two sentences about their classroom (one ⊞ and one ⊟) and two about their school, and then practise saying them.

4 VOCABULARY & SPEAKING *in, on, under*

a Focus on the pictures of the boxes and balls. Give Sts time to write the correct preposition under each picture.

Check answers.

1 in	2 on	3 under

Highlight with examples and demonstrations the difference between *on* and *in*. *In* is used when something is inside a closed or semi-closed space (e.g. *My phone is in my pocket. The book is in the drawer.*) whereas *on* is used when something is on the surface of something else (e.g. *The picture is on the wall. The book is on the table.*).

Extra idea

- You could practise these prepositions further by placing an object, e.g. your mobile phone, in different places in the classroom and asking *Where's my phone?* (e.g. *It's on the table, it's under the chair, it's in your bag*, etc.).

b Focus on the six pictures. In each one the remote control is in a different place.

Focus on the speech bubbles and picture 1. Model and drill the question and answer in chorus and individually.

Get a pair of Sts to demonstrate the activity.

Then put Sts in pairs and give them time to ask and answer the questions.

Monitor and help.

Check answers.

> 2 It's on the bed
> 3 It's in the (coffee) cup.
> 4 It's under the bed.
> 5 It's under a towel, on the chair.
> 6 It's in the suitcase.

c Put Sts in pairs, **A** and **B**. Tell them to go to **Communication** *Is there a TV? Where is it?*, **A** on *p.78* and **B** on *p.82*.

Focus on the instructions and make sure Sts are clear about what they have to do. Establish that **A** is going to first ask **B** questions about picture 1. For each object, if **B** answers *Yes, there is | are*, **A** then has to ask *Where is it? | Where are they?* and draw the object in the correct place or write the word there.

Demonstrate by taking the role of **A** and asking one of the **B**s *Is there a coat?* and eliciting *Yes, there is.* Then ask *Where is it?* and elicit *It's on the chair.* Then tell all the **A**s to draw a coat on the chair.

Get the **A**s to continue with the questions and then to swap roles.

As soon as a pair has finished, tell them to compare their pictures.

Extra idea

- You could get fast finishers to write sentences about their picture, e.g. *There's a laptop on the bed. There are some keys on the table*, etc.

WORDS AND PHRASES TO LEARN

4 61)) Tell Sts to go to *p.131* and focus on the **Words and phrases to learn** for **10A**. Make sure Sts understand the meaning of each phrase. If necessary, remind them of the context in which the words and phrases came up in the lesson. If you speak your Sts' L1, you might like to elicit a translation for the words | phrases for the Sts to write next to them. Play the audio, pausing after each phrase for Sts to repeat. You may also like to ask Sts to test each other on the phrases.

G past simple: *be*
V *in*, *at*, *on*
P *was* and *were*; sentence rhythm

10B Before they were famous...and after

Lesson plan

What some well-known celebrities did before they were famous provides the context to introduce and practise the past simple of the verb *be* (*was* / *were*).

First, Sts try to guess the previous jobs of four celebrities and then they listen to see if they were right. In Reading Sts read about a child actor who was in the Italian film *Cinema Paradiso* and they find out what he did after he was famous. The vocabulary focus in the lesson is on prepositions with places, *in*, *at*, and *on* (e.g. *at school*, *in bed*, *on a bus*).

In Pronunciation, Sts practise the strong and weak forms of *was* and *were*, and sentence rhythm. In the final speaking activity grammar, pronunciation, and vocabulary are brought together when Sts ask and answer questions about where they were at various times the previous day.

STUDY LINK

* Workbook 10B
* iTutor
* iChecker on iTutor
* www.oup.com/elt/englishfile

Extra photocopiable activities

* **Grammar** past simple: *be* p.158
* **Communicative** Where were you yesterday? *p.197* (instructions *p.170*)
* www.oup.com/elt/teacher/englishfile

Optional lead-in (books closed)

* Tell Sts that you are going to say a sentence about a person and they have to say what the person's job is.

* Say the sentences below to elicit the jobs from the class:
  1 This man works in a restaurant and you say to him 'A table for two, please.' (He's a waiter.)
  2 This woman works in a restaurant. She brings you your food. (She's a waitress.)
  3 This man works in films and in the theatre. (He's an actor.)
  4 This person plays music on the radio and in a club. (He / She is a DJ.)

1 GRAMMAR past simple: *be*

a Books open. Focus on the instructions and make sure Sts understand the meaning of *famous*. Model and drill pronunciation. Then point to the photo of Lady Gaga and ask *What does she do?* (She's a singer and an actor).

Now put Sts in pairs to ask and answer about the rest of the people in the photos. They should say if each person is a singer or an actor. Remind Sts that a woman can be an actor or an actress.

Check answers by calling on individual Sts to say what the people do.

> Brad Pitt is an actor.
> Pink is a singer and an actor.
> Russell Crowe is a singer and an actor.

b Focus on the title of the lesson, *Before they were famous…and after*, and see if Sts can work out what it means. If necessary, use L1 to check.

Now focus on the instructions and tell Sts that they are going to guess what the celebrities' jobs were before they were famous. If you didn't do the **Optional lead-in**, you might want to explain / elicit what a *DJ* is.

Give Sts time to read the text and complete each gap with a name.

Deal with any new vocabulary.

c (4 9)) Play the audio, pausing after each sentence to give Sts time to check their answers or complete the sentences. This is the first time Sts have seen *was* and *were*, but they should be able to guess the meaning from context.

Check answers.

> 1 Lady Gaga   3 Russell Crowe
> 2 Pink   4 Brad Pitt

> (4 9))
> **Before they were famous…**
> They're big names today, but many celebrities' first jobs were in fast food restaurants! For example, Lady Gaga and Pink were waitresses, Russell Crowe was a waiter and a DJ, and Brad Pitt was a chicken, standing in the street to attract customers!

d Do this as an open-class activity and elicit the answers from the class.

> He **was** a waiter.   They **were** waitresses.

e (4 10)) Tell Sts to go to **Grammar Bank 10B** on *p.110*.

Focus on the example sentences and play the audio for Sts to listen and repeat (see the **Pronunciation notes** for the pronunciation of *was* / *were*). Pause the audio as necessary.

Go through the rules with the class using the expanded information in the **Additional grammar notes** below to help you. You may want to use Sts' L1 here.

Additional grammar notes
past simple: *be*

* *Was* is the past of *am* and *is*. *Were* is the past of *are*. Like *is* and *are*, *was* and *were* can be used to describe permanent and temporary states, e.g. *I was a teacher.* / *I was at home last night.*

* *Was* and *were* are used exactly like *is* and *are*, i.e. they are inverted to make questions (e.g. *he was* → *was he?*) and *not* (*n't*) is added to make negatives (*wasn't*, *weren't*).

- The past simple is used to talk about finished time, especially with past time expressions, e.g. *last night*, *last week*. It is used to refer to both the near and distant past.

! Highlight that past time expressions do **not** have an article, i.e. *last week* NOT ~~the last week~~.

! Some Sts tend to remember *was* and forget *were*.

Focus on the exercises for **10B** on *p.111* and get Sts to do them individually or in pairs. If they do them individually, get them to compare answers with a partner.

Check answers, getting Sts to read the full sentences.

> a
> 1 Were you at school yesterday?
> 2 James wasn't very well yesterday.
> 3 We were on the plane at 4.00.
> 4 Were they in class yesterday?
> 5 David wasn't very happy last night.
> 6 I was in a meeting until 7.00 last night.
> 7 Was your sister in London last week?
> 8 It was a terrible film.
> b
> 1 was   5 Was   8 Were   11 Was
> 2 weren't   6 wasn't   9 weren't   12 wasn't
> 3 were   7 was   10 were   13 was
> 4 wasn't

Tell Sts to go back to the main lesson **10B**.

Extra support
- If you think Sts need more practice, you may want to give them the Grammar photocopiable activity at this point or leave it for later as consolidation or revision.

f   Focus on the instructions and the example. Play the first sentence, pausing after the prompt (*She's a waitress.*) for Sts to say the past form in chorus. Now continue playing the audio for Sts to hear the answer.

Play the rest of the audio, pausing after each prompt for Sts to make the sentence in the past.

> (4 11))
> 1 She's a waitress. (*pause*) She was a waitress.
> 2 Is he an actor? (*pause*) Was he an actor?
> 3 We aren't very happy. (*pause*) We weren't very happy.
> 4 It isn't expensive. (*pause*) It wasn't expensive.
> 5 They're terrible. (*pause*) They were terrible.
> 6 Are you a student? (*pause*) Were you a student?
> 7 I'm not tired. (*pause*) I wasn't tired.
> 8 You're in my class. (*pause*) You were in my class.

Then repeat the activity, eliciting responses from individual Sts.

Extra challenge
- You may want to encourage Sts to use the weak forms *was* /wəz/ and *were* /wə/ in positive sentences (See **Pronunciation notes**) although Sts at this low level are likely to find it easier to use strong forms.

2 READING

a   Focus on the instructions. Do the two questions as an open-class activity. <u>Don't</u> tell Sts if they are right.

Now play the audio for Sts to listen and read at the same time.

Check answers. Find out if any Sts have seen the film.

> 1 *Cinema Paradiso*
> 2 Salvatore Cascio / the boy in the first photo

> (4 12))
> See the article in the Student's Book on *p.60*

b Focus on the instructions and questions 1–6, making sure Sts understand all the questions.

You might want to pre-teach some lexis, e.g. *a game*, *a smile*, *winner*, *memories*, *dreams*, etc., or you may prefer to deal with it in context.

Give Sts time to read the article and answer the questions. Deal with any vocabulary problems if you didn't pre-teach any new lexis.

Get Sts to compare with a partner and then check answers.

> 1 He was eight.   4 It means 'The Oscar for flavour'.
> 2 in 1990.   5 No, it wasn't.
> 3 No, he isn't.   6 He says the film is about dreams.

c Do this as an open-class activity.

3 VOCABULARY *in, at, on*

a Focus on the instructions and sentences.

Get Sts to complete the gaps.

Check answers.

> 1 in   2 at

b Write IN, AT, and ON on the board. Highlight that we often use these prepositions with places.

Focus on the chart. Explain that all of the words in each column use the same preposition.

Get Sts to complete the gaps at the top of the chart with *in*, *at*, or *on*. They should be able to do this as they have seen examples of these prepositions earlier in the Student's Book.

c (4 13)) Play the audio once for Sts to check their answers and repeat the sentences.

> 1 at   2 in   3 on

> (4 13))
> **Where were you yesterday at 7 p.m.?**
> 1 I was at home.   I was at school.
>   I was at work.   I was at university.
> 2 I was in bed.   I was in the street.
>   I was in the kitchen.   I was in a café.
>   I was in my car.   I was in a museum.
>   I was in London.   I was in a shopping centre.
>   I was in the park.   I was in a restaurant.
> 3 I was on a bus.   I was on a train.   I was on a plane.

Explain that the best way to learn prepositions is by remembering them in phrases, e.g. *at home*, *in the office*. However, the following are some simple guidelines Sts can use:

– Use *at* for set phrases, e.g. *home, school, work, university*.
– Use *in* for towns, countries, rooms, buildings, and *bed*.
– Use *on* for transportation with *bus, train, plane, ship*, but use *in* with *cars*.

! Sometimes you can use *in* or *at* with a building, but with a small difference in meaning, e.g. *We were at a restaurant last night* (= this could be inside or outside). *We were in a restaurant* (= definitely inside), but it is better at this level to give Sts a clear (if incomplete) rule.

d Focus on the instructions and the example. Demonstrate the activity by saying a word from the chart. Elicit the correct prepositional phrase. Repeat with two or three more words.

Put Sts in pairs, **A** and **B**. Tell **A**s to look at the chart. Tell **B**s to close their books. **A** tests **B** on the phrases.

After a few minutes, get them to swap roles.

e **4 14))** Focus on the instructions. Explain that Sts are going to hear sound effects on the audio that will tell them where Jason was yesterday at the times in the exercise. They have to complete the sentences with *he was* and the place.

Play the audio, pausing after the first sound effect and get Sts to look at the example.

Then play the next sound effect and pause the audio. Ask *Where was Jason at eight o'clock?* (He was in a / his car). Get Sts to write it.

Continue playing the audio, pausing after each sound effect for Sts to write their answers.

Get Sts to compare with a partner and then play the audio again, pausing after each sound effect and eliciting answers from individual Sts.

2 he was in a / his car
3 he was on a plane
4 he was on a train
5 he was in the street
6 he was in a restaurant
7 he was in bed

4 14))
(Sound effects)
1 at six o'clock in the morning: *man snoring*
2 at eight o'clock in the morning: *car door closing and car starting*
3 at eleven o'clock in the morning: *pilot's announcement, plane taking off*
4 at three o'clock in the afternoon: *a train*
5 at five o'clock in the afternoon: *street noises*
6 at seven o'clock in the evening: *restaurant noises*
7 at ten o'clock at night: *snoring again*

4 PRONUNCIATION & SPEAKING *was* and *were*; sentence rhythm

Pronunciation notes

• Native speakers use two different pronunciations of *was* and *were* depending on whether they are stressed or not, i.e. they can have a strong or weak pronunciation.

• *was* and *were* always have a strong pronunciation in short answers and negatives, and can have a strong pronunciation in *yes* / *no* questions, e.g. *Was he at home last night?*). The pronunciation is /wɒz/ and /wɜː/.

• *was* and *were* tend to have a weak pronunciation in ⊞ sentences and are pronounced /wəz/ and /wə/, e.g. *He was a teacher* /wəz/, *They were waitresses* /wə/.

• It is useful for Sts at this level to be aware of these differences, but unrealistic to expect them to be able to use them properly and Sts will probably use mostly strong forms of *was* and *were*.

• Pronunciation of strong and weak forms tends to occur quite naturally when there is good sentence stress and rhythm, so it is worth working on this.

a **4 15))** Focus on the dialogue and play the audio once the whole way through for Sts just to listen.

Explain the meaning of *remember* and *alone*. You could point out that *was* and *were* are not usually stressed in the positive, the policeman stresses the first *were* for emphasis.

4 15))
See the dialogue in the Student's Book on *p.61*

Now play the audio again, pausing after each line for Sts to listen and repeat. Encourage them to copy the rhythm. Give more practice as necessary.

Extra support
• Put Sts in pairs and get them to practise the dialogue.

b Focus on the questions. Demonstrate the activity by getting Sts to ask you questions 1 and 2. Sts should ask separate questions when two times are given, e.g. *Where were you yesterday at 7.00 in the morning?*

In pairs, Sts ask and answer the questions. Monitor and help , making note of any problems.

Get feedback by asking individual Sts to tell the class a sentence about their partner, e.g. *Maria was in the kitchen at 7.00 in the morning yesterday.*

WORDS AND PHRASES TO LEARN

4 61)) Tell Sts to go to *p.131* and focus on the **Words and phrases to learn** for **10B**. Make sure Sts understand the meaning of each phrase. If necessary, remind them of the context in which the words and phrases came up in the lesson. If you speak your Sts' L1, you might like to elicit a translation for the words / phrases for the Sts to write next to them. Play the audio, pausing after each phrase for Sts to repeat. You may also like to ask Sts to test each other on the phrases.

For instructions on how to use these pages see *p.36*.

STUDY LINK
• iTutor

Test and Assessment CD-ROM

• Quick Test 10
• File Test 10

GRAMMAR

1	b	6	a	11	b
2	a	7	b	12	a
3	b	8	b	13	b
4	a	9	b	14	a
5	a	10	a	15	b

VOCABULARY

a
1 waiting   3 carrying   5 wearing
2 phoning   4 arriving

b
1 dress   3 shirt   5 suit
2 jacket   4 skirt   6 trousers

c
1 reception   3 gift shop   5 car park
2 lift   4 bathroom

d
1 in   2 on   3 at, at

e
1 under   3 on   5 in
2 on   4 under

PRONUNCIATION

a
1 <u>tra</u>vel   3 <u>res</u>taurant   5 re<u>cep</u>tion
2 a<u>rrive</u>   4 <u>cup</u>board

b
/ɜː/ bird   /eə/ chair   /iː/ tree
/e/ egg   /ɪə/ ear

CAN YOU UNDERSTAND THIS TEXT?

a 1 F   2 C   3 A   4 E   5 D   6 B

▶ CAN YOU UNDERSTAND THESE PEOPLE?

4 16))) 1 a   2 c   3 a   4 c   5 b

4 16)))
See the script in the Student's Book on *p.89*.

Remind Sts that they can watch the short film on *iTutor*.

> VIDEO Available as MP3 on CD4
>
> **Short film: An Unusual Hotel in Oxford**
>
> Hi! I'm Gemma. Welcome to Oxford. I'm visiting the Old Bank Hotel. It's an unusual hotel in the centre of the city.
>
> The Old Bank is in the High Street, in the centre of Oxford. Today it's a luxury hotel, but these buildings – from number 92 to number 94 – have a very interesting history. In the 16th century they were part of Christ Church College. In the 18th century they were different shops.
>
> And we know that in 1808 the buildings were one business – a bank. There was a bank here for almost 200 years, but today it's a famous Oxford hotel. Would you like to go in and look? Let's go.
>
> The Old Bank Hotel has a beautiful reception and a fantastic restaurant. There are 42 bedrooms and they're all very comfortable. They have great views of Oxford's famous colleges. This room has a large bed, two chairs, a table, a television, and a cupboard. It has a beautiful marble bathroom, too.
>
> But there are other rooms that visitors to the hotel don't usually see. These secret rooms are here in the cellar, under the hotel. These are the old bank vaults. When the hotel was a bank, all the money was here. The rooms were small and the doors weren't easy to open! They were very, very strong and on each one there was a large lock. Today, these old vaults are store rooms. The hotel keeps its wine collection in here, so it's very, very safe!
>
> 92 to 94 High Street is a part of Oxford's history. And today, If you want to visit Oxford, the Old Bank is a fantastic place to see!

G past simple: regular verbs
V regular verbs
P regular past simple endings

11A It changed my life

Lesson plan

This lesson introduces the past simple of regular verbs in the context of a student's real experience of the Erasmus programme (a European study programme where Sts do part of their course in another country). These are presented through a short picture story about a Spanish student, Clara, who went to Uppsala in Sweden to do part of her university course. Sts then focus closely on the different pronunciations of the *-ed* ending and go on to practise this in a speaking activity. The lesson finishes with Sts reading about Clara's time in Uppsala.

NB Clara's story is based on a real person and the actress reading the first person account has a slight Spanish accent. However, a native-speaker model is provided for drilling pronunciation of the new language.

STUDY LINK
- Workbook 11A
- iTutor
- www.oup.com/elt/englishfile

Extra photocopiable activities
- **Grammar** past simple: regular verbs *p.159*
- **Communicative** Guess how many *p.198* (instructions *p.171*)
- www.oup.com/elt/teacher/englishfile

Optional lead-in (books closed)
- Write IT CHANGED MY LIFE on the board. Tell Sts that this is the title of this lesson and elicit what the sentence means.

- Now write CLARA, MADRID, UPPSALA, ERASMUS underneath on the board and tell them these are the names and places in the story. You may need to elicit / explain that Uppsala is a city in Sweden.

- Elicit ideas from the class as to what the lesson might be about.

1 GRAMMAR past simple: regular verbs

a ●4 18)) Books open. Focus on the instructions and deal with any vocabulary problems, e.g. *every year, foreign*. Highlight the silent *g* in *foreign* /ˈfɒrən/ and model and drill the pronunciation. You could tell Sts that the Erasmus programme is a European Union (EU) student exchange programme, which was established in 1987.

Go through sentences 1–3 and make sure the two options are clear in each case.

Focus on the text and elicit / explain the meaning of the title, *Following my dream.*

Play the audio once the whole way through for Sts to listen and read at the same time. If Sts ask about the *-ed* ending on the verbs, e.g. *wanted, talked*, ask them if they think this is the present or the past (the past).

> ●4 18))
> See the text in the Student's Book on *p.64*

Now focus on 1–3 and give Sts time to choose **a** or **b**.

Check answers.

```
1 a    2 a    3 b
```

Deal with any vocabulary problems that arose, e.g. *Computer Science, abroad*, etc. Model and drill pronunciation.

Extra idea
- If you have a map in class, point to (or get a student to do this) Spain / Madrid and Sweden / Uppsala.

b Focus on picture 1 and ask *Where's Clara?* (at home on the internet). Repeat the question for picture 2 (at the airport) and picture 6 (in Uppsala / at university).

Now focus on the sentences and establish that they are all in the past simple and that all the ones with yellow highlighting are regular verbs. Elicit / explain the meaning of *weather, nervous,* and *excited*, and deal with any other vocabulary problems.

Put Sts in pairs and give them time to try and match pictures 1–6 with the sentences. Sts should be able to do this from words they know / recognize and using a bit of imagination. Monitor and help.

c ●4 19)) Play the audio once the whole way through for Sts to listen and check.

Check answers with the whole class by asking individual Sts to read out the sentences in order. Find out how many Sts got it right. Encourage Sts to pronounce the *-ed* ending as correctly as possible although this will be focussed on in more detail in **Pronunciation**.

See script 4.19

117

4 19)))

1 I booked my ticket online, Madrid to Stockholm.
2 I arrived in Stockholm at three o'clock.
3 I didn't like the weather! It was very cold and dark!
4 I travelled to Uppsala by bus.
5 I talked in English to the students on the bus.
6 We started classes the next day. I was nervous but excited.

d Focus on the instructions and elicit the past simple of the first sentence, *book* (booked). Give Sts time to write the other past simple forms. They can look back at the sentences in **b** to help them.

Check answers by copying the present and past forms on the board.

I **booked** my ticket.
I **arrived** in Stockholm.
I **didn't** like the weather.

Get Sts to look at the verbs again and ask them what letters they add to a verb to make the past form for regular verbs.

To make a ⊞ past form add *-ed* or *-d* (if the verb ends in *e*).

Now ask them how the negative form is made.

To make a ⊟ past form, use *didn't* + infinitive.

e **4 20)))** Tell Sts to go to **Grammar Bank 11A** on *p.112*.

Focus on the example sentences and play the audio for Sts to listen and repeat. Pause the audio as necessary.

Go through the rules with the class using the expanded information in the **Additional grammar notes** below to help you. You may want to use Sts' L1 here.

Additional grammar notes
past simple: regular verbs

• The past simple is used for finished actions and states in the past however distant or recent. For example, we can say *I phoned you yesterday* and *I phoned you earlier today*. This may be different in your Sts' L1.

• The past simple of regular verbs is very easy. There is no third person change. The basic rule is to add *-ed* to the infinitive.

• Negative sentences use the auxiliary *did* + *not* (*didn't*) + the infinitive.

• Questions use the formula (*Wh-*) + *did* + subject + infinitive. In other words, they follow the same pattern as questions in the present simple: (**Qu**) + **A** + **S** + **I**. For information on the acronyms **QuASI** and **ASI** see the **Additional grammar notes** in 7A.

• Most verbs in English are regular, although some of the most common verbs happen to be irregular, e.g. *go*, *have* (see **11B**).

Spelling rules

• The basic rule for forming the past tense in positive sentences with regular verbs is add *-ed* (e.g. *worked*) or *-d* with verbs ending in *e* (e.g. *lived*).

• Highlight that you do <u>not</u> add *-ed | -d* to regular past verbs in questions and negatives. Typical mistakes: *Did you worked yesterday? I didn't lived in London*.

Focus on the exercises for **11A** on *p.113* and get Sts to do them individually or in pairs. If Sts do the exercises individually, get them to compare answers with a partner.

Check answers, getting Sts to read the full sentences. Get them to spell any verbs where the spelling in the past changes.

a
1 They worked in a bank.
2 He finished work late.
3 We lived in Brazil.
4 I carried a big bag.
5 She walked to work.
6 The train stopped in Barcelona.
7 We played tennis.
8 You talked a lot!
9 I relaxed at the weekend.
10 He waited for the bus.
11 They travelled by train.
12 She needed a new coat.

b
1 did...park, parked
2 Did...finish, didn't finish
3 did...study, studied
4 Did...like, didn't like
5 Did...watch, watched
6 Did...close, closed
7 Did...cry, cried
8 did...arrive, arrived

Tell Sts to go back to the main lesson **11A**.

Extra support

• If you think Sts need more practice, you may want to give them the Grammar photocopiable activity at this point or leave it for later as consolidation or revision.

f Focus on the instructions, the example, and the questions.

Give Sts a few minutes to work out how to form the questions and how to answer them. Elicit the questions and answers from the class, and model and drill pronunciation.

Put Sts in pairs and get them to ask and answer the questions. One student could ask the first four and the other student the next four.

Get some feedback from the class.

1 Did Clara want to be an Erasmus student?
   Yes, she did.
2 Did she talk to her mother?
   Yes, she did.
3 Did her parents help her with the money?
   Yes, they did.
4 Did she want to go to Sweden at first?
   No, she didn't.
5 Did she book her flight online?
   Yes, she did.
6 Did she arrive in Stockholm in the morning?
   No, she didn't.
7 Did she like the weather?
   No, she didn't.
8 Did she talk to other students in Spanish?
   No, she didn't.

Extra challenge

• Get Sts to answer using short answers and then where possible they should expand their answers, e.g. for 2, *Yes, she did. She talked to her mother and her father.*

2 PRONUNCIATION regular past simple endings

Pronunciation notes

• The regular past simple ending -*ed* can be pronounced in three different ways:
   1 -*ed* is pronounced /d/ with verbs which end in a **voiced*** sound, e.g. *arrive → arrived, learn → learned.*
   2 -*ed* is pronounced /t/ with verbs which end in an **unvoiced*** sound: /k/, /p/, /f/, /s/, /ʃ/, /tʃ/, e.g. *talk → talked, finish → finished, watch → watched.*
   3 -*ed* is pronounced /ɪd/ after verbs ending in the sound /d/ or /t/, e.g. *want → wanted, need → needed.*
   * For an explanation of **voiced** and **unvoiced** sounds, see the **Pronunciation notes** in **3A** on *p.39.*

• In practice, the difference between /t/ and /d/ is very small and at this level we recommend you do not spend too much time on this. However, the difference between /ɪd/ and the other two is significant (it is an extra syllable) and Sts sometimes tend to add the /ɪd/ ending to all regular verbs. Highlight this difference emphasizing that the -*e* in -*ed* is only pronounced when there is a *t* or a *d* before it, e.g. *waited, ended,* and make sure you always correct Sts when they add the extra syllable to verbs from groups 1 and 2.

a **(4 21))** Explain that there are three different ways of pronouncing -*ed*: /d/, /t/, and /ɪd/.

Focus on the exercise and play the audio once the whole way through for Sts just to listen.

> **(4 21))**
> See the sounds and sentences in the Student's Book on *p.65*

Focus on the first sound picture *dog.* Play the audio to model and drill the word and sound (pause after the sound).

Now focus on the two example sentences after *dog.* Play the audio, pausing after each sentence for Sts to listen and repeat.

Now repeat the same process for *tie* /t/ and the /ɪd/ sound.

Point out that /d/ and /t/ are very similar, but /ɪd/ is very different (see **Pronunciation notes**). Remind Sts that we pronounce -*ed* as /ɪd/ when the preceding letter is a *d* or a *t*. Stress that this is the only time that -*ed* is a separate syllable.

If these sounds are difficult for your Sts, model them yourself so that Sts can see your mouth position, and get Sts to repeat them a few more times.

Give further practice as necessary.

Finally, get Sts, in pairs, to practise saying the sentences.

Extra support

• If you are using an interactive whiteboard, you can focus on each sound individually before moving on to the next one.

b **(4 22))** Focus on the instructions. Then play the audio for Sts to listen and repeat the sentences in **1b**. Tell them to focus on pronouncing the past forms correctly.

> **(4 22))**
> 1 I booked my ticket online, Madrid to Stockholm.
> 2 I arrived in Stockholm at three o'clock.
> 3 I didn't like the weather! It was very cold and dark!
> 4 I travelled to Uppsala by bus.
> 5 I talked in English to the students on the bus.
> 6 We started classes the next day. I was nervous but excited.

Now put Sts in pairs. Tell them to cover the sentences, look at the pictures, and take turns saying the sentences to tell Clara's story.

Extra support

• Ask for volunteers to tell Clara's story by looking at the pictures. Get Sts to cover the sentences and then ask a volunteer *What happened in this picture?* If the student makes a mistake, encourage the class to help. Continue with the other pictures until Sts have retold the whole story.

3 SPEAKING

a Focus on the instructions. Give Sts time to read the phrases and deal with any new vocabulary.

Demonstrate the activity by saying a few true positive and negative sentences about yourself using the phrases in the chart, e.g. *I listened to the radio this morning. I didn't watch TV last night.*

Put Sts in pairs to say true sentences about themselves with the phrases. Monitor and check that Sts are saying both positive and negative sentences. Remind Sts to tick and cross the phrases depending on whether their partner did the activity – explain that they will be using this information in the next activity. Make sure also that Sts are saying the sentences and <u>not</u> writing them.

b Focus on the instructions and examples. Get Sts to change partners. Explain that they are now going to ask questions about the previous partners, using the phrases in the chart and giving short answers.

Tell Sts that they must first tell their new partner who they worked with in **a**.

Get Sts to ask and answer the questions with their new partner. Monitor and check that Sts are using the infinitive of the main verb in the question.

4 READING & SPEAKING

a (4 23)) Sts are now going to read what happened when Clara, the student from **1a**, arrived in Uppsala for her Erasmus programme. Focus on the task and make sure Sts know what *a blog* is. Focus on the instructions and give Sts time to read the possible problems and deal with any questions about vocabulary, e.g. *transport*. Point out that the first one has been done for them.

Now play the audio once the whole way through for Sts to listen and read at the same time.

> (4 23))
> See the blog in the Student's Book on *p.65*

Give Sts time to read the blog again if necessary and write *yes* or *no* next to each option. Remind them that when they read they should try to focus on the words they know, and try to guess the meaning of new words.

Get Sts to compare with a partner and then check answers.

> Only the weather was a problem.

! If you do **4 Reading & Speaking** in a later class when you did **1 Grammar**, you may want to revise the first part of Clara's story before you start. Elicit the eight sentences that are in **1b**, encouraging Sts to pronounce the *-ed* endings correctly.

b Now tell Sts to read the blog again and this time look for reasons why the things in **a** were or weren't a problem for Clara.

Get Sts to compare with a partner and then check answers.

> 1 The transport wasn't a problem because everybody travels by bike and Clara rented a bike.
> 2 The other students weren't a problem because they were very nice.
> 3 The teachers weren't a problem because they helped Clara a lot.
> 4 The university wasn't a problem because it was beautiful with a very big library.
> 5 The food wasn't a problem because there was a lot of fish and Clara really liked it.
> 6 The weather was a problem because it was very, very cold. In the winter it snowed a lot and it was dark very early.
> 7 Money wasn't a problem because Ericsson sponsored Clara's project.

c Focus on the highlighted words. Put Sts in pairs to guess their meanings.

Sts can use dictionaries to check the meaning of any words they are still unsure of. Or, if dictionaries are not available, explain the words yourself.

Then with the whole class ask Sts about their guesses. Encourage Sts to use English if possible, but they may need to use L1 at times.

Deal with any other vocabulary problems that arose.

d Do this as an open-class activity.

If your Sts are at secondary school or university, you could ask them if they would be interested in doing the Erasmus programme.

WORDS AND PHRASES TO LEARN

(4 61)) Tell Sts to go to *p.131* and focus on the **Words and phrases to learn** for **11A**. Make sure Sts understand the meaning of each phrase. If necessary, remind them of the context in which the words and phrases came up in the lesson. If you speak your Sts' L1, you might like to elicit a translation for the words / phrases for the Sts to write next to them. Play the audio, pausing after each phrase for Sts to repeat. You may also like to ask Sts to test each other on the phrases.

G past simple irregular verbs: *do, get, go, have*
V verb phrases with *do, get, go, have*
P sentence rhythm

11B Life in a day

Lesson plan

This lesson introduces the past simple of the four most common irregular verbs in English: *do*, *get*, *go*, and *have*.

The lesson begins by revising the vocabulary for daily routines. The new grammar is presented through the context of a conversation between a father who arrives back early from work and is surprised to find his teenage daughter at home. Sts learn the past form of the verbs *do*, *get*, *go*, and *have*.

In the second half of the lesson, Sts read an article about a film, *A Life in a Day*, which was made using videos showing daily life around the world on one particular day. In Pronunciation Sts focus on sentence rhythm in questions and answers in the past. Finally, Sts interview a partner about their 'life in a day' and then write a blog post about a typical day in their own lives.

STUDY LINK
- Workbook 11B
- iTutor
- iChecker on iTutor
- www.oup.com/elt/englishfile

Extra photocopiable activities
- **Grammar** past simple irregular verbs: *do, get, go, have p.160*
- **Communicative** Life in a day *p.199* (instructions *p.171*)
- www.oup.com/elt/teacher/englishfile

Optional lead-in (books closed)
- Test Sts on the verb phrases they know using *have* and *go* from **Vocabulary Bank *A typical day*** on *p.125* like this:

  T *breakfast*
  Sts *have breakfast*
  T *work*
  Sts *go to work*, etc.

1 VOCABULARY verb phrases with *do, get, go, have*

a Books open. Focus on the instructions and give Sts time to complete the verb phrases.

Get Sts to compare with a partner.

b (4 24)) Play the audio for Sts to listen and check.

Check answers by asking individual Sts to read the whole phrase.

See the verbs in **bold** in script 4.24

(4 24))
1	**get** up	8	**go** home
2	**have** breakfast	9	**go** shopping
3	**have** a shower	10	**do** homework
4	**go** to school	11	**do** sport
5	**have** a coffee	12	**have** dinner
6	**have** lunch	13	**go** to bed
7	**get** a bus	14	**have** a nice day

Extra support
- You could now play the audio again for Sts to listen and repeat.

Now tell Sts to cover the verbs and get them to test themselves on the verbs. They can do this individually or with a partner.

Extra idea
- If you didn't do the **Optional lead-in**, put Sts in pairs, **A** and **B**. **A** (book open) tests **B** (book closed) on 1–7 and then **B** (book open) tests **A** (book closed) on 8–14.

2 LISTENING

a (4 25)) Focus on the task. Highlight that Ben is a businessman and that Linda is his daughter. Ask *Where was Ben?* (in Paris), *Where's he now?* (at home), *Where's Linda?* (at home).

Focus on the list of places and check that Sts can remember what they mean.

Focus on the instructions and get Sts to cover the conversation with a piece of paper.

Play the audio once the whole way through for Sts to tick the places where Linda was during the day. Play the audio again as necessary.

Get Sts to compare with a partner and then check answers. Ask *Was Linda at school?* (No, she wasn't) *Was she in a café?* (Yes, she was), etc.

Sts should tick: in a café, in a museum.

4 25))

B = Ben, L = Linda

B Hi. I'm back. Linda! What are you doing at home?
L Hi, Dad. You're very early.
B Yes, I got an early flight. Why aren't you at school?
L We didn't have classes today. We went to the British Museum in the morning. It was great. And then we had lunch in the café there.
B Why didn't you go to school this afternoon?
L We had a free afternoon.
B What did you do?
L I did homework. I had a lot of work.
B Good girl. When are your exams?
L They're next week.
B Where's your mother?
L She went out. I think she went shopping.
B What's that?
L What?
B That noise.

b Tell Sts to uncover the conversation. Focus on the conversation and the instructions. Tell Sts they are going to listen to the conversation again and they need to complete the gaps. Give them time to see if they can remember any of the missing words.

Play the audio again for Sts to listen and complete the gaps. Play again as necessary.

Get Sts to compare with a partner.

Check answers by playing the audio again, pausing after each answer, and writing the words on the board.

1	home	6	free
2	flight	7	homework
3	classes	8	week
4	British	9	mother
5	lunch	10	shopping

Go through the conversation with Sts and elicit / explain any new words or phrases. Also explain / elicit that:
– *got* is the past of *get*
– *went* is the past of *go*
– *had* is the past of *have*
– *did* is the past of *do* and *do* is used both as a main verb and as an auxiliary.

c **4 26))** Focus on the instructions and the question. Make sure Sts understand the word *noise*.

Elicit some ideas from Sts, but <u>don't</u> tell them if they are right or not.

Play the audio once the whole way through for Sts to listen and answer the question.

Get Sts to compare with a partner and then check the answer.

The noise is a boy (Dylan) in Linda's room.

4 26))

B = Ben, L = Linda, D = Dylan

B Hmm! And who are you?
L Um, Dad, this is Dylan.
B What are you doing here, Dylan?
D Well, er... You see... Linda and I wanted to do our homework together.
B Oh did you? And what kind of homework was it, exactly?

3 GRAMMAR past simple irregular verbs:
do, get, go, have

a Focus on the chart. Highlight that the sentences in the left-hand column are in the present simple and those in the right-hand column are in the past simple.

Focus on the conversation in **2b** and elicit the word missing from the first gapped sentence in the chart (*did*).

Give Sts time to complete all the sentences in the chart.

Get Sts to compare with a partner.

b **4 27))** Play the audio for Sts to listen and check.

Check answers.

I **did** my homework.
I **got** a flight.
We **went** to a museum.
We **had** lunch in the café.

4 27))

I do my homework.	I did my homework.
I get a flight.	I got a flight.
We go to a museum.	We went to a museum.
We have lunch in the café.	We had lunch in the café.

Now play the audio again for Sts to listen and repeat.

Then repeat the activity, eliciting responses from individual Sts.

Highlight that all four verbs are irregular in the past tense (i.e. you don't add -*ed* – the verbs change their form).

Highlight too that *did* here is a main verb, but remind Sts that *did* is also used as an auxiliary verb to make questions in the past simple, e.g. *Did you go to school?*

c **4 28))** Tell Sts to go to **Grammar Bank 11B** on *p.112*.

Focus on the example sentences and play the audio for Sts to listen and repeat. Pause the audio as necessary.

Go through the rules with the class using the expanded information in the **Additional grammar notes** below to help you. You may want to use Sts' L1 here.

Additional grammar notes
past simple irregular verbs: *do, get, go, have*

• A small number of verbs (several of which are very common) are irregular in the past simple. The change of form can be just one or two letters, e.g. *get → got*, or can be a completely new word, e.g. *go → went*.

• As with regular verbs, irregular verbs are only irregular in positive sentences. In negative sentences *didn't* is used with the infinitive (not the past) and questions are formed using *did* + infinitive.
Some typical mistakes include: *Did you went to the cinema? I didn't had breakfast.*

• As with regular verbs all forms are the same for all persons.

Focus on the exercises for **11B** on *p.113* and get Sts to do them individually or in pairs. If they do them individually, get them to compare answers with a partner.

Check answers, getting Sts to read the full sentences.

> a
> 1 I had eggs for breakfast this morning.
> 2 Did she go to Spanish classes last year?
> 3 We didn't have lunch at home last week.
> 4 Mike didn't go to work by car yesterday.
> 5 They went to school by bus yesterday.
> 6 What time did you get up this morning?
> 7 Did you do sport or exercise last weekend?
> 8 You didn't do the housework yesterday.
> 9 I didn't get up early this morning.
>
> b
> 1 did...have, had
> 2 Did...do, did
> 3 did...go, didn't go
> 4 did...get up, got up
> 5 did...have, didn't have, had
> 6 Did...go, went, didn't go

Tell Sts to go back to the main lesson **11B**.

Extra support
• If you think Sts need more practice, you may want to give them the Grammar photocopiable activity at this point or leave it for later as consolidation or revision.

Extra idea
• Get Sts to practise the conversation in **2b** on *p.66*, with one student taking the part of Ben (the father) and the other student the part of Linda and then swapping roles. You could rehearse the conversation before you start with Sts repeating the conversation after you or the audio.

4 READING

a Focus on the instructions and read the introduction with the class (up to *24th July*). Elicit / explain any new vocabulary, e.g. *life* (and the irregular plural *lives*), *to film*.

Ask the question to the class.

> They filmed their lives.

b (4 29)) Focus on the instructions and the photos. Remind Sts that when they read, they should try to focus on the words they know and guess the meaning of new words.

Play the audio for Sts to listen and read at the same time.

> (4 29))
> See the article in the Student's Book on *p.67*

Give Sts time to read the article again if necessary and write the numbers of the photos in the squares.

Get Sts to compare with a partner and then check answers.

> 1 E   2 C   3 B   4 A   5 D

c Focus on the instructions and two questions. Elicit / explain that *normal* refers to things people usually or often do and that *unusual* means 'not usual'.

Give Sts time to read the article again and then answer the questions. You could ask Sts to make two lists, headed *Normal* and *Unusual*.

Get Sts to compare with a partner and then check answers. Note that shaving is a normal activity for most men, but shaving for the first time is special. If Sts have different answers, get them to explain.

> Sts' own answers

Deal with any other new vocabulary problems, e.g. *incredible*, *thousands*, etc.

Extra idea
• You could focus on the photos again and elicit from the class what happened in each photo, e.g. *in photo A, a woman did a skydive; in photo B, a man arived in Kathmandu on his bike*, etc.

d Focus on the instructions and get Sts to cover the article. You could get Sts to do this in pairs or you could call out each verb and get the class to tell you the past simple.

If Sts worked in pairs, check answers.

> open → opened   go → went
> get up → got up   work → worked
> wash → washed   do → did
> have → had

Extra support
• Write the answers on the board to help Sts with exercise **e**.

e Focus on the instructions and give Sts time to complete each gap with a verb from **d**.

Get Sts to compare with a partner and then check answers.

> 1 got up   3 did   5 went, had
> 2 opened   4 worked   6 washed

5 PRONUNCIATION sentence rhythm

Pronunciation notes
• Remind Sts that in English the words that carry the important information are said more strongly than others, e.g. in *What did you do last night? What, do,* and *last night* are stressed more strongly than *did* and *your*

• For more information on **Sentence rhythm**, see the **Pronunciation notes** in **2B**.

(4 30)) Focus on the instructions and the four questions and answers. Remind Sts that the words in bigger font are the ones which are stressed (because they carry the important information). Also remind them that the underlined syllables in the multi-syllable words are stressed more.

Play the audio once the whole way though for Sts just to listen.

4 30))
See the questions and answers in the Student's Book on *p.67*

Then play the audio again for Sts to listen and repeat the questions and answers, copying the rhythm. Encourage them to pronounce the bigger bold words more strongly and the other words as lightly as possible.

Extra support

• Put Sts in pairs, **A** and **B**, and get them to practise the questions and answers. Make sure they swap roles.

6 SPEAKING & WRITING

a Tell Sts to go to **Communication** *Life in a day* on *p.79*.

Focus on the instructions and the example. Explain that Sts have to use the prompts to make questions in the past. Point out that there are both *Wh-* and *yes | no* questions, e.g. *What time did you get up yesterday?* and *Did you have a shower?*

Elicit three or four example questions from the class. Check that Sts understand what information the questions are asking for. Model and drill the pronunciation of some or all of the questions, encouraging Sts to use good rhythm by stressing the important words in the sentence as in the previous pronunciation exercise.

Put Sts in pairs and get them to takes turns interviewing each other. They write their partner's answers in the **Your partner** column.

Monitor and check that Sts are using correct question format. Make notes of any problems to focus on later.

When Sts have finished interviewing each other get some feedback from various Sts.

Extra support

• Elicit all the questions in the past before Sts interview each other. You could get them to interview you first.

Extra idea

• When Sts have finished interviewing each other put them in small groups of four or five. Try to arrange this so that Sts are not in the same group as their partner. In groups, Sts tell the others about their first partners' day yesterday.

Tell Sts to go back to the main lesson **11B**.

b Tell Sts to go to **Writing** *A blog post* on *p.85*.

Focus on the instructions for **a** and read the title of the blog and the introduction. You might want to pre-teach the word *colleague*. Model and drill pronunciation.

Give Sts time to read the blog post and complete the task. Point out that the first one has been done for them.

Get Sts to compare with a partner and then check answers.

2 Then I had a shower and had breakfast. I didn't eat...
3 After that, I went to my new office. I got a taxi, because...
4 When I arrived, the boss introduced me...
5 I didn't go out for lunch – I had a sandwich in the office...
6 I went home at 5.30. I had a pizza for dinner...
7 I went to bed early, at 9.30. I was really tired, but...

Now go to **b**. Focus on the *Showing the order of events* box and go through it with the class. Elicit / explain that we use these words to show the order in which things happen.

Highlight that *Then* and *After* have the same meaning. *After* must be followed by a noun, e.g. *After lunch*. You can't use *after* by itself. Typical mistake: *We had lunch. After, we went shopping*. It should be *After lunch | After that we went shopping*.

Now go to **c**. Explain that Sts are going to write a blog post about their day yesterday.

Write this sentence on the board: YESTERDAY WAS A _____ DAY FOR ME. Ask a few Sts what word they would put in the gap. Suggest words like *normal*, *unusual*, *interesting*, *big*.

Tell Sts to use this sentence to begin their blog and make it true for their day. Then they should explain what they did using time-order words to put the events in order. Make sure Sts understand that they don't have to say everything they did, just the most interesting or important events in their day.

Get Sts to work individually to write their blog posts. Set a time limit that will allow most Sts to finish, but will not be too long. Monitor and help as needed. If short of time, you could set this for homework.

Check that Sts are using *Then*, *after that*, etc., and telling events in the order they happened.

Extra idea

• If you have corrected their blogs, you could get Sts to 'post' them by putting them on the wall in the classroom. Then get Sts to walk around the room and read each other's blogs.

WORDS AND PHRASES TO LEARN

4 61)) Tell Sts to go to *p.131* and focus on the **Words and phrases to learn** for **11B**. Make sure Sts understand the meaning of each phrase. If necessary, remind them of the context in which the words and phrases came up in the lesson. If you speak your Sts' L1, you might like to elicit a translation for the words / phrases for the Sts to write next to them. Play the audio, pausing after each phrase for Sts to repeat. You may also like to ask Sts to test each other on the phrases.

Asking for and giving directions
Prepositions of place
Sentence rhythm and polite intonation

PRACTICAL ENGLISH
Episode 6 Is there a bank near here?

Lesson plan

In this **Practical English** lesson, Sts learn how to understand and give simple directions in the street. They begin by learning six new prepositions of place and then some very basic language for directions, which is practised through a role-play. The focus is more on asking for and understanding directions than giving directions, as the latter is quite challenging for Sts at this level. The lesson ends with a song.

STUDY LINK
- **Workbook** Is there a bank near here?
- **iTutor**
- www.oup.com/elt/englishfile

Extra photocopiable activities
- **Communicative** Where are you? *p.200* (instructions *p.171*)
- **Song** *Somewhere Over the Rainbow p.233* (instructions *p.227*)

Test and Assessment CD-ROM
- **Quick Test 11**
- **File Test 11**
- www.oup.com/elt/teacher/englishfile

Optional lead-in (books closed)
- Write the prompt phrase PLACES IN A TOWN on the board. Give Sts two minutes in pairs to brainstorm words for places in a town, e.g. *school, bank, museum*, etc.
- Elicit words from the pair with the longest list and write them on the board. Tell the other Sts to listen and check the words on their list.
- Continue eliciting more words from different pairs. Try to elicit all the words for the places in the map on *p.68*.

1 SAYING WHERE PLACES ARE

a **4 31)))** Books open. Focus on the prepositions of place and the phrases.

Play the audio once the whole way through for Sts just to listen.

> **4 31)))**
> See the words and phrases in the Student's Book on *p.68*.

Now play it again, pausing after each item for Sts to listen and repeat. Give further practice as necessary, modelling and drilling the pronunciation yourself, or using the audio, and getting choral and individual responses.

Highlight that:
- *opposite* means face-to-face, and is used mainly for people or buildings.
- some prepositions of place are one word, e.g. *opposite*, *between*, but others are two, e.g. *next to*.
- *on the corner* can be followed by *of* + street name, e.g. *on the corner of Oxford Street*.

Extra idea
- You could give more practice with *next to, opposite*, and *between* by asking questions about things or people in the classroom, e.g. *Who's sitting next to Silvio? What's between my desk and the window?*

b **4 32)))** Focus on the instructions and the map. Give Sts time to read the names of the buildings and the streets.

Demonstrate the activity by choosing a place and describing its position yourself, e.g. *It's on the corner, next to the bookshop*, for Sts to say the place (the supermarket).

Play the audio, pausing after the man asks for the place he is looking for and elicit what it is (a coffee shop). Make sure Sts are clear they have to write *coffee shop* on the map in one of the labels A–D.

Now play the rest of the first dialogue and elicit the answer (the coffee shop is building D).

Play the rest of the audio, pausing after each dialogue to give Sts time to write the name of the place.

Check answers by playing the audio, pausing after each dialogue.

A phone shop	C park
B Chinese restaurant	D coffee shop

> **4 32)))**
>
> M = man, W = woman
>
> 1
> M Excuse me?
> W Yes?
> M Is there a coffee shop near here?
> W Yes, there's one in South Street. It's next to the cinema, on the right.
> M Thanks.
>
> 2
> M Excuse me. Is there a Chinese restaurant near here?
> W Yes, there's one in King Street, between the bank and the gym.
> M Thank you.
>
> 3
> M Excuse me. Is there a phone shop near here?
> W Yes, there's one in North Street, next to the hotel, on the left.
> M Thanks.
>
> 4
> M Excuse me. Where's the park?
> W It's in London Road opposite the gym.
> M Oh great. Thank you.

Extra support
- Model and drill the question *Where's the cinema?* Then say other places from the map for Sts to substitute, e.g.
  T *bookshop*   **Sts** *Where's the bookshop?*
- Demonstrate the activity by asking a few questions to individual Sts, e.g. *Where's the supermarket?* (It's next to the bookshop).

- In pairs, Sts ask and answer questions about the map to practise the prepositions of place in **1a**.
- Monitor and help, correcting pronunciation and prepositions as necessary.

c (4 33)》 Focus on the instructions and the map again. Model and drill the street names.

Focus on the dialogue and remind Sts that the bigger words in bold are pronounced more strongly. Also highlight that the speakers use polite intonation with a wide voice range. Play the audio once the whole way through for Sts to listen to the rhythm and intonation.

> (4 33)》
> See the dialogue in the Student's Book on *p.68*

Highlight the use of *Excuse me* /ɪksˈkjuːz miː/ in the dialogue as a polite way of attracting a stranger's attention (we don't use *Please!* or *Sorry!*). Also point out that polite intonation in English tends to be higher than normal intonation.

Now play the audio again, pausing after each line, for Sts to listen and repeat, encouraging them to copy the rhythm and intonation on the audio.

d Go through the instructions and focus on the example in the speech bubbles. Remind Sts we use *Is there a* for singular places and *Are there any* for plural places.

Model and drill the question *Is there a bank near here?* Then say other places on the map for Sts to substitute, e.g.: **T** *gym* **Sts** *Is there a gym near here?*

Demonstrate the activity by asking one student about a place and elicit an answer, e.g. *Excuse me. Is there a gym near here?* (Yes, there's one in King Street, next to the Chinese restaurant.)

Put Sts in pairs and get them to ask and answer questions about the places on the map. Monitor and help.

2 ◼️ ASKING FOR & GIVING DIRECTIONS
VIDEO

a (4 34)》 Focus on the pictures and directions, and give Sts time to match them.

Then play the audio once for Sts to listen and check.

Check answers.

See script 4.34

> (4 34)》
> 1 C Go straight on.   2 A Turn right.   3 B Turn left.

Now play the audio again for Sts to listen and repeat. Give further practice as necessary, modelling and drilling the pronunciation yourself, or using the audio, and getting choral and individual responses.

Use gestures to elicit the phrases, e.g. *go straight on*, by making an appropriate gesture, e.g. putting both hands together and pointing forwards with them, *turn right* (the gesture could be pointing right with your right hand), and *turn left* (the gesture could be pointing left with your left hand). These gestures will be easier for your Sts to see if you turn sideways to the class.

Extra idea
- If you have room in the classroom, get Sts to stand up and follow directions. You could include *Stop!*, too.

b (4 35)》 Focus on the instructions and the question. Elicit the meaning of *cash machine*.

Tell Sts to cover the dialogue and look at the small map. Make sure Sts know where Rob is standing and play the video or audio twice for them to follow the directions to the cash machine.

Get Sts to compare with a partner and then check the answer.

Bank B

> (4 35)》
> See the dialogue in the Student's Book on *p.69*

Now tell Sts to uncover the dialogue and go through it line by line. You could play it again for Sts to listen and read at the same time. Highlight:
- the difference between *Turn left* and *It's on the left*.
- responding to *Thanks very much* / *Thanks* with *You're welcome*.

c Play the dialogue in **b** again, pausing after each sentence for Sts to repeat.

Now put Sts in pairs and get them to practise the dialogue.

Monitor and help as needed. Make sure they swap roles.

d (4 36)》 Focus on the instructions and make sure Sts understand why Rob needs to find another bank. Make sure Sts know that Rob is now standing outside Bank B.

Play the audio once the whole way through for Sts to listen and answer the question. Play again as necessary.

Check the answer.

Bank C

> (4 36)》
> (script in Student's Book on *p.89*)
> **R** Oh ****. I don't believe it. Excuse me, this cash machine isn't working. Is there another one near here?
> **M** Yeah, there's one in HSBC. Go straight on, turn right. Go straight on for a bit and it's on the left.
> **R** Thanks.

Extra support
- If there's time, you could play the audio again while Sts read the script on *p.89*, so they can see what they understood / didn't understand. Translate / explain any new words or phrases.

e Put Sts in pairs, **A** and **B**, and tell them to go to **Communication** *Excuse me. Can you help me?*, **A** on *p.79* and **B** on *p.83*.

Focus on the instructions and give Sts time to read their roles and look at their maps. Explain that they each have to ask for directions to two places and then label the buildings.

Tell the **A**s to start by asking the **B**s for directions to the bus station. You could point out to the **A**s that they can't see a bus station on their map and to the **B**s that they can see one. Monitor and make a note of any problems Sts are having.

Tell Sts to swap roles when the **A**s have written their first label. Now **B** asks **A** for directions to the university. Monitor and help, making a note of any general problems Sts are having and deal with these on the board at the end.

When they have finished asking for their places get Sts to compare maps to check their labels.

Extra support
• You could get Sts to write the directions down before they give them orally to their partner.

Tell Sts to go back to the main lesson **PE6**.

3 ◼◀ WHERE'S JENNY'S HOTEL?

a (4 37))) Focus on the instructions and question.

Play the video or audio once the whole way through for Sts to listen and answer the question.

Check the answer.

> To check she got his email about the hotel.

> (4 37)))
> (script in Student's Book on *p.90*)
> R = Rob, J = Jenny
> J Hello?
> R Hi, Jennifer?
> J Yes?
> R This is Rob Walker from *London24seven*. I'm phoning to check you got the email I sent you.
> J Er, what was it about?
> R It was the information about your hotel for next week.
> J Just a second. Yes here it is. Hotel Indigo, London Street. Where is it exactly?
> R It's very near Paddington Station. You can get the Heathrow Express train from the airport to the station. It only takes about fifteen minutes.
> J OK, that's great. Can I walk to the hotel from the station?
> R Yes, it's very near. Can you see it on the map?
> J Er, yes, I have it now.
> R Turn left when you leave the station. Then go straight on for a bit and turn right into London Street. The hotel's opposite Norfolk Square.
> J Great.
> R I can come to the hotel in the morning on your first day. We can walk to the office together.
> J OK. See you then.
> R Bye.
> J Bye.

b Focus on the instructions and Jenny's notes about her hotel. Give Sts time to read them. Point out that number 1 has been one for them.

Play the video or audio again for Sts to listen and complete the task. Play again as necessary.

Get Sts to compare with a partner and then check answers.

> 2 London   5 15   8 right
> 3 Station   6 left   9 opposite
> 4 airport   7 straight on

Extra support
• If there's time, you could play the audio again while Sts read the script on *p.90*, so they can see what they

understood / didn't understand. Translate / explain any new words or phrases.

Extra idea
• As this is the last episode of Rob and Jenny on the video, if your Sts have enjoyed it, you might want to ask them what they think happens when Jenny comes to London, and tell them that they can find out in *English File* Elementary!

4 ◼◀ USEFUL PHRASES

(4 38))) Focus on the phrases and make sure Sts understand what each one means.

Play the video or audio once the whole way through for Sts just to listen.

> (4 38)))
> See the phrases in the Student's Book on *p.69*

Now play the video or audio again, pausing after each phrase for Sts to listen and repeat.

Give further practice as necessary, modelling and drilling the pronunciation yourself, or using the video or audio, and getting choral and individual responses.

5 (4 MP3))) SONG *Somewhere Over the Rainbow*

For Sts of this level all authentic song lyrics will include language that they don't know.

This song was recorded by Hawaiian singer Israel Kamakawiwo'ole in 1993. For copyright reasons this is a cover version.

If you want to do this song in class, use the photocopiable activity on *p.233*.

You will find the songs as MP3 files on CD4 of the Class audio CD.

> (4 MP3)))
> ***Somewhere Over the Rainbow***
> Somewhere over the rainbow
> Way up high
> And the dreams that you dream of once in a lullaby
>
> Oh somewhere over the rainbow
> Bluebirds fly
> And the dreams that you dream of, dreams
> Really do come true
>
> Some day I'll wish upon a star
> Wake up where the clouds are far behind me
> Where trouble melts like lemon drops
> High above the chimney top
> That's where you'll find me
>
> Oh somewhere over the rainbow
> Bluebirds fly
> And the dreams that you dare to
> Oh why, oh why can't I?
>
> Oh, someday I'll wish upon a star
> Wake up where the clouds are far behind me
> Where trouble melts like lemon drops
> High above the chimney top
> That's where you'll find me
>
> Oh somewhere over the rainbow
> Way up high
> And the dreams that you dare to
> Why, oh why can't I?

G past simple: regular and irregular verbs (revision)
V more irregular verbs
P irregular verbs

12A Strangers on a train

Lesson plan

In this lesson, Sts revise the past simple (regular and irregular verbs) and learn some more irregular verbs in the context of a short story with a surprise ending about two strangers who meet on a train. Sts first read and listen to the story. Then in Vocabulary and Pronunciation Sts learn some new high frequency irregular verbs. In Grammar, Sts revise the past simple of regular and irregular verbs including the past of the verb *be*. Finally, the lesson ends with a speaking activity in which Sts ask and answer questions about what they did in the morning, previous evening, and previous week.

STUDY**LINK**
- Workbook 12A
- iTutor
- www.oup.com/elt/englishfile

Extra photocopiable activities
- **Grammar** past simple: regular and irregular verbs *p.161*
- **Communicative** Past tense questions *p.201* (instructions *p.172*)
- www.oup.com/elt/teacher/englishfile

Optional lead-in (books closed)
- Write the following on the board:

  THE LAST TIME YOU TRAVELLED BY TRAIN / BUS
  WHERE DID YOU GO?
  WHEN WAS IT?
  WHO DID YOU GO WITH?
  WHAT DID YOU DO ON THE TRAIN?

- Put Sts in pairs and give them a few minutes to answer the questions.

- Get feedback by getting a couple of Sts to tell the class about their partner, e.g. *Sabina went from here to Paris by train last month. She went with her family. They had lunch on the train.*

1 READING & LISTENING

a (4 40))) to (4 43))) Books open. Pre-teach the following vocabulary to help Sts with the story. Draw a train on the board and elicit the word *train*. Now elicit / teach words connected with travelling by train, e.g. *platform, seat, station, ticket*. Write them on the board and drill pronunciation.

Focus on the title of the story, *Strangers on a train*, and elicit / explain that *a stranger* is a person you don't know, NOT a person from another country (which is *foreigner*). NB The word *stranger* in English may be similar to the word for *foreigner* in your Sts' languages.

(4 40))) Now focus on **Part 1**. Tell Sts that they are going to read and listen at the same time. Tell them that they should try to guess the meaning of the verbs which are highlighted in yellow. These verbs will be focussed on later in the lesson. They are all past simple forms of verbs, which Sts know in the present.

Play the audio once the whole way through for Sts to read and listen to **Part 1**.

Focus on questions 1–4 and get Sts to answer them in pairs. Tell them to use the pictures to help them.

Check answers.

1 He saw her at the station / on the platform.
2 Chanel Number 5
3 They talked about (classical) music.
4 They had (a cup of) coffee.

(4 40)))
See Part 1 in the Student's Book on *p.70*

Elicit / teach the meaning of any words in the story you think Sts may not have understood, e.g. *blonde, move, full* (elicit the opposite *empty*), *nice smell*, etc.

(4 41))) Now focus on **Part 2**. Play the audio for Sts to read and listen at the same time.

Focus on questions 5–8 and give Sts time to answer them in pairs.

Check answers.

5 She works in property – flats and houses. (= she buys and sells them.)
6 He works for Citibank.
7 He lives in Chelsea / in London / in an expensive part of London.
8 She lives near him / Chelsea..

(4 41)))
See Part 2 in the Student's Book on *p.70*

Elicit / teach the meaning of any words or phrases you think Sts may not have understood, e.g. *property, That's interesting, time to go.*

(4 42))) Now focus on **Part 3**. Play the audio for Sts to read and listen at the same time.

Focus on questions 9–12 and give Sts time to answer them in pairs.

Check answers.

9 She had a BMW.
10 I really want to c u again! Friday?
11 She had two tickets for a Beethoven concert.
12 She wanted to meet in the bar at 7.30.

(4 42)))
See Part 3 in the Student's Book on *p.71*

Elicit / explain that the text message in 10 means *I really want to see you again*; in text messages people often use *c* instead of *see* and *u* instead of *you*.

Elicit / teach the meaning of any words you think Sts may not have understood, e.g. *box office*. You could tell Sts that the Royal Albert Hall is a famous concert hall in London.

(4 43))) Now focus on **Part 4**. Play the audio for Sts to read and listen at the same time.

Focus on questions 13–16 and give Sts time to answer them in pairs.

Check answers. For question 17, elicit opinions, but don't tell Sts if they are right or not.

> 13 He arrived at 7.00.
> 14 He got a text message from Olivia. He left her ticket at the box office and went to his seat in the concert hall.
> 15 He phoned Olivia and sent her a text message.
> 16 He left the concert hall and went home.
> 17 Sts' own answers

> **(4 43)))**
> See Part 4 in the Student's Book on *p.71*

Elicit / explain that the man's text says *Where are you?* and that the letter *r* is often used in text messages instead of *are*. Also elicit / teach the meaning of any words you think Sts may not have understood, e.g. the use of *get* in *got the tickets*, *angry*, *turn on*.

Extra support

• You could let Sts listen and read (or just read) the whole story again from the beginning.

b **(4 44)))** Focus on the questions and elicit some opinions about what David saw when he opened the door to his flat.

Now play the audio for Sts to find out what happened.

Get them to compare with a partner and then play the audio again.

Check the answer to the first question.

> (He saw that) there was no TV and there weren't any pictures on the walls. His laptop wasn't in his bedroom.

> **(4 44)))**
> Part 5
> I opened the door of my flat and turned on the light. Oh no! My flat looked very different. There was no TV and there weren't any pictures on the walls. I went into my bedroom. My laptop wasn't there. But there was a nice smell. Chanel Number 5.

Now ask Sts *Who do you think took the things from his flat?* (Olivia). *How did he know?* (Because there was a smell of Chanel No.5 perfume).

Finally, elicit whether Sts think the ending of the story is good or not.

Extra support

• If there's time, you could play the audio again while Sts read the scripts, so they can see what they understood / didn't understand. Translate / explain any new words or phrases.

Extra idea

• You could give Sts extra listening practice by getting them to close their books and <u>listen</u> to (not read) the whole story on audio.

2 VOCABULARY & PRONUNCIATION

more irregular verbs

> **Pronunciation notes**
>
> • Some verbs which are irregular in the past tense have quite tricky pronunciation, e.g. *buy – bought* /bɔːt/, *say – said* /sed/ (NOT /sed/), *see – saw* /sɔː/, *tell – told* /təʊld/.
>
> • As these verbs are very high frequency it is worth spending some time on making sure Sts can pronounce the past simple forms correctly.

a Focus on the verbs and elicit / explain that they are all verbs which are irregular in the past tense. Check that Sts understand their meaning.

Give Sts a few minutes to find the past forms in the story.

b **(4 45)))** Play the audio for Sts to listen and check.

Check answers and get Sts to spell the words to you as you write them on the board.

> See script 4.45

> **(4 45)))**
>
> | | | | |
> |---|---|---|---|
> | buy → bought | say → said | see → saw | tell → told |
> | leave → left | sit → sat | send → sent | write → wrote |

Write the word *bought* on the board and say it /bɔːt/. Ask Sts *What do you notice about the spelling and pronunciation of this word?* Elicit that the letters *gh* are not pronounced. They are silent. Highlight also that the pronunciation of *said* is /sed/, not /seɪd/.

Play the audio again, pausing after each verb for Sts to listen and repeat.

c **(4 46)))** Focus on the task and the example. Tell Sts they will hear the infinitive and they must say the past simple.

Play the first verb, pausing the audio for Sts to say *said* in chorus.

Play the rest of the audio for Sts to listen and say the past simple of the verb.

> **(4 46)))**
>
> | | |
> |---|---|
> | 1 say (*pause*) said | 5 leave (*pause*) left |
> | 2 tell (*pause*) told | 6 send (*pause*) sent |
> | 3 buy (*pause*) bought | 7 see (*pause*) saw |
> | 4 write (*pause*) wrote | 8 sit (*pause*) sat |

Finally, repeat the activity, eliciting responses from individual Sts.

3 GRAMMAR past simple:
regular and irregular verbs (revision)

a This exercise tests Sts on what they have learnt about the past simple in English so far. Focus on the task and the two conversations.

Give Sts time to read the conversations and choose the correct form.

Get Sts to compare with a partner.

b (4 47)) Play the audio for Sts to listen and check.

Check answers. You could get pairs to read the conversations out loud.

See verbs in **bold** in script 4.47

(4 47))

1 **A** Where did you **go** on Saturday?
   B I **went** shopping for clothes.
   A What did you **buy**?
   B I **bought** a new jacket.
   A **Was** it expensive?
   B No, it **wasn't**.

2 **A** What **did you do** last night?
   B I **saw** a film – it was a comedy with Brad Pitt.
   A **Did** you **like** it?
   B No, I **didn't like** it much. It **was** very slow.

Extra idea

• Put Sts in pairs and get them to practise the conversations. Make sure they swap roles.

c (4 48)) to (4 50)) Tell Sts to go to **Grammar Bank 12A** on *p.114*.

Highlight that this **Grammar Bank** is revision of what they have learnt about the past simple in recent Files.

Focus on the example sentences and play the audio for Sts to listen and repeat. Pause the audio as necessary.

Go through the rules with the class using the expanded information in the **Additional grammar notes** below to help you. You may want to use Sts' L1 here.

Additional grammar notes

past simple: regular and irregular verbs (revision)

• Remind Sts:
  – that you don't use the auxiliaries *did / didn't* to make questions with the verb *be* in the past tense, e.g. *Were you at home last night?* NOT *Did you be at home last night?*
  – regular verbs add *-ed* or *-d* to the infinitive in positive sentences
  – most verbs are regular (e.g. *like*, *live*), but some common verbs are irregular and change their form in the past simple (e.g. *go – went*, *have – had*)
  – use *did / didn't* + infinitive to make questions and negatives with all verbs except *be* (and *can*), e.g. *Did you like it? Did you go?* NOT *Did you liked it? Did you went?*

• (4 62)) (4 63)) Refer Sts to the **Appendix** on *p.132*, listing the regular and irregular verbs which have been taught in the Beginner Student's Book.

Focus on the exercise for **12A** on *p.115* and get Sts to do it individually or in pairs. If they do it individually, get them to compare answers with a partner.

Check answers, getting Sts to read the full sentences.

1	rented	11	answered	21	told
2	was	12	saw	22	waited
3	did	13	looked	23	went
4	went	14	was	24	was
5	visited	15	wasn't	25	had
6	stayed	16	did...see	26	did...leave
7	had	17	asked	27	were
8	were	18	Did...talk	28	wanted
9	arrived	19	didn't speak	29	was
10	said	20	said		

Tell Sts to go back to the main lesson **12A**.

Extra support

• If you think Sts need more practice, you may want to give them the Grammar photocopiable activity at this point or leave it for later as consolidation or revision.

4 SPEAKING

a Focus on the task and then give Sts time to complete each question with *was*, *were*, or *did*.

Get Sts to compare with a partner and then check answers. Model and drill the pronunciation of some of the questions.

This morning
What time **did** you get up this morning? **Were** you tired?
Did you have breakfast at home? What **did** you have?
What time **did** you leave home to come to class today?
How **did** you come to class? **Were** you late?

Last night
Were you at home all evening?
Did you watch TV?
Did you study English? **Was** it difficult?
What **did** you have for dinner? **Was** it nice?
What time **did** you go to bed?

Last week
Did you see a film last week?
Which film **was** it? **Was** it good?
Did you go shopping last week?
What **did** you buy? **Was** it expensive?
Did you do any exercise?

---

b Demonstrate the activity by getting Sts to ask you some or all of the questions first.

Now put Sts in pairs and get them to ask and answer the questions, giving as much information as possible. Get some feedback.

Extra idea

• Put Sts in new pairs and get them to tell their new partner a few things about their first partner.

WORDS AND PHRASES TO LEARN

(4 61)) Tell Sts to go to *p.131* and focus on the **Words and phrases to learn** for **12A**. Make sure Sts understand the meaning of each phrase. If necessary, remind them of the context in which the words and phrases came up in the lesson. If you speak your Sts' L1, you might like to elicit a translation for the words / phrases for the Sts to write next to them. Play the audio, pausing after each phrase for Sts to repeat. You may also like to ask Sts to test each other on the phrases.

G present continuous for future
V future time expressions
P the letters *ea*

12B A weekend in Venice

Lesson plan

This lesson introduces Sts for the first time to a future form (the present continuous used with a future meaning, e.g. *I'm leaving tomorrow*). The context for the lesson is a woman telling her friend about her forthcoming trip to Venice.

The lesson starts with a focus on future time expressions in Vocabulary. Then in Grammar the present continuous to describe future arrangements is presented through a conversation between two friends. In Pronunciation the focus is on different pronunciations of the letters *ea* in words such as *leave*, *weather*, etc. Sts then listen to three people talking about trips they have planned for the near future. Finally, in a speaking activity, Sts plan and talk about their own 'dream city break'.

On *p.129* of the Student's Book there is a group board game, which revises the main language Sts have learnt in *English File* Beginner. You could do this activity before or after **Revise and Check**.

STUDY LINK
- **Workbook 12B**
- iTutor
- iChecker on iTutor
- www.oup.com/elt/englishfile

Extra photocopiable activities
- **Grammar** present continuous for future *p.162*
- **Communicative** Holidays *p.202* (instructions *p.172*)
  Revision questions *p.203* (instructions *p.172*)
- www.oup.com/elt/teacher/englishfile

Optional lead-in (books closed)
- Write the sentences below on the board and then complete the title with a place you recently went to for the weekend:

  A WEEKEND IN _____
      WHEN DID YOU GO THERE?
      HOW DID YOU GO? (BY CAR, BUS, ETC.)
      WHO DID YOU GO WITH?
      WHERE DID YOU STAY? (WITH FAMILY, HOTEL, ETC.)
      WHAT DID YOU DO THERE?

- Get Sts to ask you the questions and give simple answers.

- Now put Sts in pairs and get them to write the sentence *A weekend in _____* and complete it with a real place they went to recently. They then take turns to ask each other the five questions to find out about their partner's weekend.

- Get some feedback from some pairs by asking about their weekends.

1 VOCABULARY future time expressions

a Books open. Focus on the time expressions in the list and the examples on the timeline. Elicit / remind Sts of the meaning of *now*, *tonight*, and *the future*.

Tell Sts they have to write the time expressions in order on the timeline. Point out the examples already done.

Put Sts in pairs and give them a few minutes to complete the rest of the timeline.

b (4 51)) Play the audio for Sts to listen and check.

Check answers and model and drill pronunciation. Highlight that we do not usually use *the* with these expressions, e.g. *next week* NOT ~~the next week~~.

> 2 tomorrow
> 4 the day after tomorrow
> 5 next weekend

> **(4 51))**
> 1 tonight
> 2 tomorrow
> 3 tomorrow night
> 4 the day after tomorrow
> 5 next weekend
> 6 next month

2 GRAMMAR present continuous for future

a Focus on the task. Elicit / explain the meaning of *advertisement* and *a city break*. (Sts should already be familiar with *break* = a short period of time when you stop and rest, e.g. *a coffee break*). Model and drill pronunciation. Ask Sts where Venice is (Italy) and find out if any of them have had a holiday there.

Get Sts to read the advertisement (or read it aloud to them) and ask them if they would like to go there or if they have been, would they like to go again.

Elicit opinions.

Deal with any vocabulary problems that arose.

b (4 52)) Get Sts to cover the conversation. Focus on the instructions and give Sts time to read sentences 1–5.

Play the audio once the whole way through for Sts to listen and circle **a** or **b**. Play again as necessary.

Get Sts to compare with a partner and then check answers.

> 1 a   2 b   3 b   4 a   5 a

(4 52)))

F = Fiona, L = Lisa

F Next weekend's a long weekend. Are you doing anything?
L I'm going to Venice for three nights.
F Lucky you! When are you leaving?
L On Friday morning. My flight's at 8.40.
F Are you going with somebody?
L No. I like travelling alone. I can do all my favourite things –
   go to art galleries, go shopping... But I'm meeting an old
   school friend. She works in Padua, and that's very near.
F Where are you staying?
L I'm staying at a little hotel near St Mark's Square. The Aqua
   Palace. It looks nice, and it isn't very expensive.
F What are you planning to do there?
L On Saturday morning I'm going to Murano – that's the
   island where they make beautiful glass. Then I'm having
   lunch at a lovely restaurant called *Ca d'Oro*—
F Stop, stop, you're making me really jealous!

---

c Get Sts to uncover the conversation and look at the
verbs in the list. Give them a few minutes to read
the conversation and complete each gap with one of
the verbs. Point out that the first one has been done for
them.

Now play the audio again for Sts to listen and check.

Check answers.

2	going	5	meeting	8	going
3	leaving	6	staying	9	having
4	going	7	staying		

Go through the conversation line by line, making
sure Sts understand it. Highlight that *a long weekend*
is a weekend when either the previous Friday or the
following Monday is a public holiday. Deal with any
other new vocabulary, e.g. *somebody, alone, art gallery,
island, glass, lovely, jealous*, etc.

d Do this as an open-class activity and elicit the answer
from the class.

2 (in the future)

e **(4 53)))** Tell Sts to go to **Grammar Bank 12B** on *p.114*.

Focus on the example sentences and play the audio for
Sts to listen and repeat. Pause the audio as necessary.

Go through the rules with the class using the expanded
information in the **Additional grammar notes** below
to help you. You may want to use Sts' L1 here.

Additional grammar notes
Present continuous for future

- This is the first time that Sts meet a future form
  in English. At this level we think that this is the
  easiest one to learn as Sts already know the form
  of the present continuous and how to use it to talk
  about things which are happening now.

- Some Sts, depending on their L1, may find this
  future use (e.g. *What are you doing at the weekend?*)
  strange as in their language the present simple may
  be used for this.

- Typical mistakes include: *What do you at the
  weekend? I go to the cinema after the class tonight.*

- Highlight that this form of the future is used to
  talk about our plans and arrangements for the near
  future, the kind of things we would write in our
  diary for the immediate future.

Focus on the exercises for **12B** on *p.115* and get Sts to do
them individually or in pairs. If they do them individually,
get them to compare answers with a partner.

Check answers, getting Sts to read the full sentences.

a
1 Are...meeting
2 'm not cooking, 're going
3 isn't coming
4 are...going
5 Are...flying, 're getting
6 is leaving
7 are...staying, aren't staying, 're renting

b
1 are...wearing
2 is...leaving
3 are...doing
4 are...coming
5 are...going, 'm meeting
6 am playing

Tell Sts to go back to the main lesson **12B**.

Extra support

- If you think Sts need more practice, you may want to
  give them the Grammar photocopiable activity at this
  point or leave it for later as consolidation or revision.

f Focus on the instructions and two examples. Either do
this as an open-class activity and elicit the sentences
onto the board or put Sts in pairs and get them to write
the sentences.

If Sts worked in pairs, elicit Lisa's trip from the class.

Suggested answers
She's travelling alone.
She's going to art galleries and she's going shopping.
She's meeting an old friend.
She's staying in a hotel for three nights.
She's going to Murano.
She's eating lunch at a lovely restaurant.

g Focus on the instructions and the questions in
the questionnaire. Now focus on the example and
demonstrate the activity by getting a student to ask
you the question (*Where are you going after class?*) and
answer it.

Then get Sts to form the other questions in the
questionnaire and ask you. Give clear simple answers,
which you could write on the board.

Now put Sts in pairs and get them to ask and answer
the questions. Monitor and help.

Get some feedback from the class.

Extra support

- Put Sts in pairs and get them to write the questions
  first. Check the questions with the class before Sts
  ask and answer them.

3 PRONUNCIATION the letters *ea*

Pronunciation notes
- The combination of vowels *ea* has several possible pronunciations.
- The most common is /iː/, e.g. *speak*. /e/ is less common, e.g. *breakfast*. /eɪ/ is very rare, and the only common *ea* words with this sound are *great*, *break*, and *steak*.

a (4 54))) Read the **Pronunciation notes** and decide how much of the information you want to give your Sts.

Focus on the *ea* box and go through it with the class.

Now focus on the exercise and play the audio once the whole way through for Sts just to listen.

> (4 54)))
> See the words and sounds in the Student's Book on *p.73*

Now focus on the sound picture *tree*. Play the audio to model and drill the word and the sound (pause after the sound).

Then focus on the words after *tree*. Remind Sts that the pink letters are the /iː/ sound. Play the audio, pausing after each word for Sts to listen and repeat.

Now repeat the same process for *egg* /e/ and *train* /eɪ/.

If these sounds are difficult for your Sts, model them yourself so that Sts can see your mouth position, and get Sts to repeat them a few more times.

Play the audio again from the beginning, pausing after each group of words for Sts to repeat.

Give further practice as necessary.

Finally, get Sts, in pairs, to practise saying the words.

Extra support
- If you are using an interactive whiteboard, you can focus on each sound individually before moving on to the next one.

b (4 55))) Play the audio once the whole way through for Sts just to listen.

> (4 55)))
> See the sentences in the Student's Book on *p.73*

Then play it again, pausing after each sentence for Sts to listen and repeat.

Then repeat the activity, eliciting responses from individual Sts.

4 LISTENING

a (4 56))) Focus on the instructions and the chart.

Tell Sts they are now going to listen to Carol talking to a colleague about her travel plans and they must complete as much of the chart as possible.

Play the audio once the whole way through for Sts just to listen.

Give Sts some time to see if they can complete any information in the chart and then play the audio again.

Check answers.

Carol
1. Scotland
2. Saturday morning
3. by train
4. her husband
5. with some friends

> (4 56)))
> (script in Student's Book on *p.90*)
> C = colleague, Ca = Carol
>
> C   Are you going on holiday next week?
> Ca Yes, we are.
> C   Where are you going?
> Ca We're going to Scotland.
> C   When are you leaving?
> Ca We're leaving on Saturday morning, very early.
> C   How are you travelling there?
> Ca We're going by train. I love trains!
> C   Are you going with the children?
> Ca No, I'm going with my husband, Jim – just the two of us.
> C   How nice. Where are you staying?
> Ca We're staying with some friends who have a house near Edinburgh.

b (4 57))) (4 58))) Now repeat the process for Martin and play audio 4.57.

Martin
1. Paris
2. Monday afternoon
3. by train
4. his girlfriend
5. in a hotel

> (4 57)))
> (script in Student's Book on *p.90*)
> C = colleague, M = Martin
>
> C Are you going anywhere next weekend?
> M Yes, I'm going to Paris.
> C Lucky you! When are you leaving?
> M On Monday afternoon.
> C Are you flying?
> M No, I'm going by train. On the Eurostar. I hate flying!
> C Who are you going with?
> M With my girlfriend.
> C Where are you staying?
> M In a hotel near the Eiffel Tower. It looks very nice.
> C Have a great trip.

Finally, repeat the process for Sebastian and play audio 4.58.

Sebastian
1. Spain
2. Saturday morning
3. by car
4. three friends
5. They're camping.

4 58)))

(script in Student's Book on *p.90*)

C = colleague, S = Sebastian

C   Would you like to have dinner next week?
S   Sorry, I can't. I'm going on holiday.
C   Oh. Where are going?
S   To Spain – to the Costa Brava.
C   Great. When are you leaving?
S   On Saturday morning.
C   Are you flying there?
S   No, we're driving.
C   Who are going with?
S   Three friends from university.
C   That's nice. Where are you staying?
S   We're camping.
C   Well, I hope you have good weather!
S   Oh, me too.

Finally, ask Sts whose holiday they would like to go on.

Extra support

- If there's time, you could play the audio again while Sts read the scripts on *p.90*, so they can see what they understood / didn't understand. Translate / explain any new words or phrases.

5 SPEAKING

a   Focus on the photos and ask Sts what cities they are (Top, left to right: Berlin, Prague, and Paris; bottom: Dublin, Rome, Barcelona). Then ask if Sts would like to go to these places for a city break.

Write DREAM CITY BREAK on the board and elicit the meaning.

Tell Sts they are going to plan their own dream weekend away. Focus on the questions and give Sts time to think of their own answers.

Extra support

- Elicit the questions before putting Sts in pairs:
  Where are you going?   *Who are you going with?*
  When are you going?   *Where are you staying?*
  How are you travelling?

b   Put Sts in small groups and get them to ask and answer the questions, giving as much information as possible. When they have asked each other all the questions, they should decide whose trip they prefer.

Get some feedback from various groups, finding out where they chose and why.

WORDS AND PHRASES TO LEARN

4 61))) Tell Sts to go to *p.131* and focus on the **Words and phrases to learn** for **12B**. Make sure Sts understand the meaning of each phrase. If necessary, remind them of the context in which the words and phrases came up in the lesson. If you speak your Sts' L1, you might like to elicit a translation for the words / phrases for the Sts to write next to them. Play the audio, pausing after each phrase for Sts to repeat. You may also like to ask Sts to test each other on the phrases.

Extra support

- If you would like to end the last lesson with a fun and motivating revision activity, use the board game pn *p.129* (see instructions in the right hand column).

FILES 1–12 THE BOARD GAME

The group board game on *p.129* revises the main language Sts have learnt in *English File* Beginner. As well as providing a final revision, it allows Sts to measure their own progress over the course in a fun and motivating way.

> **LANGUAGE**
> Grammar and vocabulary of the book

Divide the class into groups of three or four. Tell each group to use one copy of the game on *p.129*, and give each group a coin and a counter for each student.

Tell Sts what the two sides of a coin are called, *heads* and *tails*. Then write on the board: HEADS = MOVE ONE SQUARE, TAILS = MOVE TWO SQUARES. As a demonstration, ask a confident student to toss the coin and move that number of squares from the start. Get another member of their group to read out the question. The student who tossed the coin then answers the question. Ask the rest of the group *Was that OK?* to encourage Sts to listen to and evaluate what the others in their group say. If the rest of the group say no, ask them what the problem is. If they are happy with the performance, pass the coin to the next student. Tell all groups to start in the same way.

Monitor as the groups play, but don't interfere unless you hear Sts fail to pick up on a serious error. You could make notes on errors to deal with later in class if you like.

Sts continue to play until one student reaches the finish and is the winner. They must throw the exact number needed to land on the finish. If, for example, they need a one, but throw a two, they must move to the finish and then one back, to number 16.

Groups that finish fast can look back through the squares, taking turns to do the ones that were not landed on in the game.

Extra support

- If you would like to end the last lesson without the Student's Book, there is a **Communicative** revision questions photocopiable activity on *p.203* (instructions *p.172*).

For instructions on how to use these pages see *p.36*.

STUDY LINK
- iTutor

Test and Assessment CD-ROM

- Quick Test 12
- File Test 12
- Progress Test 7-12
- End -of-course Test

GRAMMAR

1 b	6 a	11 a
2 a	7 a	12 b
3 b	8 b	13 a
4 a	9 a	14 b
5 b	10 b	15 b

VOCABULARY

a 1 next to   3 on the corner   5 on the right
   2 between   4 on the left

b ask, asked   help, helped   snow, snowed
   buy, bought   leave, left   start, started
   carry, carried   miss, missed   stay, stayed
   change, changed   need, needed   study, studied
   cry, cried   say, said   talk, talked
   do, did   send, sent   tell, told
   have, had   sit, sat   write, wrote

PRONUNCIATION

a 1 <u>o</u>pposite   3 de<u>ci</u>de   5 t<u>o</u>morrow
   2 be<u>tw</u>een   4 uni<u>ve</u>rsity

b /ɒ/ clock   /eɪ/ train   /t/ tie
   /ə/ computer   /d/   dog

CAN YOU UNDERSTAND THIS TEXT?

a England and France. There is a tunnel.

b 1 by plane or by train and boat
   2 nine (hours)
   3 It opened in 1994.
   4 It is 37.9 kilometres long.
   5 about three hours
   6 They first thought of it in 1802.
   7 because the snow caused electrical problems

CAN YOU UNDERSTAND THESE PEOPLE?

(4 59))) 1 a   2 b   3 c   4 a   5 b

> (4 59)))
> See the script in the Student's Book on *p.91*)

Remind Sts that they can watch the short film on *iTutor*.

> VIDEO Available as MP3 on CD4
>
> **Short film: Erasmus**
>
> Hi, I'm John and I'm a student. I'm from Canterbury in the UK. At the moment I'm studying at the Erasmus University Rotterdam, in Holland. The university opened in 1913 and today it has over 20,000 students.
>
> I'm studying here for one year. The study programme is called the Erasmus programme. The Erasmus University and the Erasmus programme – so who was Erasmus?
>
> Desiderius Erasmus Roterodamus was born here in Rotterdam in 1466. When he was nine he went to school. He studied religion and languages, like Latin and Greek. His teachers were excellent. The young Erasmus was very clever and he learnt quickly. When he was 25 he became a catholic priest. But he didn't work as a priest for very long. Instead, he continued studying. He went to universities all over Europe, including Paris, Turin, and Cambridge. He studied languages and made new translations of the Bible in Latin and Greek. He also wrote a lot of books.
>
> Erasmus believed in peace and understanding and his ideas became popular all over Europe. He died in Basel, Switzerland, in 1536.
>
> Today there are places all over the world with Erasmus's name. For example, there's the Erasmus Bridge in Rotterdam and there's the Erasmus Hall in Brooklyn, New York.
>
> Erasmus is a good name for the programme because Erasmus worked and studied all over Europe. And he believed that people work well when they work together.

Photocopiable activities

Contents

Photocopiable material

- There is a **Grammar activity** for each main (A and B) lesson of the Student's Book.
- There is a **Communicative activity** for each main (A and B) lesson of the Student's Book as well as for each Practical English section.
- There is a **Vocabulary activity** for each section of the Vocabulary Bank of the Student's Book.
- There are six **Songs activities.** The recording of the song can be found in the Practical English lessons on the Class CD.

Using extra activities in mixed ability classes

Some teachers have classes with a very wide range of levels, and where some students finish Student's Book activities much more quickly than others. You could give these fast finishers a photocopiable activity (Grammar, Vocabulary, or Communicative) while you help the slower students. Alternatively, some teachers might want to give faster students extra oral practice with a communicative activity while slower students consolidate their knowledge with an extra grammar activity.

Tips for using Grammar activities

The grammar activities are designed to give students extra practice in the main grammar points from each lesson. How you use these activities depends on the needs of your students and the time available. They can be used in the lesson if you think your entire class would benefit from the extra practice, or you could assign them as homework for some or all of your students.

- All of the activities start with a writing stage. If you use the activities in class, get students to work individually or in pairs. Allow students to compare before checking the answers.
- All of the activities have an Activation section. Some of them have a section that gets students to cover the sentences and to test their memory. If you are using the activities in class, students can work in pairs and test their partner. If you set them for homework, encourage students to use this stage to test themselves.
- If students are having trouble with any of the activities, make sure they refer to the relevant **Grammar Bank** in the Student Book.
- Make sure that students keep their copies of the activities and that they review any difficult areas regularly. Encourage them to go back to activities and cover and test themselves. This will help with their revision.

Tips for using Photocopiable activities with iTools

All the Teacher's Book photocopiables are available on iTools.

- Before an activity:
  When setting up a task, click the 📄 icon to display the Language box for all Communicative photocopiables. If you don't want students to see the activity page while teaching the language for the task, you can cover it up with the Screenshade tool. The pop-up window with the Language box will still be visible.
- During the activity:
  You can enlarge part of an activity using the Zoom tool. This will help focus students' attention on the relevant activity or the pictures they should be looking at.
- Check answers:
  Click on the 🔑 icon to display the answers to each activity on the page. You can choose to reveal the answers one by one or all the answers at the same time.

Grammar activity answers

1A verb *be* (singular): *I* and *you*

a 2 you 3 I 4 I 5 you

b 2 'm / am 3 Are 4 'm / am 5 'm / am 6 are / 're

c 1 you 2 am 3 I 4 you

1B verb *be* (singular): *he, she, it*

a 2 Is 3 isn't 4 he 5 is 6 he 7 isn't 8 's
9 Where 10 Is 11 it 12 Is 13 isn't 14 's
15 Is 16 is 17 is 18 from 19 she 20 isn't
21 Is 22 is 23 Is 24 isn't 25 's

2A verb *be* (plural): *we, you, they*

a 2 Are; 're 3 Are; 're 4 Are; aren't; 're
5 aren't; 're 6 Are; aren't; 're 7 are; aren't
8 Are; aren't; 're

b 3 No, they aren't. They're Egyptian.
4 Yes, they are.
5 No, they aren't. They're American.
6 Yes, they are.
7 No, they aren't.
8 No, they aren't. They're Scottish.

2B *Wh-* and *How* questions with *be*

a 2 Who is he? 3 How old is he? 4 What's your first
name? 5 What's your surname? 6 How do you spell
it? 7 How old are you? 8 What's your address?
9 What's your postcode? 10 What's your home
phone number? 11 What's your mobile number?

3A singular and plural nouns; *a / an*

a 3 chairs 4 a photo 5 an umbrella 6 windows

b 3 What are they? They're watches.
4 What are they? They're dictionaries.
5 What is it? It's a credit card.
6 What is it? It's a camera.
7 What are they? They're mobile phones.
8 What is it? It's a wallet.

3B *this / that / these / those*

2 That 3 these 4 this 5 these 6 these
7 that 8 this 9 This 10 That 11 these

4A possessive adjectives; possessive *s*

a 2 your 3 his 4 our 5 my 6 their 7 its 8 my

b 2 Sarah's cat 3 Pablo's sister 4 Mr White's room

4B adjectives

a 2 's old 3 's big 4 is long 5 are cheap 6 're slow.

b 2 expensive laptops 3 a new coat 4 a tall man
5 a small table 6 fast cars

5A present simple + and -: *I, you, we, they*

3 have 4 don't read 5 have 6 speak
7 don't live 8 don't like 9 don't like 10 go
11 eat 12 need

5B present simple ?: *I, you, we, they*

a 2 live 3 work 4 Do, go 5 don't like 6 go
7 Do, read 8 don't read 9 read 10 do, do
11 watch

b 2 Do you live 3 Do you have children?
4 Do they work? 5 Do you speak French?

6A present simple: *he, she, it*

a 3 works 4 doesn't work 5 starts 6 doesn't have
7 speaks 8 has 9 finishes 10 studies
11 doesn't read 12 watches

6B adverbs of frequency

a 2 sometimes 3 never 4 usually 5 always

b 6 always has 7 usually finishes 8 sometimes goes
9 sometimes watches 10 never goes 11 usually has

7A word order in questions: *be* and
present simple

a 2 What's your surname?
3 How do you spell it?
4 Do you always take the number 10 bus?
5 Where do you work?
6 Are you a teacher?
7 Do you like your job?
8 What time do you finish work?
9 What do you do at the weekends?
10 Where do you go?
11 What music do you like?

7B imperatives; object pronouns: *me,
him*, etc

a 2 it 3 me 4 them 5 her 6 us 7 him 8 you

b 2 Close 3 Phone 4 sit 5 Relax 6 Don't speak
7 Open 8 Don't drink

8A *can / can't*

a 2 can't 3 Can 4 can't 5 can 6 Can

b 2 Can, help 3 can study 4 can't wear 5 Can,
swim 6 can watch

8B *like, love, hate* + verb + *-ing*

a 2 loves making 3 like travelling 4 hates waiting
5 loves doing 6 like camping
7 doesn't like swimming 8 hates flying
9 loves reading 10 like playing
11 don't like running 12 loves painting

9A present continuous

a 2 What are you doing? I'm doing my homework.
3 What are they doing? They're having a party.
4 What's he doing? He's studying Spanish.
5 What's she doing? She's relaxing.
6 What are you doing? I'm having a shower.
7 What are they doing? They're playing ice hockey.
8 What are you doing? I'm making lunch.

9B present continuous or present simple?

a 3 go 4 're staying 5 have 6 'm drinking
7 's raining 8 rains 9 do 10 aren't doing
11 wear 12 'm wearing 13 watches
14 's reading 15 listens 16 's listening

10A *there's a... / there are some...*

a 3 There are some pillows. 4 There's a shower.
5 There aren't any lamps. 6 There isn't a bath.
7 There are some towels. 8 There isn't a cupboard.

b 3 Is there a gym? No, there isn't.
4 Is there a gift shop? Yes, there is.
5 Is there a swimming pool? Yes, there is.
6 Are there any lifts? No, there aren't.
7 Is there a garden? Yes, there is.
8 Is there a good view? No there isn't.
9 Are there any toilets? Yes, there are.

10B past simple: *be*

a 2 wasn't 3 was 4 was 5 Were 6 wasn't
7 were 8 was 9 Was 10 wasn't 11 was
12 Was 13 was 14 were 15 was 16 weren't
17 were

11A past simple: regular verbs

a 2 They travelled to Costa Rica.
3 They stayed in a hotel in the jungle.
4 They arrived at the hotel in a small boat.
5 They carried their bags to the hotel.
6 They didn't check their email.
7 They walked in the jungle with a guide.
8 They didn't watch TV.
9 They relaxed on the beach.
10 They enjoyed their holiday very much.

11B past simple irregular verbs:
do, get, go, have

a 2 went 3 did, do 4 went 5 had 6 did, have
7 had 8 Did, go 9 got 10 got up 11 Did, have
12 didn't have 13 Did, get up 14 didn't do
15 Did, go 16 got

12A past simple: regular and irregular verbs

a 2 left 3 didn't have 4 were 5 saw 6 opened
7 phoned 8 said 9 phoned 10 gave 11 did, do
12 talked 13 told 14 worked 15 did, get
16 bought 17 went 18 was 19 went
20 had 21 sent 22 invited 23 did, go
24 went 25 had

12B present continuous for future

a 2 'm staying 3 are, going 4 Are, going
5 're going 6 are, leaving

b 1 is / 's, going 2 's going 3 is, visiting
4 is / 's, staying 5 isn't staying 6 is, staying
7 isn't coming

1A GRAMMAR verb *be* (singular): *I* and *you*

a Complete the conversation with *I* or *you*.

Miranda Hi, ¹*I* 'm Miranda. Are ²_____ Monica?

Sally No, ³_____'m not, ⁴_____'m Sally.

Miranda Nice to meet ⁵_____ !

b Complete the conversation with *am*, *'m*, *are*, or *'re*.

Student Excuse me, ¹*am* I in room 2?

Receptionist What's your name?

Student I ²_____ Caroline.

Receptionist ³_____ you Caroline Herzog?

Student No, I ⁴_____ not. I ⁵_____ Caroline Fuchs.

Receptionist You ⁶_____ in room 3.

Student Thank you.

c Complete the conversation.

Charlotte Are ¹_____ Paolo Galli?

Paolo Yes, I ²_____ .

Charlotte Hi, ³_____'m Charlotte from the Dover School of English.

Paolo Oh, hello!

Charlotte Nice to meet ⁴_____ .

activation

d Practise the conversations with a partner.

1B GRAMMAR verb *be* (singular): *he, she, it*

a Complete the conversation. Use contractions where possible.

A ¹ *Where* 's Michael Fassbender from?
² _____ he from the UK?

B No, he ³ _____ .

A Is ⁴ _____ from Germany?

B Yes, he ⁵ _____ .

A Where in Germany?
Is ⁶ _____ from Berlin?

B No, he ⁷ _____ .
He ⁸ _____ from Heidelberg.

A ⁹ _____ 's dim sum from?
¹⁰ _____ it from the USA?

B No, ¹¹ _____ isn't.

A ¹² _____ it from Japan?

B No, it ¹³ _____ .
It ¹⁴ _____ from China.

A ¹⁵ _____ sushi from Japan?

B Yes, it ¹⁶ _____ .

A Where ¹⁷ _____ Cate ¹⁸ _____ ?
Is ¹⁹ _____ from the United States?

B No, she ²⁰ _____ .

A ²¹ _____ she from Australia?

B Yes, she ²² _____ .

A Where in Australia?
²³ _____ she from Sydney?

B No, she ²⁴ _____ .
She ²⁵ _____ from Melbourne.

activation

b Practise the conversations with a partner.

2A GRAMMAR verb *be* (plural): *we, you, they*

a Look at the pictures. Complete the sentences with the correct form of *be*. Use contractions where possible.

1 We _'re_ in Rio de Janeiro.

2 _____ they Italian?
No, they _____ Spanish.

3 _____ they Turkish?
No, they _____ Egyptian.

4 _____ they on holiday?
No, they _____. They _____ on business.

5 Are you Japanese?
No, we _____. We _____ American.

6 _____ we in room 10?
No, you _____ in room 10. You _____ in room 9.

7 Sorry, _____ we late?
No, you _____.

8 _____ they English?
No, they _____. They _____ Scottish.

b Look at the pictures. Write ⊞ or ⊟ short answers. If the answer is ⊟, write the correct sentence.

1 Are they in Mexico? *No, they aren't. They're in Brazil.*

2 Are the cars Spanish? *Yes, they are.*

3 Are they Turkish? _____

4 Are they on business? _____

5 Are the women Japanese? _____

6 Are they in room 9? _____

7 Are they late? _____

8 Are they English? _____

activation

c Work with a partner. Ask and answer the questions in **b** about the pictures.

2B GRAMMAR *Wh-* and *How* questions with *be*

a Put the words in the correct order to make questions.

1

Gill	Hi Anna!
Anna	Hello Gill, ¹ *how are you* ? **(you how are)**
Gill	I'm fine, thanks. ²_____? **(he who is)**
Anna	He's Sammy, my little boy.
Gill	³_____? **(old is how he)**
Anna	He's one.
Gill	He's very nice.

2

Woman	⁴_____? **(your first what's name)**
Boy	Henry.
Woman	OK. ⁵_____? **(what's surname your)**
Boy	Schultz.
Woman	⁶_____? **(spell do how it you)**
Boy	S-C-H-U-L-T-Z.
Woman	Oh, yes. ⁷_____? **(you old are how)**
Boy	I'm 18.
Woman	OK. That's fine.

3

Woman 1	⁸_____? **(your address what's)**
Woman 2	It's 72 London Road, Liverpool.
Woman 1	⁹_____? **(postcode what's your)**
Woman 2	It's L2 7BC.
Woman 1	Thank you. ¹⁰_____? **(home what's phone your number)**
Woman 2	It's 0151 496 0878.
Woman 1	OK. ¹¹_____? **(mobile your number what's)**
Woman 2	I don't have a mobile phone.

activation

b Practise the conversations with a partner.

3A GRAMMAR singular and plural nouns; *a / an*

a Look at the pictures. Complete the answers. Be careful with *a / an*.

1

What is it? It's _a coat_ .

2

What are they? They're _keys_ .

3

What are they? They're _____ .

4

What is it? It's _____ .

5

What is it? It's _____ .

6

What are they? They're _____ .

b Look at the pictures. Write questions and answers.

1

What are they?
They're pens.

2

What is it?
It's a piece of paper.

3

_____
_____

4

_____
_____

5

_____
_____

6

_____
_____

7

_____
_____

8

_____
_____

activation

c Work with a partner. Practise the questions and answers in **a** and **b**.

3B GRAMMAR *this / that / these / those*

a Complete the conversations. Use *this*, *that*, *these*, or *those*.

1

Man	Hey, Sally, is ¹ *this* your laptop?
Woman	No, it isn't.
Man	Where's your laptop?
Woman	²_____ 's my laptop – over there on the table.
Man	And the keys? Are ³_____ your keys?
Woman	Yes, they are.

2

Man	Is ⁴_____ mug from Switzerland?
Woman	No, it's from France.
Man	And ⁵_____ chocolates? Are ⁶_____ from Switzerland?
Woman	Yes, they are. And ⁷_____ picture is from Switzerland, too.

3

Woman	Excuse me. Is ⁸_____ the bus to Glasgow?
Driver	No, ma'am. ⁹_____ is the bus to Liverpool.
Woman	Oh, no! Where's the bus to Glasgow?
Driver	¹⁰_____ 's the bus to Glasgow over there – number 41. Are ¹¹_____ your bags?
Woman	Yes, they are.
Driver	Here, let me help you.

activation

b Practise the conversations with a partner.

4A GRAMMAR possessive adjectives; possessive 's

a Look at the pictures. Complete the sentences with *my, your, his, her, its, our,* or *their.*

1

Where's _my_ umbrella?

2

What's in ____ bag?

3

That's Josh and ____ wife.

4

Where are ____ coats?

5

Where are ____ sunglasses?

6

Look, I think these are ____ keys.

7

It's a great book. Now what's ____ name?

8

That's Mr Green. He's ____ French teacher.

b Complete the sentences with the name and possessive *s*.

1 This is *Amelia's husband*, Nick. (husband / Amelia)

2 Look! It's _____ ! Over there! (cat / Sarah)

3 Rosa is _____ . She's in my class. (sister / Pablo)

4 This is _____ . He's the German teacher. (room / Mr White)

c Work with a partner. Cover the sentences in **a**. Look at the pictures and say the sentences.

4B GRAMMAR adjectives

a Write sentences for the pictures. Use the correct form of *be* and an adjective from the list.

big   cheap   long   old   ~~short~~   slow

1 He *'s short* .   **2** It _____ .   **3** It _____ .

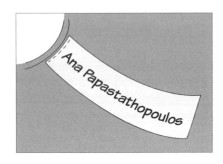

4 Ana's surname _____ .   **5** These _____ .   **6** They _____ .

b Complete the sentences for the pictures. Use an adjective and a noun from the lists.

~~beautiful~~   expensive   fast   new   small   tall   car   coat   laptop   man   table   ~~woman~~

1 She's *a beautiful woman* .   **2** They're _____ .   **3** It's _____ .

4 He's _____ .   **5** It's _____ .   **6** They're _____ .

> **activation**

c **Test your memory.** Cover the sentences. Look at the pictures and say the sentences.

5A GRAMMAR Present simple ⊞ and ⊟: *I, you, we, they*

a Write a ⊞ or a ⊟ sentence for each picture. Use the verbs from the list.

eat   go   have (x2)   ~~not have~~   not like (x2)   not live   need   not read   speak   ~~watch~~

We _watch_ TV in the evening.

I _don't have_ sugar in coffee.

We _____ tea for breakfast.

I _____ books in the evening. I listen to music.

Andy and Jane _____ two children.

We only _____ English in our class!

My parents _____ in a flat. They live in a house.

I _____ cats.

We _____ this film. It's terrible.

I _____ to English class on Tuesday and Thursday.

They _____ fast food at the weekend.

They _____ a new car.

activation

b **Test your memory.** Cover the sentences. Look at the pictures and say the sentences.

5B GRAMMAR present simple ?: *I, you, we, they*

a Complete the conversation. Use the words in brackets.

> A ¹ *Do* you *live* here in Oxford? **(live)**
>
> B Yes, I ²_____ in Oxford, but I ³_____ in London. **(live; work)**
>
> A ⁴_____ you _____ to work by car?
>
> B No, I ⁵_____ driving, I ⁶_____ to work by train. **(not like; go)**
>
> A It's a long way! ⁷_____ you _____ the newspaper on the train? **(read)**
>
> B I ⁸_____ the newspaper, but I ⁹_____ the news on my tablet every morning. **(not read; read)**
>
> A And what ¹⁰_____ you_____ on the train after work? **(do)**
>
> B In the afternoons, I just ¹¹_____ something on my tablet. **(watch)**

b Complete the conversation. Write the questions.

> A Good morning Mr Smyth.
>
> B Hello. Nice to meet you.
>
> A ¹ *Do you want coffee?*
>
> B Yes, please. Black with no sugar.
>
> A ²_____ in London?
>
> B No, I don't. I live in Birmingham.
>
> A ³_____
>
> B Yes, two. A daughter and a son. They're 20 and 22.
>
> A ⁴_____
>
> B No, they don't work. They're students.
>
> A ⁵_____
>
> B No, not French, but I speak Spanish and Italian.

activation

c Practise the conversations with a partner.

English File 3rd edition Teacher's Book Beginner Photocopiable © Oxford University Press 2015

6A GRAMMAR present simple: *he, she, it*

a Look at the pictures. Write about Mark. Use the verbs (⊞ or ⊟) in the list.

~~not drink~~	finish	have	not have	~~live~~	not read	speak	start	study	watch	work	not work

1 He _lives_ in a house.
2 He _doesn't drink_ coffee in the morning.
3 He _____ in a bank in London.
4 He _____ in an English bank.
5 He _____ work at 8.30.
6 He _____ a big lunch.

7 He _____ French to customers at work.
8 He _____ meetings at work.
9 He _____ work at 5.30.
10 He _____ French after work.
11 He _____ in the evening.
12 He _____ TV in the evening.

activation

b **Test your memory.** Work with a partner. Tell your partner to turn over his / her copy. Ask questions to test your partner's memory.

Does Mark work in a bank? ⟩ ⟨ Yes, he does.

Does he drink coffee in the morning? ⟩ ⟨ No, he doesn't.

6B GRAMMAR adverbs of frequency

a Complete the sentences with an adverb of frequency (*always*, *never*, *usually*, or *sometimes*).

always = ✓✓✓✓✓
usually = ✓✓✓✓✗
sometimes = ✓✓✗✗✗
never = ✗✗✗✗✗

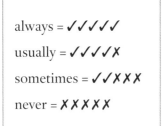

1 ✓✓✓✓✓

He *always* gets up at 7.30.

2 ✓✓✗✗✗

He _____ has breakfast.

3 ✗✗✗✗✗

He _____ goes to work by car.

4 ✓✓✓✓✗

He _____ has a sandwich for lunch.

5 ✓✓✓✓✓

He _____ does the housework on Sunday.

b Complete the sentences with an adverb of frequency and a verb.

6 ✓✓✓✓✓

She *always has* a coffee at 10.00.

7 ✓✓✓✓✗

She _____ work late.

8 ✓✓✗✗✗

She _____ to the supermarket after work.

9 ✓✓✗✗✗

She _____ TV with her husband.

10 ✗✗✗✗✗

She _____ to bed before 12.00.

11 ✓✓✓✓✗

She _____ dinner with her friends on Friday night.

activation

c Cover the sentences. Look at the pictures and say the sentences.

7A GRAMMAR word order in questions: *be* and present simple

a Put the words in the correct order to make questions.

1

Waiter	Good evening. ¹ *Do you have a reservation* ? **(have do a reservation you)**
Woman	Yes, we do.
Waiter	²_____? **(your what's surname)**
Woman	It's Leigh.
Waiter	³_____? **(spell how it you do)**
Woman	L - E - I - G - H
Waiter	Thank you. Your table is by the window. Come with me.

2

Woman	⁴_____ the number 10 bus? **(always take do you)**
Man	Yes, I do.
Woman	⁵_____? **(you where work do)**
Man	I work at the university.
Woman	⁶_____? **(teacher you are a)**
Man	Yes, I am.
Woman	⁷_____? **(like your do job you)**
Man	Yes, I do. It's great.
Woman	⁸_____? **(work you what time do finish)**
Man	I usually finish at five o'clock.

3

Boy	⁹_____? **(do do weekends what the you at)**
Girl	I usually meet my friends.
Boy	¹⁰_____? **(you do go where)**
Girl	To a bar or a disco.
Boy	¹¹_____? **(like music what you do)**
Girl	I like hip hop and R&B.

activation

b Practise the dialogues with a partner.

7B GRAMMAR imperatives; object pronouns: *me*, *him*, etc.

a Complete the sentences with a pronoun. Write it in the **PRONOUN** column.

		PRONOUN
1	I love cats. Do you like ▆?	*them*
2	This exercise is difficult. I can't do ▆.	_____
3	I always phone my brother but he never phones ▆.	_____
4	Where are the car keys? I can't find ▆.	_____
5	Paula is a very good friend. I see ▆ every weekend.	_____
6	We have a meeting with the manager. He wants to speak to ▆.	_____
7	Jack goes to your school. Do you know ▆?	_____
8	You love me but I don't love ▆!	_____

b Complete the sentences with a ⊞ or ⊟ imperative of a verb from the list.
Write it in the **IMPERATIVE** column.

close   drink   open   phone   relax   sit   speak   ~~walk~~

		IMPERATIVE
1	▆ in the park at night!	*Don't walk*
2	It's very cold in here. ▆ the window, please!	_____
3	▆ me when you arrive in Paris.	_____
4	Come in and ▆ down.	_____
5	▆! You're on holiday.	_____
6	▆ in Italian! This is an English class.	_____
7	▆ your books, please, and go to page 22.	_____
8	▆ coffee now! It's 10.00 pm.	_____

activation

c **Test your memory**. Cover the PRONOUN and IMPERATIVE columns.
Say the sentences with the missing words.

8A GRAMMAR can / can't

a Complete the sentences with *can* or *can't*.

1 You _can_ leave your bags over there.

2 I'm sorry. We _____ come to dinner tonight.

3 _____ you open the window, please?

4 You _____ use your mobile phone here.

5 We _____ go to the beach. It's a beautiful day.

6 _____ I help you?

b Complete the sentences with *can* or *can't* and a verb from the list.

help ~~park~~ study swim watch wear

1 You _can't park_ here!

2 _____ you _____ me with my homework?

3 Look! We _____ French here in the evening.

4 I'm sorry, but you _____ that hat in the classroom.

5 _____ we _____ here today?

6 Tidy your room and then you _____ TV.

8B GRAMMAR *like, love, hate* + verb + *-ing*

a Write sentences with the correct form of *like* ☺, *love* ☺☺, *don't like* ☹, or *hate* ☹☹ and the activity.

He _doesn't like cycling_ .

She _____ cakes.

They _____ .

She _____ for the bus.

He _____ exercise.

They _____ .

She _____ .

He _____ .

She _____ books in English.

They _____ computer games.

They _____ .

She _____ her nails.

activation

b **Test your memory.** Cover the sentences. Look at the pictures and say the sentences.

English File 3rd edition Teacher's Book Beginner Photocopiable © Oxford University Press 2015

9A GRAMMAR present continuous

a Look at the pictures. Write questions and answers with the present continuous.

1

(they / do?)
What are they doing?
(they / watch / football match)
They're watching football.

2

(you / do?)
_____
(I / do / my homework)
_____

3

(they / do?)
_____
(they / have / a party)
_____

4

me llamo Jack,
tengo veinte años

(he / do?)
_____
(he / study / Spanish)
_____

5

(she / do?)
_____
(she / relax)
_____

6

(you / do?)
_____
(I / have / a shower)
_____

7

(they / do?)
_____
(they / play / ice hockey)
_____

8

(you / do?)
_____
(I / make / lunch)
_____

activation

b **Test your memory.** Cover the sentences. Look at the pictures and say the questions and answers.

9B GRAMMAR present continuous or present simple?

a Write the verb in the present continuous or the present simple in the VERB column. Use contractions where possible.

VERB

1 My dad usually (go) to work by bus.   *goes*

2 Today he (drive)   *'s driving*

3 We usually (go) camping on holidays.   _____

4 Now we (stay) in a fantastic hotel.   _____

5 I usually (have) coffee for breakfast.   _____

6 Today I (drink) tea.   _____

7 Oh no! It (rain) now and we don't have an umbrella.   _____

8 It usually (rain) all September in Scotland. _____

9 The children usually (do) their homework in the evening.   _____

10 They (not do) their homework this evening, because they're on holiday.   _____

11 I usually (wear) jeans and a T-shirt at the weekend.   _____

12 I (wear) my new skirt and blouse today for the party.   _____

13 My mum usually (watch) TV after dinner.   _____

14 She (read) a book tonight.   _____

15 Gary always (listen) to classical music.   _____

16 Today he (listen) to pop music.   _____

activation

b **Test your memory.** Cover the VERB column. Say the sentences with the correct form.

10A GRAMMAR *there's a... / there are some...*

a Write ⊞ and ⊟ sentences about the hotel room.
Use *There's | There isn't a* or *There are some… | There aren't any…*.

1 TV   *There isn't a TV.*
2 chairs   *There are some chairs.*
3 pillows   _____.
4 shower   _____.
5 lamps   _____.
6 bath   _____.
7 towels   _____.
8 cupboard   _____.

b Write questions with *Is there a…?* | *Are there any…?* Then write short answers.

1 restaurants?   *Are there any restaurants?*   *Yes, there are.*
2 car park?   *Is there a car park?*   *No, there isn't.*
3 gym?   _____? _____.
4 gift shop?   _____? _____.
5 swimming pool?   _____? _____.
6 lifts?   _____? _____.
7 garden?   _____? _____.
8 good view?   _____? _____.
9 toilets?   _____? _____.

activation

c **Test your memory.** Cover the sentences. Look at the picture and say what there is and isn't in the room and the hotel.

10B GRAMMAR past simple: *be*

a Complete the conversations with *was, wasn't, were,* or *weren't.*

1

A I think he ¹ _was_ a gym teacher before he was famous.

B No, he ² _____ .

A OK, what ³ _____ he?

B He ⁴ _____ a waiter in a fast food restaurant.

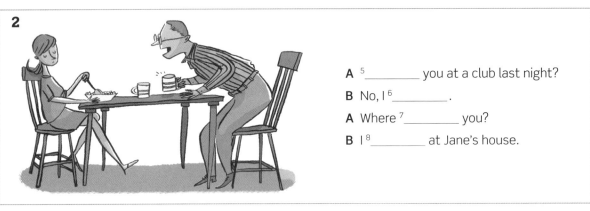

2

A ⁵ _____ you at a club last night?

B No, I ⁶ _____ .

A Where ⁷ _____ you?

B I ⁸ _____ at Jane's house.

3

A ⁹ _____ your mother an actress too?

B No, she ¹⁰ _____ . She ¹¹ _____ a nurse.

A ¹² _____ she tall?

B Yes, she ¹³ _____ very tall and beautiful.

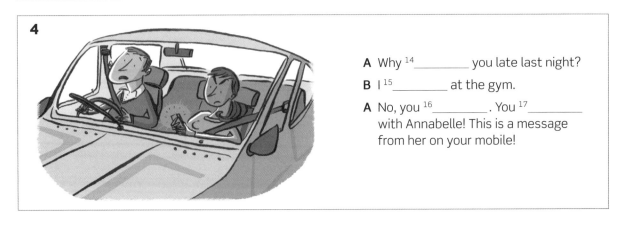

4

A Why ¹⁴ _____ you late last night?

B I ¹⁵ _____ at the gym.

A No, you ¹⁶ _____ . You ¹⁷ _____ with Annabelle! This is a message from her on your mobile!

activation

b Practise the conversations with a partner.

English File 3rd edition Teacher's Book Beginner Photocopiable © Oxford University Press 2015

11A GRAMMAR past simple: regular verbs

want a holiday

travel to Costa Rica

stay in a hotel in the jungle

arrive at the hotel in a small boat

carry their bags to the hotel

not check their email

walk in the jungle with a guide

not watch TV

relax on the beach

enjoy their holiday very much

a Look at the pictures about Adele and Tom's holiday. Write sentences in the past simple.

1 *Adele and Tom wanted a holiday.*

2 *They* _____

3 _____

4 _____

5 _____

6 _____

7 _____

8 _____ *in the evening.*

9 _____ *every day.*

10 _____

b **Test your memory.** Cover the sentences and look at the pictures. Tell the story with a partner.

11B GRAMMAR past simple irregular verbs: do, get, go, have

a Complete the conversations. Use the verbs in brackets in the past simple.

1

A Good morning, Jenny. [1] _Did_ you _have_ a good weekend? (have)

B Yes, I did. We [2]_____ to a concert on Saturday night. (go)
What [3]_____ you _____ at the weekend? (do)

A On Sunday afternoon, we [4]_____ to a football match with Beth and Dan. (go)
Then we [5]_____ dinner at their house. (have)

B What [6]_____ you _____ for dinner? (have)

A We [7]_____ Italian food. (have) It was great!

B [8]_____ you _____ to bed late? (go)

A Yes, I did. We only [9]_____ home at midnight, and then I [10]_____ at six this morning. (get; get up).

2

A Hi, darling. [11]_____ you _____ a good day? (have)

B No, I [12]_____ a good day. (not have) It was terrible!

A Why? [13]_____ the boys _____ late again? (get up)

B Yes, very late. And they [14]_____ their homework last night. (not do)

A [15]_____ you _____ to the office this morning? (go)

B Yes, but I was late, too. I [16]_____ an email from my boss about it. (get) He was angry.

A Don't worry. Tomorrow is Saturday and you can relax.

---

activation

b Practise the conversations on this page in pairs.

12A GRAMMAR past simple: regular and irregular verbs

a Complete the conversation. Use the past simple of the verbs in brackets.

A How ¹*did* you *meet* (meet) your wife?

B It's a long story. Two years ago I ²_____ (leave) my wallet on the train. It ³_____ (not have) any money in it, but my credit cards ⁴_____ (be) in it.

A Oh no! That's terrible.

B Yes, but a woman on the train ⁵_____ (see) the wallet and ⁶_____ (open) it. The name of the bank was on the credit cards. She ⁷_____ (phone) the bank and ⁸_____ (say) that she had my wallet. Then the bank ⁹_____ (phone) me and ¹⁰_____ (give) me her number.

A What ¹¹_____ you _____ (do) then?

B I ¹²_____ (talk) to the woman on the phone. She ¹³_____ (tell) me that she ¹⁴_____ (work) in an office in the city centre.

A How ¹⁵_____ you _____ (get) the wallet from her?

B The next day I ¹⁶_____ (buy) some chocolates and flowers and I ¹⁷_____ (go) to her office. She ¹⁸_____ (be) really nice so we ¹⁹_____ (go) for a coffee. We ²⁰_____ (have) a good time.

A That's great! Then what happened?

B The next day I ²¹_____ (send) her an email and I ²²_____ (invite) her out to dinner.

A Where ²³_____ you _____ (go)?

B We ²⁴_____ (go) to a romantic restaurant on the beach and ²⁵_____ (have) a great evening.

A And then?

B Well, she's now my wife!

activation

b Practise the conversation with a partner. Then cover the conversation and look at the pictues. Tell the story.

Two years ago the man left his wallet on the train...

12B GRAMMAR present continuous for future

a Complete the conversations. Use the correct form of the present continuous (verb + -ing) and the verbs in brackets.

1

A What [1] _are_ you _doing_ next weekend? (do)

B I [2]_____ with my brother in Bristol. (stay)

A Who [3]_____ you _____ with? (go)

B With my friend Laura.

A [4]_____ you _____ by train? (go)

B No, we're not. We [5]_____ by car. (go)

A When [6]_____ you _____? (leave)

B Probably on Friday night.

A Well, have a good weekend!

B Thanks. You too.

2

A Where [1]_____ Jane _____ on holiday this summer? (go)

B She [2]_____ to South America. (go)

A Wow! That sounds great. What countries [3]_____ she_____? (visit)

B Argentina first and then Chile and Brazil.

A Where [4]_____ she _____? (stay)

B She [5]_____ (not stay) in hotels because they're very expensive. Probably in cheap hostels!

A How long [6]_____ she _____? (stay)

B Three weeks. She [7]_____ home until the end of July. (not come)

activation

b Practise the conversations with a partner.

Communicative activity instructions

Tips for using Communicative activities

We have suggested the ideal number of copies for each activity. However, you can often manage with fewer, e.g. one copy per pair instead of per student.

When Sts are working in pairs, if possible, get them to sit face-to-face. This will encourage them to really talk to each other and also means that they can't see each other's worksheet.

If your class doesn't divide into pairs or groups, get two Sts to share one role, or get one student to monitor, help, and correct.

Extra idea
- If some Sts finish early, they can swap roles and do the activity again, or you could get them to write some of the sentences from the activity.

1A Are you...?
A mingle activity

Each student has to find two famous partners. Copy and cut up one sheet per 20 Sts.

Language	
Excuse me, are you...?	Yes, I am. / No, I'm not. Sorry!
Hi / Hello. I'm...	Nice to meet you.

- Give each student one card. If you have more than 20 Sts, copy the sheet twice and have some characters repeated. For smaller groups, tell them that they might only find ONE of the two famous people.
- Tell Sts they are the first famous person on their card. They must find the other two famous people and then introduce themselves.
- Write the sentences from **Language** on the board or show them on screen if using iTools. Practise the questions and the two possible responses. Demonstrate the activity with one of the better students and make sure all Sts are clear about what they have to do. Tell Sts not to worry too much about pronouncing the names correctly.
- Tell Sts to stand up and begin the activity.
- As some Sts might find their two people very quickly, you could set a time limit, e.g. five minutes. In a smaller class, you could give out unused cards to Sts who finish early.

Extra idea
- Put on some lively music in the background while Sts do the activity.

1B Where are they from?
A pairwork activity

Sts ask each other where famous people are from.

Copy one sheet per pair.

Language		
Where's she from?	She's from Mexico.	
Where's he from?	He's from Italy.	I don't know.

- Quickly revise countries in **Vocabulary Bank Countries and nationalities**, p.117.
- Put Sts in pairs and give each pair a copy of the worksheet.
- Write the sentences from **Language** on the board or show them on screen if using iTools. Revise the questions and answers. Check that Sts remember how to say *I don't know*.
- Focus on photo 1 and ask the question *Where's she from?* Elicit answers from the class and and establish that the right answer is *She's from Mexico*.
- Sts work in pairs, taking turns pointing at one of the photos and asking where the person is from.
- When Sts have finished, check answers with the class, telling them the people's nationalities if they don't know or couldn't guess them.

    1 Salma Hayek (actress) is from Mexico.
    2 Mesut Özil (football player) is from Germany.
    3 Ken Watanabe (actor) is from Japan.
    4 Roger Federer (tennis player) is from Switzerland.
    5 Vanessa Paradis (singer and actress) is from France.
    6 Dariusz Michalczewski (boxer) is from Poland.
    7 Fernando Alonso (F1 driver) is from Spain.
    8 Anna Netrebko (opera singer) is from Russia.
    9 Donatella Versace (fashion designer) is from Italy.
    10 Kate Winslet (actress) is from England.
    11 Orhan Pamuk (writer) is from Turkey.
    12 Paolo Coelho (writer) is from Brazil.

Extra support
- To help the Sts if you think they don't know the famous people, write the countries they are from on the board, but not in the order they are in the worksheet.

PE1 Who are you?
A mingle activity

Sts take on a new identity and practise asking for personal information and spelling names. Copy enough sheets for each student to have one card. Prepare a card for yourself to use as an example.

Language	
Good morning / afternoon / evening.	
What's your first name?	Marisol.
How do you spell it?	M-A-R-I-S-O-L.
What's your surname?	
Where are you from?	I'm from (Rennes) in (France).

- Tell Sts that they are going to temporarily change their identity. Give out one card to each student.

- Write the sentences from **Language** on the board or show them on screen if using iTools. Model and drill pronunciation.
- Demonstrate the activity by using a card that you have created for yourself, with a different identity. Get Sts to ask you the questions and then answer them with the information on your card. Choose a name that Sts will have to ask how to spell in order to make spelling part of the task.
- Tell Sts that they are going to walk around the room and meet some 'new' people. When they meet someone, they ask for their first and last names and where they are from. They should ask people to spell their names and the towns they are from, and should write down the information. Give them a target number of people they should meet, e.g. four or five, or set a time limit, e.g. ten minutes.
- When you are sure Sts understand what they have to do, get Sts to stand up and talk to each other.
- To follow up, ask a few Sts about one of the the new people they met, e.g. *What's his name? How do you spell his surname? Where is he from?*

2A Match the sentences
A pairwork activity

Sts work in pairs to match questions and answers. Copy one worksheet per pair and cut into **A** and **B**.

Language	
Are you from Spain?	*No, we're Italian.*
Is Anna Russian?	*Yes, she's from Moscow.*

- Write the sentences from **Language** on the board in the following way, or show them on screen if using iTools:

  1 *Are you from Spain?*   a *Yes, she's from Moscow.*
  2 *Is Anna Russian?*   b *No, we're Italian.*

- Elicit from the class which sentence goes with which and draw a line between them (1b, 2a).
- Put Sts into pairs, **A** and **B**, ideally face-to-face, and give out the sheets. Make sure Sts can't see each other's sheets.
- Ask one pair to demonstrate the activity. Student **A** reads the first sentence (*Excuse me. Are you James?*). Student **B** reads the correct response (*No, I'm not. I'm Jason*). Ask Student **A** if the response is OK.
- Sts work in pairs. **A** asks his / her questions first and then they swap roles. Monitor and ensure that Sts are not looking at each other's cards.
- When Sts have finished, check answers.

1 Excuse me. Are you James?	i No, I'm not. I'm Jason.
2 Where are Alice and Umberto from?	j They're Swiss.
3 Are you here on holiday?	f Yes, we are.
4 Is Nike English?	g No, it isn't. It's American.
5 Are they Mexican?	h No, they aren't. They're Spanish.
6 Are we late?	e No, you aren't.
7 Where are you from?	c I'm from Egypt.
8 Is Caroline French?	d Yes, she's from Paris.
9 Where are you from in Germany?	a We're from Berlin.
10 Is Kyoto in China?	b No, it's in Japan.

Extra idea
- If some Sts finish early they can swap cards with their partner and repeat the activity.

2B Remember the sentences
A pairwork activity

Sts match and then memorize sentences. Copy one sheet per student or per pair.

Language	
Hi Lola. This is Paul.	*Nice to meet you.*
How old is Karin?	*She's 38.*

- Write the sentences from **Language** on the board in the following way, or show them on screen if using iTools:

  1 *Hi Lola. This is Paul.*   a *She's 38.*
  2 *How old is Karin?*   b *Nice to meet you.*

- Cover the responses a and b, and elicit from Sts a possible response to 1 and 2. Then uncover the answers and elicit from the class which response goes with each sentence, and draw a line between them (1b, 2a).
- Put Sts in pairs and give out the sheets. Tell Sts to match sentences 3-14 to answers c-n. Give a time limit e.g. five minutes, then check the answers.

3 What's your phone number?	k It's 123 4488.
4 Nice to meet you.	n Nice to meet you, too.
5 Is she married?	a No, she's single.
6 How are you?	j Fine thanks.
7 See you tomorrow.	m Bye!
8 What's your name?	b My name's Karl.
9 Have a nice day!	f Thanks.
10 Where are you from?	i I'm from Italy.
11 When's your English class?	d On Monday and Friday.
12 Hello!	h Hi!
13 My name's Maribel, not Maria.	l Sorry.
14 What day is it today?	c It's Thursday.

- Tell Sts they now have to memorize as many answers as they can. Give them one or two minutes for this.
- When the time is up, get Sts to fold the sheet on the dotted line, so that responses c-n are not visible.
- Tell Sts they will now have to remember the original responses to 3-14 and write these in the middle column. Demonstrate by asking the class to remember number 3 (*It's 123 4488.*).
- Set a time limit, then get Sts to compare their answers with their partner before they unfold their paper to see how many they remembered correctly.

Extra challenge
- Ask Student B to turn the sheet face down. Student A says one of the sentences, at random, from 1-14 and Student B then says the response from memory.

3A The same or different?
A pairwork activity

Sts find similarities and differences between two pictures. Copy one sheet per pair **A** and **B**.

Language
A *I have one watch in my picture. The same or different?*
B *Different. I have two. I have three pencils in my picture.*
A *The same. I have three pencils, too.*

- Quickly revise the vocabulary on page 119 of the Student's Book.
- Put Sts in pairs, **A** and **B**, ideally face-to-face, and give out the sheets. Make sure Sts can't see each other's sheets.
- Write the sentences from **Language** on the board, or show them on screen if using iTools. Elicit the meaning of *too*.
- Demonstrate the activity by taking the part of Student **A**. Say *I have one watch in my bag*. Ask a Student **B** *The same or different?* Elicit the response *Different. I have two watches*. Tell Sts to write *D* (different) in the box next to the watches.
- Now take the part of Student **B**. Say *I have three pencils in my picture*. Elicit the response from a Student **A** *The same. I have three pencils, too.*
- Sts work in pairs. Tell them to take turns telling each other what they have in their pictures. When the pairs finish, get them to look at each other's pictures to check their answers.

3B *What's this? What's that?*
A pairwork or small group activity

Sts play a game making sentences with *this, that, these, those*. Copy one worksheet for each pair or small group.

There are three game options, both cut and non-cut versions. Each game can be played in pairs or in small groups of three or four Sts.

Language	
What's this? / What's that?	*It's a mobile phone.*
What are these? / What are those?	*They're pencils.*

- Write the sentences from **Language** on the board, or show them on screen if using iTools, and revise the use of the words *this, that, these,* and *those*.

Game 1: Win a card

- Cut up the worksheet and make one set of cards for each pair or group. Give each pair or group a set of picture cards. Tell Sts to spread out the picture cards face up on their desk.
- Demonstrate the activity by going to one group and picking up a card with a *this* item. Elicit from Sts the question *What's this?* then say, e.g., *It's a tablet*. Then point to a card which has a pointing finger on it but leave it on the table and elicit the question *What's that* and say, e.g. *It's an umbrella*. Explain to Sts that they will have to leave cards with a pointing finger on the table and use *that / those*, and they will have to pick up cards without the finger and use *this / these*.
- Sts play in pairs or groups. They take turns choosing a picture and saying a sentence. If a student says a correct sentence, he/she can keep the picture card. The student with the most cards at the end of the game wins.

Game 2: Win a picture

- **Non-cut alternative:** Leave the picture cards as one sheet. Sts take turns choosing a picture. For *this / these*, they touch the picture and say the sentence. For *that / those*, they point to the picture without touching it. When they 'win' a picture, they write their initials on it. The student with most pictures initialled wins the game.

PE2 Can I have an orange juice, please?
A roleplay activity

Sts roleplay ordering food in groups of three. Copy one sheet per group and cut up the menu and role cards.

Language	
Can I have a cheese sandwich?	*Here you are.*
How much is that?	*It's £4.15*
Anything else?	*No, thanks. / Yes, please, a Diet Coke.*

- Revise prices by writing a few prices on the board, e.g., *£5.65, $11.25, €0.50* and calling on volunteers to say the prices (*five pounds sixty-five, eleven dollars and twenty-five cents, fifty cents*).
- Explain to Sts that they are going to roleplay ordering food and taking orders in a pub. Elicit the phrases in **Language** and then write the sentences on the board, or show them on screen if using iTools. Model and drill pronunciation.
- Put the Sts in groups of three and give them a menu to share. Make one student the barman and give him / her the role card. Give the other two Sts the customer card to share. Give Sts a few minutes to read their roles.
- Waiters should let the customers read the menu before taking their order. They need a piece of paper to take down the orders and later to tell them how much it is.
- When the customers have read the menu, tell waiters to take orders and calculate how much it is.
- You could ask a group or groups to 'perform' in front of the others.

4A Happy families
A group card game

Sts play a card game and try to collect all the members of the same family. Cut up a set of cards for each group of four Sts.

Language	
Can I have Tom's sister, please.	*No, sorry. / Here you are.*

- Tell Sts they are going to play a family card game. (The game is similar to the game English speakers know as 'Happy Families'.) If Sts have a similar game in their countries, you might want to refer to this.
- In the game, there are five sets of cards. Write on the board *Mario's family, Monica's family, Ray's family, Charlie's family, Amy's family*. Model and drill pronunciation.
- Put Sts in groups of four or five and give each group a pack of cards. One student shuffles and deals the cards face down. In groups of four, each student should have five cards.
- Sts look at their cards. Explain that on each card they see the name of the family at the the top. The pictures at the bottom show them the four cards in the family. The large picture is the card they have. The three small pictures show them the cards they have to collect to complete the group. The winner is the first person to collect all four cards in a set.

- To collect cards, Sts ask each other for the cards they don't have. They can ask any student in the group for a card. If a student (S1) has a card from Mario's family with the word *SISTER* in capital letters, the student needs the other three Mario cards. So the student might ask another student (S2) *Can I have Mario's brother, please.* If S2 has the card he / she **must** give it to S1, saying *Here you are.* Then S1 can continue and ask the same (or a different) player for another card, etc. But if the player who is asked <u>doesn't</u> have the card he / she says *No, sorry*, then it is his / her turn to ask.

- The turn then goes to the next student on the left. Sts play until one student has collected all four cards from one family.

- Note that a student must have at least <u>one</u> card from a family in his / her hand in order to ask for the others. A common strategy in the game is for Sts to listen carefully and remember which cards the other Sts are asking for. This lets them know what cards other Sts have in their hands.

4B What is it?

A pairwork activity

Sts use adjectives to identify objects. Copy one sheet per pair and cut into **A** and **B**.

> **Language**
>
> It's expensive.   It's a watch.
> It's number three.   It's an expensive watch.

- Write the sentences from **Language** on the board, or show them on screen if using iTools. Model and drill pronunciation.

- Revise adjectives by saying an adjective and getting Sts to say the opposite, e.g. *slow – fast*. (See **Vocabulary Bank** *Adjectives*, p.121.)

- Put Sts into pairs, **A** and **B**, ideally face-to-face, and give out the sheets.

- Demonstrate the activity by taking the part of Student **A**. Say to a Student **B** *It's expensive.* Elicit the response *It's number three.* Point out that Sts can also respond by naming the object e.g. *the car*. Now get a Student **B** to choose a picture on his sheet (e.g. *the computer*) and say *It's slow.* You then say *Number 8* or *It's a computer*.

- Sts take turns saying sentences *It's* + adjectives. Their partner says the number of the picture or names the object. Make it clear that Sts should choose random pictures. They should not do them in order.

Extra idea

- When Sts finish, they could take turns saying sentences with the adjective and noun together, e.g., A (points at a picture) *What's number 3?* or *What is it?* **B** *It's an expensive watch.*

1 It's fast. / It's a fast car.	7 It's long. / It's a long name.
2 It's tall. / It's a tall tree.	8 It's slow. / It's a slow computer.
3 It's expensive. / It's an expensive watch.	9 It's new. / It's a new coat.
4 It's small. / It's a small key.	10 It's cheap. / It's a cheap car.
5 It's old. / It's an old umbrella.	11 It's easy. / It's an easy number.
6 It's big. / It's a big house.	12 It's ugly. / It's an ugly picture.

5A Talk about food

A pairwork activity

Sts answer questions about their tastes and habits in relation to food and drink. Copy one sheet per student.

> **Language**
>
> *I have orange juice for breakfast. What about you?*
> *Me, too.*
> *I don't have orange juice. I have milk.*

- Quickly revise the vocabulary in **Vocabulary Bank** *Food and drink*, p.122.

- Write the sentences from **Language** on the board, or show them on screen if using iTools. Model and drill pronunciation.

- Give out the sheets and tell Sts to look at the pictures of the food / drink and make sure they know the words. Ask them to put a tick next to the sentence if the information is true for them or a cross if it is false. Remind Sts of the meaning of a lot of and elicit the meaning of *every day*.

- Now put Sts in pairs and tell them they are going to tell each other about their sentences.

- Demonstrate the activity. Focus on the first sentence on the board / screen (*I have orange juice for breakfast*) and tick it. Say *I have orange juice for breakfast* and then ask *What about you?* Elicit the two possible answers in **Language**.

- Sts now take turns telling each other their sentences and asking their partners *What about you?*.

- Get feedback by asking a few Sts to report the things they have in common: *We like chocolate. Our favourite food is pasta*.

5B Do you…?

A group speaking activity

Sts ask and answer questions. Copy one sheet per group of three or four Sts and cut into cards.

> **Language**
>
> *Do you…?*   *Yes, I do. / No, I don't.*
> *Sorry. Can you repeat that, please?*

- Revise *Do you…?* questions by asking individual Sts and getting them to give you short answers, e.g., *Do you drink tea in the morning? Do you like rock music?* Say some questions very quietly to elicit *Excuse me. Can you repeat that, please?*

- Write the sentences from **Language** on the board, or show them on screen if using iTools. Model and drill pronunciation.

- Put Sts in groups of three or four and give each group a set of cards.

- Demonstrate by getting a student to pick a card and ask you the question. Answer the question.

- Sts work in their groups. Sts take turns to pick a card and ask the others in the group to answer. Monitor and make sure each student participates equally.

Non-cut alternative

- Sts could do this activity in pairs. Copy one sheet per student and have the Sts fold the sheet in half. A and B take turns asking the questions. A is asking the questions in the first column, and B the questions in the second column.

Extra challenge

- With a good class you could encourage Sts to say a little more when they answer a question and to react to their partner's answer, e.g. A:*Do you like cats?* B: *Yes, I do. I have two cats* Q:*What are their names?*

PE3 Time bingo

A group card game

Sts revise the time with bingo cards. Copy and cut up one card per pair or per student.

> **Language**
>
> (*It's*) *twenty past three, a quarter to six, eleven o'clock.*

- Draw a clock on the board and quickly revise the time.
- Put Sts in pairs and give each pair a bingo card.
- Rehearse the shout, *Bingo!*
- Explain you are going to dictate times, and if the time is on their card, they must cross it out (ask Sts to cross out in PENCIL so the card can be used again).
- Start calling out times, repeating them once. Keep a note of all the times you call out.
- When a pair has crossed out ALL the times on their card they call out *Bingo!*
- Ask Sts to read back the times and check they are correct.
- Play again, giving pairs different cards or getting Sts to rub out and swap cards with another pair. Call out the times in a different order.

Times to dictate: 4.15   3.20   6.25   7.50   5.25   7.30
5.45   10.55   9.35   2.50   11.10   1.05   12.10   8.40

6A What do they do? Where do they work?

A pairwork information gap activity

Sts ask each other about people's jobs and places of work. Copy one sheet per pair and cut into **A** and **B**.

> **Language**
>
> *What does Kate do?*   *She is a nurse.*
> *Where does she work?*   *She works in a children's hospital.*

- Put Sts into pairs, **A** and **B**, ideally face-to-face, and give out the sheets. Make sure Sts can't see each other's sheets.
- Explain that their sheet has missing information which their partner has.
- Focus on the question prompts on the left (*What | do?*) and elicit the first question for Kate, *What does Kate do?*
- Elicit from Sts **A** the answer (*She's a nurse*) and tell the **B**s to write *a nurse* in the space.
- Elicit from Sts **A** the question, *Where does Kate work?* Elicit the answer from **B**s (*She works in a school*) and tell the **A**s to write *in a hospital* in the space.

- Write the sentences from **Language** on the board, or show them on screen if using iTools. Model and drill pronunciation. Now ask Sts how they would ask the questions for George (*What does George do? Where does he work? etc.*).
- Sts ask and answer questions. Monitor and check that they are spelling and pronouncing the words correctly.
- When Sts have finished, tell them to turn over the sheets and ask quick questions round the class to see if they remember people's jobs and places of work.

6B What do you usually do?

A pairwork activity

Sts tell a partner about things they *always*, *usually*, *sometimes*, or *never* do. Copy one worksheet for each pair and cut into **A** and **B**.

> **Language**
>
> *I usually have cereal for breakfast. What about you?*
> *I always have cereal for breakfast. I love cereal.*

- Write the sentences from **Language** on the board, or show them on screen if using iTools. Model and drill pronunciation.
- Demonstrate the activity by giving Sts a couple more examples. Say to a student, e.g. I *sometimes have breakfast in bed on Sunday morning. What about you?* Elicit a true response from the student. Then say to another student I *usually read the newspaper in the morning. What about you?*
- Put Sts into pairs, **A** and **B**, ideally face-to-face, and give out the sheets. Make sure Sts can't see each other's sheets. Give Sts a few of minutes to read and complete the sentences on their half of the sheet. Monitor and answer any questions about vocabulary.
- When Sts have finished, tell them they will now have to say their sentences to their partner and ask *What about you?* Demonstrate the activity with a good student if necessary, using the sentences from **Language**.
- Sts work in pairs. Monitor and help as needed. Encourage Sts to add extra information to their answers as in the examples.
- Get feedback by asking a few volunteers to report what they have learned about their partner.

Extra support

- When Sts have finished, you could ask them to write three sentences about their partner.

7A Free time questionnaire

A group work activity

Sts revise word order in questions by asking each other questions about free time activities. Copy and cut up one sheet per group.

> **Language**
>
> *Do you usually go out*
>   *on Saturday night?*   *Yes, I do.*
> *What do you do?*   *I go to the cinema. What about you?*

- Quickly revise word order in questions and revise the time expressions: *in the morning | evening | at night | at the weekend*

- Put Sts in pairs or small groups. Give each pair / group of Sts a set of cards which they should put face down on the table, and explain that they are going to ask their classmates questions about their free time activities.

- Demonstrate the activity by asking a student to choose a card and ask you the question. Answer the question as fully as possible and ask the student *What about you?*

- Tell Sts that if there are two questions on their card, to ask the first one. If their partner answers *Yes, I do*, then they ask the second one.

- Sts work in their pairs / groups. Encourage Sts to try and say as much as they can as they answer the questions and encourage the questioner to react to the answer if possible with another question.

- When Sts have finished, get feedback by asking individual Sts what their answers were.

  Non-cut alternative
  - Copy one sheet per student. Put Sts in pairs and tell them to take turns in asking the questions from each other and noting down the answers Get feedback by asking Sts to say two or three facts about their partner.

7B   What do you think of...?

A pairwork activity

Sts complete a survey about things / people they like or don't like, then they interview their partner. Copy one sheet per student.

> **Language**
>
> *I like Justine Timberlake.*
> *Do you like him?*   *Yes, I do. I like him a lot.*
>   *He's OK.*
>   *No, I don't like him. He's awful.*

- Write on the board the following sentence with the name of an actor / actress you think that your Sts will know, e.g. *I like Justin Timberlake. Do you like _____?* Elicit what the missing pronoun is (*him*). Ask a student the question and elicit an answer from the **Language** box. Write the sentences from **Language** on the board, or show them on screen if using iTools.

- Give out the sheets and go through the headings in each category and make sure that Sts understand what they mean. Give them a few minutes to complete the sentences. Stress that they don't need to fill in all the categories if they can't, but set a minimum number of sentences they have to fill in (e.g. seven).

- Go round monitoring and helping with any vocabulary Sts need.

- Now put Sts into pairs and focus on **b**. Tell them they will interview their partner. They tell their partner about their preferences then ask them for their opinion and make notes about their partner's answers. Demonstrate by getting a student to ask you a question from their sheet and answer truthfully.

- Sts work in pairs, taking turns to ask and answer questions. Monitor and help where necessary.

- Get feedback by asking a few pairs to report how their answers are the same or different, e.g. *Pierre likes classical music, but I don't like it.*

Extra challenge
- Encourage the student who is answering the question to give more information where possible, and the student who is asking to try to ask extra questions where appropriate.

PE4   Famous birthdays

A pairwork information gap activity

Sts ask and answer questions about the birthdays of famous people. Copy one sheet per pair and cut into **A** and **B**.

> **Language**
>
> *When is Robert de Niro's birthday?   17th August.*

- Write the sentences from **Language** on the board, or show them on screen if using iTools. Revise dates if necessary by writing some dates on the board, e.g., *03/01, 28/05, 12/06, 09/03*. Elicit how to say them: *the third of January, the twenty-eighth of May, the twelfth of June, the ninth of March.*

- Write *Beyoncé* on the board. Elicit the question *When is Beyoncé's birthday?* Write *04/09* and elicit the response *the fourth of September.*

- Put Sts into pairs, **A** and **B**, ideally face-to-face, and give out the sheets. Make sure Sts can't see each other's sheets.

- Explain to Sts that they have to find out the birthdays of the people on their worksheet if the birthday is not given.

- Demonstrate the activity with two Sts. Have a student **B** ask about the first picture *When is Will Smith's birthday?* **A** responds with the date on the worksheet, *the twenty-fifth of September.*

- Sts take turns asking and answering questions about the birthdays. When they finish, they can compare worksheets to confirm their answers.

- Follow up by asking Sts if they found a celebrity birthday that is the same as theirs or if they know that their birthday is the same as that of another famous person.

8A   What's missing?

A pairwork activity

Sts guess the *can* phrase that's missing from their sentences. Copy one sheet per pair and cut into **A** and **B**.

> **Language**
>
> [+] *I can park here*
> [-] *I can't park here*
> [?] *Can I park here?*

- Write the sentence *I'm sorry, but you can't drink coffee in the library* in large letters on a piece of paper. Don't show it to the class. Tell Sts that you have written a sentence and they have to guess what it is. Write on the board *I'm sorry, but you _____ coffee in the library.* Tell Sts that you want them to guess what's missing in the sentence. It will be *can* or *can't* + a verb.

- Elicit ideas. If Sts make an incorrect guess, say *Sorry, try again.* When they guess the correct answer (*can't drink*), say *Yes, that's right* and write the missing words in the sentence on the board.

- Write the sentences from **Language** on the board, or show them on screen if using iTools. Remind Sts of the three forms of *can / can't* and the word order in questions. Model and drill pronunciation. You could also write *Yes, that's right / Sorry, try again* on the board and model and drill the pronunciation

- Put Sts in pairs, **A** and **B**, ideally face-to-face, and give out the sheets. Make sure Sts can't see each other's sheets.

- Explain to Sts that the sentences with blanks are the ones they have to guess. Highlight that they have to use *can / can't* + a verb and that it may be a positive, negative or a question form that is missing. The ones without blanks are the ones their partner has to guess. The answers for these are the words in bold.

- Demonstrate the activity with two good student. Get a Student **A** to read the first sentence and try to guess the missing words. Student **B** responds *Yes, that's right* or *Sorry, try again.* When **A** guesses correctly, he / she writes the missing words on the sheet. Emphasise that Sts should help each other if they are having problems guessing the missing verb forms.

- Sts take turns making guesses and completing the sentences. Monitor and help. When Sts have finished, they can compare sheets to confirm their answers and check spelling.

8B What do you like doing?
A pairwork activity

Sts guess their partner's opinion of particular activities. Copy one sheet per pair and cut into **A** and **B**.

Language
I like swimming. I think you don't like swimming.
You're right. / You're wrong. I love swimming.

- Write these activities on the board or draw simple pictures, e.g. *playing tennis, cooking.* Choose a good student and say, e.g. *Mario, I think you like playing tennis. Am I right?* and teach the answer *You're right / You're wrong.* Continue guessing a few other Sts' opinions about the activities.

- Write the sentences from **Language** on the board, or show them on screen if using iTools. Model and drill pronunciation.

- Now ask Sts to guess your opinion of *playing tennnis* and *cooking* using *I think you like / love / hate...*, and tell them if they are right or wrong.

- Put Sts in pairs, **A** and **B**, ideally face-to-face, and give out the sheets. Make sure Sts can't see each other's sheets.

- Sts individually fill in the sentences under each picture, first writing if they like / love / don't like the activity and then writing what they think for their partner.

- Sts take turns to read sentences and respond to their partner.

- Get feedback to find out who has the most correct guesses.

9A Guess what I'm doing!
A group activity

Sts mime phrases in the present continuous. Copy one sheet and cut into cards.

Language	
Are you...?	*Yes, I am. / No, I'm not.*
	Yes, we are. / No, we aren't.
You're sending a text message.	*That's right.*

- Tell Sts that they are going to act out some phrases in the present continuous for their classmates to guess. They have to do this without speaking.

- Demonstrate the activity. Put the cards face down on your desk and pick a card. Then tell Sts that you are going to act out the phrase for the class and they will have to guess what you are doing. For example, if you draw the card *making dinner*, you could pretend to be in a kitchen and to chop vegetables then put them in a pot and pretend to stir it. You could also draw a clock showing 7.00 p.m. on the board to indicate that it is dinner and not lunch you are making.

- Encourage the class to guess. Sts ask questions and you answer. Elicit the response *You're making dinner.*

- Write the sentences from **Language** on the board, or show them on screen if using iTools. Model and drill pronunciation.

- Put Sts in small groups and give them a set of cards face down. If you have a small class you could do this as a whole class activity. Sts take turns to take a card and act out what's on the card until someone in the group guesses. Then another student takes a card, etc. You could set a time limit for each person e.g. two minutes.

Extra idea
- You could make this a competitive game with teams. One member of Team 1 takes a card and has e.g. two minutes to try to make his / her team guess what is on the card. If they guess within the time limit Team 1 gets a point. Then a member of Team 2 takes a card, etc.

9B A board game
A pairwork or group work activity

Sts play a game to practise using the present simple and present continuous. Copy one sheet per pair or per group of 3–4 Sts. You will also need a coin per group and one counter per student (e.g. a paper clip, a small coin, etc.).

Language	
What are you doing now?	*I'm driving.*
Do you speak English at home?	*No, I don't. We speak Spanish.*

- Tell Sts that they are going to play a game to practise the present simple and present continuous. Write the sentences from **Language** on the board, or show them on screen if using iTools. Remind Sts of the difference between present continuous and present simple.

- Put Sts into pairs or groups of 3–4. Give each pair or group one copy of the game board. Tell Sts that they will need a coin to decide how many spaces to move. They toss the coin: heads = move one space, tails = move two spaces.
- To begin the game, Sts put their counter on the START square. Then one student tosses the coin and moves his / her counter one or two squares. Sts have to answer the question on the square they land on or follow the directions to move back or ahead one square. In that case, they answer the question on the new square. If Sts can answer the question they stay on that square. If they can't answer it they go back to the previous square.
- Sts take turns to throw the coin, answer questions, and move along the board. The first person to reach the FINISH is the winner.

Extra challenge
- Encourage the student who is answering the question to give extra information and the other Sts in the group to ask follow up questions as appropriate.

PE5 Would you like to…?

A pair activity

Sts ask a partner about things they would like to do in the future. Copy one worksheet for each pair, and cut into **A** and **B**.

Language	
Would you like to travel to Antarctica?	*Yes, I would. / No, I wouldn't.*
Why (not)?	*Because I think it's very beautiful. / Because it's very cold there.*

- Tell Sts they are going to find out what some of their classmates would like to do in the future.
- Write the sentences from **Language** on the board, or show them on screen if using iTools. Model and drill pronunciation.
- Put Sts into pairs, **A** and **B**, and give out the sheets. Give Sts a minute to read the items and answer any questions about vocabulary.
- Demonstrate the activity by getting a student to choose a phrase and ask you the question (*Would you like to…?*). Answer with a short answer, *Yes, I would* or *No, I wouldn't*, and then indicate that the student should ask *Why?* or *Why not?* Give a short, simple response that uses words and structures Sts have studied.
- Get Sts work in pairs asking and answering the questions. Monitor and help as needed. Make sure Sts are asking follow up questions with *Why*.
- Get feedback by asking a few Sts to report their findings. *Mario would like to write a book. He wants to write about his family.*

10A My hotel

A pairwork information gap activity

Sts ask each other about the facilities in two hotels. Copy one sheet per pair and cut it into **A** and **B**.

Language	
Is there a restaurant in the hotel?	*Yes, there is.*
Where is it?	*It's on the first floor.*
Are there any bars?	*No, there aren't.*

- Quickly revise the ordinal numbers 1 to 5 by writing the numbers on the board or saying them and eliciting the ordinal, e.g. *one – first*. Remind Sts that we use ordinal numbers to talk about the floors in a building, *first floor, second floor*, etc. Remind them also of *ground floor.*
- Write the sentences from **Language** on the board, or show them on screen if using iTools. Model and drill pronunciation. Remind Sts that we usually use *any* in plural questions with *Are there*, and *a / an* with singular statements and questions with *There is* and *Is there.*
- Put Sts into pairs, **A** and **B**, and give out the sheets.
- Focus on the instruction for **a**. Tell Sts they have to write one thing from the list of facilities on each floor. Highlight that they have to make choices. They can't use everything on the list, only six facilities. Give them a few minutes to do this.
- Focus on the instructions for **b** and **c**. Demonstrate the activity with a good student or get two students to demonstrate the first exchange.
- When Sts have finished, get them to compare their hotels and check their answers.

10B Where were you yesterday?

A pairwork activity

Sts practise the prepositions *on, at, in*, and ask each other what they were doing at particular times in the past. Copy one sheet per pair and cut into **A** and **B**.

Language
Were you at home at 6 o'clock last night?
Yes, I was. / No, I wasn't. What about you?

- Revise prepositions of place, e.g., *at work, on the train / bus, in the car, at the restaurant* (see Student's Book, *p.61*).
- Write the sentences from **Language** on the board, or show them on screen if using iTools. Model and drill pronunciation.
- Put Sts in pairs, **A** and **B,** and give out the sheets. Make sure they can't see each other's sheets. Ask Sts to complete the questions with the correct preposition. Monitor and correct individual mistakes as necessary.

Student A		Student B	
1	on	1	at
2	in	2	in
3	in	3	on
4	at	4	in
5	on	5	at
6	in	6	in
7	at	7	in

- Focus on **b**. Explain to Sts that they are going ask questions to find out where their classmates were at certain times.
- Demonstrate the activity by getting a student **B** to ask the first question (*Were you at a restaurant yesterday at two o'clock?*) Get student **A** to answer the question. (*Yes, I was / No, I wasn't.*) Encourage A to ask *What about you?*

- Sts work in pairs taking turns to ask each other questions. Monitor and help where necessary.
- Get feedback by asking Sts to report on the places where they and their partner were at the same time yesterday e.g. *Jan and I were in the car yesterday afternoon.*

11A Guess how many
A pairwork and mingle activity

Sts first work in pairs to guess how many Sts did the activity described on their card. Then they do a survey to find out if their guess was correct. Copy the sheet and cut it into cards. Make enough copies for each pair to have one question.

> **Language**
>
> *Did you watch TV last night?*   *Yes, I did.*
> *Did you study English this morning?*   *No, I didn't.*

- Quickly revise the past simple of regular verbs, focusing especially on the question form. Write the infinitive of a few verbs from the activity on the board. Elicit the past forms and write them on the board. Write the sentences from **Language** on the board, or show them on screen if using iTools, and revise questions and short answers.
- Put Sts in pairs and give each pair one card. If you have more than 20 Sts in the class, give some pairs the same card. Tell Sts that they need to guess how many Sts in the class did the activity that is on their card and write the number on the card where it says *Our guess*.
- Tell Sts that they now have to find out if their guess is correct by asking everyone a question using *Did you...?* e.g. *Did you watch TV last night*. Monitor and check that questions are correct.
- Pairs walk around asking their questions from memory (not reading them), and making notes of the answers. They should write the name of the person and *yes* or *no*. They need to ask everybody in the class. (As Sts are doing this, they will also be answering questions from other pairs.)
- When they have finished, get Sts to sit down and ask each pair to report the results of their survey, e.g. *Ten people watched TV last night. Our guess was eight.* Find out if any pairs' guesses were right.

11B Life in a day
A pairwork activity

Sts ask and answer questions to find three things they both did yesterday. Copy one sheet per pair and cut into **A** and **B**.

> **Language**
>
> *Did you get up at eight o'clock this morning?*   *Yes, I did.*
> *Did you have coffee after dinner last night?*   *No, I didn't.*
> *What about you?*

- Write these phrases on the board.
  / get a bus to English class today?
  / get up late last Sunday?
- Elicit the missing words Sts need to add to make a correct question (*Did you*) and write the full question on the board.

- Put Sts into pairs, **A** and **B**, and give out the sheets. Make sure Sts can't see each other's sheets. Tell them that they will have to ask their partner the questions on their sheet and tick or cross the answers. Focus on **b** and explain they will try to find things they have in common.
- Demonstrate the activity by getting a student to ask you the first question (*Did you get up at 8 o'clock this morning?*). Answer the question truthfully and then ask the student *What about you?*
- Sts take turns to ask each other the questions and note down the answers. Remind them to ask *What about you?* after answering a question.
- Monitor and correct any mistakes.
- When Sts have finished get them, in pairs, to write sentences with *We...* for the things they had in common. Get feedback by asking pairs which things they had in common e.g. *We got a bus to English class today.*

Extra challenge
- Tell Sts to get their partner to give more information, e.g. *Did you go shopping with friends last week? Yes, I did. I went shopping with Marta and Luisa.*

PE9 Where are you?
A pairwork or small group activity

Sts follow directions and use a map to find their way to a destination. Make one copy of the map and cut up one copy of the direction cards for each pair or group.

> **Language**
>
> *Go straight on.*
> *Turn right. / Turn left.*
> *It's on the corner of King Street and West Road.*
> *It's on the right.*

- Revise the language for directions by drawing a simple map on the board. Write the sentences from **Language** on the board, or show them on screen if using iTools. Model and drill pronunciation.
- Put Sts in pairs or small groups and give them a map and a set of direction cards. Focus on the map and elicit from the class all the places marked with a symbol and write them on the board.

[£] = bank	[H] = hospital
[ ] = restaurant	[ ] = car park
[ ] = school	[ ] = supermarket
[ ] = phone shop	[ ] = hotel
[ ] = book shop	[ ] = park
[ ] = factory	[ ] = cinema
[ ] = museum	

- Demonstrate the activity with the class. Read one of the cards and ask Sts to tell you where they are. Read slowly, pausing to give Sts time to follow on the map. Make sure Sts understand the preposition outside e.g. *You are outside the bank.* Draw a little diagram on the board to show this. If Sts don't understand something, encourage them to ask questions, e.g., *Do we turn left or turn right? Could you repeat that, please?*
- In their pairs or groups, Sts take turns picking cards and reading the directions aloud for the others to follow. (The correct answer is in brackets at the end of the directions.)

- Monitor and remind them to ask questions if they don't understand the directions.
- Get feedback by asking which pairs got all the directions right.

  ### Extra challenge
  - If some pairs or groups finish early, get them to make up their own directions to any place on the map or to give real directions to a place near the school.

12A Past tense questions
A pairwork or group work activity

Sts play a game to practise the past simple. Copy one sheet for each pair or for each group of 3–4 Sts. You will also need a coin per group and one counter per student (e.g. a paper clip, a small coin, etc.).

Language	
Where did you buy your shoes?	I bought my shoes in the shopping centre.
What did you do last weekend?	I went to a rock concert.

- Tell Sts that they are going to play a game to practise the past simple. Write the sentences from **Language** on the board, or show them on screen if using iTools. Model and drill pronunciation.
- Put Sts into pairs or groups of 3–4. Give each pair or group one copy of the game board. Tell Sts that they will need a coin to decide how many spaces to move. They toss the coin: heads = move one space, tails = move two spaces. Quickly go through the questions to make sure Sts understand all of them. Tell Sts that they should try to answer with full sentences so that they practise the past simple.
- To begin the game, Sts put their counter on the START square. Then one student tosses the coin and moves his / her counter one or two squares. Sts have to answer the question on the square they land on or follow the directions to move back or ahead one square. In that case, they answer the question on the new square. If they can't answer a question they go back to the previous square that they were on.
- Sts take turns answering questions, and moving along the board. The first person to reach the FINISH is the winner.

  ### Extra challenge
  - Encourage the student who is answering the question to give extra information and the other Sts in the group to ask follow up questions as appropriate.

12B Holidays
A pairwork information gap activity

Sts exchange information about different people's adventure holidays. Copy one sheet per pair and cut into **A** and **B**.

Language	
Where's she going?	She's going to Scotland.
Who's he going with?	He's going with his girlfriend.
How are they travelling	They're travelling by train.

- Revise saying dates. Write some dates on the board, e.g., *11th July*, *21st August*, Get Sts to say the dates.

- Put Sts into pairs, **A** and **B**, ideally face-to-face, and give out the sheets. Make sure Sts can't see each other's sheets.
- Tell Sts that they have information about three people's holiday plans and they need to ask their partner questions to fill in the missing information on their sheets.
- Focus on the picture of Diana and the first prompt *Where | she | go?* to elicit the question *Where's she going?* Elicit the answer *She's going on a city break to Paris.* Now focus on the second prompt and elicit the question (*Who's she going with?*), then the answer (*She's going alone.*)
- Quickly elicit the other five questions from the class with *she*. Now focus on the picture of Nick and elicit what the questions will be for him and remind Sts that they need to use *he* e.g. *Where's he going?* Finally focus on the picture of Paul and Jake and ask what the questions are for two people, e.g. *Where are they going?*
- Write the sentences from **Language** on the board or show them on screen if you are using iTools. Model and drill pronunciation.
- Demonstrate the activity with a good student, asking and answering the first four questions about Diana. Encourage Sts to answer with full sentences.
- Sts work in pairs, taking turns to ask their partners questions to complete the charts. They may have to ask each other to spell some words. When they finish, they can compare their sheets.
- Get feedback and ask Sts which holiday plan they like best.

Revision questions
A revision activity

Sts ask each other questions to revise a range of tenses, vocabulary, and verb forms from the book. This could be used as a final 'pre-test' revision activity. Alternatively, it could be used as an oral exam. Copy and cut up one set of cards per pair.

Language
Grammar and vocabulary of the course.

- Put Sts in pairs. Give each pair a set of cards that they place face down on the table. Sts take turns to pick up the top card and talk to their partner about the topic on the card, using the prompts.
- Set a time limit per card, e.g. three minutes.
- Tell Sts to keep the card they have talked about.
- When Sts have finished and if there is time, they can swap cards with their partner.
- Monitor and help where necessary.

  ### Non-cut alternative
  - Make one copy per pair. Give Sts a few moments to read through the cards. Then A chooses a number for B. B then talks about what's on the card for that number. They take turns to choose a topic for their partner to talk about.

1A COMMUNICATIVE Are you...?

You're Find...	Katy Perry Orlando Bloom Tom Hanks	You're Find...	Orlando Bloom Andy Garcia Katy Perry
You're Find...	Beyoncé Johnny Depp Cameron Diaz	You're Find...	Cameron Diaz Meryl Streep Antonio Banderas
You're Find...	Andy Garcia Shakira Victoria Beckham	You're Find...	Johnny Depp Tom Hanks Penelope Cruz
You're Find...	Meryl Streep Russell Crowe Beyoncé	You're Find...	Sandra Bullock Daniel Radcliffe Nicole Kidman
You're Find...	Penelope Cruz Sandra Bullock Russell Crowe	You're Find...	Leonardo DiCaprio Ben Affleck Shakira
You're Find...	Daniel Radcliffe Victoria Beckham Amy Adams	You're Find...	Shakira Amy Adams Orlando Bloom
You're Find...	Ben Affleck Nicole Kidman Katy Perry	You're Find...	Russell Crowe Penelope Cruz Johnny Depp
You're Find...	Tom Hanks Cameron Diaz Leonardo DiCaprio	You're Find...	Nicole Kidman Katy Perry Andy Garcia
You're Find...	Amy Adams Katy Perry Daniel Radcliffe	You're Find...	Katy Perry Antonio Banderas Sandra Bullock
You're Find...	Antonio Banderas Beyoncé Meryl Streep	You're Find...	Victoria Beckham Leonardo DiCaprio Ben Affleck

1. Salma Hayek
2. Mesut Özil
3. Ken Watanabe
4. Roger Federer
5. Vanessa Paradis
6. Dariusz Michalczewski
7. Fernando Alonso
8. Anna Netrebko
9. Donatella Versace
10. Kate Winslet
11. Orhan Pamuk
12. Paolo Coelho

PE1 COMMUNICATIVE Who are you?

First name: **Christophe**
Last name: **Moreau**
From: **Rennes, France**

First name: **Katya**
Last name: **Scheider**
From: **Leipzig, Germany**

First name: **Vicenzo**
Last name: **Giordano**
From: **Perugia, Italy**

First name: **Aleksandra**
Last name: **Kowalski**
From: **Poznan, Poland**

First name: **Natalia**
Last name: **Carvalho**
From: **Belem, Brazil**

First name: **Andrey**
Last name: **Soloyov**
From: **Grozny, Russia**

First name: **Miguel**
Last name: **Vazquez**
From: **Bilbao, Spain**

First name: **Anthony**
Last name: **Clarke**
From: **Croydon, England**

First name: **Mathilde**
Last name: **Kessler**
From: **Lucerne, Switzerland**

First name: **Yusuf**
Last name: **Endogan**
From: **Antalya, Turkey**

First name: **Stephen**
Last name: **Andersen**
From: **Memphis, USA**

First name: **Nazir**
Last name: **Hanania**
From: **Luxor, Egypt**

2A COMMUNICATIVE Match the sentences

Student A

	Answers to Student B
1 Excuse me. Are you James?	**a** We're from Berlin.
2 Where are Alice and Umberto from?	**b** No, it's in Japan.
3 Are you here on holiday?	**c** I'm from Egypt.
4 Is Nike English?	**d** Yes, she's from Paris.
5 Are they Mexican?	**e** No, you aren't.

Student B

	Answers to Student A
6 Are we late?	**f** Yes, we are.
7 Where are you from?	**g** No, it isn't. It's American.
8 Is Caroline French?	**h** No, they aren't. They're Spanish.
9 Where are you from in Germany?	**i** No, I'm not. I'm Jason.
10 Is Kyoto in China?	**j** They're Swiss.

2B COMMUNICATIVE Remember the sentences

1 Hi Lola. This is Paul.	g	*Fold here*	**a** No, she's single.
2 How old is Karin?	e		**b** My name's Karl.
3 What's your phone number?			**c** It's Thursday.
4 Nice to meet you.			**d** On Monday and Friday.
5 Is she married?			**e** She's 38.
6 How are you?			**f** Thanks.
7 See you tomorrow.			**g** Nice to meet you.
8 What's your name?			**h** Hi!
9 Have a nice day!			**i** I'm from Italy.
10 Where are you from?			**j** Fine thanks.
11 When's your English class?			**k** It's 123 4488.
12 Hello!			**l** Sorry.
13 My name is Maribel, not Maria.			**m** Bye!
14 What day is it today?			**n** Nice to meet you, too.

3A COMMUNICATIVE The same or different?

Student A

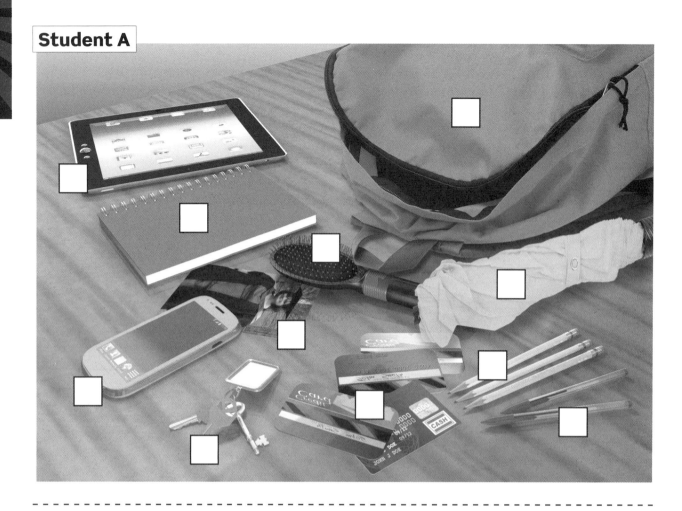

Student B

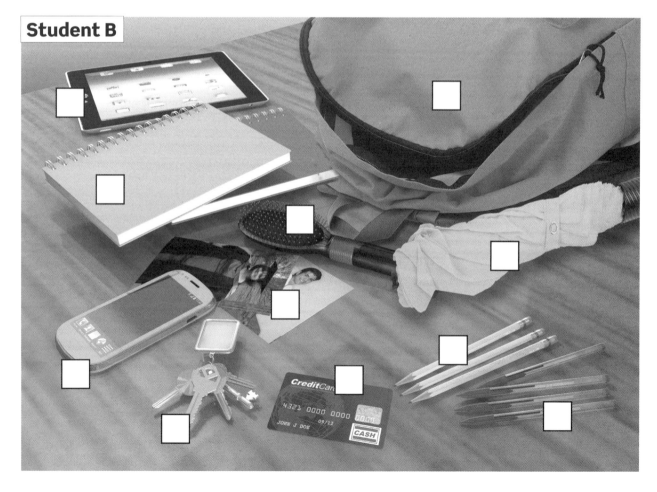

English File 3rd edition Teacher's Book Beginner Photocopiable © Oxford University Press 2015

3B COMMUNICATIVE What's this? What's that?

The Three Kings

Food

Sandwiches (cheese, chicken, or tuna)	£4.15
Burger	£4.99
Cheeseburger	£5.20
Salads (chicken or egg)	£5.95

Drinks

Coke / Diet Coke	£2.60
Orange juice	£2.80
Mineral water	£1.99
Coffee / tea	£1.95
Beer	£3.25

A You are a barman.

Welcome the customer and show them the menu.

Useful phrases:

Can I help you?

Anything else?

Here you are.

B You are a customer.

Look at the menu and choose something to eat and drink.

Useful phrases:

Can I have...?

How much is it?

Here you are.

English File 3rd edition Teacher's Book Beginner Photocopiable © Oxford University Press 2015

MARIO'S FAMILY	MARIO'S FAMILY	MARIO'S FAMILY	MARIO'S FAMILY
SISTER / brother / father / mother	sister / BROTHER / father / mother	sister / brother / FATHER / mother	sister / brother / father / MOTHER
MONICA'S FAMILY	MONICA'S FAMILY	MONICA'S FAMILY	MONICA'S FAMILY
BROTHER / daughter / sister / husband	brother / DAUGHTER / sister / husband	brother / daughter / SISTER / husband	brother / daughter / sister / HUSBAND
RAY'S FAMILY	RAY'S FAMILY	RAY'S FAMILY	RAY'S FAMILY
WIFE / brother / sister / son	wife / BROTHER / sister / son	wife / brother / SISTER / son	wife / brother / sister / SON
CHARLIE'S FAMILY	CHARLIE'S FAMILY	CHARLIE'S FAMILY	CHARLIE'S FAMILY
FATHER / wife / son / mother	father / WIFE / son / mother	father / wife / SON / mother	father / wife / son / MOTHER
AMY'S FAMILY	AMY'S FAMILY	AMY'S FAMILY	AMY'S FAMILY
MOTHER / daughter / husband / son	mother / DAUGHTER / husband / son	mother / daughter / HUSBAND / son	mother / daughter / husband / SON

4B COMMUNICATIVE What is it?

Student A

1
2
3
4

5
6
7
8

9
10
11
12

Student B

1
2
3
4

5
6
7
8

9
10
11
12

5A COMMUNICATIVE Talk about food

		You	Your friend
1 I have ___ for breakfast.		T/F	_____
2 I don't drink ___ .		T/F	_____
3 I have a ___ for lunch.		T/F	_____
4 I don't like ___ .		T/F	_____
5 My favourite food is ___ .		T/F	_____
6 I don't have ___ in ___ .		T/F	_____
7 I eat a lot of ___ .		T/F	_____
8 I like ___ .		T/F	_____
9 I don't have ___ on my ___ .		T/F	_____
10 I have ___ for breakfast at the weekend.		T/F	_____
11 I drink a lot of ___ every day.		T/F	_____
12 I don't eat ___ in the evening.		T/F	_____

5B COMMUNICATIVE Do you...?

live in a small house	drink coffee in the morning
drink water in the afternoon	eat Chinese food
eat fruit every day	like vegetables
listen to the radio in the evening	study on Saturday afternoons
speak Japanese	like cats
have a blue car	make breakfast for your family
watch TV in the morning	speak Russian
want a coffee	want a sandwich
have a tablet	like classical music
live near the school	read the newspaper in the morning
listen to music in your car	work on Saturdays
need a new phone	go to the gym

English File 3rd edition Teacher's Book Beginner Photocopiable © Oxford University Press 2015

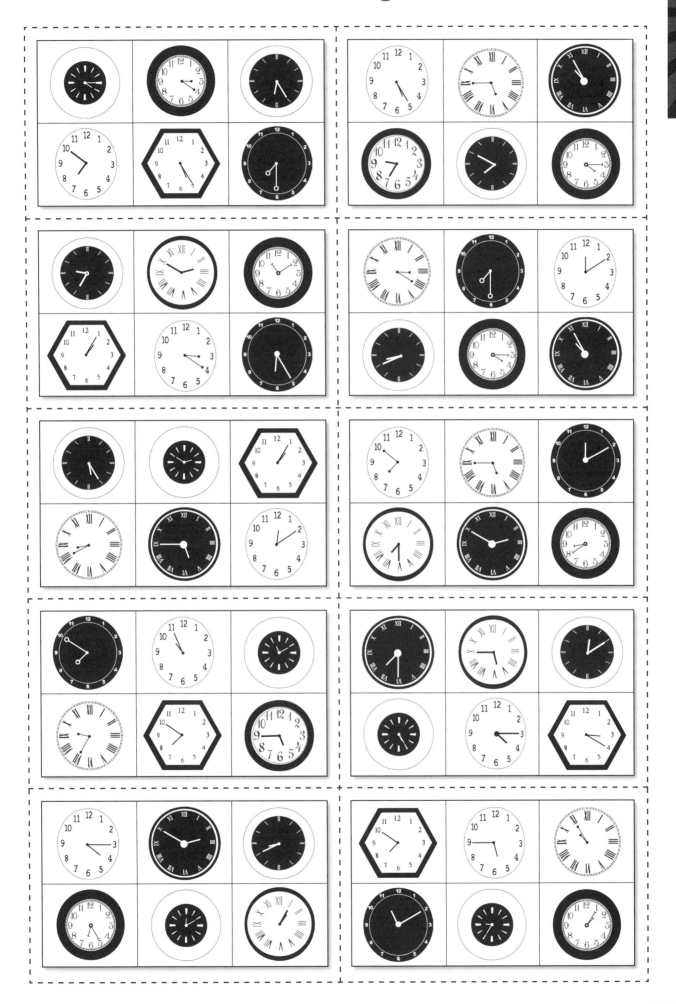

6A COMMUNICATIVE What do they do? Where do they work

Student A

What / do?

Kate	George	Jim	Liz	Julia	Maria

Where / work?

Kate	George	Jim	Liz	Julia	Maria

- -

Student B

What / do?

Kate	George	Jim	Liz	Julia	Maria

Where / work?

Kate	George	Jim	Liz	Julia	Maria

English File 3rd edition Teacher's Book Beginner Photocopiable © Oxford University Press 2015

6B COMMUNICATIVE What do you usually do?

Student A

a Complete the sentences with *always*, *usually*, *sometimes*, or *never* + verb. Make the sentences true for you.

1 I _____ cereal for breakfast.

2 I _____ TV in the evening.

3 I _____ a bath in the evening.

4 I _____ shopping on Saturday morning.

5 I _____ my homework before class.

6 I _____ to the radio in the car.

7 I _____ lunch in a restaurant.

8 I _____ coffee after dinner.

b Now tell your partner and then ask *What about you?*

- -

Student B

a Complete the sentences with *always*, *usually*, *sometimes*, or *never* + verb. Make the sentences true for you.

1 I _____ up late at the weekend.

2 I _____ to bed at about 11 o'clock.

3 I _____ a shower in the morning.

4 I _____ housework in the evening.

5 I _____ to the gym after school / work.

6 I _____ the newspaper on Sunday.

7 I _____ a sandwich for lunch.

8 I _____ breakfast in the morning.

b Now tell your partner and then ask *What about you?*

7A COMMUNICATIVE Free time questionnaire

Ask your partner the questions and write down their answers in your notebook.

1 Do you usually go out on Saturday night? What do you do?

2 Do you get up late on Sundays? What time do you get up?

3 How do you relax in the evenings?

4 When do you usually meet your friends?

5 Do you do exercise or sport? What do you do?

6 When do you study English at home?

7 Do you listen to music? What music do you listen to?

8 Do you play a musical instrument? What instrument do you play?

9 Do you watch a lot of TV? What programmes do you watch?

10 Do you go shopping at the weekend?

11 Do you cook? What's your speciality?

12 What do you never do at the weekend?

13 Where do you usually go in the summer holidays?

14 Do you read e-books? When do you usually read?

English File 3rd edition Teacher's Book Beginner Photocopiable © Oxford University Press 2015

7B COMMUNICATIVE What do you think of...?

Work with a partner. Complete two sentences (or more) in each category.

Music

I like _____ (male singer).
Do you like _____?

I don't like _____ (female singer).
Do you like _____?

I like _____ (a group).
Do you like _____?

I listen to _____ (a type of music).
Do you like _____?

Sport

I often watch _____ (a sport)
on TV. Do you watch _____?

I play _____ (a sport).
Do you play _____?

I really like _____ (sportsman).
Do you like _____?

I really like _____ (sportswoman).
Do you like _____?

Food

I love _____s (fruit plural).
Do you like _____?

I don't like _____ (food).
Do you like _____?

I sometimes eat _____ (a
nationality) food.
Do you like _____?

My favourite drink is _____
(a drink). Do you drink _____?

Student A

Will Smith   25/09

Keira Knightley _____

Rihanna   20/02

Jackie Chan _____

Katy Perry   25/10

Adele _____

Leonardo DiCaprio   11/11

Kate Middleton _____

Kanye West   08/06

Benedict Cumberbatch _____

Usain Bolt   21/08

Stephenie Meyer _____

Student B

Will Smith _____

Keira Knightley   26/03

Rihanna _____

Jackie Chan   07/04

Katy Perry _____

Adele   05/05

Leonardo DiCaprio _____

Kate Middleton   09/01

Kanye West _____

Benedict Cumberbatch   19/07

Usain Bolt _____

Stephenie Meyer   24/12

8A COMMUNICATIVE What's missing?

Student A

1 I'm sorry, but you _____ _____ photos in the museum.

2 **Can** we **use** the Wi-fi in the hotel?

3 _____ you _____ with American Express at that restaurant?

4 Where **can** I **play** tennis in this town?

5 _____ the students _____ home for lunch?

6 You **can't use** your mobile in the hospital.

7 You're late. You _____ into the class.

8 We **can park** the car here, but it costs £5 an hour!

9 It's OK. You _____ in Jane's chair. She isn't here today.

10 The children **can't swim** in the pool today. It's very cold.

11 _____ you _____ me, please? I don't understand this homework.

12 We **can get up** late today. It's Sunday!

- -

Student B

1 I'm sorry, but you **can't take** photos in the museum.

2 _____ we _____ the Wi-fi in the hotel?

3 **Can** you **pay** with American Express at that restaurant?

4 Where _____ I _____ tennis in this town?

5 **Can** the students **go** home for lunch?

6 You _____ your mobile in the hospital.

7 You're late. You **can't come** into the class.

8 We _____ the car here, but it costs £5 an hour!

9 It's OK. You **can sit** in Jane's chair. She isn't here today.

10 The children _____ in the pool today. It's very cold.

11 **Can** you **help** me, please? I don't understand this homework.

12 We _____ late today. It's Sunday!

English File 3rd edition Teacher's Book Beginner Photocopiable © Oxford University Press 2015

8B COMMUNICATIVE What do you like doing?

Student A *I love / I like / I don't like + -ing*

1
I _____
I think you _____

2
I _____
I think you _____

3
I _____
I think you _____

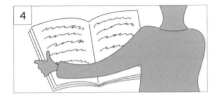

4
I _____
I think you _____

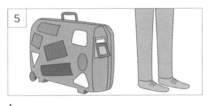

5
I _____
I think you _____

6
I _____
I think you _____

7
I _____
I think you _____

8
I _____
I think you _____

- -

Student B *I love / I like / I don't like + -ing*

1
I _____ on TV.
I think you _____

2
I _____
I think you _____

3
I _____
I think you _____

4
I _____
I think you _____

5
I _____ computer games.
I think you _____

6
I _____ clothes.
I think you _____

7
I _____ cakes.
I think you _____

8
I _____
I think you _____

making coffee	listening to music	eating pasta	cooking
carrying bags	paying by credit card	painting a room	parking a car
playing a video game	taking a photo	doing housework	cycling
walking in the mountains	crying	reading an e-book	watching football
buying a coat	packing a suitcase	getting a taxi	having a shower

9B COMMUNICATIVE A board game

START

Why are you studying English?

When do you usually do your English homework?

Go back one space. ←

What are you carrying in your bag today?

What do you like doing in your free time?

What's the teacher doing now?

Think of one person in your family. What's he / she doing now?

Move forward one space. ←

What book are you reading at the moment?

When do you usually go on holiday?

Go back one space. ←

How do you relax at the weekend?

What do you usually do after dinner?

Move forward one space. ←

What language are you speaking now?

What time does this class finish?

What are you wearing?

FINISH

PE5 COMMUNICATIVE Would you like to...?

Student A

(a) Ask **B** questions with *Would you like to...?* Then ask *Why* or *Why not?*

Would you like to travel to Antarctica? Why? (Why not?)

(b) Answer **B**'s questions.

Student B

(a) Answer **A**'s questions.

(b) Ask **A** questions with *Would you like to...?* Then ask *Why* or *Why not?*

Would you like to be a lawyer? Why? (Why not?)

	Student A		Student B
1	travel to Antarctica	1	be a lawyer
2	play in a rock band	2	meet a famous person
3	write a book	3	learn Chinese
4	be in a film	4	play tennis at Wimbledon
5	open a restaurant	5	work for a computer company
6	buy a big, fast car	6	live in a different country for a year
7	have cooking classes	7	travel around the world
8	learn to play a musical instrument	8	be famous

Student A

(a) Choose six things from the list below and write one on each floor of your hotel.

bars   gift shop   gym   reception   restaurant   spa   swimming pool   toilets

(b) Ask **B** about his / her hotel: *Is there a…? Where is it? Are there any…? Where are they?* Write the answers in the chart.

(c) Answer **B**'s questions about your hotel. *Yes, there is / are. It's / They're on the … floor.*

Your hotel

THE **Queen** HOTEL

5
4
3
2
1
G

Your partner's hotel

THE **Palace** HOTEL

5
4
3
2
1
G

- -

Student B

(a) Choose six things from the list below and write one on each floor of your hotel.

bars   gift shop   gym   reception   restaurant   spa   swimming pool   toilets

(b) Answer **A**'s questions about your hotel. *Yes, there is / are. It's / They're on the … floor.*

(c) Ask **A** about his / her hotel: *Is there a…? Where is it? Are there any…? Where are they?* Write the answers in the chart.

Your hotel

THE **Palace** HOTEL

5
4
3
2
1
G

Your partner's hotel

THE **Queen** HOTEL

5
4
3
2
1
G

10B COMMUNICATIVE Where were you yesterday?

Student A

(a) Complete the questions with *in*, *at*, or *on*.

(b) Ask **B** the questions. Then answer **B**'s questions. Remember to ask *And what about you?* Tick the box if you were in the same place.

---

1 Were you _____ a bus yesterday morning? _____

2 Were you _____ bed yesterday at nine o'clock in the morning? _____

3 Were you _____ a shopping centre with a friend yesterday afternoon? _____

4 Were you _____ work / school yesterday morning? _____

5 Were you _____ the street at ten o'clock last night? _____

6 Were you _____ London or New York yesterday? _____

7 Were you _____ a café at eleven o'clock yesterday? _____

Student B

(a) Complete the questions with *in*, *at*, or *on*.

(b) Answer **A**'s questions. Then ask **A** your questions. Remember to ask *And what about you?* Tick the box if you were in the same place.

---

1 Were you _____ a restaurant yesterday at two o'clock? _____

2 Were you _____ a museum yesterday afternoon? _____

3 Were you _____ a train yesterday morning? _____

4 Were you _____ the park last night? _____

5 Were you _____ home alone at six o'clock last night? _____

6 Were you _____ the kitchen at nine o'clock yesterday morning? _____

7 Were you _____ your car yesterday afternoon? _____

English File 3rd edition Teacher's Book Beginner Photocopiable © Oxford University Press 2015

1 Find out how many people watched TV last night.

Our guess: _____ people   The real number: _____ people

2 Find out how many people studied English last weekend.

Our guess: _____ people   The real number: _____ people

3 Find out how many people played football yesterday.

Our guess: _____ people   The real number: _____ people

4 Find out how many people cooked dinner yesterday.

Our guess: _____ people   The real number: _____ people

5 Find out how many people walked to class today.

Our guess: _____ people   The real number: _____ people

6 Find out how many people listened to the radio yesterday.

Our guess: _____ people   The real number: _____ people

7 Find out how many people waited for a bus yesterday.

Our guess: _____ people   The real number: _____ people

8 Find out how many people cleaned their room last weekend.

Our guess: _____ people   The real number: _____ people

9 Find out how many people talked to their mother this morning.

Our guess: _____ people   The real number: _____ people

10 Find out how many people travelled by train on their last holiday.

Our guess: _____ people   The real number: _____ people

11B COMMUNICATIVE Life in a day

Student A

a Ask Student **B** the questions.

1 / get up at eight o'clock this morning?	☐
2 / have a very long shower this morning?	☐
3 / get a bus to English class today?	☐
4 / do English homework ten minutes before the class?	☐
5 / go to bed very early last night?	☐
6 / get home late last night?	☐
7 / have two coffees (or more) yesterday?	☐
8 / have lunch at home yesterday?	☐
9 / have breakfast in bed last weekend?	☐
10 / go shopping with friends last weekend	☐

b How many things did the two of you (you and your partner) do?

Student B

a Ask Student **A** the questions.

1 / do exercise yesterday?	☐
2 / have cereal for breakfast today?	☐
3 / do your English homework with a friend?	☐
4 / get a bus to work / school yesterday?	☐
5 / have dinner with your family last night?	☐
6 / have a coffee after dinner last night?	☐
7 / get home very late yesterday?	☐
8 / have lunch with a friend on Saturday?	☐
9 / get up late last Sunday?	☐
10 / go shopping for food last weekend?	☐

b How many things did the two of you (you and your partner) do?

PE6 COMMUNICATIVE Where are you?

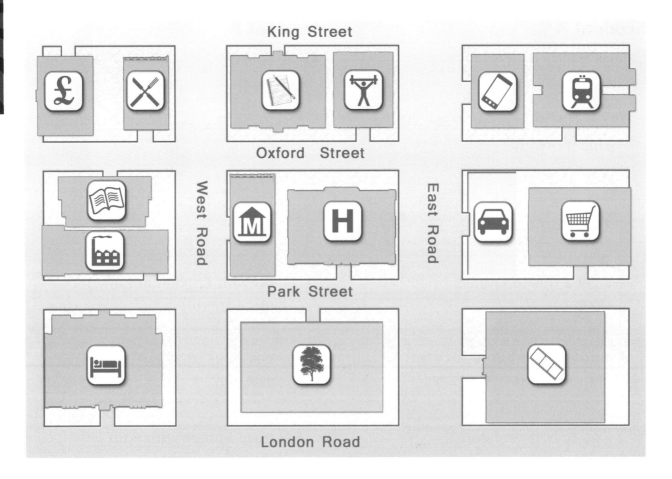

---

1 You are outside the restaurant in Oxford Street. Turn left and then turn right into West Road. Go straight on. Then left into Park Street. It's the building on the left, opposite the park. (**the hospital**)

2 You are outside the phone shop in East Road. Turn left and go straight on. Turn left into Park Street. It's the building on the left next to the car park. (**the supermarket**)

3 You are outside the bookshop in Oxford Street. Turn right and go straight on. Turn right into West Road. Go straight on. Turn right into London Road. It's on the right. (**the hotel**)

4 You are outside the hotel. Turn left and go straight on. Turn left into East Road. Go straight on and turn right into Oxford Street. It's on your left. (**the train station**)

5 You are outside the factory in Park Street. Turn left then turn left again into West Road. Go straight on. Turn right into King Street. Go straight on. It's on the corner of King Street and East Road. (**the phone shop**)

6 You are outside the museum in West Road. Turn left and then turn left again into Park Street. Go straight on. Turn right into East Road. It's on the left. (**the cinema**)

7 You are outside the cinema in East Road. Turn right and go straight on in East Road. Turn left into King Street. Go straight on. It's on the left after the gym. (**the school**)

8 You are at the supermarket. Turn right and go straight on in Park Street. Turn right into West Road, go straight on, and then turn left into Oxford Street. It's on the left opposite the restaurant. (**the bookshop**)

12A COMMUNICATIVE Past tense questions

Where did you buy your shoes?

What time did you get up today?

Go back one space. ←

Did you get a bus or a train today? Where to?

What did you have for dinner last night?

Where did you have breakfast this morning?

Move forward one space. ←

What time did you leave the house this morning?

Did you see a film on TV last night? What film?

Who did you sit next to in the last class?

Go back one space. ←

How many emails or messages did you send yesterday?

Where did you go last night / at the weekend?

Move forward one space. ←

Did you write anything by hand yesterday? What?

When did you do your English homework?

Where did you go on holiday last summer?

FINISH

12B COMMUNICATIVE Holidays

Student A

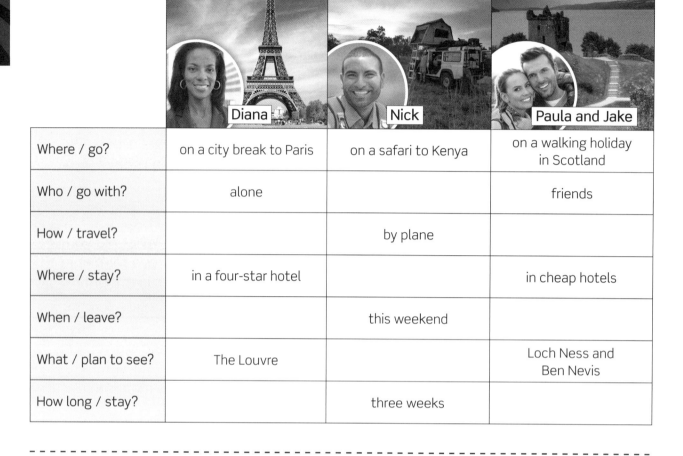

	Diana	Nick	Paula and Jake
Where / go?	on a city break to Paris	on a safari to Kenya	on a walking holiday in Scotland
Who / go with?	alone		friends
How / travel?		by plane	
Where / stay?	in a four-star hotel		in cheap hotels
When / leave?		this weekend	
What / plan to see?	The Louvre		Loch Ness and Ben Nevis
How long / stay?		three weeks	

Student B

	Diana	Nick	Paula and Jake
Where / go?	on a city break to Paris	on a safari to Kenya	on a walking holiday in Scotland
Who / go with?		his girlfriend	
How / travel?	by train		by train
Where / stay?		in a tent	
When / leave?	next Friday		tomorrow
What / plan to see?		lions and elephants	
How long / stay?	two nights		ten days

COMMUNICATIVE Revision questions

1 Personal information

What's your surname?
How do you spell it?
What's your email address?
What's your mobile number?
What's your address?
What's your postcode?

2 Talk about a friend

What's his / her name?
What does he / she do?
Where does he / she live?
How old is he /she?
Is he / she married?
Does he / she have children?

3 Food and drink

What's your favourite food and drink?
Is there any food or drink you don't like?
Which do you prefer – breakfast, lunch, or dinner? Why?
What do you usually have for breakfast?
What do you drink when you go out at night?
Do you cook? Do you like it?

4 What do you do in your free time?

How do you relax?
What do you do when you aren't at work / in class?
What do you like doing with your friends?
What sport or exercise do you do?
When do you have free time?
What do you usually do on a Saturday night?
What do you like doing in your summer holiday?

5 Your typical day (Monday to Friday)

What time do you usually get up?
How do you go to work or school?
Where do you usually have lunch?
What time do you get home in the evening?
What do you do after dinner?
What time do you go to bed?

6 What can / can't you do?

Say three things you can do in English.
Say three things you can see in this class.
Say three things you can do with a smartphone.
Say two things you can't do in English class.
Say two things you can't do on a plane.

7 Talking about the past

Were you at home last night?
Were you in bed at 8.00 this morning?
Did you go out last Saturday night?
Where did you have lunch yesterday?
Where were you at 4.00 yesterday afternoon?
When did you do your English homework?
Where did you go on your last holiday?

8 Times and dates

What time is it now?
What time does this class finish?
What days do you have English class?
When's your birthday?
What's your favourite day of the week?
When does this course finish?

9 Where do you live?

Do you live near here?
Do you live in a house or a flat?
Is it big or small?
Do you like it? Why (not)?
How many bedrooms are there?
Describe your bedroom.

10 Talking about the future

What are you doing after class today?
Are you meeting a friend after class today?
Where are you having dinner tonight?
Are you going to bed early tonight?
What are you doing this weekend?

1A Numbers 0–10 and days

A word search puzzle

Copy one sheet per student.

Language
Words for numbers 0 to 10 and days

- Put Sts in pairs and give out the sheets. Tell Sts to look for the number words from *zero* to *ten* and the days of the week. The words are either horizontal or vertical. Highlight the two examples.
- Focus on **b** and tell Sts to write the numbers and the days in the charts below.
- Check answers.

> **Numbers:** zero, one, two, three, four, five, six, seven, eight, nine, ten
> **Days of the week:** Monday, Tuesday, Wednesday, Thursday, Friday, Saturday, Sunday

T	H	R	E	E	S	Y	T	S	I	X	T
R	H	J	L	E	A	U	U	G	F	F	W
F	Y	U	E	N	T	Y	E	D	N	R	0
O	N	E	R	F	U	H	S	P	N	I	S
U	H	T	H	U	R	S	D	A	Y	D	T
R	N	V	H	B	D	P	A	T	M	A	E
T	E	N	X	T	A	A	Y	C	O	Y	I
S	N	I	N	E	Y	E	Y	H	N	U	G
W	E	D	N	E	S	D	A	Y	D	F	H
B	E	X	Z	E	R	O	V	V	A	I	T
T	I	N	A	S	E	V	E	N	Y	V	L
S	U	N	D	A	Y	J	S	P	Q	E	F

1B Countries

A pairwork activity

Copy one sheet per pair.

Language
Country names; numbers 1–10.
What's country number 1?

- Revise the country names from the **Vocabulary Bank** on *p.117*. Write the **Language** question on the board. Model and practise.
- Put Sts in pairs and give each pair a worksheet. Set Sts a time limit to try and label the map with the correct countries.
- Check answers by getting Sts to say the numbers and the countries, e.g., *Number three is Italy*. Follow up by asking Sts to find the general location of their country on the map if it is not one of the countries on the list.

1	England	6	Spain
2	Germany	7	France
3	Switzerland	8	Italy
4	Poland	9	Egypt
5	Russia	10	Turkey

PE1 Classroom language

A pairwork activity

Copy one sheet per student or per pair.

Language
Classroom language

- Quickly revise the language for teachers and students in **Vocabulary Bank** *Classroom language*, *p.118*. Then ask Sts to close their books.
- Put Sts in pairs and give out the sheets. Tell them that they have to fill in the missing word in the speech bubbles. Explain that the lines indicate the number of letters in each of the words.
- Demonstrate the activity. Focus on the example. Elicit that the teacher wants the students to sit down and that the missing word is '*down*'.
- Set a time limit for Sts do the activity in pairs.
- Check answers by asking Sts to read answers aloud and asking them to spell the missing word.

1 down		7 spell
2 open		8 repeat
3 page		9 sorry
4 stand		10 excuse
5 look		11 understand
6 close		12 know

2A Nationalities and languages
Writing nationalities and languages

Copy one sheet per student.

Language
Words for countries, nationalities and languages

- Quickly revise countries and nationalities in **Vocabulary Bank** (Student's Book *p.117*). Then ask Sts to close their books.
- Give out the sheets. Focus on **a** and the example. Get Sts to work individually or in pairs to complete the chart. If Sts work individually, get them to check their answers in pairs. Remind Sts to use capital letters for the first letter and lower case for the rest. Monitor and help where necessary. Check answers.

Brazil	Brazilian
China	Chinese
The USA	American
Egypt	Egyptian
Spain	Spanish
Turkey	Turkish
Switzerland	Swiss
Russia	Russian
Japan	Japanese
Poland	Polish
Italy	Italian
Germany	German
France	French
Mexico	Mexican

- Focus on **b** and the pictures. Get Sts, in pairs, to say the nationalities e.g. *It's Japanese.* Check answers.

2	Spanish (castanets)	6	French (bread)
3	Swiss (penknife)	7	German (car)
4	Turkish (flag)	8	Polish (flag)
5	Chinese (chopsticks)	9	Mexican (sombrero)

- Now focus on **c**. Ask Sts to complete the sentences individually, then check with their partner. Check answers with the group, encouraging Sts to use full sentences when they answer the questions.

1 Spanish	2 Arabic	3 English	
4 French, German, Italian			

2B Numbers dictation
A pairwork speaking and listening activity

Copy one sheet per pair and cut into **A** and **B**.

Language
Numbers 11 to 100

- Revise numbers from 11 to 100 by writing a few numbers on the board, e.g. *17, 34, 29, 42, 87*, and asking individual Sts to say the numbers. Then reverse the activity by asking Sts to call out numbers. As they do this, write the numbers in numerical form on the board.
- Put Sts in pairs, **A** and **B**, ideally face-to-face, and give out the sheets. Make sure Sts can't see each other's sheets. Focus on **a** and the examples on the sheets. Give Sts a few minutes to write the numbers on their half of the sheet in words. Monitor while Sts are working and correct any mistakes.

- Now focus on **b** and **c**. Tell Sts they are going to take turns dictating their numbers to their partners. Their partner will write the numbers they hear (in numerals, not in words). Demonstrate by getting a Student **A** to read the second number, *23*. Then tell the **B** Sts to write the number on their worksheet.
- Sts work in pairs to dictate numbers and write their partner's numbers. When they have finished, they should compare their sheets to make sure they wrote the correct numbers and have spelt them correctly. Monitor while Sts are doing this, make notes of any problems, and review these later with the whole class.

3A Things in the classroom
A pairwork information gap activity

Copy one sheet per pair and cut into **A** and **B**.

Language	
Words for things in the classroom and small things:	
What's number 1?	*It's a window.*
Is number 2 a board?	*Yes, it is. / No, it isn't.*
How do yo spell it?	

- Revise a few of the words for things in the classroom and small things by walking around and pointing at or holding up a variety of objects and asking *What's this?*
- Put Sts in pairs, **A** and **B**, ideally face-to-face, and give out the sheets. Give Sts a minute to look at the picture and read the list of words below it.
- Give Sts a few minutes to write the missing words on their own.
- Tell Sts that they are now going to check their answers with their partner. Demonstrate the activity with a good student. Take the part of Student **A** and ask a Student **B** Ask *What's number 2?* to get the answer board. Get a Student **B** to ask you *What's number 3?* and answer *door*. Then say *Is number 4 coat?* If **B** says *yes* then say *How do you spell it?*
- Write the sentences from **Language** on the board or show them on screen if you are using iTools. Model and drill pronunciation.
- Sts work in pairs asking and answering questions about the objects. Sts can write in the names of any objects missing from their list. Monitor and check that they are using the article *a | an*. Refer them to the conversation models on the board if necessary.
- When Sts have finished, they should compare their sheets to make sure they have the same words and have spelt them correctly.

4A People and family

A sentence completion activity

Copy one sheet per student.

> **Language**
> Words for people

- Focus on **a**. Tell Sts to work individually or in pairs to look at the pictures and complete the sentences. If Sts work individually, ask them to compare their answers with a partner when they finish.

> 2 girl   3 boy   4 children   5 woman
> 6 men   7 man   8 women

- Now focus on **b**. Tell Sts to work individually or in pairs to look at the pictures and complete the sentences.

> 2 husband   7 sister
> 3 mother   8 brother
> 4 father   9 girlfriend
> 5 daughter   10 boyfriend
> 6 son

- When Sts have finished, get feedback from the class by asking individuals or pairs to read out their answers. Encourage Sts to use full sentences.

4B Colours and common adjectives

A hidden word chain and crossword

Copy one sheet per student.

> **Language**
> Words for colours and opposite adjectives

- Give out the sheets and focus on **a**. Ask Sts to find and circle the colour words in the word chain.

> blue   white   grey   green   red   brown
> pink   orange   yellow

- Now focus on **b**. Tell Sts to match the colours to the objects in the pictures. Note that it is not necessary to teach the words for the objects in order for Sts to complete the exercise.
- Sts work individually, writing the appropriate colours under each object. When they have finished, ask Sts to compare their answers with a partner. Then check the answers with the whole class. Get Sts to say, e.g. *It's black*, etc.

> 2 orange   3 pink   4 red   5 brown   6 green
> 7 grey   8 yellow   9 white   10 blue

Extra challenge

- Sts will probably not know all of the English words for the things in the pictures. Teach the words for the things in the pictures and write them on the board: *a raven, carrots, a flamingo, strawberries, a tree (trunk), a tree, an elephant, a snowman, the sun, the sky.* Then get Sts to say sentences, e.g. *The raven is black, The sky is blue,* etc.
- Now focus on **c**. Ask Sts to look at the first word *difficult* and ask *What's the opposite of difficult?* Elicit that the answer is *easy*, and ask Sts to write the word in the squares in the puzzle.

- Sts work individually completing the puzzle with the opposites of the words on the left.
- Check answers by getting Sts to tell you the opposite of each adjective.

> 2 short   3 cheap   4 ugly   5 slow   6 new
> 7 small   8 bad

Extra challenge

- Get Sts to say full sentences, e.g. *The opposite of difficult is easy.*

5A Food and drink

A matching activity with anagrams

Copy one sheet per student.

> **Language**
> Words for food and drink

- Put Sts into pairs and give out the sheets. To demonstrate the activity, write this on the board *s-h-i-f f____*. Ask the class to use the four letters to make a word for something you can eat. Explain that the first letter is given. Elicit the answer *fish*.
- Put Sts into pairs and give out the sheets. Focus on **a** and the example. Give Sts time individually or in pairs to un-jumble all the letters to make the food words. If Sts are 'stuck' on a word give them a clue such as the first two letters.
- Check answers.

> a fish   h chocolate   o cereal
> b eggs   i vegetables   p water
> c fruit   j potatoes   q juice
> d sugar   k bread   r pasta
> e tea   l butter   s rice
> f milk   m cheese   t coffee
> g meat   n sandwich

- Now focus on **b** and get Sts to match the words with the pictures. Elicit all the words from the class and correct pronunciation.

> a 2   h 15   o 9
> b 3   i 12   p 18
> c 13   j 6   q 19
> d 14   k 8   r 11
> e 16   l 4   s 7
> f 17   m 5   t 20
> g 1   n 10

5B Common verb phrases

A wordsearch puzzle and gap-fill activity

Copy one sheet per student.

> **Language**
> Common verb phrases

- Put Sts in pairs and give out the sheets. Focus on **a**. Tell Sts to look for 14 verbs horizontally and vertically. Emphasise that the words must be verbs.
- You can make this part of the activity a race by setting a time limit of, e.g. ten minutes.
- Now focus on **b**. Tell Sts to complete the sentences with one of the verbs they have found in the wordsearch puzzle.
- Check answers by getting Sts to read out the completed sentences.

2 live		9 speak	
3 have		10 have	
4 watch		11 work	
5 listen		12 study	
6 read		13 go	
7 eat		14 like	
8 drink		15 need	

Y	P	L	I	V	E	K	L	G	O
D	R	I	N	K	W	H	I	N	W
S	E	S	X	N	N	A	K	O	A
T	E	T	L	U	R	V	E	O	T
U	N	E	E	D	W	E	C	H	C
D	W	N	D	Z	O	R	W	W	H
Y	T	R	J	N	R	E	A	S	D
S	S	P	E	A	K	A	N	L	F
I	V	V	Z	L	L	D	T	N	V
X	R	X	L	E	A	T	J	S	K

6A Jobs and places of work

A pairwork activity

Copy one sheet per pair or per student.

> **Language**
> Words for jobs and places of work

- Give out the sheets and focus on **a**, the photo and the sentences about Linda. Explain that Sts are going to work in pairs to complete the sentences on the worksheet. They have to write what each person does and where he / she works.
- Give Sts time to complete the missing information and get them to compare their answers with another student. Check answers.

2 journalist / office	
3 teacher / school	
4 policeman / street	
5 nurse / hospital	
6 waiter / restaurant	
7 taxi driver / street	
8 doctor / hospital	
9 receptionist / hotel	
10 factory worker / factory	

- Now focus on **b** and highlight the example. Sts cover the sentences with a piece of paper and look only at the photos. They try to remember the people's jobs and where they work.

6B What's the word?

A vocabulary game

Copy one sheet per student.

> **Language**
> Words used to describe daily activities

- Quickly revise a few common daily activities by asking Sts questions, e.g. *What do you usually do in the morning? What about the afternoon? And in the evening?* Elicit answers from several Sts. They can refer to the **Vocabulary Bank** on *p.125* if necessary.
- Put Sts into pairs and give out the sheets. Tell Sts they have to complete the column on the right with the missing words. Explain that the number of lines indicates the number of letters in the missing word.
- Check answers by getting Sts to read out the completed sentences.

2	work	10	gym
3	sandwich	11	finish
4	shopping	12	get
5	housework	13	bed
6	shower	14	coffee
7	dinner	15	breakfast
8	have	16	watch
9	bath	17	school

- Focus on **b**. Get Sts to cover the WORD column and look at the sentences. Sts work in pairs and try to say the sentences including the missing words.

Extra idea

- You could make the activity a race by setting a time limit, e.g. ten minutes. The first pair to write all the words correctly wins.

7A Common verb phrases 2: free time

A gap-fill activity

Copy one sheet per pair.

> **Language**
> Common verbs phrases: free time

- Quickly revise the verb phrases related to free time by asking a few of Sts *What do you usually do in your free time?* Elicit answers from several Sts. They can refer to the **Vocabulary Bank** on *p.126* if necessary
- Put Sts into pairs and give out the sheets. Tell Sts they have to complete the column on the right with the correct verbs from the list.
- Focus on the example sentence and elicit that the verb that goes with *in the mountains* is *walk*.
- Sts work in pairs to fill in the gaps. Monitor and help Sts where necessary.
- Check answers by getting Sts to read out the completed sentences.

2	go out	8	meet
3	play	9	relax
4	do	10	travel
5	go	11	play
6	play	12	stay
7	play		

- Now focus on **b** and get Sts to cover the VERB column and look at the sentences. Sts in pairs. try to say the sentences including the missing verbs

PE4 Months and ordinal numbers

A hidden message puzzle

Copy one sheet per student.

> **Language**
> The months and ordinal numbers

- Give out the sheets and focus on **a**. Tell Sts they have to complete the puzzle with the months of the year. The number of squares for each word and the letters included in the puzzle will help them decide which month to write. Explain that when they have finished the puzzle, they will find the Secret Message in the shaded column going down. Tell Sts to write these words in the question at the end of the puzzle.
- Students work individually or in pairs to complete the puzzle. Suggest that they fill in the "easy" months first and then work on the harder ones.
- When they have finished check answers and ask *What is the secret message?*

2	October	8	September
3	June	9	March
4	January	10	December
5	November	11	August
6	April	12	July
7	February		

Secret Message: When is your birthday?

- Focus on **b** and the examples in the chart. Numbers are given in pairs and one number from each pair is missing. Focus on the third line of the chart. Ask Sts *What number goes in the second column?* and elicit the answer (*third*)
- Sts work individually to complete the chart with the missing numbers. Check answers, correcting and practising pronunciation as necessary.

9A Common verb phrases 2: travelling

A matching activity

Copy one sheet per student.

> **Language**
> Common verb phrases: travelling

- Give out the sheets. Tell Sts they will have to choose a verb from the list to make verb phrases. Set a time limit, e.g. ten minutes, to complete the activity.
- Put Sts into pairs and tell them to compare their answers before you check them with the whole class.

2 stay	3 carry	4 get	5 wait	6 leave	7 arrive
8 pack	9 buy	10 book	11 rent	12 wear	

- Focus on **b**. Tell Sts to work in pairs and take turns in testing each other by covering the verb column and saying the phrases.

10A Draw it!

A vocabulary group game

Copy one sheet per group. Cut up the worksheet into cards.

> **Language**
> Words for things and places in a hotel

- Put Sts into small groups of three or four. Give out a set of cards to each group and ask them to put the cards face down on the desk.
- Demonstrate the activity by choosing an object that is not on the worksheet, e.g. a window, and drawing it on the board. Ask Sts to guess what you are drawing. Don't say anything. Just gesture to indicate if guesses are wrong, right, or nearly right. (Make your drawing very simple to show Sts that even someone who is not an artist can do a simple drawing.)
- Tell Sts that they are going to do the same thing in their groups. They will take turns picking a card, then they will draw the word for their classmates to guess. Emphasize that the person doing the drawing must not speak. When a student guesses correctly, that student gets to keep the card. The student who ends up with the most cards when all the cards are finished is the winner.

Non-cut alternative

- Give out a complete worksheet to each group. Sts take turns to choose a word from the worksheet without letting their classmates know which word they have chosen. They then draw the object on the card for their classmates to guess. When a student guesses correctly, that student writes his / her name on the square with the object. Set a time limit for the activity. The person who has guessed the most objects in that time is the winner.

a Find the words for numbers 0–10 and the days of the week.

T	H	R	E	E	S	Y	T	S	I	X	T
R	H	J	L	E	A	U	U	G	F	F	W
F	Y	U	E	N	T	Y	E	D	N	R	O
O	N	E	R	F	U	H	S	P	N	I	S
U	H	T	H	U	R	S	D	A	Y	D	T
R	N	V	H	B	D	P	A	T	M	A	E
T	E	N	X	T	A	A	Y	C	O	Y	I
S	N	I	N	E	Y	E	Y	H	N	U	G
W	E	D	N	E	S	D	A	Y	D	F	H
B	E	X	Z	E	R	O	V	V	A	I	T
T	I	N	A	S	E	V	E	N	Y	V	L
S	U	N	D	A	Y	J	S	P	Q	E	F

b Write the words in the charts.

Numbers

0 _____zero_____   6 _____

1 _____   7 _____

2 _____   8 _____

3 _____   9 _____

4 _____   10 _____

5 _____

Days of the week

M _onday_

T _____

W _____

T _____

F _____

S _____

S _____

1B VOCABULARY Countries

Look at the map. With a partner write the names of the countries on the map.

Egypt   England   France   Germany   Italy   Poland   Russia   Spain   Switzerland   Turkey

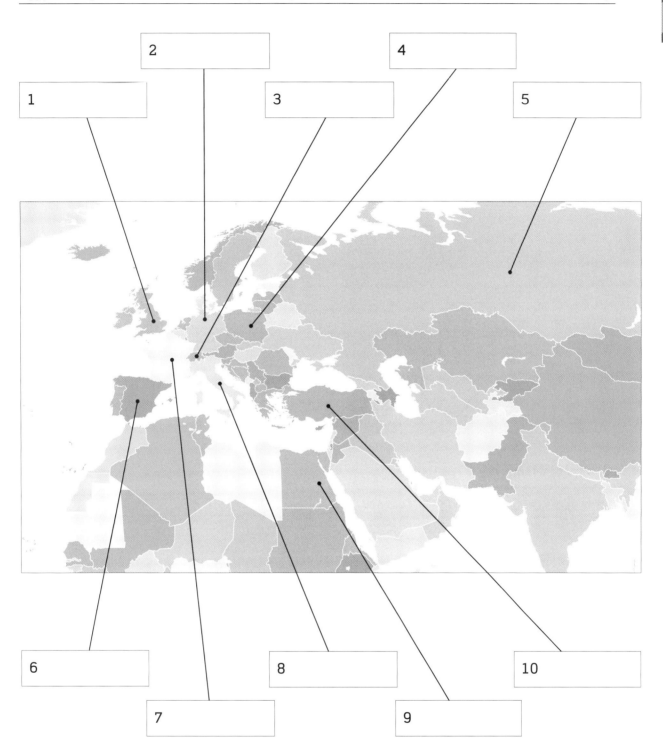

PE1 VOCABULARY Classroom language

Look at the pictures. Complete the missing words in the sentences.

The teacher says:

1
Please sit d o w n.

2
O _ _ _ _ your books.

3
Go to p _ _ _ _ 5.

4
St _ _ _ _ up, please.

5
L _ _ _ _ at the board, please.

6
C _ _ _ _ _ _ your book.

The student says:

7
How do you s p _ _ _ _ 'dictionary'?

8
Today is Friday and tomoro
Can you r _ _ _ _ _ _ that, please?

9
S _ _ _ _ _ _ I'm late.

10
E _ _ _ _ _ _ _ me. What's 'grazie' in English?

11
Rob is on holiday in Poland and
Sorry. I don't u _ _ _ _ _ _ _ _ _ _ _.

12
What's the capital of Switzerland?
I don't k n _ _ _.

2A VOCABULARY Nationalities and languages

a Complete the chart with the nationalities.

Country	Nationality
Brazil	_B r a z i l i a n_
China	_ _ _ _ _ _ _ ☐
The USA	_ _ _ _ _ _ _ _ _
Egypt	_ _ _ _ _ _ _ _
Spain	_ _ _ _ _ _ _ ☐
Turkey	_ _ _ _ _ _ _ ☐
Switzerland	_ _ _ _ _ _ ☐
Russia	_ _ _ _ _ _ _
Japan	_ _ _ _ _ _ _ _ _ _1_
Poland	_ _ _ _ _ _ _ ☐
Italy	_ _ _ _ _ _ _
Germany	_ _ _ _ _ _ _ ☐
France	_ _ _ _ _ _ _ ☐
Mexico	_ _ _ _ _ _ _ ☐

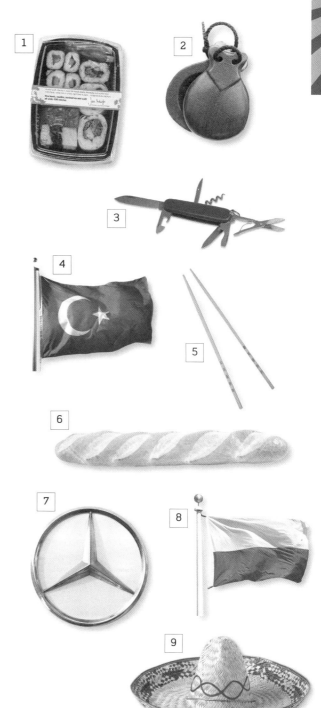

b Match the pictures with the nationalities. Write the numbers in the boxes.

c Complete the sentences with the correct languages.

1 In Mexico they speak _____.

2 In Egypt they speak _____.

3 In the UK and the USA they speak _____.

4 In Switzerland they speak _____, _____, and _____.

2B VOCABULARY Numbers dictation

Student A

a Write the numbers in words in the 'Your numbers' column.

Your numbers	B's numbers
15 _fifteen_	11
23 _____	
37 _____	
48 _____	
56 _____	
61 _____	
79 _____	
84 _____	
92 _____	

b Dictate your numbers to **B**.

c Listen to **B**. Write **B**'s numbers in the chart.

- -

Student B

a Write the numbers in words in the 'Your numbers' column.

Your numbers	A's numbers
11 _eleven_	15
27 _____	
31 _____	
43 _____	
54 _____	
69 _____	
78 _____	
82 _____	
96 _____	

b Listen to **A**. Write **A**'s numbers in the chart.

c Dictate your numbers to **A**.

English File 3rd edition Teacher's Book Beginner Photocopiable © Oxford University Press 2015

3A VOCABULARY Things in the classroom

Student A

a Look at the picture. Write the missing words.

1 window	5 umbrella	9 dictionary	13 mobile phone	17 notebook
2 _board_	6 _____	10 _____	14 _____	18 _____
3 door	7 chair	11 piece of paper	15 ID card	19 watch
4 _____	8 _____	12 _____	16 _____	20 _____

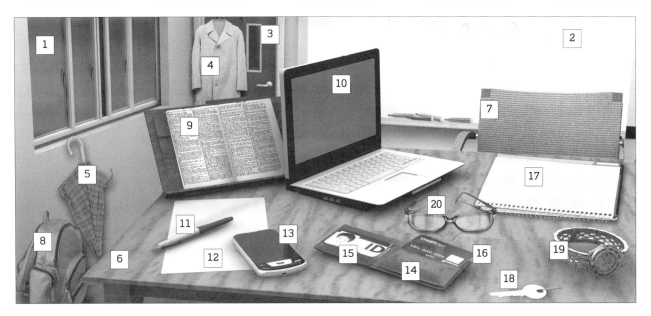

b Check your answers with **B**.

What's number 2? It's a board.

Student B

a Look at the picture. Write the missing words.

1 _window_	5 _____	9 _____	13 _____	17 _____
2 board	6 table	10 laptop	14 wallet	18 key
3 _____	7 _____	11 _____	15 _____	19 ___ ___
4 coat	8 bag	12 pen	16 credit card	20 glasses

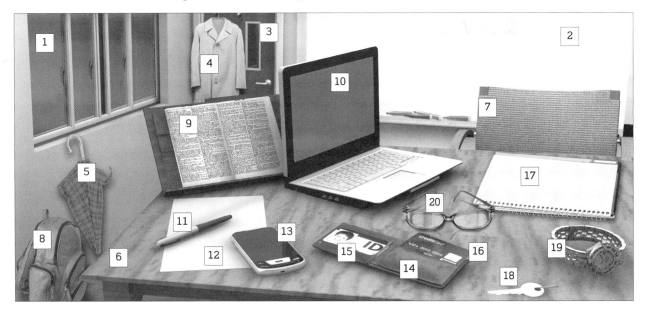

b Check your answers with **A**.

What's number 1? It's a window.

4A VOCABULARY People and family

a Complete the sentences. Use the words in the list.

boy   children   friends   girl   man   men   woman   women

Fabio and Anna are _friends_ .

Kim is a _____ .

Alex is a _____ .

Megan and Dan are _____ .

Mrs DeSouza is a _____ .

George and Michael are _____ .

Mr Husson is a _____ .

Jessica and Helena are _____ .

b Complete the sentences. Use the words in the list.

boyfriend   brother   daughter   father   girlfriend   husband   mother   sister   son   wife

1 Rita is Bob's _wife_ .
2 Bob is Rita's _____ .
3 Rita is Ryan and Brenda's _____ .
4 Bob is Ryan and Brenda's _____ .
5 Brenda is Rita and Bob's _____ .
6 Ryan is Rita and Bob's _____ .
7 Brenda is Ryan's _____ .
8 Ryan is Brenda's _____ .
9 Molly is Ryan's _____ .
10 Josh is Brenda's _____ .

4B VOCABULARY Colours and common adjectives

a Find the colour words.

blackmblueoawhitehgreysegreentreredwbrowngupinksiforangexoyellow

black

b Match the words in **a** to the pictures.

| 1 | 2 | 3 | 4 | 5 |

black _____ _____ _____ _____

| 6 | 7 | 8 | 9 | 10 |

_____ _____ _____ _____ _____

c Write the opposites of words 1–8.

1 difficult	E	A	S	Y	
2 tall					
3 expensive					
4 beautiful					
5 fast					
6 old					
7 big					
8 good					

5A VOCABULARY Food and drink

a Put the letters in order to make food words.

a	shif	**f** _ish_ ☐		**k**	drabe	**b** _____ ☐
b	gegs	**e** _____ ☐		**l**	tutreb	**b** _____ ☐
c	truif	**f** _____ ☐		**m**	sheece	**c** _____ ☐
d	rugas	**s** _____ ☐		**n**	cashwind	**s** _____ ☐
e	eat	**t** _____ ☐		**o**	lceare	**c** _____ ☐
f	klim	**m** _____ ☐		**p**	trawe	**w** _____ ☐
g	tame	**m** _____ ☐		**q**	cijue	**j** _____ ☐
h	coclhaoet	**c** _____ ☐		**r**	atpsa	**p** _____ ☐
i	beetsglave	**v** _____ ☐		**s**	crie	**r** _____ ☐
j	taesotop	**p** _____ ☐		**t**	foefce	**c** _____ ☐

b Then match the words to the pictures. Write the number of the picture in the box.

English File 3rd edition Teacher's Book Beginner Photocopiable © Oxford University Press 2015

5B VOCABULARY Common verb phrases

a Find 14 verbs.

Y	P	L	I	V	E	K	L	G	O
D	R	I	N	K	W	H	I	N	W
S	E	S	X	N	N	A	K	O	A
T	E	T	L	U	R	V	E	O	T
U	N	E	E	D	W	E	C	H	C
D	W	N	D	Z	O	R	W	W	H
Y	T	R	J	N	R	E	A	S	D
S	S	P	E	A	K	A	N	L	F
I	V	V	Z	L	L	D	T	N	V
X	R	X	L	E	A	T	J	S	K

b Complete the sentences with a verb from **a**.

1 I don't _want_ coffee, thanks.

2 I _____ in a big house with my wife Katya and our children.

3 Do you _____ a big breakfast in the morning?

4 I don't _____ TV. The programmes are terrible!

5 We _____ to music in the car.

6 I don't _____ the newspaper in English. It's difficult!

7 We don't _____ meat. We're vegetarians.

8 I don't _____ coffee in the evening.

9 Excuse me? Do you _____ English?

10 Do you _____ brothers and sisters?

11 I _____ in a bank in London.

12 Do you _____ English at university?

13 I _____ to English classes on Tuesdays and Thursdays.

14 Do you _____ this song? I think it's great!

15 I _____ a new computer. My computer is very old.

6A VOCABULARY Jobs and places of work

a Look at the people in the photos and complete the sentences about their jobs.

1. Linda is a _shop assistant_ . She works in a souvenir _shop_ . She speaks French and Spanish with customers.

2. Amanda is a _____ . She works in the _____ of an important newspaper. She writes articles about education.

3. Daniel is a _____ . He works in a big secondary _____ . He teaches history.

4. Gary is a _____ . He works in the _____ . He works with his dog, Rex.

5. Sophie is a _____ . She works in a children's _____ . She usually works in the morning, but sometimes she works at night.

6. Richard is a _____ . He works in an Italian _____ . He usually works at the weekend.

7. Roger is a _____ in London. He works in the _____ . He drives a black cab.

8. Eric is a _____ . He works in a children's _____ . He works with Sophie.

9. Diana is a _____ . She works in a _____ in Manchester. She meets a lot of people every day.

10. Julie is a _____ . She works in a cheese _____ . She starts work at 6:30 every morning.

b Work with a partner. Cover the sentences. Talk about the people in the pictures.

Linda is a shop assistant. She works in a souvenir shop.

6B VOCABULARY What's the word?

a Read the sentences and write the missing words in the WORD column.

WORD

1   I usually go ▆ at five o'clock.   *h o m e*

2   Do you go to ▆ by train?   _ *o r* _

3   I always have a ▆ for lunch.   *s* _ _ _ *w* _ _ _

4   We sometimes go ▆ on Saturday.   _ _ _ *p* _ _ _ *g*

5   Do you do the ▆ in your house?   *h* _ _ _ _ *w* _ _ _

6   Mike has a ▆ every morning.   _ _ *o w* _ _

7   The Wilson family has ▆ at six o'clock every evening.   _ *i* _ _ _ *r*

8   When do you usually ▆ lunch?   _ *a* _ _

9   I'm tired. I want to have a nice hot ▆.   *b* _ _ *h*

10 We need exercise. Let's go to the ▆.   _ *y* _

11 They ▆ work at six o'clock every day.   _ *i* _ _ *s* _

12 We never ▆ up early on Sundays.   _ *e* _

13 We usually go to ▆ late on Saturday night.   _ _ *d*

14 In the morning, I go to a café and have a ▆ and
    a croissant.   _ *o* _ *f* _ _

15 We sometimes have ▆ in bed on Saturday morning.   *b* _ _ _ *k* _ _ _ _

16 I never ▆ TV in the morning.   _ _ *t* _ *h*

17 The children go to ▆ by bus.   _ *c* _ _ *o* _

b **Test your memory.** Cover the WORD column. Look at the sentences.
Can you remember the words?

a Complete the sentences with a verb from the list. Write your answers in the VERB column.

do   go   go out   meet   play [x3]   relax   stay   swim   travel   ~~walk~~

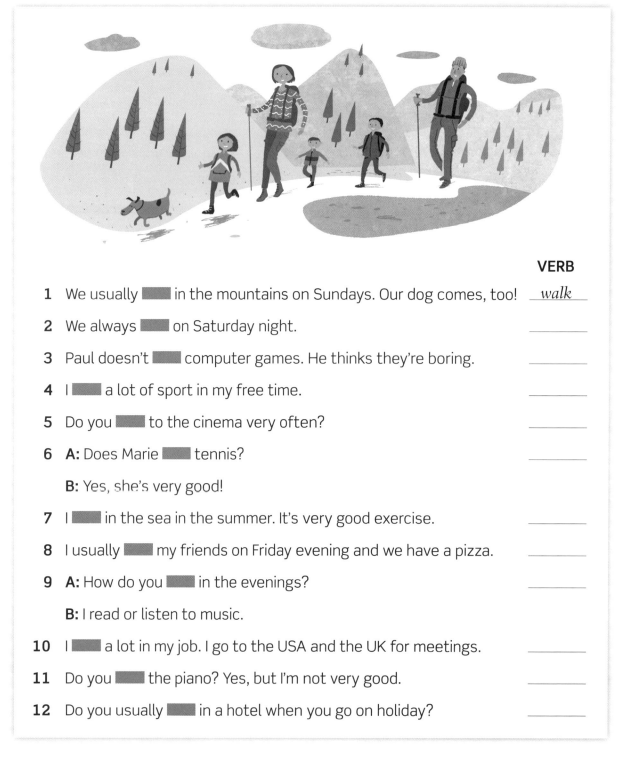

VERB

1   We usually ▆▆▆ in the mountains on Sundays. Our dog comes, too!   *walk*

2   We always ▆▆▆ on Saturday night.   _____

3   Paul doesn't ▆▆▆ computer games. He thinks they're boring.   _____

4   I ▆▆▆ a lot of sport in my free time.   _____

5   Do you ▆▆▆ to the cinema very often?   _____

6   **A:** Does Marie ▆▆▆ tennis?   _____

    B: Yes, she's very good!

7   I ▆▆▆ in the sea in the summer. It's very good exercise.   _____

8   I usually ▆▆▆ my friends on Friday evening and we have a pizza.   _____

9   **A:** How do you ▆▆▆ in the evenings?   _____

    B: I read or listen to music.

10   I ▆▆▆ a lot in my job. I go to the USA and the UK for meetings.   _____

11   Do you ▆▆▆ the piano? Yes, but I'm not very good.   _____

12   Do you usually ▆▆▆ in a hotel when you go on holiday?   _____

b **Test your memory.** Cover the VERB column. Look at the sentences. Can you remember the verbs?

PE4 VOCABULARY Months and ordinal numbers

a Write the months of the year in the crossword. When the puzzle is complete, you can read the secret message going down. There are some letters in the puzzle to help you.

The Secret Message: When is _____ ?

b Write the missing numbers in the chart.

one	first		eleventh
two	second	twelve	
three		thirteen	
	fourth		fourteenth
five		fifteen	
	sixth	sixteen	
	seventh		seventeenth
eight		eighteen	
nine			nineteenth
	tenth	twenty	
		thirty	

9A VOCABULARY Common verb phrases 2: travelling

a Match the verbs in the list to phrases 1–12. Write them in the VERB column.

arrive   book   buy   carry   get   leave   pack   ~~phone~~   rent   stay   wait   wear

	VERB	
1	*phone*	home, your family
2	_____	in a hotel, in a hostel
3	_____	a suitcase, a bag, an umbrella
4	_____	a taxi, a train, a bus
5	_____	for a flight, for a bus, for a friend
6	_____	the house in the morning, work at 5.00
7	_____	in London, at the airport
8	_____	a suitcase, a bag
9	_____	a present, a souvenir
10	_____	tickets, a table in a restaurant
11	_____	a car, a flat
12	_____	a coat, jeans

b **Test your memory.** Cover the VERB column. Say phrases 1–12.

English File 3rd edition Teacher's Book Beginner Photocopiable © Oxford University Press 2015

10A VOCABULARY Draw it!

a bed	a pillow	a table	a lamp
a remote control	a cupboard	a floor	a bathroom
a bath	a shower	a towel	a swimming pool
a car park	a bar	a garden	a lift
a gift shop	reception	a gym	a lamp

Song activity instructions

The songs can be found on CD4 of the Class audio CD as MP3 files.

PE1 All Together Now
Identifying words (4) MP3)))

- Copy one sheet per student.
- Put Sts in pairs and give out the sheets. Focus on **a**. Give pairs a few minutes to match the pictures and the words.
- Check answers.

  2 e   3 c   4 g   5 b   6 f   7 a

- Now focus on **b** and the example. Tell Sts that they are going to listen to the song and they have to write down the numbers of the pictures in the order as they hear them. Make sure they cover the song lyrics first.
- Play the song once or twice, as necessary, for Sts to number the pictures check answers.

  4 7 2 5 6 3

- Now go through the song with the class, helping Sts understand the meaning, and using the **Glossary** to help. Then go through the **Song facts**.
- Finally, if you think your Sts would like to hear the song again, play it to them one more time. If your class likes singing, they can sing along.

PE2 That's How Much
Listening for extra words (4) MP3)))

- Copy one sheet per student.
- Give out the sheets and focus on the task and the example. Explain that Sts have to listen and cross out the extra word. Tell Sts that all the lines numbered 1–10 have an extra word, but the lines without numbers are correct.
- Play the song once for Sts to try and cross out the extra words. Play the audio again, this time pausing after each line, and replaying if necessary.
- Check answers.

  1 lucky   2 then   3 all   4 please   5 big
  6 sometimes   7 planet   8 here   9 sunny   10 now

- Go through the song with the class, helping Sts understand the meaning and using the **Glossary** to help.
- Ask Sts to read the **Song facts**.
- Finally, if you think your Sts would like to hear the song again, play it to them one more time. If your class likes singing, they can sing along.

PE3 Stop the Clock
Remembering words and matching rhyming words (4) MP3)))

- Copy one sheet per student.
- Give out the sheets and focus on **a**. Explain that Sts have to write the word under each picture. The number of lines represents the number of missing letters. Ask sts to compare their answers and then check.

  1 baby   2 clock   3 train   4 three

- Now focus on **b**. Tell sts to cover **a** and look at the pictures in the song lyrics. Ask them if they can remember what the pictures represent. Play the song once, pausing the audio from time to time just before a picture word for Sts to say the word.
- Now focus on **c** and go through the words in each circle, eliciting the pronunciation and meaning. Then get Sts to match the rhyming pairs. Check answers.

  1 c   2 a   3 b

- Go through the song with the class helping Sts undrestand the meaning, and using the **Glossary** to help. Then go through the **Song Facts**.
- Finally, if you think your Sts would like to hear the song again, play it to them one more time. If your class likes singing, they can sing along, trying to remember the picture words.

PE4 Calendar Girl
Listening for specific words (4) MP3)))

- Copy one sheet per student.
- Give out the sheets and focus on **a**. Highlight that the highlighted clues will help Sts to decide what the missing words are when they listen.
- Play the song once for Sts to try and write the missing words, pausing as necessary to give Sts time to write the words. Play the song again for Sts to listen and check their answers, replaying individual lines as necessary. Check answers.

  1 start   2 Valentine   3 smile   4 dad
  5 beach   6 sixteen   7 Halloween   8 tree

- Go through the song with the class helping Sts undrestand the meaning, and using the **Glossary** to help. Then go through the **Song Facts**.
- Finally, if you think your Sts would like to hear the song again, play it to them one more time. If your class likes singing, they can sing along.

PE5 Song I'd Like to Sing
Listening for specific words 4 MP3)))

- Copy one sheet per student.
- Give out the sheets. Go through the words and phrases at the ends of the lines and check the meaning and pronunciation of each one. Tell Sts they have to circle the word they hear.
- Play the song once and Sts circle the words they hear. Then play the song again for them to complete their answers. Replay any lines as necessary.
- Check answers with the whole class and get Sts to write the words in the song.

2 know	9 know	15 last
3 always	10 a	16 want
4 good	11 mother	17 a
5 the	12 woman	18 pretty
6 sing	13 together	19 sing
7 take	14 until	20 love
8 this		

- Go through the song with the class, helping Sts understand the meaning, and using the **Glossary** to help. Then go through the **Song Facts**.
- Finally, if you think that your Sts would like to hear the song again, play it to them one more time. If your class likes singing, they can sing along.

PE6 Somewhere Over the Rainbow
Identifying words 4 MP3)))

- Copy one sheet per student.
- Give out the sheets and focus on **a**. Give Sts a few minutes to match the pictures with the words, individually or in pairs. Check answers.

2 d	3 a	4 e	5 g	6 b	7 h	8 c

- Now focus on **b** and the example. Tell Sts to write down the letter of the pictures as they hear them. Make sure they cover the song lyrics first.
- Play the song once or twice as necessary for Sts to number the pictures. Then check answers.

c	h	g	d	a	e	b

- Now focus on **c**. Go through the words in each circle, eliciting the pronunciation and meaning. Then get Sts to match the rhyming pairs. Check answers.

1 c	2 a	3 b

- Go through the song with the class, helping Sts understand the meaning, and using the **Glossary** to help. Then go through the **Song Facts**.
- Finally, if you think your Sts would like to hear the song again, play it to them one more time. If your class likes singing, they can sing along.

PE1 SONG All Together Now ④ MP3))

a Match the pictures with the words.

a a tree ☐

b a cup of tea ☐

c a friend ☐

d 'I love you' *1*

e a rope ☐

f a bed ☐

g a ship ☐

b Listen to the song. Write the number of the picture in the order you hear them.

1 ☐ ☐ ☐ ☐ ☐ ☐

All Together Now

One, two, three, four
Can I have a little more?
Five, six, seven, eight, nine, ten
I love you

A B C D
Can I bring my friend to tea?
E F G H I J
I love you

Sail the ship,
Chop the tree,
Skip the rope,
Look at me (Look at me)

All together now
(All together now)
All together now
(All together now)
All together now
(All together now)
All together now
(All together now)

Black, white, green, red
Can I take my friend to bed?
Pink, brown, yellow, orange
    and blue
I love you

All together now
(All together now)
All together now
(All together now)
All together now
(All together now)
All together now
(repeat)

Sail the ship,
Chop the tree,
Skip the rope,
Look at me (Look at me)

All together now
(All together now)
All together now
(repeat)

GLOSSARY

sail the ship

chop the tree

skip the rope

SONG FACTS

This song was written by John Lennon and Paul McCartney, and it appeared in the Beatles' film *Yellow Submarine* (1968).

PE2 SONG That's How Much 🔊 4 MP3))

Listen to the song. Cross out the extra words in lines 1–10.

That's How Much

That's how much
That's how much
Yeah, yeah, yeah
That's how much
I love you
(Yeah, I love you)
1 Pick a ~~lucky~~ number from one to ten
2 Double it and then add a million
That's how much
That's how much
Yeah, yeah, yeah
That's how much
I love you
(Yeah, I love you)
3 Count all the miles from here to Mars
4 Please triple it and add a trillion
That's how much
That's how much
Yeah, yeah, yeah
That's how much
I love you
(Yeah, I love you)

5 Although I'm not a big mathematical genius
6 At least I sometimes know the score
7 Who cares how far to planet Venus
8 When you live here right next door
9 Count the pebbles on every sunny beach
10 Triple it and now add a trillion
That's how much
That's how much
Yeah, yeah, yeah
That's how much
I love you
(Yeah, I love you)

Who cares how far to Venus
When you live right next door
(Yeah, yeah, yeah)
(Right next door)
Count the pebbles on every beach
Triple it and add a trillion
That's how much
That's how much
Yeah, yeah, yeah
That's how much
I love you
(Yeah, I love you)

SONG FACTS

That's How Much was a hit for the American singer Bryan Hyland in 1960.

GLOSSARY

double = multiply by two
triple = multiply by three
add = put together two numbers e.g. 2+2
know the score = know what is important

Who cares....? = it isn't important
next door = the house/flat next to your house/flat
pebbles = small stones

PE3 SONG Stop the Clock (4) MP3))

a Look at the pictures. What are the words?

1 b _ _ _   **2** c *l* _ _ _ _   **3** t *r* _ _ _ _   **4** t *h* _ _ _ _

b Listen to the song. Can you remember the picture words?

Stop the Clock

Tick-tock, stop the

Tick-tock, stop the

Time keeps moving on

Soon my will be gone

Away, poor me

Tick-tock, stop the

Tick-tock, stop the

She's gonna catch the at

That'll be the end of me

Tick-tock, stop the

Tick-tock, stop the

Tick-tock, stop the

For my would be mine

If I could just turn back the time

Tick-tock, stop the

Tick-tock, stop the

Tick-tock, stop the

Time keeps moving on

Soon my will be gone

Tick-tock, stop the

Tick-tock, stop the

Tick-tock, stop the

For my would be mine

If I could just turn back the time

Tick-tock, stop the

c Match the words in groups **A** and **B** that have the same sound. Can you say them correctly?

A
1 stop ☐
2 me ☐
3 mine ☐

B
a three
b time
c clock

SONG FACTS

Stop the Clock was a hit for the American rhythm and blues singer Fats Domino in 1962. He sold 100 million copies and was a big influence on the Beatles, The Rolling Stones and many other artists.

GLOSSARY

keeps moving on = doesn't stop
baby = girlfriend/wife
gonna = going to (future, informal)

That'll be = That will be (future)
turn back the time = go back to the past

PE4 SONG Calendar Girl 4 MP3))

Listen to the song and write the missing words 1–8. Use the highlighted clues to help you.

Calendar Girl

I love, I love, I love my calendar girl
Yeah, sweet calendar girl
I love, I love, I love my calendar girl
Each and every day of the year

(January)
You ¹_____ the year all fine   *a verb*
(February)
You're my little ²_____   *14th February*
(March)
I'm gonna march you down the aisle
(April)
You're the Easter bunny
When you ³_____   *a verb*

Yeah, yeah
My heart's in a whirl
I love, I love, I love my little calendar girl
Every day (every day)
Every day (every day)
Of the year (every day of the year)

(May)
Maybe if I ask your ⁴_____ and mom
   a family member
(June)
They'd let me take you to the junior prom
(July)
Like a firecracker
I'm aglow
(August)
When you're on the ⁵_____ you
   steal the show   *a place*

Yeah, yeah
My heart's in a whirl
I love, I love, I love my little calendar girl
Every day (every day)
Every day (every day)
Of the year (every day of the year)

Whoo!

Yeah, yeah
My heart's in a whirl
I love, I love, I love my little calendar girl
Every day (every day)
Every day (every day)
Of the year (every day of the year)

(September)
I light the candles at your sweet ⁶_____
   a number
(October)
Romeo and Juliet on ⁷_____   *31st October*
(November)
I'll give thanks that you belong to me
(December)
You're the present beneath my Christmas
   ⁸_____   *a thing*

Yeah, yeah
My heart's in a whirl
I love, I love, I love my little calendar girl
Every day (every day)
Every day (every day)
Of the year (every day of the year)

I love, I love, I love my calendar girl
Yeah, sweet calendar girl
I love, I love, I love my calendar girl
Yeah, sweet calendar girl

SONG FACTS

Neil Sedaka had a hit with this song in 1961. It reached number 4 in the US Billboard charts. A 'calendar girl' is a girl who appears in a photo on a calendar.

GLOSSARY

gonna = going to (future, informal)
march = walk like a soldier
aisle = a way between lines of seats in a church
Easter = a religious festival in March or April
bunny = a little rabbit

in a whirl = moving in a circle very quickly
junior prom = a school dance at the end of the year
a firecracker = a small firework
aglow = shining with happiness
beneath = under

PE5 SONG Song I'd Like to Sing (4 MP3)))

a Listen and circle the correct word in each pair 1–20.

b Listen again and check. Write the words in the song.

Song I'd Like to Sing

There's ¹_____ song I'd like to sing

Do you ²_____ the song I mean?

It don't ³_____ sound the same

But it's always ⁴_____ to sing.

Anyone can say ⁵_____ words

Anyone can ⁶_____ the tune

If you ⁷_____ a little time

I can teach ⁸_____ song to you.

And we can get to ⁹_____ each other

Like a sister and ¹⁰_____ brother

Like a father and a ¹¹_____

Like a ¹²_____ and a man.

And ¹³_____ we can sing along

Just enjoy ¹⁴_____ it's over

It don't need to ¹⁵_____ forever

If we ¹⁶_____ it to it can.

Maybe it don't mean ¹⁷_____ thing

It's a ¹⁸_____ little tune.

It's a song I like to ¹⁹_____

That I'd ²⁰_____ to sing with you.

(la la la la)

1	one / (a)
2	know / like
3	always / usually
4	great / good
5	the / those
6	like / sing
7	give / take
8	the / this
9	love / know
10	a / her
11	mother / mum
12	lady / woman
13	tomorrow / together
14	when / until
15	last / be
16	need / want
17	a / some
18	nice / pretty
19	write / sing
20	love / like

SONG FACTS

Song I'd Like to Sing is from Kris Kristofferson and Rita Coolidge's 1973 album, *Full Moon*. They won two Grammy awards for their albums.

GLOSSARY

anyone = any person

a tune = the music of a song

last (verb) = to continue for a long time

forever = for all time

English File 3rd edition Teacher's Book Beginner Photocopiable © Oxford University Press 2015

PE6 SONG Somewhere Over the Rainbow (4 MP3))

a Match the pictures with the words.

a
b
c
d
e
f
g
h

1 rainbow *f*
2 bluebird
3 star
4 clouds

5 lullaby
6 chimney
7 dream
8 high (*adj.*)

b Listen to the song. Write the letter of the pictures in the order you hear them in the song.

f

Somewhere Over the Rainbow

Ooo ooo ooo etc.

Somewhere over the rainbow
Way up high
And the dreams that you dream of once in a lullaby

Oh somewhere over the rainbow
Bluebirds fly
And the dreams that you dream of, dreams
Really do come true

Some day I'll wish upon a star
Wake up where the clouds are far behind me
Where trouble melts like lemon drops
High above the chimney top
That's where you'll find me

Oh somewhere over the rainbow
Bluebirds fly
And the dreams that you dare to
Oh why, oh why can't I?

Oh, someday I'll wish upon a star
Wake up where the clouds are far behind me
Where trouble melts like lemon drops
High above the chimney top
That's where you'll find me

Oh somewhere over the rainbow
Way up high
And the dreams that you dare to
Why, oh why can't I?

Ooo ooo ooo etc.

---

c Match the words in groups **A** and **B** that have the same sound.

A
1 high
2 drop
3 star

B
a top
b far
c lullaby

SONG FACTS

Somewhere over the Rainbow is originally from the film *The Wizard of Oz*. Israel Kamakawiwo'ole recorded his version in 1993 and it has been used in films and TV shows including the popular series *Glee*.

GLOSSARY
dream = (noun and verb) something you want to happen
to come true = to become reality
to melt = to become liquid
lemon drops = yellow sweets